# Bond Portfolio Immunization

# Bond Portfolio Immunization

**Michael R. Granito**
The Morgan Bank

**LexingtonBooks**
D.C. Heath and Company
Lexington, Massachusetts
Toronto

**Library of Congress Cataloging in Publication Data**

Granito, Michael R.
  Bond portfolio immunization.

  Includes index.
  1. Bonds. 2. Portfolio management. I. Title
HG4651.G75   1984                    332.63'23                    83–49012
ISBN 0–669–07660–0   (alk. paper)

Published simultaneously in Canada

Printed in the United States of America

International Standard Book Number: 0–669–07660–0

Library of Congress Catalog Card Number: 83–49012

# Contents

# Figure and Tables

# Acknowledgments

This book was written over the period 1979 through 1983, a time of rapidly rising interest rates and heightened interest in documenting assured rates of return. The work began as a collection of research studies intended to assist clients of the Morgan Bank in understanding the investment issues underlying the techniques of bond immunization that were just then emerging in the U.S. financial markets. It was a time when academic analysis of immunization lagged behind applications that had been made urgent by market conditions, leaving to practitioners the task of demonstrating the empirical and even, on occasion, the theoretical properties of immunization techniques.

I wish to thank the management of the Morgan Bank, whose resolve to serve client interests underscores a belief in research. I especially wish to thank Nick Potter, Dave Brigham, Kim Schappert, and Pierre Daviron for providing the resources and encouragement necessary for completing this work. My colleagues in the Fixed Income Investment group at Morgan regularly provided constructive advice on the content and presentation of this work at its various stages of development. In this regard, special thanks go to the immunization specialists in the Fixed Income area, without whose general efforts this work would not have been possible. I wish to thank Pat Bihn, Larry Smith, and especially Janet Kappenberg, my co-worker of three years, who helped more than anyone else in developing and implementing the immunization procedures at Morgan.

# 1 Introduction

Bond portfolio immunization refers to a mathematically precise scheme for investing in bonds so that fluctuations in interest rates do not prevent the attainment of long-term target returns. The target return is stated at the outset of the investment period on the basis of yields available in the market and the horizon of the program. The investment objective could be the attainment of a fixed compound rate over a known horizon, as may be the case if a single liability is to be financed in the future; or, in the case of multiple liabilities, the objective would be a target internal financing rate on the overall liability stream.

The concept of immunization was first developed in the British actuarial literature about 1950 and was separately introduced in the U.S. literature about 1970.[1] Actual applications of the concepts were evidently infrequent and limited to the insurance community until 1980, when two developments brought immunization into the forefront of institutional investment thought and practice. First, the mathematical tractability of the topic attracted considerable academic research, which in turn popularized the approach. Second, and far more important, record high real and nominal interest rates available since the fall of 1979 inspired interest in immunization of all forms for targeting high rates. This motivation was dramatized by the rather poor fixed income portfolio performance over the previous several years and by the fact that, at a time when corporate profits were poor, U.S. pension plans could reduce contributions to their funds insofar as the immunized rate, which is locked up, could be used to increase the actuarial assumption used in valuing projected liabilities.

These developments set the stage for an extraordinary growth in the use of the immunized asset form since 1979. In responding to the challenge of making immunization work in practice, money managers encountered several difficulties. First, while immunized methods would work perfectly under certain theoretical assumptions, it was not clear that the historical tests which suggested good performance in practice were adequate. Specifically, the historical results reflected returns on theoretically selected hypothetical portfolios, not actual portfolios. Second, interest rates were far more volatile than in the pre-1979 era, making earlier performance data questionable. Finally, immunization was no longer an intellectual exercise, but a business subject to intense competition. Consequently, efforts were made to improve on the earliest techniques recommended to provide higher returns with less risk. Along with improved operational methods, at least one new variant on the basic immunization concept emerged, as well as applications of the same concepts to other investment media.

In the spirit of such inquiry, this book presents a series of studies that examine each of the major forms of immunization for the purpose of improving the practical implementation of these strategies. It is in this sense a practitioner's guide developed during a research effort for managing large institutional portfolios. The book is divided into four parts. Chapters 2 through 4 discuss classic or bullet immunization. Chapters 5 and 6 cover contingent immunization. Chapter 7 discusses dedicated portfolios. Chapters 8 and 9 cover the application of immunization analysis to new investment media—financial futures and foreign exchange, respectively. In the remainder of this chapter we summarize the issues and findings of each section.

## Bullet Immunization

In bullet or classic immunization, the objective is to manage a portfolio of coupon bonds to achieve the return profile of a pure discount (zero coupon) bond maturing at a specified investment horizon. That is, a sum of money is to be invested at the outset, no additions or withdrawals made during the period, and a predetermined amount withdrawn on the horizon. This implies that the compound return on the original investment is certain and known as of the start of the period. Why not simply buy a pure discount bond in the first place? In part, these instruments were a response to the phenomenon of immunization. But to date, the supply of corporate zero coupon bonds has not been adequate to achieve proper diversification, or they have not generally been available at the desired maturity dates, or they have noncompetitive yields. For many purposes, the U.S. Treasury zero coupon bonds that have been artificially created through coupon stripping have yields which are quite low compared with immunized target returns, or are objectionable because of the form of ownership. Similarly, insurance contracts offering this same return profile are generally illiquid, implying substantial penalties for early withdrawal, although yields normally exceed those available using public bonds of similar overall credit.

The theoretical concept behind why bullet immunization can work at all is nontrivial. We buy coupon bonds knowing that the income must be reinvested at an unknown future rate through to the horizon, yet we stipulate an unqualified target return that is expected to be achieved with great accuracy. The insight that such a promise is possible arises out of a mathematical assumption about the behavior of yield curves. The earliest work on the subject (see Fisher and Weil) focused on the concept of forward rates, which are implicit in any particular yield curve and from which a full yield curve can be derived.[2] In a world of perfect certainty, the forward rate, measured as of today $t$ and applying to a future time $t + s$ is the short-term rate of interest that will prevail at time $t + s$. If we take a yield curve, compute the forward rates out into the future, and then compound these rates from today through some future time $T$, we will derive (after appropriate annualization of the total return) the market's implicit indication of the yield on a $T$ year pure discount (zero coupon) bond. This rate is called the $T$ year spot rate.

Fisher and Weil showed that if forward rates shift once in a parallel fashion then it is possible to initially structure a coupon bond portfolio in such a fashion that the initially estimated spot rate will be earned, regardless of the shift. The structure required is simply that the duration of the portfolio equal the remaining time remaining until the end of the horizon, where duration is the present value-weighted average maturity of the portfolio in which both coupon and principal receipt dates are separately counted. In fact, they point out a relationship between their work and earlier findings. If forward rates do not shift, precisely the spot rate is earned, whereas any actual shift implies a total return in excess of the spot rate. This phenomenon has to do with the fact that, with the exception of a zero coupon bond, the duration of a bond or bond portfolio is itself a function of rates. In particular, as rates rise, duration falls; conversely, as rates fall, duration rises. Therefore, for any discrete shift in rates, a portfolio that initially has target duration shortens during a rate increase or lengthens during a rate decline, compared with the duration behavior of the zero coupon alternative.

To offer the immunization approach as a complete strategy, Fisher and Weil point out but do not prove that to account for multiple rate shifts we need merely maintain through time a portfolio duration equal to the remaining horizon. Because each individual shift is accounted for, rebalancing after any shift (or after any other event that interrupts the quality of duration and horizon) will imply a dynamic immunization. This immunization has the property that the spot rate will be the minimum return that will be earned only if there is no shift in forward rates at all.

The work of Fisher and Weil is the seed from which has grown an extensive academic literature on bullet immunization in three broad areas. First, the original results and certain more recent results have been cast in a continuous time analysis in which rate shifts are assumed to be continuous but infinitesimal. Second, multiple horizon (or liability) dates have been considered. Third, and most important, attempts have been made to relax the requirement that only parallel shifts can be immunized. Specifically, it is quite clear that parallel shifts do not characterize actual markets. Yet the simplicity of the original immunization rule made it desirable to manage a single parameter in performing the immunization. Consequently, researchers sought to define more general patterns of rate shifts for which we could also define a single measurement of maturity such that immunization would be achieved by managing this new measure. The efforts of Cox, Ingersoll and Ross and Khang are most notable.[3]

In light of these general efforts, by the time bullet immunization had become popular as a practical investment vehicle, a disconcertingly large number of techniques had been recommended for improving on the original Fisher and Weil techniques. The essential tenet of each technique was to keep duration equal to the remaining horizon through rebalancing. However, different recommendations existed for the definition of duration as well as for the definition of the target rate. Moreover, the concept of how to structure the portfolio was even less precise in the following sense. The theoretical treatments of immunization clearly imply that a diversity of ways could exist to get the proper duration. However, a systematic relationship between return and variation in portfolio construction is not generally identified either because of the arbitrariness of the factors that give rise to such a relationship and the implication of arbitrage opportunities, which, when eliminated, would invalidate the underlying interest-rate process; or because all immunizing portfolios are expected to provide the same return.

Notwithstanding these facts, return differences resulting from variation in composition exist in actual markets so that the practitioner must optimize some criterion subject to the duration constraint. Intuitively, however, each of a bewildering diversity of optimization criteria possesses some logic—for example an objective measurement, such as average yield, could be optimized, as could a subjective element, such as expected return. If a parallel shift is actually expected, one could choose bonds that are as unlike a zero-coupon bond as possible to underscore the fact that the target return would then be the minimum. Alternatively, a safer route could be to choose bonds that replicate the zero coupon bond cash flow to the greatest possible extent, thereby mitigating the effect of shifts in general.

Chapter 2 employs a detailed prospective simulation analysis to identify which bullet immunization techniques appear to work best in a volatile rate environment. For this purpose, the best or risk-minimizing strategy refers to the combination of duration definition, target rate definition, objective optimization criterion, and rebalancing frequency that compacts returns most tightly about the target rate. In an experimental design, we tested a wide diversity of assumptions. We simulated increasing, stable, and declining rates. These simulations yielded several broad conclusions. A rebalancing frequency of three to six months is quite adequate; defining duration as Macaulay duration and defining portfolio duration as the weighted-average

Macaulay duration worked approximately as well as anything else and considerably better than at least one choice; the target return that worked best was the spot rate, although initial portfolio yield to maturity worked nearly as well; and the best optimization criterion is one that minimizes the variance of portfolio cash flow about the horizon.

Chapter 2 has several other findings. First, other techniques that employ only objective information in the optimization (which we generically call *objective immunization*) can significantly outperform the risk minimization variants, although less reliably. This finding serves as an introduction to chapters 3 and 4, where we systematically evaluate the efficacy of objective methods in identifying the risk-return tradeoff that pure theory fails to address. Second, we considered several forms of optimization based on subjective information (yield curve forecasts of varying accuracy) and compared the results of these tests to the risk minimizing returns. The subjective optimizations were simply (1) immunization where we maximize expected return resulting from a yield curve forecast, subject to the duration constraint; and (2) maximization of expected return, but subject to no duration constraint. We call these latter strategies *active immunization* and *active management,* respectively.

The purpose of these simulations was to determine how well we must forecast yield before active immunization or active management outperforms the risk minimizing approach. Generally, if managers can forecast the direction of rate change 60 percent of the time and at least 25 percent magnitude of the change, active immunization will outperform the risk minimizing technique, and active management (without regard to immunization) will outperform active immunization despite great volatility of yields and yield curve shape changes.

In chapters 3 and 4 we seek to identify a risk-return tradeoff among immunized portfolios that connects the risk minimizing strategy developed in chapter 2 with the higher expected return variants whose existence is implicit in the fact that first, actual markets do not obey any particular shift pattern; and second, some theoretical developments imply that if we do get the theoretically appropriate shifts, the immunized return is the minimum return that will be earned. It is pointed out that a theory of this tradeoff is inaccessible because if one starts from a theoretical yield curve process that predicts that immunization is possible, the existence of at least two points along a tradeoff, both of which are immunized, implies that arbitrage is possible. This would only highlight the implausibility of the interest rate process that was chosen.

To avoid this problem, we adopt an alternative approach and simply characterize the form of total compound return for an arbitrary portfolio with no particular assumption regarding yield curve shifts. This is done in chapter 4. When the formula is specialized to the assumption that the portfolio is a bullet immunization (with Macaulay portfolio duration set equal to remaining horizon), total compound return equals the initial yield to maturity plus a term related to the curvature of the yield curve. A natural approach to immunization is therefore implied: Maximize portfolio yield to maturity, set Macaulay duration equal to target, and minimize the curvature term. If the curvature term is adequately minimized, the initial yield to maturity will serve as a target. As a practical matter, minimization of the curvature term implies selecting securities that mature near the horizon date. This will serve to minimize the differences in yields among securities purchased, thus maximizing the effective flatness of the yield curve. Although these developments are central to our agreement, chapter 4 is quite mathematical and may be difficult for many readers. Consequently, the results of this mathematical analysis are applied in chapter 3 prior to being presented in detail in chapter 4.

With the results of chapter 4 in mind, chapter 3 merges the techniques of risk minimization with yield maximization. The disadvantage of the literal application of the technique developed in chapter 4 is that the curvature term is not a simple linear function of the portfolio weights, Macaulay portfolio duration is employed, rather than the weighted average of Macaulay durations, and the portfolio yield to maturity is maximized rather than a simple weighted-average yield. To remedy this, chapter 3 observes that the risk minimization criterion of minimizing the variance of the cash flow around the horizon is a simple linear criterion. Moreover, it has the effect of choosing bonds maturing near the horizon. Hence, it tends to replicate the curvature minimization strategy, although for a different reason. Similarly, when a simple direct test of the new strategy was discussed in chapter 2, we found that the weighted average of the Macaulay durations was not significantly different from the portfolio Macaulay duration. Finally, an additional finding of chapter 4 is that a very close (first-order) approximation to the portfolio yield to maturity is the duration-weighted yield. This is not a simple weighted-average yield in which we sum the portfolio capitalization weights times the respective bond's yield. Instead we sum the capitalization weights times the bond's yield times the ratio of the bond's Macaulay duration to the average Macaulay duration (which, in virtue of our second assumption, we have just defined to be the portfolio duration).

Summarizing these modifications to our proposed strategy, we maximize duration-weighted yield, set average Macaulay duration equal to target, and minimize the cash flow variance term. When cash flow variance is controlled, the initial yield could be expected to be a reasonable target estimate. Thus, at each rebalancing our strategy has the desirable property of maximizing the target return from that point on. This dynamic optimality could be expected to perform well as a device for extracting a risk-reward tradeoff when only objective data are employed in the optimization. Moreover, although this entire approach is intuitive, it arose out of a theoretical characterization of immunized returns that did not presume any particular variety of yield curve shift.

The burden of chapter 3 is an empirical estimation of the risk-return tradeoff we have postulated. For consistency the same simulated yields and prices as were used in chapter 2 are used here also. Specifically, because all parameters of the design (duration-weighted yield, weighted-average duration, and the cash flow variance term) are linear functions of the portfolio weights, we employed a linear program as follows: maximize duration-weighted yield to maturity, subject to the constraint that the weighted-average duration equal the remaining horizon, and subject to a successively relaxed constraint on cash flow variance. The extremes of the tradeoff were defined by minimizing cash flow variance subject to the duration constraint; and maximizing duration-weighted yield subject to the duration constraint and no constraint on cash flow variance—that is, this constraint is completely relaxed. The outcome of these tests is a risk-return tradeoff that is highly significant and readily measured. We believe that the variables (appropriately measured) yield and cash flow variance define the critical interplay for practical bullet immunization analysis using objective data.

**Contingent Immunization**

First discussed by Leibowitz and Weinberger, contingent immunization is a hybrid of active management and bullet immunization in which the portfolio is run actively over a defined horizon until an event triggers the portfolio into the immunized mode for the balance of the horizon.[4] At the inception of the portfolio, the immunized target return is estimated and a floor or minimum acceptable return over the horizon is stated. For example, the immunized target over a 5-year horizon could be estimated as 12 percent and the floor stipulated to be 10 percent. The 10 percent floor return can be converted into a minimum acceptable market value on termination date $T$. Call this amount $V(T, 10\%)$. At inception, therefore, the portfolio has a market value larger than what would be necessary to obtain a 10 percent compound return on the entire investment.

Consider the difference between the actual market value at time $t$ and the amount just necessary (when using the immunized rate at time $t$) to provide a 10 percent return on the original investment. We call this difference the excess market value at time $t$. It is simply equal to the actual market value at time $t$ minus the present value as of time $t$ of $V(T, 10\%)$ at the prevailing immunized rate. As long as this value is positive, the manager could take an active bet on the market by allowing portfolio duration to depart from the immunized target duration in accordance with the manager's interest rate outlook. If the manager is correct, the excess market value increases; if he is incorrect, it declines. If it were to decline to zero, the manager stops making active bets and runs the portfolio in a bullet immunized mode for the balance of the horizon. When the excess market value falls to zero, by definition immunization at prevailing rates will produce exactly $V(T, 10\%)$ at time $T$, or the minimum acceptable terminal value.

This form of immunization is attractive to many investors because it allows upside potential but has a fixed lower bound on return where the lower bound is a decision variable. Although the analysis of the return distribution in a contingent portfolio is mathematically tractable, and in fact comparatively interesting, it has not attracted much interest from the academic community. This is partially because of the newness of the idea; but perhaps is more closely related to the fact that a contingent immunization does not emerge as an optimal strategy based on the theories of behavior that economists normally ascribe to investors. These theories predict smooth or continuous changes in investment profiles, rather than discontinuous ones. In some respects, the same argument can be made regarding bullet immunization in the sense that it has not been derived as an optimal strategy. However, its role as a long-term risk-free asset—a long-term pure discount bond—puts it on a solid normative footing. As a vehicle for any investor with a very long horizon, both strategies suffer from the critical role played by the fixed termination date, which is normally far shorter than the investor's true horizon.

Specifically, actually carrying a bullet immunization to term (where toward the end the portfolio is all cash and cash equivalents) may be less important than the effect of having initiated the program over the first few years of its life, and having captured the certainty of a general level of return in an ongoing planning process. This is more of the substance of the investment than carrying through to the very end, unless of course, a specific liability is being targeted or actuarial guideline fulfilled. Similarly, if a contingent portfolio is actually triggered, it seems unlikely that an investor with a long-term horizon would wish to leave it immunized (depending perhaps on the remaining term), thus abandoning the original style of having a degree of activeness and risk-taking, unless a specific liability is to be paid or a guideline fulfilled.

Notwithstanding these qualifications, the return profile of contingent immunization may be rigorously analyzed. Chapters 5 and 6 develop, respectively, a purely mathematical approach and a simulation approach to this problem. The intent of this work is to parameterize the return distribution of a contingent portfolio in terms of the critical parameters: horizon, difference between immunized return and floor, aggressiveness or bet size, and forecasting accuracy. By varying the decision variables we then sketch out a risk-return tradeoff that may be helpful in deciding which combinations of parameter settings are most attractive to different investors.

In both the mathematical and simulation studies, we allow variations in bet size, manager yield change forecasting accuracy, and the difference between immunized return and floor. In the mathematical study we also vary the horizon, whereas in the simulation study we fix the horizon but allow variation in yield volatility. The most significant difference between the two approaches is how the bet size is defined, by which we mean the extent of the risks incurred by the manager, measured in terms of either the total portfolio value or the excess market value defined previously. Certainly a variety of assumptions could be adopted. In a broad sense the thrust of modern financial control theory is the identification of the optimal bet size as a potentially complicated function of market expectations, market value, interest rates, remaining horizon, and even investor risk preference. Rather than adopt this approach we consider in chapters 5 and 6 two representative but different definitions of bet size, and then regard the respective sizes as a parameter in the experimental design for the purpose of measuring a risk-return tradeoff.

Specifically, in the mathematical analysis of chapter 5, contingent portfolio returns in a given period are defined as the corresponding immunized return plus (with probability $p$) or minus (with probability $1 - p$) a fixed positive quantity $d$. Thus, a correct bet is made with probability $p$ and incorrect with probability $1 - p$. Moreover, within a particular simulation $p$ is a constant over time, independent of prior successes or failures, as is $d$. The number $d$ is our measurement of bet size. In the simulation analysis of chapter 6, forecast accuracy is also independent from period to period and within a given simulation. The probability of a correct forecast is constant over time as is the bet size. But here bet size is defined as the percentage of the excess market value that the manager can lose if yields move by one standard duration in the wrong direction. In chapters 5 and 6, both forecast accuracy and bet size (given its basic definition) are varied across simulations, along with other parameters, to trace out the effects of such parameter changes on the contingent portfolio return distribution.

While our definitions of bet size assume particular management styles that, as we have indicated, may not be optimal, they do reflect the range of thought for how such programs should be run and are representative in this sense. In both analyses, the portfolio return generation process was assumed to be a discrete time phenomenon rather than a continuous process. This is modified in an appendix to chapter 5 where a continuous-time diffusion model is assumed. This model is actually a limiting version of the discrete model employed in the chapter and has the same interpretation regarding bet size. Although this approach is cleaner in some respects, allowing a more explicit treatment of the effects of changes in parameter values, much of the intuition is lost. Investors tend to think in terms of discrete bets and probabilities of success, rather than in terms of mean and standard deviation of incremental return. Thus, we rely more heavily on the discrete model.

Our conjecture at the outset is that while the mathematical and simulation approaches differ, mainly with respect to bet definition, the broad conclusions regarding the risk–return tradeoff within a contingent immunization will be similar. This is borne out by the statistical tables supporting each chapter. The general findings are that expected return increases and the probability of triggering decreases with increases in forecasting accuracy and the difference between the immunized return and the floor. This was expected.

However, increasing the bet size may not be the best way to increase expected return unless the probability of a correct forecast is quite high. That is, with large and statistically independent bets, there is a large probability of triggering even if the probability of correct forecasts is high enough to be regarded as representing insight, but not very high. Basically, with modest but not great insight regarding rate changes, an investor requires many opportunities to make bets for the law of large numbers to reflect forecasting insight in returns reliably. It bets are too large, the probability of triggering is too great and the law of large numbers, in a sense, does not have a chance to work. This implies that a general prescription for the management of a contingent immunization, where forecasting accuracy can only be assumed to represent reasonable insight, is to make modest bets and to increase expected returns by reducing the floor. This is made somewhat more reasonable by an observation apparent in the statistical tables that while the floor may be reduced in this way, the probability of being between the original floor recommendation and the new lower one is small compared with the increase in expected return, as long as forecasting insight is positive.

**Dedicated Bond Portfolios**

Dedicating a bond portfolio is an investment technique in which a particular set of bonds is matched with a set of liabilities to be paid in the future. There are different interpretations regarding what constitutes a match. The most common is the *cash match,* in which bonds are chosen so that the cash flows from the portfolio (principal plus coupon) very nearly equal the liabilities in both timing and amount. The problem with this approach is its inflexibility. The procedure may select bonds that are unattractive as investments except for their maturity characteristics. Moreover, this technique often precludes future swap activity insofar as the universe of acceptable substitutes is correspondingly restricted. The obvious benefit of cash matching is the virtual elimination of reinvestment rate risk.

*Duration matching* is the conceptual alternative to cash matching. This approach makes use of immunization theory by recognizing that a portfolio whose duration equals the duration of the liabilities will finance the payments with small reinvestment rate risk. (The duration constraint must be maintained through appropriate rebalancing over time.) This approach adds considerable flexibility in the choice of bonds and in future swap activity, but at the expense of greater uncertainty. That is, reinvestment rate risk is not eliminated to the same degree as with cash matching, although it is largely eliminated. It is often possible to hybridize the cash match and duration match approaches to obtain a blend that suits the investor's risk requirements, without undue sacrifice of overall yield or latitude for future swap activity. Such hybrids are sometimes called multiperiod immunization. These techniques generally involve the identification of theoretical measurements that, when constrained in performing a duration match, help reduce reinvestment rate risk. As additional constraints are added, the solution begins to approach a cash match. A theoretical analysis of this type is presented in chapter 9 and summarized in the last section of this chapter.

Contrary to popular supposition, there is a substantial role for portfolio management after the dedicated portfolio is created. There is the normal credit and call risk monitoring function. Less appreciated are the opportunities for swap and general periodic reoptimization that occur when conditions in the bond market and in the portfolio itself change (as it matures). Taking advantage of these opportunities can add return equal to or even larger than the fee normally charged for dedicated portfolio services. It is important to employ a definition of asset-liability match that gives ample latitude for this type of management activity.

The decision to dedicate involves both actuarial and asset mix considerations. It is important to understand that, under certain conditions, there is strong justification for dedicated assets being a normal portion of the fund, but that in the absence of those conditions, dedicating may only be a cosmetic change (perhaps for the purpose of increasing the assumed rate and reducing contributions). A positive role for dedication emerges when we couple two distinct principles. First, as the funding level of a plan improves, there is a tendency toward a less risky posture because upside potential is then a less effective inducement to accepting downside risk. Second, as any institution's risk aversion increases, the theoretically optimal behavior regarding a future liability is to move toward a locked-up posture, even if a more aggressive management of the same assets remains attractive to others.

Taken together, these statements imply that as the funded level of a plan increases, a growing role for dedicated assets is quite plausible. A pattern is expected to emerge in which particular assets are targeted toward liabilities whose horizons complement the asset's risk control attributes. Thus, dedicated bonds would finance predictable nearby liabilities and risk is totally managed. Equities and active bonds (and other risky assets) are targeted to less predictable distant liabilities that have horizons for which the compound returns on those assets are more predictable. The proportion in dedicated assets would be adjusted primarily in accordance with the funding level of the plan and the relative attractiveness of dedicated versus riskier assets. In particular, a high funding level alone would not justify dedicated assets if their relative returns were unattractive.

Against this backdrop the decision to dedicate is, or should be, a standard consideration for many plans. Gradual adjustment in the portion dedicated is predicted to be a normal event. More substantial changes are predicted whenever perceptions change regarding the relative attractiveness of dedicated versus other assets, or the funding level of the plan. Although it is not absolutely necessary, there is the presumption that a change in the effective asset mix (that is, its overall aggressiveness) would attend an appreciable change in the dedicated portion.

Our remarks thus far focus on alterations in the dedicated portion of a fund for the purpose of maintaining an optimal asset mix. There may also be an effect on contributions. In fact, we would (in theory) expect that the asset mix, actuarial rate, and contribution rate would be jointly optimized so that a change in contribution (and assumed rate) would attend any change in the dedicated portion. This focus on dedication as a valid investment vehicle contradicts a commonplace (and cynical) perception of dedication as simply a device to reduce contributions. This perception views dedicated assets as "just a bond portfolio" and disregards its long-term risk control element. The origin of this perception is that high interest rates (which often occur along with and are often felt to be ultimately responsible for falling corporate profits) has created opportunities for firms to reduce contributions (and thereby increase net income) by raising the actuarial assumption on the dedicated portion of the fund. Often the perceived asset mix has not changed since the basic allocation to fixed income and the structure of the bond portfolio has not been materially changed. Contributions have thus been manipulated through a cosmetic change in investment vehicles. If there is not a genuine belief that the assumed actuarial rate should be higher, reduced contribution today implies that it must be increased in the future.

Numerous considerations come into play when deciding what the effect on contribution should be when dedicating. Other things being equal, a significant increase in rates is normally justification for an increase in the assumed rate as long as the change reflects the time over which rates are expected to be higher and as long as the asset mix implies that the higher rates will be captured (as in dedication). (Among other things, this statement assumes that there is no offsetting change in the salary growth assumption, as may be the case if a change in inflation causes the change in rates.) Whether contributions are affected is another matter that involves questions of business strategy. Thus a firm that expects to achieve a fully funded status over a particular horizon may wish to reduce contribution to maintain that horizon. Another firm in the same position may wish to take advantage of the higher rates, maintain (or even increase) contribution, and shorten the horizon. This involves the question of which management generation should be the beneficiary of the high rates.

During 1981 and 1982, we suspect that actuarial assumptions lagged the high rates of return available in the markets. As a consequence, many plans may have been better funded than they appeared, so that a jump in the low risk dedicated portion of the fund was entirely warranted, without any implication that the reduced contributions (caused by a higher effective actuarial rate) would necessitate an increase in contribution (or at least not as large an increase) later. However, it must be stressed that simply because interest rates may have risen sharply relative to actuarially assumed rates (so that additional fixed income investments or dedicated bonds are desired), an increase in the assumed actuarial rate is not necessarily appropriate. This is because fixed income securities generally (and dedicated bonds in particular) are capable of locking in the financing rate on a particular liability stream through time. This will be merely one component of the total liability stream. The uncertainty within the other components may be related to such factors as inflation or growth rates in differing economic sectors. The overall actuarial rate is a weighted-average rate that, in principle, reflects risk-adjusted expected returns on assets targeting all of the various components of liability. If interest rates rise and we can assert that expected returns on other asset types have not changed, an increase in the assumed rate may be warranted. However, an increase in rates may coincide with a decline in expected return on other assets. For example, the expected returns on assets used as inflation hedges (which finance the component in the total liability stream that is sensitive to inflation) may have fallen. Thus, the justification for an increase in the assumed rate may actually be far weaker than appears on the surface.

Where dedication is performed as part of an optimal asset mix, the foregoing remarks imply that we cannot scrutinize the operations solely in terms of its effects on contribution. When the impact on contribution is the objective however, there is a simple methodology for making the decision to dedicate. When reduced contribution today is at the known expense of future contribution, we are, in effect, borrowing from the pension fund. This will be beneficial if the aftertax earnings on the investment into which the saved funds are invested exceed what would have been earned had the money been left in the fund. This is because we will be able to replenish the fund (with appropriate interest) and still leave a residual for distribution to shareholders. This computation can be difficult and involves many of the subtleties encountered in general capital budgeting analysis. The analysis is clearest when we assume that the existing asset mix is optimal and that no effective change in the asset mix is being made through dedicating. The cost of borrowing from the fund is better understood here than when dedicating leaves the fund in a suboptimal risk–reward posture. When suboptimality is created we must consider not only the earnings on the fund if the full contribution had been made, but what the fund would have earned had the asset mix not been changed. Overall, analysis suggests that borrowing from the pension fund will not be desirable unless some special factors are present.

Just as a prolonged period of high rates may imply that an increased actuarial assumption is warranted, the weak economy, poor profits, and high cost of external capital that often attend high rates also imply that some firms may wish to defer contributions, even if actuarial and asset mix positions correctly reflect available market returns. That is, the capital budgeting analysis discussed earlier may favor borrowing from the pension plan for some firms under such conditions.

**Extensions to Other Investment Media**

Chapters 8 and 9 extend the application of immunization concepts to new investment media—foreign exchange and financial futures, respectively. Along with integrating futures into the analysis, chapter 9 develops a general model for handling nonparallel yield shifts, which implies the need to control several duration-like measures at once. This is the price paid for allowing nonparallel shifts. The analyses in both chapters are more mathematical than those in previous chapters. However, the intuition behind the results is clear and quite simple.

In chapter 8 we consider the problem of someone with an expected payoff in a foreign currency at some point in the future. Suppose, for instance, that a Japanese investor purchases a five-year bullet immunization in the United States; he will therefore have a predictable dollar position (say $1 million) in five years that is to be converted into yen. Assume that the investor does not wish to incur any exchange rate risk. If a forward market existed far enough into the future, the dollars could be sold forward at the prevailing rate on such a contract. Alternatively, if futures contracts existed with the proper horizon, we could short $1 million face amount in yen–dollar exchange rate contracts with the required expiration date. (Even this would ignore having to mark to market.)

Suppose, however, that neither futures nor forward markets existed with long enough horizons. In this case, chapter 9 demonstrates that the position will be hedged if the investor rolls over the appropriate short position in the foreign exchange market. For this purpose, a short position in the nearby yen–dollar exchange rate future could be employed. The number of dollars to be short should precisely equal the present value of the future dollar exposure, but valued using the Japanese interest rate. The intuition behind this statement is developed by imagining that there could only be one shift in the exchange rate. If this shift occurred immediately, the true cost to the Japanese of not being hedged is simply equal to the present value (using the Japanese interest rate) of the future dollar position times the change in the yen–dollar rate. To remedy this, we maintain a short position in the yen–dollar exchange rate equal to the present value of the dollar exposure. As long as the change in the exchange rate future picks up the full change in the spot rate, we will be fully hedged. If we maintain this posture throughout time, at each point we will be correctly hedged for the next shift, and we are thereby hedged against multiple exchange rate shifts.

The similarity between this technique and bullet immunization is intriguing. Suppose the time until the end of the horizon of an arbitrary portfolio is $T - t$. If rates shift upward by 1 percent, intuitively our total return will be enhanced by 1 percent times the remaining time or $1\% \times (T - t)$. But if yields rise we will experience a capital loss that offsets this gain. Mathematical analysis of yields demonstrates that this loss approximately equals the negative of the duration $D$ times the yield change, or $- D \times 1\%$. Hence the total effect of a 1 percent increase in yields on total return is the reinvestment effect plus the capital loss effect, or $(T - t) \times 1\% - D \times 1\%$. Now, in a bullet immunization, we set duration equal to the remaining horizon so that the impact total return of the yield change is $(T - t) \times 1\% - (T - t) \times 1\% = 0$. Thus, we are immunized. Setting the duration equal to the remaining horizon causes the reinvestment effect to perfectly offset the capital gain (loss) effect so that the target total return is unaffected by interest rate changes. If after any shift and throughout time, we keep duration equal to the remaining horizon we are always ready for the next shift. Thus, we are immunized against multiple shifts. (Of course, we have implicitly assumed in this discussion parallel shifts in forward rates.)

In the foreign exchange case, instead of equating capital gains (losses) with changes in earnings over the balance of the program, we equate capital gains (losses) with changes in the future value of the dollar position if exchanged into yen in the future. The mathematics are identical. In fact, it was a comparison of the underlying equations that demonstrated the conceptual relationship between immunization and foreign exchange hedging. We could easily transform these results to demonstrate that the present value of the position (as of the horizon date) is also hedged through maintaining the same short position. That is, we can view this approach as either a vehicle for locking in the present or the future value of a foreign currency exposure at the exchange rates prevailing at the outset of the horizon.

These statements are rigorously developed in chapter 8 where we assume that the exchange rate moves in a continuous fashion (that is, multiple shifts are allowed) and that the currency to be exchanged is actually a flow over time as opposed to a single lump sum. In more advanced treatments we have extended these results to uncertainty in interest rates and currency flows. Although the precise value of the exchange rate that is locked in may become more complicated, the rule continues to be to maintain a short position equal to the present value of the future long position.

Turning to financial futures and a technique for handling nonparallel forward rate curve shifts, chapter 9 adopts a different methodology for performing immunization. As we have remarked earlier, researchers on bullet immunization sought to find categories of nonparallel forward rate shifts that would allow the use of a single duration measure to achieve immunization. That is, we would manage the portfolio so that this single measure would equal the target. It has long been understood, however, that if more than one measure is allowed, nonparallel shifts could be accounted for more easily. This awareness was implicit in some of the earliest work, and even in the original paper by Redington where the concept of immunization was first introduced formally in the form of a duration-match approach to financing liabilities.[5] We pursue this latter approach by developing a general model for interest-rate shifts from which we can derive generalized duration measures that allow us to achieve immunization. The role of financial futures is then brought into the analysis.

We begin by recognizing that the most general formula to represent the shift in forward rates would simply be the assumption of a continuous curve added to the existing forward rate structure. That is, instead of assuming that at time $t$ the forward rates for all future times $t + h$ shift by a constant amount, we assume that at time $t$ they shift by an amount dependent on $h$. We then use the fact that any such curve (shift) can be mathematically represented as a polynomial of potentially infinite degree. Put in this general form, the coefficients of the polynomial uniquely determine the shift in forward rates. The interpretation of this formula is that any actual shift in forward rates can be represented as a linear combination of a series of more basic shifts: a constant or parallel shift, a shift proportional to $h$, a shift which is quadratic in $h$, and so forth.

We next make the critical assumption that shifts in forward rates occur because of continuous variation in the coefficients of the polynomial. This allows us to use differential calculus to represent the change in the present value of any asset or liability as equal to a sum of terms, one term for each coefficient in the polynomial. Each respective term in the sum captures the effect on present value of a shift in the coefficient of the respective type of yield shift—parallel, linear, quadratic, and so forth. A particular term will equal the sensitivity of present value (for any asset) to a change in only that component or type of shift within the total shift, times the change in the coefficient for that type of shift in the polynomial. Thus, we have represented the total change in present value as a sum of price sensitivities to each type of yield shift times the change in the coefficient for that type of yield shift. Each of these price sensitivities is, in effect, a different type of duration measurement.

Now, to achieve immunization we must make sure that the overall or total price sensitivity of the actual portfolio equals the overall price sensitivity of the benchmark asset or liability that we are seeking to replicate. At this point, the theory does not draw any distinction between whether we are performing a bullet immunization or a dedication. In either case, we compute the price sensitivity of either the zero coupon benchmark or a liability stream, respectively. Specifically, we must compute the price sensitivity or duration of the benchmark with respect to each type of yield shift that composes the overall yield shift. To achieve immunization we must rebalance the actual portfolio so that the price sensitivity or duration for each type of yield shift is the same for both the portfolio and the benchmark. This equality must be maintained over time through rebalancing.

To summarize, we have allowed greater generality in the nature of yield shifts at the expense of greater complexity in our measurement of risk. Specifically, we have developed a yield shift model that represents the total yield shift as a sum of different kinds of shifts. We then developed a duration measure that would immunize against each type of shift individually. To be totally immunized, we must set portfolio duration of each type equal to the corresponding benchmark statistic. At this point of generalization, we see that the theory is the same whether we are doing a bullet immunization or a dedication. In a bullet immunization we compute the appropriate duration measures for a zero coupon bond and set the actual portfolio duration measures equal to these amounts. In particular, the first measure of duration (the original concept) for a zero coupon bond is simply the time remaining until the end of the horizon. In a dedicated portfolio we set the duration measures of the liabilities equal to the corresponding measures of the assets. It will be recalled that a conceptual alternative to a cash match is a duration match. We point our earlier in this chapter and in chapter 7 that a conventional duration match alone is often believed to be too risky because of the prospect and impact of nonparallel forward rate shifts. Instead, we remarked that additional constraints to reduce risk were sometimes added. In practice, the constraints are the generalized duration measures that we have identified here.

As a practical matter, it is normal to assume explicitly or implicitly that only the first few coefficients of the polynomial model are nonzero, which is to say that only the first few generalized duration measures are necessary to provide adequate defense against nonparallel rate shifts. Also as a practical matter, there is no guarantee that we can always achieve immunization even using the generalized approach we have laid out here. The reason is that the set of generalized duration measures possessed by the benchmark may be impossible to achieve using the securities in the available universe. It is in this circumstance that financial futures may be of some help.

For our present purposes, two characteristics of financial futures are relevant to their use in immunization. First, they require no investment other than margin, which can be held in the form of earning assets. Second, they possess generalized duration measures as do any other bond. In light of these statements the use of futures in immunized portfolios is clear. If it is either impossible or inefficient to achieve immunization using the portfolio assets alone, and if futures can be used, one simply sets the generalized duration of the portfolio, plus the contribution to this statistic from the futures, equal to the required level. This is done for each such generalized measure. A simple formula for the optimal number of futures emerges when one is only concerned with parallel yield shifts. In this case, only the original duration measure is required and the portfolio can be left alone with all rebalancing to maintain target duration being accomplished with the futures contracts. In general, if it is desired to handle all rate shift risk in the futures market, an additional futures instrument must be added for each additional generalized duration measure to be controlled. Of course, we require independence of the respective futures in the sense that their generalized duration profiles are not too similar. If they were too similar, a redundancy would emerge and we would not be able to achieve target on all duration measures. In this connection, the only characteristic of the futures contract that is used is its price sensitivity or generalized duration. In particular, we do not require expiration of the future near any particular cash flow within the benchmark cash flow profile unless motivated by price sensitivity.

**Notes**

1. See F.M. Redington, "Review of the Principles of Life-Office Valuations," *Journal of the Institute of Actuaries* 78:3 (1952), pp. 286-340; Irwin T. Vanderhoof, "The Interest Rate Assumption and the Maturity Structure of the Assets of a Life Insurance Company," *Transactions of the Society of Actuaries* 24 (1972), pp. 157-192; Lawrence Fisher and Roman L. Weil, "Coping with the Risk of Interest-Rate Fluctuations: Returns to

Bondholders from Naive and Optimal Strategies," *Journal of Business* 44 (October 1971), pp. 408–431.

2. Ibid.

3. J.C. Cox, J.E. Ingersoll, Jr., and S.A. Ross, "Duration and the Measurement of Basis Risk," *Journal of Business* (1981), pp. 57–61; Chulsoon Khang, "Bond Immunization when Short-Term Rates Fluctuate More than Long-Term Rates," *Journal of Financial and Quantitative Analysis* (December 1979).

4. Martin L. Leibowitz, and Alfred Weinberger, "Contingent Immunization: A New Procedure for Structured Active Management," Salomon Brothers, (January 1981).

5. Redington, "Review of the Principles of Life-Office Valuations."

# 2

# Bullet Immunization and Active Management

Chapter 1 outlines the basic concepts and issues underlying the various forms of bond immunization. As we described there, bullet immunization seeks to provide a fixed (prespecified) compound return on an initial investment over a predefined horizon. All such immunizations have the basic management rule of keeping (through periodic rebalancing) the duration of the portfolio equal to the time remaining until the end of the horizon. However, within this general guideline, considerable variation exists as to the precise method for bond selection. In practice, we normally rebalance a bullet portfolio by optimizing some criterion subject to the constraint that portfolio duration equals the time remaining until the end of the horizon. Two broad categories of optimization criteria may be identified. The first employs only market-observable information in the analysis, for example, bond yields. Thus we might maximize average portfolio yield subject to the duration constraint. We shall call bullet immunization of this type *objective immunization* because no forecast quantities are employed. The second category of immunization employs forecasts in the optimization, and for this reason will be called *active immunization*. For example, using a yield curve forecast we may compute expected returns on each security and maximize expected portfolio return subject to the duration constraint. By employing this active immunization formulation but relaxing the duration constraint we approach what is normally called *active management*. This management style is employed by many fixed income money managers. It simply involves optimization based on yield curve forecasts. No explicit promise is made regarding returns over any particular horizon and no rigid constraint regarding duration or maturity is normally employed, although implicit (self-imposed) constraints can often be discerned.

This chapter employs a detailed simulation analysis to document the relative performance of various bullet immunization strategies against numerous alternative strategies. The study clarifies the relationship among the many objective immunization methods (and related issues) that have been proposed, showing which techniques work best in differing interest rate environments. Based on analysis in chapter 4, a new objective approach is discussed and tested. In addition, we compare the performance of these general methods to that of active immunization and active management under numerous assumptions regarding the ability to forecast yields. These results provide strong evidence on the question of how well we must be able to forecast yields before an active approach can outperform immunized returns over prolonged horizons. Through these analyses we seek to answer the major investment questions associated with executing and marketing bullet immunization methods. In the course of this work we develop evidence pertaining to several other questions. In particular, evidence is obtained illustrating the risk-reward tradeoff of active management. The breadth of the results on performance of alternative strategies may be useful in helping an investor select the appropriate index for performance appraisal.

Our broad intent in this chapter is to verify the existence of objective techniques that will work well in practice, and to compare these generally to active immunization and active management. Although many objective strategies are considered, we do not seek to provide a complete description of the risk-return tradeoff within the objective class. Efforts along these lines are made in chapter 3.

## Design of the Study

In broad terms, the research study was conducted as follows. First, we simulated interest rates into the future. Three scenarios were developed: secularly rising rates, secularly declining rates, and level rates. In each case, a business cycle was also assumed to be present. For each point in the future, a bond universe was specified. Finally, numerous portfolios were managed through time according to differing concepts of optimality and differing constraints placed on the management process. Relative performance was recorded.

### Horizon and Rebalancing Frequency

Because many immunization analyses employ a five-year horizon, we chose this as our horizon also. The theoretical research design does not depend on this, however. We examine results under monthly, quarterly, and annual rebalancing intervals. That is, interest rates, bond universes, and portfolio selections were updated monthly, quarterly, and annually. Most of the comparative strategy analysis was conducted using quarterly rebalancing because this is an appropriate interval for studying active management.

### Interest Rates

Three interest rate scenarios were developed: (1) rising rates consistent with a 12 percent long run inflation; (2) declining rates consistent with a 4 percent long-run inflation; and (3), level rates consistent with an 8 percent long-run inflation. In each case, rates were developed through simulating an econometric model for the three-month rate, the three-year rate, the ten-year rate, and the thirty-year rate. Other points on the yield curve were derived by interpolation.

*Bond Universes*

Given interest rates for each period, we developed a corresponding universe of bonds for each period by assuming an initial coupon–maturity curve based on outstanding securities, then assuming that a new long-term bond is issued at par every six months. Bonds thus drop out of the universe at the short end as they mature and are added every six months at the long end. At each point, sixty bonds are in the universe with equally spaced maturities. At the starting point for the simulation, maturity ranges from six months to thirty years. The maturity of all bonds decline steadily through time with one maturing and one issued every six months. We have made no provision for unexpected elimination from the universe through default or call. Thus we implicitly assume a high-grade bond yield curve in the case of default.

In the case of call, we implicitly assume that, in practice, new bonds are issued with shorter maturities than the thirty years that would be substituted for those called or that an adequate supply of discount bonds is always available. Alternatively, we could view the universe as consisting of government securities with insignificant call risk. To reduce the magnitude of the computer time required, we assumed that at each point in time a thirty-bond subset of the sixty in the universe would actually be employed. Every other maturity was selected from the sixty bonds to form the list of thirty. The qualitative and quantitative rate of return characteristics of this sample were thus virtually identical to the complete set.

*Immunization Strategies*

Although numerous theoretical variations exist, immunization strategies found in practice are conceptually similar and may be analyzed along four dimensions. First, three general definitions for the target return are employed: (1) the spot rate or the implied rate on a pure discount bond with maturity equal to the horizon; (2) the initial portfolio yield to maturity; or (3) the initial portfolio yield adjusted for roll along the yield curve and reinvestment of cash flows. Minor variations on these three also exist. Second, one of two definitions of duration is usually employed: (1) Macaulay duration or (2) duration computed from forward rates. Third, two basic variations exist on the manner in which portfolio duration is constrained to the target value. A capitalization-weighted average of the duration of the bonds in the fund is constrained to the target value (that is, a linear constraint); or a more complicated weighting method is employed (a nonlinear constraint). Finally, the optimization criterion is varied in numerous ways. Typically, we optimize either a linear function of bond characteristics, such as weighted-average yield or weighted-average expected return; or a nonlinear function. When a nonlinear function is employed, it has been a cash flow variability concept—that is, a measure of the variance of portfolio cash flows around the duration target. Such a measure is theoretically related to the error in an immunization due to nonimmunizable yield shifts.

In our work, we compare all portfolio returns to each of the target returns mentioned. We test both duration definitions. We have employed numerous versions of the linear optimization criterion in conjunction with simple linear duration constraints, including a close linear approximation to the nonlinear (variability) optimization criterion. We have employed the nonlinear duration constraint in a special two-bond universe. In this case we have developed the exact mathematical analysis underlying this method and presented it in chapter 4. This analysis and the associated technique represent new insights into bullet immunization theory and are further summarized later in this chapter.

*Transaction Costs and Other Portfolio Constraints*

For several reasons, the portfolio selection mechanisms available to us were not appropriate for handling the effects of transaction costs and other portfolio constraints as to, for example, credit sector or maturity. For transaction costs, actual costs depend on numerous factors including the size of the fund, market conditions, and sector composition. In our model we were not able to control for these complex variables. Even a conceptually simple penalty based on the volume of transactions would have lead to complicated and time-consuming optimization methods that would have precluded the breadth of analysis. Moreover, such solutions are invariably imperfect and thus bias comparisons of strategies that differ in portfolio turnover. Thus we uniformly made no correction for transaction costs. As a practical matter, the portfolio manager should judge the transaction costs associated with a particular immunized fund and adjust the theoretical target rate accordingly. Results show, as expected, that active strategies have much higher turnover than the less active, so that the raw results bias performance in favor of the active strategies.

Again for lack of adequate control parameters, the bulk of our results place no constraints on such factors as sector allocation or diversification. The only realistic constrains at our disposal, beside duration constraints, were maturity or time diversification constraints. We could constrain investments to be in certain broad maturity ranges or constrain a particular maturity to be no more than a fixed percentage of the portfolio. But these constraints, applied in our model, would not have the same effect they do in practice. Because we have only one security in each maturity category, any diversification constraint is a maturity diversification constraint rather than a credit diversification constraint. We have no facility for making credit diversification since we have no credit sectors. We could have constrained any portfolio maturity to being no more than a fixed percentage of the portfolio, but this would have been somewhat arbitrary and would diminish the comparability of strategies that differ only in yield-forecasting ability. Moreover, such constraints are risk constraints, which are analogous to the duration constraints. Including them could easily confound the impact of the duration constraint that we wished to isolate in this study. Thus, it was decided to omit time diversification constraints in most of our tests.

For comparative purposes, some quarterly tests in all three interest rate scenarios were conducted with and without a diversification constraint in which no single maturity in excess of two years could represent more than 20 percent of the portfolio. As expected, this constraint had the effect of diminishing return for any strategy with explicitly or implicitly good forecasting ability but improving returns to any strategy with explicitly or implicitly poor forecasting ability. The immunization strategy that minimizes cash flow variability was slightly improved in general in the limited simulations run with and without such constraints. Active management with accurate forecasts was diminished by approximately 50 to 100 basis points.

## Summary of the Study

In this study some 351 different strategies were evaluated over successive five-year horizons assuming increasing, decreasing, and level yield scenarios realistic for today's markets. Monthly, quarterly, and annual rebalancing intervals were considered as well as all of the significant technical specifications for performing immunization. Much time was spent in developing and analyzing several new immunization methods. We divide the research findings into four categories: first, procedural immunization questions—how well does immunization work in general, and what are the best of the standard (objective) immunization techniques? Second, active immunization versus objective techniques—under what conditions does actively managed immunization (that is, emphasizing yield forecasts) outperform standard methods? Third, active management versus immunization—under what conditions does active management (that is, strategy based on yield forecasts without regard to immunization) outperform objective or active immunization methods?

### Procedural Questions About Objective Immunization

It has been documented that many immunization methods work fairly well on an historical basis. The picture is not so clear if we project future rates to be as volatile as they have been since the fall of 1979. Under such conditions we must reexamine such questions as rebalancing interval, duration definition, and precise duration matching rule.

*General Performance.* When interest rates are enormously volatile, capable of moving hundreds of basis points at either the long or short end each and every quarter, many immunization strategies that worked well before no longer work. For example, one strategy based on a simple weighted-average yield to maturity maximization subject to a duration constraint, which worked well under smaller rate variations, underperformed its target (often substantially) fourteen of twenty times in a simulated environment of yields moving secularly down. Nonetheless, certain strategies are quite effective despite volatile yields. Using one such technique with quarterly rebalancing, we found the worst performance out of 20 rising, 20 level, and 20 declining rate environments to be 7 basis points (bp), 16 bp, and 14 bp short of target, respectively. On average the technique was over its target in these cases by 7 bp, 7 bp, and 9 bp, respectively. Using an alternative method under slightly modified assumptions, largest shortfalls were 1 bp, 16 pb, and 7 bp; on average, the technique was over target by 6 bp, under target by 4 bp, and on target, respectively. We conclude that immunized returns can indeed be offered in environments with large and frequent rate shifts.

*Rebalancing Frequency.* Technical analysis of immunization suggests that more accurate results obtain when we rebalance portfolios more frequently, especially when yields are volatile. In fact, when the best performing techniques were examined under monthly, quarterly, and annual rebalancing schemes, the results were qualitatively and quantitatively similar. This result conforms with what other researchers have found. Larger errors were found for still less frequent rebalancing, however. We conclude that considerable latitude is possible in the management of immunized funds, but that they must be managed. In respect of these results, most subsequent analysis was conducted assuming a quarterly rebalancing interval to compare results to that of active portfolio management.

*Duration Definition.* Duration is the key measurement of bond maturity when employing immunization techniques. Two definitions of duration are in common use, among a larger number that have been proposed by either theorists or practitioners. The principal definitions are Macaulay duration and duration computed on the basis of forward rates. Duration based on forward rates is the original concept that is theoretically correct for parallel forward rate shifts. Another concept, Khang's log-duration, also employs concepts of forward rates but seeks to immunize against nonparallel rate shifts of a certain type. We have tested these definitions and several variations on them in our simulations. Log-duration was found to produce generally inferior results compared to the other definitions. The remaining two produced very similar results. Since Macaulay duration is somewhat more intuitive, is the theoretically correct basis for our internally developed methods, and avoids problems that forward rates encounter when mixtures of high-grade and lower-grade bonds are used, we have decided to conduct our remaining work using this definition. This decision would not have been made if Macaulay duration had not performed as well as it had in the immunization simulations. We believe that this measure provides an accurate basis for illustrating the accuracy of immunization and for comparing immunization to other strategies. In particular applications, some improvement may be possible using refinements of this concept or still other as yet undiscovered methods.

*Immunization Technique.* Immunization operates in a manner similar to other optimized investment strategies: We maximize a criterion subject to constraints. The constraint that is always present in immunization is the duration constraint. Often this is presented as a linear constraint: A capitalization-weighted average of the duration of the bonds in the fund is set equal to the remaining time to the horizon. When portfolio Macaulay duration is used, the portfolio duration is not such a simple weighting, so a more complicated nonlinear constraint is required in theory, but this is often simplified to the linear constraint. We often add other constraints to the problem in addition to the duration constraint. The objective function, or criterion to be maximized, is not clearly specified by theory as is the duration constraint. The quantities maximized in practice are either measures of expected return or technical quantities whose optimization improves the ability of immunization to hit the target return. Either capitalization-weighted averages of bond-specific quantities or more complicated weightings are used.

In our analysis we examined numerous versions of the objective function and both linear and nonlinear duration constraints. When linear duration constraints were employed, two linear specifications of the objective function were found to work the best. Both had the effect of creating immunized portfolios using bonds with small coupon payments, although both outperformed the strategy of minimizing current income subject to the duration constraint. The first specification was a simplification (linearization) of a more complicated nonlinear method. This method sought to select bonds whose cash flows are tightly compacted around the horizon.

The second method was simply the strategy of minimizing the average bond price in the portfolio. This method substantially outperformed the former technique except in one case in twenty in the declining rate scenario when it underperformed by 38 bp. Beside this single case, the minimize average bond price technique outperformed its competitor by an average of 220 bp, 249 bp, and 201 bp in the decreasing, level, and increasing yield scenarios respectively. This is somewhat impressive in light of the fact that our previous discussion of the general performance of immunization referred primarily to the performance record of the first method described here. The other methods we considered (for example, minimize current yield subject to the duration constraint) that often worked well for smaller yield shifts worked poorly here. Either these methods had generally lower returns for one or more rate scenarios, or had high or higher returns but with excessive variability in the decreasing, level, or increasing yield scenarios, respectively. Intuitively, the minimize average price technique works well because it is a combination of the first technique and the strategy of maximizing yield to maturity.

Considerable effort spent was in developing a new immunization technique, which we describe fully in chapter 4. This analysis begins by deriving the formula for the total return on a bond portfolio over a particular horizon. When this result is specialized to a bullet immunization, in which portfolio Macaulay duration is kept equal to the remaining horizon, the total return is shown to equal the initial yield to maturity on the portfolio plus a term related to the curvature of the yield curve over time (as well as the effect of discontinuities in portfolio yield). Consequently, a reasonable immunization strategy would be to maximize portfolio yield to maturity and set Macaulay duration equal to target, but to use bonds with adjacement maturities so that the assumption of parallel movements (less curvature effect) is more accurate. This latter restriction implies a minimization of the curvature term in the total return formula. Evidently, a tradeoff exists between yield maximization and curvature minimization. That is, one could seek larger returns at the expense of risk if greater curvature exposure is allowed. This concept is explored in chapter 3. At present our hypothesis is that the concept at least suggests a technique for highly reliable returns.

In testing this hypothesis, we constrain the portfolio Macaulay duration to equal the remaining horizon. As previously indicated, this is not the same as the capitalization-weighted average of the Macaulay durations of the bonds in the portfolio. To simplify the experiments, we chose to operate with portfolios consisting of two bonds. To have adjacent maturities, we chose five-year and eight-year bonds to do the immunization. These bonds were selected because even for any plausible yield shift, some combination of them can still be used to create the desired portfolio duration; they are also close enough in maturity so that in general their yields move together. Given the same dramatic yield shifts as were employed in our previous tests, this method produced the most accurate results. That is, realized returns over the twenty successive immunizations for each of the three rate scenarios were closer to their target values for this method than for any other method.

Our conclusions regarding immunization method are that a great deal of attention must be paid to exactly how portfolios are optimized if we want assurance of being close to the target return when yields are highly volatile. Generally, a technique that minimizes the variance of portfolio cash flows around the horizon is necessary. This variance concept has intuitive appeal since a zero variance would imply a pure discount (zero coupon) bond, which would provide a perfect immunization. The theory behind this concept is further developed in chapter 3, along with its relation to curvature minimization. Use of either linear or nonlinear duration constraints seems capable of producing adequate accuracy despite highly volatile yields. The nonlinear method we have developed (that is, using portfolio Macaulay duration) shows great promise as its clear mathematical derivation allows identification of bond characteristics likely to improve immunization accuracy. It is worth noting that the minimize cash flow variability approach and the way we applied our new approach predictably led to qualitatively similar portfolios and we are not surprised by the similarity of results. However, the analytical developments are quite different, as is the extent of the intuition that underscores the nonlinear method.

*Target Return Selection.* Several quantities have been proposed as the appropriate target return for an immunization strategy. The three primary targets are: (1) the spot rate, or the implied rate on a pure discount bond with maturity equal to the horizon; (2) the initial portfolio yield to maturity; or (3) the realized return on the portfolio assuming no shifts in the yield curve. The first two targets have theoretical support; they are the targets recommended by the bulk of the immunization literature and the new approach we have developed, respectively. That is, literature points out that the spot rate will be the minimum return if yields shift in a particular way. The latter approach makes no assumption regarding yield shifts but does not state that the yield to maturity will be the minimum. It shows, however, that returns will be quite close to this quantity if yield differences of bonds used in the portfolio are small.

The third target has little to recommend it beside the fact that it is the logical extension of the following statement: The immunized return is that which would be received if the yield curve does not shift over the horizon. This statement is a modified version of the correct statement: The spot rate is that which would be received if the rates predicted at the start of the program by the forward rate curve are in fact realized. It is not hard to see why the watered-down version came into existence; this latter statement makes little sense to nonspecialists. Nonetheless, the target return arising out of the simplified statement has no strong theoretical support. Beside these three targets, several modifications have been used in practice, but they do not represent substantive conceptual innovations.

After extensive testing, we have found that the first and second targets perform the best. Defining the objective immunized return as the return on the strategy that minimizes variability of portfolio cash flow about the horizon, in the declining rate scenario across twenty trials, largest shortfalls of realized versus target return were 9.00 bp, 7.01 bp, and 78.83 bp using the three targets, respectively; on average, returns were over target by 23.39 bp, 22.00 bp, and 28.25 bp, respectively. Under the level rate scenario, largest shortfalls were 13.78 bp, 16.26 bp, and 18.17 bp; while on average, returns were over target by 19.70 bp, 19.47 bp, and 51.57 bp. In the increasing rate scenario, largest shortfalls were 14.93 bp, 14.12 bp, and 21.91 bp; while average returns exceeded target by 25.45 bp, 24.30 bp, and 54.86 bp, respectively. Root-mean-squared errors showed a quantitatively similar performance pattern as the largest shortfalls. On the basis of these data, the first and second targets substantially outperform the third, with the performance of the first two about equal. The first target based on the spot rate had a very slight edge over the second method. These conclusions differ somewhat from the finding of other researchers using historical data. Historical analyses typically find a closer correspondence of realized return to target return than we have found. However, the yield swings we have simulated here are more volatile than historical movements.

For purpose of defining objective immunized returns for further comparison to active immunized returns and to active management returns, we chose the immunization technique in which we minimize the variability of cash flows about the horizon. This technique is the most accurate method that is directly comparable to the other strategies we examined. That is, this method has a linear duration constraint so that it is comparable in its treatment of duration to, for example, the active immunization strategies based on yield curve forecasts. The strategy of minimizing average price subject to a linear constraint also satisfied this requirement and outperformed the chosen technique, but had far more variable results. The definition of objective immunized return that should be taken as the benchmark is that which most clearly matches the theoretical target determinable at the start of the program. Thus, when selecting a return target, we really are simultaneously selecting the target and a technique capable of hitting it with high probability. A target that cannot be reliably attained by any technique is not useful; nor is an immunization strategy that does not systematically hit some predictable value. Thus we favor the minimum cash flow variability definition of benchmark return as it reliably achieves returns close to the target. The minimize average price technique will be recommended in many applications for its dominance over the benchmark. It is not the benchmark itself.

### Active Immunization Versus Standard Techniques

We have identified several useful objective immunization techniques. One technique reliably earns the target return and is usually somewhat above the target. Another technique, the minimize average price strategy, tends to be substantially above target. Can active immunization outperform these strategies? To test this hypothesis we must simulate an environment in which, at each rebalancing point, a yield curve forecast is made. For example, under quarterly rebalancing, a three-month forecast is made every three months. Given the yield forecast, expected returns on each security are computed using current prices and coupons. We then choose a portfolio to maximize expected return subject to the duration constraint. Assuming quarterly rebalancing, this computation would be made twenty times in a given five-year program. Realized quarterly returns are compounded and then annualized to be compared to the immunized return. This entire computation is performed twenty times over twenty successive five-year horizons in each of a declining, level, and increasing yield scenario. In all, we will have sixty annualized active immunized returns on sixty five-year programs that can be compared to the sixty corresponding returns for the more objective immunization techniques. This defines the experimental design.

The next step is to define what we mean by an interest rate forecast. In this study we adopt a two-step approach. To compare active immunization of a given yield forecasting accuracy to a simpler alternate strategy, we endow management with forecasts that are right a given percentage of the time and wrong the remaining percentage. We then vary what we mean by right versus wrong. Although an infinite number of possibilities exist for such a designation, we tested fourteen different combinations to reflect the range of plausible forecasting abilities. To accomplish this, we said that a correct forecast was one of, or a combination of three basic forecasts for yields for the end of the current period: (1) the naive or no foresight forecast, which was taken to be simply the current yield curve; (2) the perfect foresight forecast, which was taken to be actual yields as of the end of the current period; or (3), the distant view forecast, which was taken to be the actual yield curve at the end of the following period. Thus, with quarterly rebalancing, the three forecasts for yields in three months would be today's yield curve, the actual curve in three months, and the actual curve in six months. Combinations of the first two (that is, averages of the first two) produce a forecast that has the direction of change uniformly correct but the magnitude of change is understated; yields move faster than forecast. Conversely, combinations of the latter two produces forecasts that have the direction correct but yields are forecast to move faster than they actually do.

We define an incorrect or wrong forecast as one or a combination of three basic forecasts for yields for the end of the current period: (1) the completely wrong or wrong direction forecast, in which yields are forecast to move in the direction opposite to the actual move that takes place during the period and to the same degree; (2) the no foresight forecast just defined; and (3) perfect foresight forecast as just defined. Thus, with quarterly rebalancing and assuming yields go up in three months 100 bp at the short end and 50 bp at the long end, the three forecasts for yields in three months would be: (1) today's yields less 100 bp at the short end and less 50 bp at the long end; (2) today's yields; and (3), the actual yield curve in three months. Combinations of the first two (that is, averages of the first two) produce a forecast in which the direction is uniformly wrong. Combinations of the latter two produce a forecast that has the direction right but that, for certain purposes, is called an incorrect forecast when compared to the forecast called correct.

Given these definitions of correct and incorrect forecasts, we formed fourteen pairings of incorrect with correct forecasts and tested the results of being correct 0 percent of the time, 10 percent of the time, and so on up to 100 percent of the time. Thus, one pairing was no foresight and perfect foresight. For this pair we would test the consequence of having perfect foresight 0 percent of the time and no foresight 100 percent; perfect foresight 10 percent and no foresight 90 percent; and so on up to perfect foresight 100 percent of the time and no foresight 0 percent. The same was done for thirteen other combinations.

The results of these tests are striking. When active immunization is compared to the minimize cash flow variability strategy, and when correct is defined as perfect foresight versus incorrect, defined as no foresight, a 20 percent forecasting accuracy outperforms objective immunization. Outperform here is taken to mean produce a higher return in all sixty trials; or produce a higher return in the vast majority of trials, never have a large shortfall of realized versus target, and average substantially higher than target. If a correct forecast is defined as an average of perfect foresight and no foresight, and incorrect as defined as a weighting of the wrong direction and no foresight forecasts, then a forecasting accuracy of 60 percent dominates objective immunization. This figure corresponds to a .75 weighting on no foresight versus .25 on perfect foresight for the correct forecast; and .75 on the wrong direction forecast versus .25 on no foresight for in incorrect forecast. While this 60 percent figure may be too low for—say .9 versus .1 weightings rather than .75 versus .25—the figures for .5 versus .5 and for .25 versus .75 were only 50 percent. These weightings correspond to underestimates of the yield change when a correct forecast is made and the direction incorrect when an error is made.

If we continue to define errors in this way but define a correct forecast as a weighting of the perfect foresight forecast and the distant view forecast, figures of 60 percent accuracy are generally sufficient to dominate objective immunization. Only 20 percent is necessary when the correct forecast is defined as the distant view and incorrect is defined as no foresight; but this jumps to 70 percent when we define correct to be only .75 of the distant view versus .25 of perfect foresight and .25 of the wrong direction forecast versus .75 of the no foresight forecast. When both the incorrect forecast and the correct forecasts have any predictive content, a 0 percent forecasting accuracy outperforms objective immunization.

To summarize these statements, when correct forecasts have a nontrivial predictive content (when they get the direction right and at least 25 percent of the magnitude of the change), a 60 percent forecasting accuracy is sufficient to outperform objective immunization. This is true even if the forecasts are fairly bad when incorrect. As incorrect forecasts come closer to the no foresight forecast and as correct forecasts come closer to perfect foresight, the required accuracy drops below 60 percent. A forecasting accuracy of greater than 60 percent can be required if correct forecasts pick up too little of the magnitude of the change, although 25 percent of the change appears sufficient. (If the correct forecast has no foresight and the incorrect errs on direction, no forecasting accuracy beats immunization.) Conversely, if correct forecasts are too heavily weighted on the distant view forecast, greater than 60 percent may be required.

In short, regardless of the error (assuming errors imply an error on direction), 60 percent accuracy is sufficient as long as correct forecasts get the direction right and enough but not too much of the magnitude. One way to characterize the magnitude requirement is to say that if rates move gradually through time, the forecast for rates in three months must equal the realized curve anywhere between three weeks and eighteen weeks from the date of the forecast for 60 percent accuracy to be sufficient. At the long end, more than eighteen weeks can require as much as 70 percent accuracy and less than three weeks may require considerably more. When we cite 60 percent accuracy as being sufficient to outperform objective immunization, we of course mean that 50 percent would not outperform it. Mathematically, a breakeven point exists between 50 percent and 60 percent where financial theory suggests that an investor would be indifferent between being offered active immunization and objective immunization. This point is exceedingly difficult to identify and we do not attempt to put a precise value on it. Likely values supplied by intuition conform, however, with what other researchers have found regarding the forecasting accuracy required to outperform simple strategies using such other investment vehicles as common stock.

The foregoing discussion compared active immunization to the objective immunization strategy of minimizing the variability of cash flows about the target. What if we compare active immunization to the minimize average price strategy? As one would expect, required accuracy is greater in this case. Here, an 80 percent forecasting accuracy is required to dominate when correct forecasts are in the three- to eighteen-week band and incorrect forecasts err on direction. Required accuracy increases rapidly outside the band on the distant side to the point that no forecasting accuracy outperforms. As before, on the short side of the band, if the correct forecast has no foresight and the incorrect errs on direction, no forecasting ability outperforms. Also as before, if both correct and incorrect forecasts have predictive content, a 0 percent forecasting ability beats objective immunization.

*Active Management Versus Objective Immunization*

Earlier in this chapter, we analyzed standard (objective) immunization strategies and then compared standard strategies to active immunization. Active immunization consists of maximizing expected return subject to a duration constraint, given a particular yield curve forecasting ability. In this section we compare objective methods to active management, but where active management is no longer constrained by duration. Thus, we compare objective immunization to active management as it is ordinarily practiced.

The impact of removing the duration constraint conforms to intuition. When forecasting ability is good, returns improve. When it is bad, returns are worse. The changes are sizable, showing that the duration constraint has considerable force. When comparing active management to the minimize cash flow variability definition of immunization, we again find that a 60 percent accuracy dominates immunization for a wide range of forecasting abilities. This range is even wider than in the comparisons of the objective methods to active immunization. Thus, when correct forecasts have the direction right and at least 25 percent of the magnitude of the change, 60 percent accuracy was sufficient to outperform objective immunization regardless of the nature of incorrect forecasts. In effect, using the three- to eighteen-month range employed in the previous section, we still have the three-week requirement, but no discernable upper limit, given the tests we employed. That is, as long as the forecast for rates in three-months forecasts the actual curve realized within the next three to twenty-four weeks, 60 percent forecasting accuracy is sufficient. (Twenty-four weeks was the outer limit of our study.) As before, if less than 25 percent of the magnitude is picked up, greater than 60 percent may be required. If the correct forecast is the no foresight forecast, and if incorrect forecasts err on direction, no forecasting ability outperforms objective immunization. Again, as in the comparison of objective techniques to active immunization, if both correct and incorrect forecasts have predictive ability, a 0 percent forecasting ability outperforms objective immunization; and as correct forecasts approach perfect foresight and incorrect approach approaches no foresight, required accuracy drops below 60 percent.

In contrast to the comparison of objective immunization and active immunization, we find here that, with a 60 percent forecasting accuracy, active management still outperforms the minimize average price strategy. Indeed, we found only one instance in which the accuracy required in this case was larger than for the minimize cash flow variability method. This one instance was where the correct forecast had a .75 weight on the distant view forecast and .25 on perfect foresight, while the incorrect forecast had a .25 weight on the wrong direction forecast and .75 on no foresight. Here 70 percent accuracy was required rather than 60 percent. The reason for the pervasiveness of the 60 percent figure is the impact of the duration constraint. When accuracy is at least 60 percent, and the constraint is removed, returns improve enough to generally outperform the minimize average price immunization performance. The constraint holds back performance when accuracy is at least 60 percent.

Several naive, nonimmunization strategies were also evaluated over the three interest rate scenarios. These strategies were laddered, barbell, long-term bonds, intermediate bonds, and short-term bonds. On average, each of these strategies except the short-term portfolio had higher returns than the minimize cash flow variability immunization method, but often had large shortfalls. Thus they did not outperform objective immunization in the sense we mean here. Because all five strategies had average returns less than the minimize average price immunization method, they also failed to outperform this method.

**The Risk-Return Tradeoff**

Chapter 2 outlined the findings of a detailed simulation analysis regarding the relative performance of alternative bullet immunization techniques. Both objective techniques (those which do not use any forecast data in the optimizations) as well as active techniques (those which do use forecast data) were compared, as were active management techniques (optimizations based on yield forecasts without any duration constraint). The purpose of that study was to establish some basic facts about the practical aspects of immunization: Which objective techniques work the best in volatile rate environments? How well must we forecast rates before active immunization outperforms the objective methods? How well must we forecast rates before active management outperforms immunization?

In making these comparisons, chapter 2 also outlined the concepts underlying the new immunization approach developed in chapter 4. That analysis began with the formula for total compound return on a general bond portfolio that was then specialized to a bullet immunization. The resulting formula equaled the initial yield to maturity plus a term summarizing the curvature of the yield curve. This implied an immunization technique in which we maximize portfolio yield to maturity, set Macaulay duration equal to horizon, and minimize the curvature term. Although we acknowledged that higher-risk-higher-return strategies could emerge from this approach, we only tested the low-risk (curvature minimization) version, which we found to be highly accurate.

In chapter 2 we did not seek to specify a risk-reward tradeoff within the objective techniques, although we tested various strategies that led to the belief that such a tradeoff exists. Instead we verified the existence of objective techniques, which were highly reliable, for further comparison to more active methods. In this chapter we document a risk-return tradeoff within the objective class. To do this we illustrate the relationship between the new approach developed in chapter 4 and the standard techniques. Specifically, we consider the relationship between cash flow variability and curvature, the two quantities that, when minimized, produced the most reliable results. We then show that the relationship between the yield maximization concept underlying (or representing one aspect of) the new approach and risk (curvature or cash flow variability) minimization emerges as a risk-return tradeoff that is readily measured and of practical significance. The first section of this chapter summarizes our earlier findings, along with some introductory material, and introduces the concept behind the tradeoff. The second section outlines the analysis, and the third section provides the results of the simulation. The principal conclusion of this work is that the proposed tradeoff is, in concept and result, the appropriate framework for practical bullet immunization analysis, both from its strong theoretical underpinnings and empirical measurement.

**The Tradeoff Concept**

*Summary of Earlier Work*

Detailed mathematical analysis by numerous researchers has verified the possibility of perfectly immunizing a portfolio under certain conditions pertaining to the nature of interest rate movements. Several categories of rate movements have been identified that allow such strategies. For each such category a different measure of duration has been identified as appropriate. That is, corresponding to each rate movement variety, the immunization strategy will work only for the particular definition of duration that arises out of the mathematical calculations. This definition may be non-intuitive, bearing little resemblance to the familiar Macaulay definition.

Unfortunately, actual rate movements are far more varied than the theoretical categories that have been proved immunizable. This has motivated the study of the performance of the various immunization strategies in actual markets. When rate movements are immunizable, one merely makes sure that the appropriately defined duration of the portfolio equals the time remaining until the horizon. If there is more than one way to accomplish this, all possibilities will produce the same return. In simulations of plausible rate movements, all possibilities will not produce the same return. Thus, the main purpose of such an exercise is to search for that objective immunization technique which provides returns closest to target, where *objective* means that no forecast data is used in the analysis, only observable data. One normally simulates the management process where at each step some criterion is maximized subject to the constraint that portfolio duration equals the time remaining until the end of the horizon.

The best technique is actually the simultaneous selection of objective optimization criteria—rebalancing frequency, duration definition, and target definition—that produce the best results in terms of being able to compact returns tightly about the target. A study along these lines is presented in chapter 2. This analysis produced (among other things) the following conclusions. Rebalancing frequency more often than three to six months added little value and could even be detrimental after transaction costs, while a frequency as low as annual was often adequate. The Macaulay duration for individual bonds performed as well as any other definition, along with defining portfolio duration as the weighted average of the Macaulay durations of the individual bonds. The definition of target return that performed the best was the spot rate, although the initial yield to maturity performed nearly as well. The optimization criterion that performed the best (in terms of centering returns tightly about the target) was a risk minimization criterion. The use of this combination of techniques produced immunized returns exceedingly close to target despite great yield volatility.

*Comparing Cash Flow Variance Minimization*
*and Curvature Minimization*

The risk minimization criteria that produced the results in the previous section came from two sources. The first minimization criterion is a linear function of bond characteristics which was independently developed here, as well as by several other authors. Fong and Vasicek provide probably the most rigorous analysis of this statistic, which is given by equation 3.1.[1]

$$\frac{\displaystyle\sum_i \sum_T \frac{N(i)C(i,\ t)(t - D^*)^2}{(1 + y(i))^t}}{\displaystyle\sum_i N(i)P(i)} \tag{3.1}$$

where $y(i)$ is the yield on the $i$th bond, $N(i)$ is the number of bonds of type $i$ held, $C(i, t,)$ is the cash flow from the $i$th bond at period $t$ in the future, $P(i)$ is the price of the $i$th bond, and $D^*$ is the target duration of the portfolio (where duration is given by Macaulay duration). If portfolio duration is defined as the weighted average of the Macaulay durations of the bonds within the portfolio, it is simple to show that (if in fact the portfolio duration equals the target duration, $D^*$) this statistic reduces to

$$\left\{\sum_i X(i)D_2(i)\right\} - D^{*2}$$

where

$$D_2(i) \equiv \frac{\displaystyle\sum_i \frac{C(i,\ t)t^2}{(1 + y(i))^t}}{P(i)}$$

and $X(i)$ is the percentage of the portfolio in bond $i$. That is, the statistic is a linear function of the $X(i)$ and may thus be incorporated in a conventional linear program as the criterion to be optimized or as a constraint.

Fong and Vasicek demonstrate that the error in hitting the target return in a bullet immunization is, as a first-order approximation, proportional to this quantity. This makes sense intuitively because the statistic is literally equal to the variance of portfolio cash flows around the horizon; and if this variance is zero, the portfolio must be a perfectly immunizing zero coupon (pure discount) bond. Fong and Vasicek do not point out an equally significant fact that is of great significance for many theoretical applications as well as an important source of intuition. Simple calculations show that for an individual bond or a bond portfolio, the statistic is precisely equal to the negative of derivative of the Macaulay duration with respect to true portfolio yield to maturity when yields are continuously compounded. Under discrete compounding, the statistic is proportional to the negative of the derivative where the proportionality factor is $1/(1+y)$. This derivative can only be zero for a zero-coupon bond. These facts strongly support the rationale for why this variability concept should, when minimized, produce reliable returns.

The second source for a risk minimizing criteria arises from the analysis developed in chapter 4. There we develop a formula for the total compound return on an arbitrary portfolio that, when specialized to the case of a bullet immunization, reduces to two terms: (1) the initial yield to maturity on the portfolio; and (2) an expression measuring the curvature of the yield curve over time (as well as certain discontinuities in portfolio yield). The formula, which is given by equation 4.20, implies the following technique for bullet immunization. Maximize yield to maturity, set Macaulay duration equal to the remaining horizon, and minimize the curvature term. Clearly, the most reliable results will occur if one simply minimizes the curvature term without regard to yield. Examination of this term reveals that it will be minimized when the bonds in the portfolio have similar yields over time. Consequently, restricting the universe of securities to bonds that are adjacent on the yield curve (and for which the yield curve is more nearly flat) can be expected to produce reliable results. This approach was tested in chapter 2 and found to be quite accurate.

Both risk concepts normally lead to the same type of portfolio: bonds whose cash flows are tightly compacted around the horizon. The respective theories behind each approach, however, are separate, although the reliability of the simulated returns benefit from both sources of logic. Specifically, the curvature approach always seeks bonds for which the assumption of a flat yield curve is best. The cash flow variance approach always seeks to construct a portfolio for which cash flows are as similar as possible to that of a pure discount bond with maturity equal to the horizon. This latter concept will not construct a portfolio for which the yield curve is as flat as possible. Instead, it will (as its theoretical objective) lead to a mitigation of the effects of nonparallel shifts in general. Thus, the concepts are related but the type of yield shift that each seeks to protect against are different—nonflat versus nonparallel.

The foregoing comparison of the cash flow variance and curvature minimization approaches illustrates why both produce reliable results. Our interpretation of a curvature-minimizing strategy as one where maturities are compacted around the horizon is, of course an ex ante (or heuristic) optimization because we are led to it by first principles regarding yield curve shapes in practice, rather than by an evaluation of the current yield levels that might suggest a different strategy for avoiding a nonflat pattern. However, any useful alternative approach would likely involve a conjecture about the future shape of the yield curve and would cease to be an objective technique, thus making it noncomparable to cash flow variance minimization. Thus our objective application of curvature minimization renders it operationally similar and *more* conceptually similar to cash flow variance minimization than it would otherwise be. These facts, along with the statistical tests, imply that the approaches, as we have applied them, are virtually the same.

*Developing the Risk-Return Tradeoff*

Notwithstanding the findings of the similarity between cash flow variance minimization and our application of pure curvature minimization, the full strategy outlined in chapter 4 (set Macaulay duration equal to target, maximize yield to maturity, and minimize curvature exposure) is not equivalent to others that we have tested. Rather, the analysis provides a theoretical basis for unifying the two most intuitively interesting approaches that are commonly used: yield maximization and risk minimization. Specifically, equation 4.20 implies a tradeoff between yield and curvature that will depend on the nature of the yield curve shape over time.

The principal objective of this chapter is to perform an empirical analysis of this risk-return tradeoff. Three earlier findings will be of assistance. First, because the cash flow variance minimization criterion, which has strong theoretical justification of its own, is qualitatively and quantitatively similar to the curvature measure, as we have applied it, and as importantly, because the associated statistic is a linear function of bond characteristics, we will employ this quantity as the risk control.

Second, we demonstrate in chapter 4 that the duration-weighted yield is a close underestimate of the true yield to maturity. This statistic is given by equation 3.2:

$$\sum_i X(i) \frac{D(i)}{D} y(i) \qquad (3.2)$$

where

$$\bar{D} \equiv \sum_i X(i)D(i) \qquad (3.3)$$

where $X(i)$ is the percentage of the portfolio in the $i$th bond, and $D(i)$ is the Macaulay duration of the $i$th bond.

If $\bar{D}$ (the capitalization-weighted average of the Macaulay durations) is constrained to a particular value, then equation 3.2 is a linear function of $X(i)$.

Third, because the results for both the linear and nonlinear duration constraints in chapter 2 are similar, we shall define the portfolio duration to be the simple weighted average of the Macaulay durations of the bonds in the portfolio. This statistic is given by equation 3.3 and is a linear function of the $X(i)$.

We may now organize these factors and outline the experimental design. By virtue of the linearity of our analytical criteria in portfolio allocations, the $X(i)$, we may employ linear programming to measure the risk-return tradeoff. At one extreme we minimize cash flow variability subject to the duration constraint that $\bar{D}$ (equation 3.3) equal the remaining horizon. The minimum value of cash flow variance $V0$ is saved. At the other extreme we maximize duration-weighted yield (equation 3.2) subject to the duration constraint. The minimum value of cash flow variance $V1$ is computed and also saved. In between, we maximize duration-weighted yield subject to the duration constraint and subject to the constraint that cash flow variance equal a value between $V0$ and $V1$. By altering this value, we sketch the risk-return tradeoff.

This formulation is highly intuitive and enjoys a presumption for theoretical soundness even in the absence of analytical support from chapter 4. However, chapter 4 takes this further in a way that suggests that this trade-off construction is the appropriate one for the practical application of objective immunization. In particular, equation 4.20 shows total return equal to initial yield to maturity plus the curvature term. Thus, when curvature is minimized, the initial yield is a target measure. In our simulations at each step, we maximize yield subject to a constraint on risk or curvature. Thus at each point in the life of a single portfolio we maximize (subject to a risk constraint) its target return from that point on! This maximization, which has an apparent dynamic optimality, could be expected to impart the most significant upward slope to any risk-return frontier, making it the appropriate measurement.

## Design of the Simulation

Our starting point was a simulation of yields. For consistency we employed the same simulated data as was employed in chapter 2. To review, we simulated short, intermediate, and long yields using simple econometric techniques and assigned other points along the yield curve through interpolation. Starting from an initial yield curve with yields near 8 percent, three patterns were simulated: secularly increasing yields (to stabilize near 12 percent); secularly stable yields (remaining near 8 percent); and secularly declining yields (to stabilize near 4 percent). New yield curves were generated each quarter. Appendix 3A shows the yields for each scenario for selected points along the yield curve. (In all, sixty points were used to describe each curve ranging from three months to thirty years). As can be seen, great yield volatility was assumed to exist. The mean absolute change from one quarter to the next for the selected yields is included in appendix 3A. To develop a bond universe, we began with an initial coupon distribution that reflects actual markets. In the course of the simulation we assumed that as bonds matured, new long-term bonds were issued at par.

The actual tests involved simulating the performance of immunized portfolios. Results were developed for portfolios with three-, five- and seven-year horizons. Each portfolio was assumed to be reoptimized quarterly. For each horizon we simulated sixty portfolios: twenty under increasing yields, twenty under stable yields, and twenty under declining yields. For example, in the five-year horizon case for increasing yields we would optimize a portfolio using prices and yields for the first period. Returns under the optimal strategy were recorded where security returns were derived from the first- and second-period prices for the universe. Reoptimization was made using second-period prices and yields and return to the optimal strategy was again recorded using second- and third-period prices. This process continued for twenty periods (quarters). The twenty returns would be converted to a single (annualized) five-year return.

At the outset of the simulation we would record several measures of target return for comparison to actual return. One simulation for a five-year immunization would involve use of data from twenty-one yield curves (say the first twenty-one). To develop additional observations as well as to randomize the starting point, we would then perform an identical five-year simulation using yield curves 2 through 22, and so on. Twenty such simulations would be performed, ultimately using curves 20 through 40 for the last portfolio. A similar exercise would be done in the five-year case for stable and declining yields. The entire exercise would be repeated for three- and seven-year horizons. Results would thus consist of 180 simulated returns (three- five- and seven-year horizons with twenty increasing, twenty stable, and twenty declining yield scenarios each) and several target return measures to compare with each of the 180 returns.

The 180 returns would be generated for a particular optimization technique. The main purpose of our work, of course, is to test the effect of differences in technique. In all, we generated 180 returns for each of five different techiques (for a total of 900 simulated returns). These techniques were related to one another in a way that we will now review.

At one extreme was risk minimization. There we always minimized the cash flow variance statistic given in equation 3.1. At the other extreme was yield maximization. There we always maximized the yield statistic given by equation 3.2. This is not the same as the simple weighted-average yield statistic tested in chapter 2 and found to produce poor results. The empirical conjecture of the simulation analysis is that the extremes of risk minimization and yield maximization are appropriately connected by constrained yield maximization. That is, if we maximize yield subject to successive maximum levels of risk (as well as to a duration constraint), we will sketch out a risk-return frontier. If the risk and yield constraints are close to their true theoretical representations, as we believe they are, then the tradeoff that emerges is not a frontier, but the frontier. That is, it is the best empirical depiction of its theoretical counterpart.

In the simulations actually performed for each of the 180 cases, we developed five points on the proposed risk-reward tradeoff: risk minimization, yield maximization, and three points in between representing equally spaced intermediate levels of risk from lowest to highest. We developed two target measures of return for each point as well. The results of the simulation are described in the next section, particularly the ability of this framework to define a useful risk-return frontier, differences in the frontier for different horizons, and the relative performance of different measures of target return.

## Simulation Results

In this section we examine the three questions posed in the preceding analysis. Does the framework developed define a useful risk-return frontier for immunized portfolios? If so, how do the results depend on the horizon? What is the relative performance of different target measures?

Beginning with the results on defining a frontier, table 3-1 shows the mean and standard deviations of annualized compound returns of the simulated portfolios for three-, five-, and seven-year horizons. Increasing, stable, and decreasing yield scenarios are indicated separately and combined. Within each group portfolio, returns are listed according to the risk constraint—most binding to least binding. Higher risk unambiguously produces a higher mean return in every case. However, the standard deviation of return does not increase uniformly except in the case of increasing yields. Based on this evidence alone, the linear risk measurement employed in the optimization is directly linked to mean return but not to the normal measurement of return risk, standard deviation. This is actually not a problem because return risk in an immunized portfolio normally refers to the

**Table 3-1**
**Mean and Standard Deviation of Return**

| Risk | Decreasing Mean | Decreasing Standard Deviation | Stable Mean | Stable Standard Deviation | Increasing Mean | Increasing Standard Deviation | Combined Mean | Combined Standard Deviation |
|---|---|---|---|---|---|---|---|---|
| | *Decreasing* | | *Stable* | | *Increasing* | | *Combined* | |
| *Risk* | *Mean* | *Standard Deviation* | *Mean* | *Standard Deviation* | *Mean* | *Standard Deviation* | *Mean* | *Standard Deviation* |
| | | | | *Three-year Horizon* | | | | |
| 1 | 6.90 | 2.75 | 9.31 | 1.96 | 12.68 | 2.04 | 9.63 | 3.28 |
| 2 | 7.86 | 2.75 | 9.71 | 1.94 | 13.60 | 2.33 | 10.39 | 3.35 |
| 3 | 8.40 | 2.76 | 9.80 | 1.91 | 13.88 | 2.47 | 10.69 | 3.33 |
| 4 | 8.91 | 2.73 | 10.04 | 1.89 | 14.09 | 2.70 | 11.01 | 3.31 |
| 5 | 9.31 | 2.74 | 10.26 | 1.89 | 14.28 | 2.98 | 11.28 | 3.34 |
| | | | | *Five-year Horizon* | | | | |
| 1 | 6.91 | 2.78 | 9.56 | 1.85 | 12.91 | 1.94 | 9.79 | 3.31 |
| 2 | 8.50 | 2.71 | 10.71 | 1.88 | 14.27 | 1.87 | 11.16 | 3.22 |
| 3 | 9.38 | 2.67 | 11.03 | 1.78 | 15.12 | 2.02 | 11.84 | 3.25 |
| 4 | 10.21 | 2.61 | 11.39 | 1.73 | 15.72 | 2.27 | 12.44 | 3.24 |
| 5 | 10.81 | 2.59 | 11.69 | 1.70 | 16.19 | 2.55 | 12.89 | 3.29 |
| | | | | *Seven-year Horizon* | | | | |
| 1 | 7.01 | 2.74 | 9.76 | 1.66 | 13.11 | 1.80 | 9.96 | 3.26 |
| 2 | 8.69 | 2.87 | 11.05 | 1.62 | 14.44 | 1.81 | 11.39 | 3.20 |
| 3 | 9.78 | 2.91 | 11.70 | 1.61 | 15.52 | 1.85 | 12.33 | 3.24 |
| 4 | 10.90 | 2.90 | 12.26 | 1.59 | 16.47 | 1.88 | 13.21 | 3.22 |
| 5 | 11.65 | 2.89 | 12.68 | 1.59 | 17.15 | 2.01 | 13.83 | 3.26 |

deviation of return from target, as opposed to dispersion about mean return.

Table 3-2 is identical to table 3-1 except that the standard deviation now refers to the standard deviation of return less the target return where target is defined as the estimate of the initial (annualized) yield to maturity of the immunized portfolio. (This also equals the value of the objective function after the first optimization for each portfolio). It is quite clear that a well-defined risk-reward frontier emerges from the analysis which is significant and which has the appropriate slope whether yields are increasing, decreasing, or stable (although the steepness of the slope is affected). Moreover, mean return increases (with increasing risk) on an ex ante basis as well because, by construction, the target return increases as the risk constraint is relaxed. Thus the ex post results agree with the ex ante prediction arising out of the theory underlying the simulation.

We now consider the usefulness of the two measures of target return on an absolute and relative basis: the yield to maturity estimate employed above versus the spot rate. Obviously, we would like the target to be a good estimate of realized return. In particular, we would like the target to approx-

**Table 3–2**
**Mean and Standard Deviation of Return Minus Target**

| Risk | Decreasing | | Stable | | Increasing | | Combined | |
|---|---|---|---|---|---|---|---|---|
| | Mean | Standard Deviation | Mean | Standard Deviation | Mean | Standard Deviation | Mean | Standard Deviation |
| | | | *Three-year Horizon* | | | | | |
| 1 | 6.90 | 0.25 | 9.31 | 0.20 | 12.68 | 0.27 | 9.63 | 0.26 |
| 2 | 7.86 | 0.44 | 9.71 | 0.43 | 13.60 | 0.69 | 10.39 | 0.62 |
| 3 | 8.40 | 0.58 | 9.80 | 0.65 | 13.88 | 1.09 | 10.69 | 0.94 |
| 4 | 8.91 | 0.73 | 10.04 | 0.86 | 14.09 | 1.54 | 11.01 | 1.26 |
| 5 | 9.31 | 0.88 | 10.26 | 1.07 | 14.28 | 2.02 | 11.28 | 1.57 |
| | | | *Five-year Horizon* | | | | | |
| 1 | 6.91 | 0.16 | 9.56 | 0.17 | 12.91 | 0.17 | 9.79 | 0.18 |
| 2 | 8.50 | 0.23 | 10.71 | 0.29 | 14.27 | 0.18 | 11.16 | 0.33 |
| 3 | 9.38 | 0.32 | 11.03 | 0.49 | 15.12 | 0.46 | 11.84 | 0.64 |
| 4 | 10.21 | 0.51 | 11.39 | 0.72 | 15.72 | 0.90 | 12.44 | 0.99 |
| 5 | 10.81 | 0.67 | 11.69 | 0.93 | 16.19 | 1.37 | 12.89 | 1.30 |
| | | | *Seven-year Horizon* | | | | | |
| 1 | 7.01 | 0.11 | 9.76 | 0.18 | 13.11 | 0.11 | 9.96 | 0.15 |
| 2 | 8.69 | 0.16 | 11.05 | 0.41 | 14.44 | 0.25 | 11.39 | 0.37 |
| 3 | 9.78 | 0.24 | 11.70 | 0.60 | 15.52 | 0.34 | 12.33 | 0.57 |
| 4 | 10.90 | 0.31 | 12.26 | 0.81 | 16.47 | 0.42 | 13.21 | 0.83 |
| 5 | 11.65 | 0.43 | 12.68 | 1.04 | 17.15 | 0.60 | 13.83 | 1.06 |

imate the mean returns in table 3–2; more precisely, we would like the mean of the difference between actual return and target to be close to zero (and of course we would like this difference to have a small standard deviation). Tables 3–3 and 3–4 reproduce table 3–2 but show means and standard deviations of actual minus target. Table 3–3 employs the yield target while table 3–4 employs the spot rate.

Except for several cases of risk minimization when using the yield target, both targets substantially underestimate return. In every case the underestimate is monotonic. As risk increases, the extent of underestimation increases. This pattern is necessary in the case of the spot rate. In this case the target is the same regardless of the risk level because it is by definition the rate for the appropriate maturity taken from the term structure. Hence, if realized returns increase with increasing risk, so must the mean deviation when using the spot rate. The underestimate need not increase when using the yield method if the optimal objective function value (for yield) increases rapidly enough as the risk constraint is relaxed. While the mean target does increase, as table 3–5 shows, it clearly does not rise as rapidly.

**Table 3–3**

**Mean and Standard Deviation of Return Minus Yield Target**

| Risk | Decreasing | | Stable | | Increasing | | Combined | |
|---|---|---|---|---|---|---|---|---|
| | Mean | Standard Deviation | Mean | Standard Deviation | Mean | Standard Deviation | Mean | Standard Deviation |
| | | | *Three-year Horizon* | | | | | |
| 1 | 0.10 | 0.25 | −0.13 | 0.20 | −0.17 | 0.27 | −0.06 | 0.26 |
| 2 | 0.84 | 0.44 | 0.05 | 0.43 | 0.56 | 0.69 | 0.49 | 0.62 |
| 3 | 1.24 | 0.58 | −0.01 | 0.65 | 0.69 | 1.09 | 0.64 | 0.94 |
| 4 | 1.64 | 0.73 | 0.09 | 0.86 | 0.77 | 1.54 | 0.83 | 1.26 |
| 5 | 1.93 | 0.88 | 0.17 | 1.07 | 0.83 | 2.02 | 0.98 | 1.57 |
| | | | *Five-year Horizon* | | | | | |
| 1 | 0.05 | 0.16 | −0.06 | 0.17 | −0.11 | 0.17 | −0.04 | 0.18 |
| 2 | 1.46 | 0.23 | 0.90 | 0.29 | 1.08 | 0.18 | 1.14 | 0.33 |
| 3 | 2.23 | 0.32 | 1.09 | 0.49 | 1.79 | 0.46 | 1.70 | 0.64 |
| 4 | 2.96 | 0.51 | 1.32 | 0.72 | 2.27 | 0.90 | 2.18 | 0.99 |
| 5 | 3.46 | 0.67 | 1.50 | 0.93 | 2.63 | 1.37 | 2.53 | 1.30 |
| | | | *Seven-year Horizon* | | | | | |
| 1 | 0.07 | 0.11 | −0.04 | 0.18 | −0.10 | 0.11 | −0.02 | 0.15 |
| 2 | 1.64 | 0.16 | 1.14 | 0.41 | 1.14 | 0.25 | 1.30 | 0.37 |
| 3 | 2.64 | 0.24 | 1.68 | 0.60 | 2.13 | 0.34 | 2.15 | 0.57 |
| 4 | 3.67 | 0.31 | 2.15 | 0.81 | 2.99 | 0.42 | 2.93 | 0.83 |
| 5 | 4.35 | 0.43 | 2.47 | 1.04 | 3.60 | 0.60 | 3.47 | 1.06 |

**Table 3–4**

**Mean and Standard Deviation of Return Minus Spot Rate Target**

| | Decreasing | | Stable | | Increasing | | Combined | |
|---|---|---|---|---|---|---|---|---|
| | Mean | Standard Deviation | Mean | Standard Deviation | Mean | Standard Deviation | Mean | Standard Deviation |
| | | | *Three-year Horizon* | | | | | |
| 1 | 0.39 | 0.40 | 0.28 | 0.43 | 0.39 | 0.53 | 0.35 | 0.45 |
| 2 | 1.35 | 0.50 | 0.68 | 0.62 | 1.31 | 1.05 | 1.11 | 0.81 |
| 3 | 1.90 | 0.61 | 0.77 | 0.68 | 1.59 | 1.35 | 1.42 | 1.04 |
| 4 | 2.41 | 0.71 | 1.01 | 0.85 | 1.80 | 1.75 | 1.74 | 1.31 |
| 5 | 2.80 | 0.82 | 1.23 | 1.03 | 1.99 | 2.18 | 2.01 | 1.58 |
| | | | *Five-year Horizon* | | | | | |
| 1 | 0.23 | 0.25 | 0.20 | 0.23 | 0.25 | 0.31 | 0.23 | 0.26 |
| 2 | 1.82 | 0.29 | 1.35 | 0.40 | 1.61 | 0.39 | 1.59 | 0.41 |
| 3 | 2.70 | 0.35 | 1.67 | 0.50 | 2.46 | 0.62 | 2.28 | 0.67 |
| 4 | 3.53 | 0.46 | 2.02 | 0.70 | 3.07 | 1.04 | 2.87 | 0.99 |
| 5 | 4.13 | 0.57 | 2.33 | 0.90 | 3.53 | 1.49 | 3.33 | 1.29 |

*Table 3–4 (continued)*

| Risk | Decreasing Mean | Decreasing Standard Deviation | Stable Mean | Stable Standard Deviation | Increasing Mean | Increasing Standard Deviation | Combined Mean | Combined Standard Deviation |
|------|------|------|------|------|------|------|------|------|
| | | | | *Seven-year Horizon* | | | | |
| 1 | 0.23 | 0.21 | 0.22 | 0.26 | 0.24 | 0.32 | 0.23 | 0.26 |
| 2 | 1.91 | 0.35 | 1.51 | 0.42 | 1.58 | 0.42 | 1.67 | 0.43 |
| 3 | 3.00 | 0.45 | 2.16 | 0.58 | 2.66 | 0.49 | 2.60 | 0.61 |
| 4 | 4.12 | 0.51 | 2.72 | 0.78 | 3.61 | 0.57 | 3.48 | 0.85 |
| 5 | 4.87 | 0.57 | 3.14 | 1.00 | 4.29 | 0.73 | 4.10 | 1.06 |

## Table 3–5
## Results of Yield Target

| Risk | Decreasing Mean | Decreasing Standard Deviation | Stable Mean | Stable Standard Deviation | Increasing Mean | Increasing Standard Deviation | Combined Mean | Combined Standard Deviation |
|------|------|------|------|------|------|------|------|------|
| | | | | *Three-year Horizon* | | | | |
| 1 | 6.80 | 2.88 | 9.43 | 2.08 | 12.85 | 2.10 | 9.69 | 3.42 |
| 2 | 7.02 | 2.85 | 9.65 | 1.97 | 13.04 | 1.99 | 9.90 | 3.36 |
| 3 | 7.16 | 2.84 | 9.81 | 1.88 | 13.19 | 1.90 | 10.05 | 3.33 |
| 4 | 7.28 | 2.82 | 9.95 | 1.79 | 13.32 | 1.84 | 10.18 | 3.30 |
| 5 | 7.38 | 2.82 | 10.09 | 1.71 | 13.45 | 1.79 | 10.30 | 3.29 |
| | | | | *Five-year Horizon* | | | | |
| 1 | 6.87 | 2.82 | 9.62 | 1.93 | 13.02 | 1.99 | 9.83 | 3.39 |
| 2 | 7.04 | 2.79 | 9.81 | 1.82 | 13.19 | 1.89 | 10.01 | 3.34 |
| 3 | 7.15 | 2.77 | 9.95 | 1.73 | 13.33 | 1.83 | 10.14 | 3.32 |
| 4 | 7.26 | 2.76 | 10.07 | 1.66 | 13.45 | 1.79 | 10.26 | 3.30 |
| 5 | 7.35 | 2.77 | 10.19 | 1.59 | 13.56 | 1.75 | 10.36 | 3.29 |
| | | | | *Seven-year Horizon* | | | | |
| 1 | 6.95 | 2.79 | 9.80 | 1.79 | 13.21 | 1.85 | 9.98 | 3.36 |
| 2 | 7.05 | 2.76 | 9.91 | 1.72 | 13.31 | 1.79 | 10.09 | 3.33 |
| 3 | 7.14 | 2.75 | 10.02 | 1.65 | 13.40 | 1.75 | 10.18 | 3.31 |
| 4 | 7.23 | 2.74 | 10.12 | 1.59 | 13.48 | 1.71 | 10.28 | 3.29 |
| 5 | 7.30 | 2.75 | 10.21 | 1.54 | 13.55 | 1.68 | 10.35 | 3.28 |

Why this occurs in the case of the yield target is not completely clear. It should be kept in mind that, theoretically, the accuracy of the yield as a target diminishes as risk increases. This, however, does not explain the pervasive monotonic underestimation. Underestimation in the case of either target definition (although far more severe for the spot rate definition) appears to be related to the fact that for certain categories of yield movements, the target return is the minimum return, and if a stochastic shift occurs, actual return will be larger. The constrained yield maximization appears to be a strong vehicle for optimizing with respect to the actual stochastic shifts that the simulation generated (which were extraordinarily diverse).

Given that neither target closely predicted mean return, the yield target performed better, as tables 3–3 and 3–4 show. Mean errors were generally smaller regardless of the horizon length or the direction of yield movement. The standard deviation of actual minus target was also generally smaller regardless of horizon or yield change direction, but less dramatically so. Mean errors were negative in a few cases of pure risk minimization when using the yield target, suggesting that in such cases the spot rate could be preferred. Before drawing such a conclusion, however, it should be noted that the absolute mean deviation was universally smaller for the yield target. Moreover, the choice of target (from the point of view of an asymmetric loss function for being above versus below target) depends on a consideration of order statistics (as well as means and variances) to which we now turn.

Tables 3–6 to 3–11 show various return statistics for three-, five-, and seven-year horizons. In each case results are presented separately for increasing, stable, declining, and combined yields. Within each group there are four columns of data (each row corresponding to a different risk level in an immunized portfolio). The first column shows the number of cases (in the particular simulation) when actual return fell short of target. The second column shows the value of the largest shortfall. The third column is the average shortfall, and the fourth column is the average excess when returns exceeded target. Tables 3–6 through 3–8 employ the yield definition of target while tables 3–9 to 3–11 employ the spot rate definition.

**Table 3–6**
**Order Statistics for Yield Target and Three-Year Horizon**

| Risk | Number | Worst | Average if Under | Average if Over |
|------|--------|-------|------------------|-----------------|
| | | *Decreasing Yields* | | |
| 1 | 8 | −0.40 | −0.13 | 0.26 |
| 2 | 0 | 0.07 | 0.00 | 0.84 |
| 3 | 0 | 0.39 | 0.00 | 1.24 |
| 4 | 0 | 0.35 | 0.00 | 1.64 |
| 5 | 0 | 0.24 | 0.00 | 1.93 |
| | | *Stable Yields* | | |
| 1 | 13 | −0.45 | −0.24 | 0.08 |
| 2 | 10 | −0.63 | −0.31 | 0.42 |
| 3 | 10 | −0.98 | −0.56 | 0.54 |
| 4 | 10 | −1.21 | −0.65 | 0.82 |
| 5 | 10 | −1.45 | −0.74 | 1.08 |

*Table 3-6 (continued)*

| Risk | Number | Worst | Average if Under | Average if Over |
|---|---|---|---|---|
| | | *Increasing Yields* | | |
| 1 | 14 | -0.67 | -0.29 | 0.12 |
| 2 | 4 | -0.71 | -0.56 | 0.84 |
| 3 | 7 | -1.11 | -0.48 | 1.33 |
| 4 | 9 | -1.52 | -0.65 | 1.93 |
| 5 | 9 | -1.96 | -1.00 | 2.34 |
| | | *Combined Yields* | | |
| 1 | 35 | -0.67 | -0.11 | 0.12 |
| 2 | 14 | -0.71 | 2.08 | 2.62 |
| 3 | 17 | -1.11 | 2.27 | 4.56 |
| 4 | 19 | -1.52 | 2.63 | 7.11 |
| 5 | 19 | -1.96 | 3.09 | 10.68 |

**Table 3-7**
**Order Statistics for Yield Target and Five-Year Horizon**

| Risk | Number | Worst | Average if Under | Average if Over |
|---|---|---|---|---|
| | | *Decreasing Yields* | | |
| 1 | 9 | -0.27 | -0.09 | 0.16 |
| 2 | 0 | 1.00 | 0.00 | 1.46 |
| 3 | 0 | 1.64 | 0.00 | 2.23 |
| 4 | 0 | 1.89 | 0.00 | 2.96 |
| 5 | 0 | 1.98 | 0.00 | 3.46 |
| | | *Stable Yields* | | |
| 1 | 14 | -0.42 | -0.14 | 0.12 |
| 2 | 0 | 0.55 | 0.00 | 0.90 |
| 3 | 0 | 0.61 | 0.00 | 1.09 |
| 4 | 0 | 0.56 | 0.00 | 1.32 |
| 5 | 0 | 0.48 | 0.00 | 1.50 |
| | | *Increasing Yields* | | |
| 1 | 15 | -0.48 | -0.16 | 0.07 |
| 2 | 0 | 0.69 | 0.00 | 1.08 |
| 3 | 0 | 0.96 | 0.00 | 1.79 |
| 4 | 0 | 0.75 | 0.00 | 2.27 |
| 5 | 0 | 0.48 | 0.00 | 2.63 |
| | | *Combined Yields* | | |
| 1 | 38 | -0.48 | -0.14 | 0.13 |
| 2 | 0 | 0.55 | 0.00 | 1.14 |
| 3 | 0 | 0.61 | 0.00 | 1.70 |
| 4 | 0 | 0.56 | 0.00 | 2.18 |
| 5 | 0 | 0.48 | 0.00 | 2.53 |

**Table 3-8**
**Order Statistics for Yield Target and Seven-Year Horizon**

| Risk | Number | Worst | Average if Under | Average if Over |
|------|--------|-------|------------------|-----------------|
| | | *Decreasing Yields* | | |
| 1 | 3 | − 0.13 | − 0.10 | 0.10 |
| 2 | 0 | 1.37 | 0.00 | 1.64 |
| 3 | 0 | 2.27 | 0.00 | 2.64 |
| 4 | 0 | 3.07 | 0.00 | 3.67 |
| 5 | 0 | 3.61 | 0.00 | 4.35 |
| | | *Stable Yields* | | |
| 1 | 12 | − 0.37 | − 0.15 | 0.13 |
| 2 | 0 | 0.59 | 0.00 | 1.14 |
| 3 | 0 | 0.99 | 0.00 | 1.68 |
| 4 | 0 | 1.22 | 0.00 | 2.15 |
| 5 | 0 | 1.27 | 0.00 | 2.47 |
| | | *Increasing Yields* | | |
| 1 | 17 | − 0.36 | − 0.13 | 0.07 |
| 2 | 0 | 0.70 | 0.00 | 1.14 |
| 3 | 0 | 1.46 | 0.00 | 2.13 |
| 4 | 0 | 2.24 | 0.00 | 2.99 |
| 5 | 0 | 2.48 | 0.00 | 3.60 |
| | | *Combined Yields* | | |
| 1 | 32 | − 0.37 | − 0.13 | 0.10 |
| 2 | 0 | 0.59 | 0.00 | 1.30 |
| 3 | 0 | 0.99 | 0.00 | 2.15 |
| 4 | 0 | 1.22 | 0.00 | 2.93 |
| 5 | 0 | 1.27 | 0.00 | 3.47 |

**Table 3-9**
**Order Statistics for Spot Target and Three-Year Horizon**

| Risk | Number | Worst | Average if Under | Average if Over |
|------|--------|-------|------------------|-----------------|
| | | *Decreasing Yields* | | |
| 1 | 5 | − 0.18 | − 0.09 | 0.55 |
| 2 | 0 | 0.62 | 0.00 | 1.35 |
| 3 | 0 | 1.05 | 0.00 | 1.90 |
| 4 | 0 | 1.42 | 0.00 | 2.41 |
| 5 | 0 | 1.64 | 0.00 | 2.80 |
| | | *Stable Yields* | | |
| 1 | 9 | − 0.26 | − 0.15 | 0.63 |
| 2 | 3 | − 0.54 | − 0.34 | 0.86 |
| 3 | 2 | − 0.56 | − 0.46 | 0.91 |
| 4 | 2 | − 0.50 | − 0.40 | 1.17 |
| 5 | 3 | − 0.45 | − 0.27 | 1.49 |

*Table 3-9 (continued)*

| Risk | Number | Worst | Average if Under | Average if Over |
|------|--------|-------|------------------|-----------------|
| | | *Increasing Yields* | | |
| 1 | 6 | −0.35 | −0.21 | 0.64 |
| 2 | 4 | −0.65 | −0.42 | 1.74 |
| 3 | 3 | −0.83 | −0.66 | 1.98 |
| 4 | 4 | −1.06 | −0.65 | 2.41 |
| 5 | 4 | −1.29 | −0.86 | 2.70 |
| | | *Combined Yields* | | |
| 1 | 20 | −0.35 | −0.15 | 0.61 |
| 2 | 7 | −0.65 | −0.39 | 1.31 |
| 3 | 5 | −0.83 | −0.58 | 1.60 |
| 4 | 6 | −1.06 | −0.56 | 1.99 |
| 5 | 7 | −1.29 | −0.60 | 2.35 |

**Table 3-10**
**Order Statistics for Spot Target and Five-Year Horizon**

| Risk | Number | Worst | Average if Under | Average if Over |
|------|--------|-------|------------------|-----------------|
| | | *Decreasing Yields* | | |
| 1 | 3 | −0.09 | −0.06 | 0.28 |
| 2 | 0 | 1.36 | 0.00 | 1.82 |
| 3 | 0 | 1.93 | 0.00 | 2.70 |
| 4 | 0 | 2.59 | 0.00 | 3.53 |
| 5 | 0 | 2.97 | 0.00 | 4.13 |
| | | *Stable Yields* | | |
| 1 | 6 | −0.14 | −0.07 | 0.31 |
| 2 | 0 | 0.73 | 0.00 | 1.35 |
| 3 | 0 | 0.76 | 0.00 | 1.67 |
| 4 | 0 | 0.78 | 0.00 | 2.02 |
| 5 | 0 | 0.80 | 0.00 | 2.33 |
| | | *Increasing Yields* | | |
| 1 | 7 | −0.15 | −0.07 | 0.43 |
| 2 | 0 | 0.99 | 0.00 | 1.61 |
| 3 | 0 | 1.23 | 0.00 | 2.46 |
| 4 | 0 | 1.23 | 0.00 | 3.07 |
| 5 | 0 | 1.20 | 0.00 | 3.53 |
| | | *Combined Yields* | | |
| 1 | 16 | −0.15 | −0.07 | 0.34 |
| 2 | 0 | 0.73 | 0.00 | 1.59 |
| 3 | 0 | 0.76 | 0.00 | 2.28 |
| 4 | 0 | 0.78 | 0.00 | 2.87 |
| 5 | 0 | 0.80 | 0.00 | 3.33 |

**Table 3-11**
**Order Statistics for Spot Target and Seven-Year Horizon**

| Risk | Number | Worst | Average if Under | Average if Over |
|------|--------|-------|------------------|-----------------|
| | | *Decreasing Yields* | | |
| 1 | 3 | −0.13 | −0.10 | 0.10 |
| 2 | 0 | 1.37 | 0.00 | 1.64 |
| 3 | 0 | 2.27 | 0.00 | 2.64 |
| 4 | 0 | 3.07 | 0.00 | 3.67 |
| 5 | 0 | 3.61 | 0.00 | 4.35 |
| | | *Stable Yields* | | |
| 1 | 4 | −0.29 | −0.12 | 0.31 |
| 2 | 0 | 0.66 | 0.00 | 1.51 |
| 3 | 0 | 1.00 | 0.00 | 2.16 |
| 4 | 0 | 1.19 | 0.00 | 2.72 |
| 5 | 0 | 1.24 | 0.00 | 3.14 |
| | | *Increasing Yields* | | |
| 1 | 5 | −0.18 | −0.14 | 0.37 |
| 2 | 0 | 0.98 | 0.00 | 1.58 |
| 3 | 0 | 1.99 | 0.00 | 2.66 |
| 4 | 0 | 2.80 | 0.00 | 3.61 |
| 5 | 0 | 3.18 | 0.00 | 4.29 |
| | | *Combined Yields* | | |
| 1 | 12 | −0.29 | −0.12 | 0.32 |
| 2 | 0 | 0.66 | 0.00 | 1.67 |
| 3 | 0 | 1.00 | 0.00 | 2.60 |
| 4 | 0 | 1.19 | 0.00 | 3.48 |
| 5 | 0 | 1.24 | 0.00 | 4.10 |

With a five- or seven-year horizon, shortfalls occurred only when pure risk minimization was employed; in this case they occurred regardless of target definition. In the seven-year case, shortfalls had the same rough magnitude regardless of target, while in the five-year case shortfalls using the yield target were roughly twice as large as with the spot rate. In the three-year case, shortfalls occurred for pure risk minimization only when yields declined (regardless of target) but occurred throughout for stable or increasing yields. In the risk minimization case, shortfalls were larger for the yield definition of target—in some cases nearly twice as large. Shortfalls in the stable and increasing yield cases exceeded all others by a wide margin. For increasing yields, worst shortfalls (column 2) were greater (by roughly 50 percent) for the yield target although the average shortfall was the same or only slightly larger for this definition. For stable yields, both the average and worst shortfalls were substantially larger for the yield target.

These results, along with tables 3-3 and 3-4, suggest that the yield definition of target generally performs as well or better than the spot rate. It is clearly superior for intermediate and long horizons when anything other than pure risk minimization is employed. For these horizons, and when minimizing risk, the spot rate has fewer and smaller shortfalls although absolute mean errors are larger (tables 3-3 and 3-4). For short horizons, these same remarks apply when yields are declining. For stable or increasing yields, both the spot rate and yield targets have large shortfalls. Here the spot rate produces generally smaller shortfalls for all risk levels, although absolute mean errors are larger.

On balance, it would appear desirable to use the yield target for intermediate to long horizons. The spot rate could be used in these cases when risk immunization is employed and when small shortfalls and small excess returns are asymmetrically valued. For short horizons, the spot rate appears to dominate if a yield forecast (as to increasing, stable, or declining yields) is unavailable for conditioning the decision. If yields are expected to decline, the preference for target is similar to that expressed for longer horizons. (Of course, if such a forecast were available it could be used in the optimization process as well, which could meaningfully alter the results).

As a practical matter, it is often difficult to estimate the spot rate so that the yield target would be a frequent starting point. This is especially true when using corporate securities of differing credit levels. As a consequence, where the spot rate is desired it may be best to estimate it through an adjustment to the yield target based on the shape of the yield curve.

As a final note, our results bear on a question that is the subject of some confusion. Does risk in an immunized portfolio increase or decrease as the horizon is increased? Pure theory casts little light on this issue because such analyses typically deal with circumstances where immunization is perfect. The time dimension in risk depends on whether the deviations from perfect immunization caused by actual yield shifts are of a nature that accumulate or diversify as the horizon lengthens. Our results, which are generated from volatile yield movements whose shape changes accord with practice, suggest that risk decreases as the horizon increases when yields generally change (secularly) from their starting level. Risk remains approximately the same when yields remain (secularly) near their starting levels. This somewhat paradoxical result follows from examining in table 3-4 the uniform and significant decline in risk in the increasing and decreasing yield scenarios but the stable risk in the stable rate scenario. Without conditioning on a particular yield shift scenario, it appears prudent to predict some decline in risk.

## Conclusions

The principal conclusions of this chapter are as follows:
First, drawing on theoretical analyses of risk minimization and general

return representation, a risk-reward tradeoff for immunized portfolios can be empirically determined that is significant and that agrees in shape with ex ante predictions.

Second, the yield to maturity definition of target return outperforms the spot rate definition in many cases, especially for intermediate and long horizons. However, it does not dominate this definition.

Third, as a general matter, risk in immunized portfolios appears to decline as the horizon is increased. This is evidently the result of the diversification of errors over time.

Finally, we may now give some interpretation to an objective criterion developed in chapter 2 that frequently outperformed the cash flow variance minimization approach although with less reliability: the strategy of minimizing the average price per bond. It was pointed out in chapter 2 that this method combines the logic of buying discount bonds (which reduces cash flow variance) with the logic of maximizing yield. (This is simply because these are the two ways to get a low price.) Although this combination is nonlinear and could not be exactly replicated by the techniques developed in this chapter, it is evident that this strategy is represented by the tradeoff developed.

**Note**

1. Gifford Fong, and Oldrich Vasicek, "A Risk Minimizing Strategy for Multiple Liability Immunization," unpublished manuscript, September 15, 1980.

# Appendix 3A
# Simulated Yields for
# Selected Maturities

| PERIOD | | | MATURITY | | | |
|---|---|---|---|---|---|---|
| | 1 | 3 | 5 | 10 | 20 | 30 |
| 1 | 8.27 | 9.00 | 9.26 | 9.90 | 10.05 | 10.20 |
| 2 | 13.21 | 12.86 | 12.70 | 12.38 | 12.19 | 12.02 |
| 3 | 12.52 | 11.80 | 11.76 | 11.65 | 11.58 | 11.50 |
| 4 | 7.04 | 8.75 | 9.18 | 9.78 | 10.31 | 10.83 |
| 5 | 4.91 | 6.48 | 6.73 | 7.35 | 8.02 | 8.69 |
| 6 | 3.56 | 5.17 | 5.58 | 6.18 | 6.74 | 7.29 |
| 7 | 4.97 | 5.76 | 5.77 | 5.80 | 5.83 | 5.85 |
| 8 | 4.65 | 5.70 | 5.99 | 6.45 | 6.69 | 6.92 |
| 9 | 6.23 | 7.16 | 7.28 | 7.57 | 7.72 | 7.87 |
| 10 | 8.78 | 9.08 | 9.00 | 8.67 | 8.48 | 8.31 |
| 11 | 6.80 | 6.48 | 6.49 | 6.53 | 6.56 | 6.59 |
| 12 | 2.80 | 2.74 | 2.92 | 3.45 | 3.96 | 4.46 |
| 13 | 0.47 | 1.70 | 1.84 | 2.18 | 2.54 | 2.90 |
| 14 | 0.93 | 2.62 | 2.86 | 2.94 | 3.01 | 3.08 |
| 15 | 5.52 | 5.35 | 5.22 | 4.91 | 4.69 | 4.47 |
| 16 | 9.37 | 7.03 | 6.56 | 6.05 | 5.77 | 5.51 |
| 17 | 10.78 | 8.13 | 7.93 | 7.44 | 7.21 | 6.98 |
| 18 | 7.81 | 6.53 | 6.44 | 6.64 | 6.75 | 6.86 |
| 19 | 5.02 | 5.60 | 5.69 | 5.92 | 6.09 | 6.25 |
| 20 | 5.21 | 5.18 | 5.05 | 4.68 | 4.31 | 3.95 |
| 21 | 6.20 | 5.03 | 4.88 | 4.51 | 4.13 | 3.74 |
| 22 | 2.06 | 2.11 | 2.24 | 2.59 | 2.94 | 3.28 |
| 23 | 4.57 | 5.08 | 5.08 | 5.09 | 5.10 | 5.11 |
| 24 | 3.20 | 5.07 | 5.34 | 5.48 | 5.55 | 5.63 |
| 25 | 4.76 | 5.05 | 5.10 | 5.23 | 5.30 | 5.36 |
| 26 | 7.42 | 7.31 | 7.31 | 7.37 | 7.40 | 7.43 |
| 27 | 8.88 | 7.04 | 6.96 | 6.75 | 6.61 | 6.46 |
| 28 | 8.70 | 6.86 | 6.43 | 5.89 | 5.37 | 4.87 |
| 29 | 3.60 | 4.55 | 4.53 | 4.48 | 4.42 | 4.37 |
| 30 | 2.06 | 3.14 | 3.36 | 3.58 | 3.80 | 4.00 |
| 31 | 3.97 | 4.32 | 4.31 | 4.29 | 4.27 | 4.26 |
| 32 | 5.18 | 5.96 | 6.10 | 6.23 | 6.30 | 6.37 |
| 33 | 7.57 | 6.99 | 7.01 | 7.07 | 7.10 | 7.12 |
| 34 | 9.05 | 8.05 | 7.80 | 7.44 | 7.24 | 7.05 |
| 35 | 4.10 | 5.31 | 5.45 | 5.80 | 6.02 | 6.25 |
| 36 | 5.30 | 5.39 | 5.38 | 5.31 | 5.24 | 5.18 |
| 37 | 1.59 | 3.61 | 3.69 | 3.89 | 4.09 | 4.30 |
| 38 | 0.51 | 2.51 | 2.88 | 3.25 | 3.61 | 3.96 |
| 39 | 3.35 | 4.66 | 4.56 | 4.31 | 4.13 | 3.94 |
| 40 | 4.02 | 4.83 | 5.00 | 5.19 | 5.32 | 5.43 |
| 41 | 4.29 | 5.97 | 5.97 | 5.97 | 5.96 | 5.96 |
| 42 | 3.98 | 5.44 | 5.73 | 6.04 | 6.21 | 6.37 |
| 43 | 5.00 | 4.92 | 4.98 | 5.14 | 5.25 | 5.37 |
| 44 | 2.22 | 3.25 | 3.35 | 3.27 | 3.19 | 3.11 |
| 45 | 2.35 | 2.31 | 2.38 | 2.56 | 2.75 | 2.94 |
| 46 | 0.35 | 1.69 | 2.05 | 2.62 | 3.16 | 3.70 |
| 47 | 4.91 | 4.21 | 4.21 | 4.22 | 4.22 | 4.23 |
| 48 | 4.23 | 6.11 | 6.36 | 6.40 | 6.42 | 6.44 |
| 49 | 8.37 | 8.36 | 8.33 | 8.26 | 8.22 | 8.19 |
| 50 | 6.55 | 8.05 | 8.19 | 8.03 | 7.95 | 7.87 |

MEAN ABSOLUTE QUARTERLY CHANGE

| | 2.16 | 1.43 | 1.33 | 1.18 | 1.09 | 1.01 |
|---|---|---|---|---|---|---|

| PERIOD | 1 | 3 | MATURITY 5 | 10 | 20 | 30 |
|---|---|---|---|---|---|---|
| 1 | 8.27 | 9.00 | 9.26 | 9.90 | 10.05 | 10.20 |
| 2 | 10.89 | 11.56 | 11.73 | 11.97 | 12.10 | 12.21 |
| 3 | 12.65 | 12.09 | 12.05 | 11.96 | 11.91 | 11.85 |
| 4 | 8.52 | 10.18 | 10.40 | 10.44 | 10.47 | 10.50 |
| 5 | 7.33 | 9.38 | 9.54 | 9.92 | 10.31 | 10.70 |
| 6 | 5.22 | 7.50 | 8.00 | 8.62 | 9.21 | 9.79 |
| 7 | 5.47 | 7.82 | 8.00 | 8.46 | 8.82 | 9.19 |
| 8 | 7.57 | 9.93 | 10.24 | 10.28 | 10.30 | 10.32 |
| 9 | 9.93 | 9.11 | 9.42 | 10.19 | 10.58 | 10.97 |
| 10 | 8.16 | 10.02 | 10.42 | 10.88 | 11.12 | 11.35 |
| 11 | 6.10 | 8.67 | 8.89 | 9.45 | 9.79 | 10.13 |
| 12 | 5.59 | 7.36 | 7.73 | 8.15 | 8.50 | 8.84 |
| 13 | 2.82 | 5.26 | 5.56 | 6.31 | 7.09 | 7.88 |
| 14 | 2.64 | 5.09 | 5.60 | 6.16 | 6.74 | 7.30 |
| 15 | 5.21 | 7.14 | 7.14 | 7.13 | 7.13 | 7.13 |
| 16 | 8.03 | 8.70 | 8.76 | 8.67 | 8.61 | 8.55 |
| 17 | 9.35 | 10.36 | 10.31 | 10.17 | 10.10 | 10.03 |
| 18 | 13.42 | 12.15 | 11.82 | 11.33 | 11.08 | 10.84 |
| 19 | 11.47 | 11.41 | 11.36 | 11.24 | 11.16 | 11.08 |
| 20 | 9.64 | 10.36 | 10.39 | 10.20 | 10.05 | 9.91 |
| 21 | 6.42 | 6.62 | 6.79 | 7.22 | 7.64 | 8.06 |
| 22 | 5.07 | 6.46 | 6.64 | 6.64 | 6.65 | 6.66 |
| 23 | 5.92 | 7.41 | 7.42 | 7.46 | 7.49 | 7.52 |
| 24 | 5.17 | 8.32 | 8.84 | 9.19 | 9.41 | 9.63 |
| 25 | 10.78 | 11.53 | 11.39 | 11.06 | 10.90 | 10.74 |
| 26 | 12.88 | 12.38 | 12.15 | 11.69 | 11.45 | 11.23 |
| 27 | 9.29 | 10.45 | 10.60 | 10.97 | 11.22 | 11.47 |
| 28 | 7.06 | 8.83 | 9.14 | 9.37 | 9.58 | 9.78 |
| 29 | 4.77 | 7.40 | 7.57 | 8.00 | 8.46 | 8.91 |
| 30 | 3.97 | 5.88 | 6.20 | 6.44 | 6.70 | 6.95 |
| 31 | 5.63 | 6.76 | 6.94 | 7.38 | 7.72 | 8.07 |
| 32 | 10.17 | 9.85 | 9.80 | 9.75 | 9.73 | 9.70 |
| 33 | 12.87 | 10.95 | 10.82 | 10.48 | 10.30 | 10.12 |
| 34 | 12.09 | 11.92 | 11.86 | 11.75 | 11.69 | 11.63 |
| 35 | 9.42 | 10.44 | 10.38 | 10.21 | 10.09 | 9.98 |
| 36 | 5.46 | 6.66 | 6.97 | 7.41 | 7.87 | 8.31 |
| 37 | 7.61 | 7.96 | 7.92 | 7.83 | 7.74 | 7.64 |
| 38 | 6.06 | 7.17 | 7.35 | 7.46 | 7.57 | 7.68 |
| 39 | 7.91 | 7.77 | 7.92 | 8.30 | 8.55 | 8.80 |
| 40 | 9.08 | 9.63 | 9.85 | 10.27 | 10.50 | 10.72 |
| 41 | 14.01 | 12.53 | 12.40 | 12.07 | 11.92 | 11.76 |
| 42 | 12.14 | 11.52 | 11.54 | 11.81 | 11.96 | 12.10 |
| 43 | 11.35 | 12.33 | 12.23 | 11.97 | 11.80 | 11.63 |
| 44 | 10.64 | 9.05 | 8.90 | 9.04 | 9.16 | 9.27 |
| 45 | 6.00 | 7.28 | 7.39 | 7.65 | 7.92 | 8.19 |
| 46 | 4.71 | 7.08 | 7.45 | 7.67 | 7.87 | 8.07 |
| 47 | 4.38 | 7.63 | 7.88 | 8.53 | 8.97 | 9.41 |
| 48 | 6.91 | 9.78 | 10.14 | 10.14 | 10.14 | 10.15 |
| 49 | 6.70 | 10.57 | 10.83 | 11.50 | 11.80 | 12.11 |
| 50 | 7.85 | 10.51 | 11.08 | 11.79 | 12.15 | 12.48 |

MEAN ABSOLUTE QUARTERLY CHANGE

| 2.09 | 1.46 | 1.35 | 1.16 | 1.07 | 1.04 |

| PERIOD | | | MATURITY | | | |
|---|---|---|---|---|---|---|
| | 1 | 3 | 5 | 10 | 20 | 30 |
| 1 | 8.27 | 9.00 | 9.26 | 9.90 | 10.05 | 10.20 |
| 2 | 12.04 | 12.46 | 12.47 | 12.37 | 12.31 | 12.26 |
| 3 | 12.27 | 12.09 | 12.02 | 11.85 | 11.73 | 11.60 |
| 4 | 7.45 | 9.73 | 10.26 | 10.95 | 11.60 | 12.23 |
| 5 | 7.84 | 10.30 | 10.44 | 10.80 | 11.17 | 11.55 |
| 6 | 9.79 | 10.64 | 10.82 | 11.04 | 11.24 | 11.44 |
| 7 | 9.98 | 12.49 | 12.59 | 12.84 | 12.99 | 13.15 |
| 8 | 13.78 | 14.79 | 14.95 | 15.04 | 15.09 | 15.13 |
| 9 | 14.17 | 15.33 | 15.40 | 15.57 | 15.65 | 15.74 |
| 10 | 12.15 | 14.58 | 15.02 | 15.44 | 15.70 | 15.94 |
| 11 | 9.56 | 13.25 | 13.46 | 13.99 | 14.42 | 14.84 |
| 12 | 8.27 | 10.67 | 11.22 | 11.95 | 12.62 | 13.26 |
| 13 | 10.35 | 11.34 | 11.44 | 11.70 | 11.96 | 12.22 |
| 14 | 10.13 | 10.01 | 10.19 | 10.76 | 11.24 | 11.70 |
| 15 | 10.36 | 11.36 | 11.51 | 11.87 | 12.09 | 12.32 |
| 16 | 14.35 | 14.15 | 14.12 | 14.11 | 14.11 | 14.10 |
| 17 | 14.01 | 14.83 | 14.86 | 14.95 | 14.99 | 15.04 |
| 18 | 17.23 | 15.38 | 15.05 | 14.76 | 14.58 | 14.40 |
| 19 | 13.90 | 13.54 | 13.52 | 13.47 | 13.44 | 13.40 |
| 20 | 11.78 | 12.22 | 12.25 | 12.19 | 12.12 | 12.06 |
| 21 | 8.03 | 10.13 | 10.40 | 11.08 | 11.73 | 12.39 |
| 22 | 14.64 | 13.83 | 13.57 | 13.12 | 12.73 | 12.36 |
| 23 | 11.44 | 12.52 | 12.61 | 12.82 | 12.95 | 13.08 |
| 24 | 13.45 | 13.59 | 13.73 | 14.07 | 14.25 | 14.41 |
| 25 | 15.67 | 14.71 | 14.86 | 15.21 | 15.38 | 15.56 |
| 26 | 14.33 | 15.28 | 15.33 | 15.15 | 15.04 | 14.93 |
| 27 | 12.52 | 13.47 | 13.54 | 13.73 | 13.89 | 14.04 |
| 28 | 13.18 | 13.26 | 13.19 | 12.97 | 12.73 | 12.50 |
| 29 | 12.54 | 12.09 | 12.00 | 11.78 | 11.55 | 11.32 |
| 30 | 10.51 | 10.91 | 11.07 | 11.36 | 11.59 | 11.82 |
| 31 | 10.90 | 11.60 | 11.80 | 12.31 | 12.61 | 12.92 |
| 32 | 13.31 | 14.04 | 14.10 | 14.02 | 13.97 | 13.93 |
| 33 | 14.43 | 14.93 | 14.96 | 15.04 | 15.07 | 15.11 |
| 34 | 13.13 | 13.91 | 14.05 | 14.16 | 14.24 | 14.31 |
| 35 | 10.62 | 11.91 | 12.03 | 12.33 | 12.59 | 12.85 |
| 36 | 8.10 | 9.89 | 10.30 | 10.83 | 11.41 | 11.98 |
| 37 | 11.24 | 11.26 | 11.42 | 11.81 | 12.19 | 12.57 |
| 38 | 11.87 | 12.50 | 12.58 | 12.57 | 12.57 | 12.57 |
| 39 | 12.93 | 12.83 | 12.97 | 13.30 | 13.51 | 13.71 |
| 40 | 13.12 | 13.93 | 14.20 | 14.66 | 14.90 | 15.12 |
| 41 | 15.39 | 15.99 | 15.88 | 15.62 | 15.49 | 15.36 |
| 42 | 14.31 | 15.09 | 15.28 | 15.55 | 15.71 | 15.85 |
| 43 | 13.01 | 13.70 | 13.86 | 14.24 | 14.54 | 14.83 |
| 44 | 12.08 | 12.68 | 12.76 | 12.78 | 12.79 | 12.81 |
| 45 | 8.45 | 9.56 | 9.81 | 10.44 | 11.10 | 11.75 |
| 46 | 11.57 | 11.49 | 11.39 | 11.13 | 10.90 | 10.68 |
| 47 | 11.22 | 12.24 | 12.23 | 12.22 | 12.21 | 12.20 |
| 48 | 14.07 | 14.06 | 13.99 | 13.82 | 13.72 | 13.63 |
| 49 | 12.02 | 12.93 | 13.18 | 13.81 | 14.12 | 14.43 |
| 50 | 14.29 | 14.59 | 14.55 | 14.35 | 14.23 | 14.12 |

MEAN ABSOLUTE QUARTERLY CHANGE

| | 1.97 | 1.43 | 1.29 | 1.06 | 0.95 | 0.96 |
|---|---|---|---|---|---|---|

# 4

# A New Approach to Immunization Mathematics

This chapter rigorously derives the new concepts employed in chapter 2, and especially in chapter 3. Because the treatment is mathematical, we have presented this material after those applications, which are more relevant than the proofs for many purposes. The material here is not required for an understanding of chapters 5 through 9.

In this chapter we develop a new approach to the mathematical representation of bond portfolio returns. Under general conditions and with no special assumption regarding yield curve shifts, a formula is derived for the total compound return on an arbitrary portfolio over a given horizon. Several applications of the formula are then made. First, when the portfolio is assumed to be a bullet immunization, the formula reduces to the initial yield to maturity on the portfolio plus a term related to the curvature of the yield curve over time. This finding implies a new objective immunization technique in which yield to maturity is maximized, the Macaulay duration of the portfolio is kept equal to the remaining horizon, and bonds are selected so that the curvature term is minimized. When curvature is minimized to the greatest possible extent, the initial yield to maturity of the portfolio is then likely to be a reasonable selection for the target return, and the technique is expected to be quite reliable as tested in chapter 2. As yield is maximized at the expense of curvature exposure, a risk-return tradeoff is likely to emerge as tested in chapter 3.

As a second application, we specialize the general formula to the case in which a single bond is purchased and held to maturity, with all coupons reinvested in this same security. The total compound return is shown to be equal to two principal terms plus a residual where the first two terms are a weighted average of the initial bond yield to maturity and the average reinvestment rate. The weights sum to one and the weight on the initial yield is equal to the ratio of the Macaulay duration of the bond at purchase divided by its maturity at purchase.

A final accomplishment of this chapter is to develop a close linear approximation to the yield to maturity of a bond or bond portfolio that is theoretically (and in fact) closer than the weighted average yield. We are able to demonstrate that under all but pathological conditions, this estimate is actually an underestimate of the true yield to maturity. This is of considerable use when employing any procedures requiring frequent computation of true yield, such as using the immunization technique proposed here. We develop the basic theory first, and then follow with applications.

## The Total Differential of Price

Consider a bond portfolio with value $V(t)$ at time $t$, and discrete cash flows

$$C_{s-t}, s \geq t$$

Yield to maturity $y(t)$ is defined by

$$V(t) \equiv \sum_{s \geq t} C_{s-t} e^{-y(t)(s-t)} \tag{4.1}$$

The total nonstochastic differential of $V$ is then

$$dV = V_y dt - VD dy \tag{4.2}$$

or

$$\frac{dV}{V} = y dt - D dy \tag{4.3}$$

where $D$ is the bond's Macaulay duration:

$$D(t) \equiv \frac{1}{V(t)} \sum_{s \geq t} C_{s-t} e^{-y(t)(s-t)}(s - t) \tag{4.4}$$

Our results in this section are motivated by the following observation. Proceeding heuristically, suppose that $y(t)$ is a continuous deterministic function. That is, the portfolio is managed in such a fashion that, along with continuity in deterministic yields on underlying assets, the portfolio yield to maturity is continuous in time. Because $V(t)$ is nonnegative, we may employ the log transform, $Z(t) = \ln(V(t))$, so that

$$dZ = \frac{dV}{V} \tag{4.5}$$

and

$$Z(t) = \int_0^t dZ \tag{4.6}$$

Substituting equation 4.3 into 4.6 and exponentiating yields

$$V(t) = V(0)e^{\int_0^t y dt - \int_0^t D dy} \tag{4.7}$$

Over any horizon of length $T$, the continuously compounded return is given by

$$\frac{\ln{(V(T)/V(0))}}{T} = \frac{1}{T}\left\{ \int_0^T y dt - \int_0^T D dy \right\} \tag{4.8}$$

This result is somewhat compelling once it is recognized that $D$ may be controlled through the investment process. For example, suppose the portfolio is managed in accordance with the requirement that Macaulay duration equal the remaining investment horizon, or

$$D(t) = T - t \tag{4.9}$$

This is the usual immunization strategy using Macaulay duration rather than the definition that employs forward rates. Theorem 4.1 in appendix 4A shows that in this case

$$\frac{1}{T}\left\{ \int_0^T y dt - \int_0^T D dy \right\} = y(0) \tag{4.10}$$

and hence

$$\frac{\ln{(V(T)/V(0))}}{T} = y(0)$$

That is, the compound return equals a constant, the initial yield to maturity, regardless of the actual time path of portfolio yield.

Equation 4.7 states the main idea of this paper. The distribution of total return may be examined through analysis of the time path of yield to maturity and Macaulay duration. Equation 4.10 suggests the usefulness of this approach by proving an immunization theorem that makes no assumption regarding yield shifts. The developments in this section were heuristic and intended to illustrate the approach taken. Strictly speaking, the results are true only for a pure discount bond. A precise analysis of $y(t)$ and other quantities is required for a rigorous restatement of equations 4.2 to 4.10 that renders them applicable to more general conditions. In the remainder of this section, we develop an integral representation of total return that corrects equation 4.7 for factors ignored in the preceding development.

*A Closer Look at the Problem*

The developments in the previous section were provided to illustrate the approach taken for computing returns. They must be modified in two ways. First, it is apparent that the assumption that the portfolio yield $y(t)$ be continuous is not valid. Even if yields on underlying securities are continuous and the proportion of funds invested in each security are continuous, discontinuities in $y(t)$ will in general exist; for example, whenever a coupon is received and a duration rule is being employed. Second, even if $y(t)$ is continuous, its movement over the differential $dt$ will be attributed to two sources: (1) changes in yields on underlying securities and (2) changes in portfolio composition. Changes in yield because of changes in portfolio composition do not affect total return in a way suggested by equation 4.3. Clearly a rigorous analysis of the function $y(t)$ is necessary for a proper specification of equation 4.7.

In developing a total return formula, we shall make several assumptions. First, the yield to maturity on each underlying asset is a continuous Lipschitz function of time. Second, the proportionate holding of each asset is a piecewise continuous function of time, with at most a countable number of jump discontinuities. Over continuous regions we shall also assume this function to be a Lipschitz function. Third, the portfolio is managed continuously through time. These assumptions are compatible with a wide range of control rules so that the results are capable of describing total returns for many portfolio management rules including, for example, immunization. The analysis will be deterministic, leaving to future work extensions to diffusion process representation of asset yields and portfolio holdings.

We begin our analysis by considering the total return on the portfolio over an interval of time $t_a \leq t \leq t_b$, in which no coupons or principal are received. Under this assumption we have the following theorem, which requires continuity of underlying asset yields $y_i(t)$ and asset proportions $x_i(t)$ for $i = 1, \ldots, B + 1$, but, in fact, neither of the Lipschitz assumptions.

THEOREM 4.2. *Under the given conditions, the portfolio yield $y(t)$ over the interval $t_a \leq t \leq t_b$ is a continuously differentiable function of the portfolio proportions ($x_i$, $i = 1, \ldots, B + 1$), the underlying bond yields ($y_i$, $i = 1, \ldots, B + 1$) and time $t$:*

$$y = y(x_i, y_i, t; i = 1, \ldots, B + 1)$$

Noting the constraint that

$$\sum_{i=1}^{B+1} x_i = 1$$

so that we may define

$$x_{B+1} \equiv 1 - \sum_{i=1}^{B} x_i$$

we may also write

$$y = y^c(x_j, y_i, t; j = 1, \ldots, B, i = 1, \ldots, B + 1)$$

and

$$y_{x_i} = \frac{1}{D(t)} \frac{P_i(y)}{P_i(y_i)} \quad i = 1, \ldots, B + 1$$

$$y^c_{x_i} \equiv y_{x_i}\bigg|_{\Sigma x_i = 1} = \frac{1}{D(t)} \left\{ \frac{P_i(y)}{P_i(y_i)} - \frac{P_{B+1}(y)}{P_{B+1}(y_{B+1})} \right\}$$

$$dy\bigg|_{\substack{dy_i = 0, \forall i \\ dt = 0 \\ d\Sigma x_i = 0}} \equiv \sum_{i=1}^{B} y^c_{x_i} dx_i = \sum_{i=1}^{B+1} y_{x_i} dx_i \qquad (4.11)$$

where $D(t)$ is the portfolio Macaulay duration and $P_i (\cdot) (i = 1, \ldots, B + 1)$ denotes the price of the bond evaluated at the given yield to maturity and where for simplicity we have abbreviated

$$P_i(\cdot, t) = P_i(\cdot) \quad i = 1, \ldots, B + 1$$

$$D(y_i, x_i, t; i = 1, \ldots, B + 1) = D(t)$$

*Proof.* See appendix 4A.

The import of the theorem is seen through examining figure 4.1. Suppose that the fund is rebalanced at time $t$ and $t + h$ where $(t_a \leq t \leq t + h \leq t_b)$ and suppose that $h$ is a very small number. We will examine the total return over the interval $t$, $t + h$ as $h$ approaches zero. The curve in figure 4.1 represents the time path of yield to maturity. Portfolio yield after rebalancing at time $t$ is $y(t)$. Between $t$ and $t + h$, units of each asset held are those purchased at time $t$. The $y_i$ vary continuously over the interval and hence the $x_i$ do also, in a passive unmanaged fashion. Thus portfolio yield $y$ varies accordingly. Defining $y(t + h)$ as the portfolio yield to maturity after rebalancing at $t + h$, letting

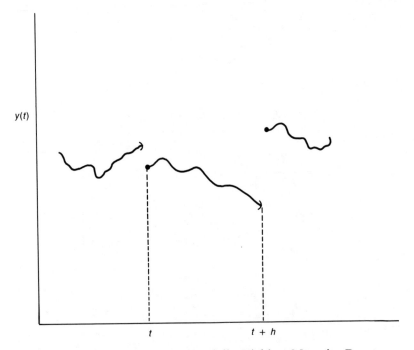

**Figure 4-1.** Discontinuities in Portfolio Yield to Maturity Due to
Rebalancing at Times $t$ and $t + h$

$$y^*(t + h) = \lim_{s \to t+h} y(s)$$

and using equation 4.3, the total return on the portfolio over the interval, $t$, $t + h$ is given by

$$y(t)h - D(t)(y^*(t + h) - y(t)) + o(y^*(t + h) - y(t)) + o(h) \tag{4.12}$$

We rewrite this as

$$y(t)h - D(t)(y(t + h) - y(t)) + D(t)(y(t + h) - y^*(t + h))$$
$$+ o(y^*(t + h) - y(t)) + o(h) \tag{4.13}$$

Now, consider the differential $y(t + h) - y^*(t + h)$. Theorem 4.3 in appendix 4A demonstrates that this may be written as

$$\sum_{i=1}^{B+1} y_{x_i}(t)\{x_i(t + h) - x_i(t)\}$$

$$-\sum_{i=1}^{B+1} \left(y_{x_i}(t) - \frac{1}{D(t)}\right) x_i(t) \frac{(P_i(t + h) - P_i(t))}{P_i(t)} + o(h)$$

$$(4.14)$$

where $x_i(t + h)$ is the portfolio proportion after rebalancing at $t + h$, and $P_i(\cdot)$ is now evaluated assuming $y_i$. Substituting equations 4.11 into 4.14 and 4.14 into 4.13, the total return over the interval $t$, $t + h$ may be written

$$y(t)h - D(t)dy(t, t + h) + \sum_{i=1}^{B+1} Z_i(t)dx_i(t, t + h)$$

$$-\sum_{i=1}^{B+1} (Z_i(t) - 1)x_i(t) \frac{dP_i(t, t + h)}{P_i(t)} + o(h)$$

$$(4.15)$$

where   $dP_i(t, t + h) = P_i(t + h, y_i(t + h)) - P_i(t, y_i(t))$

$Z_i(t) = P_i(y)/P_i(y_i)$

$dy(t, t + h) = y(t + h) - y(t)$

$dx_i(t, t + h) = x_i(t + h) - x_i(t)$

$dx_{B+1} = -\sum_{i=1}^{B} dx_i$

$x_{B+1} = 1 - \sum_{i=1}^{B} x_i$

Having defined the total return over the interval $t$, $t + h$, decompose the interval $t_a$, $t_b$ into $N$ subintervals of equal length with the points $t_j$, $j = 1, \ldots, N + 1$; $t_a = t_0$; $t_{N+1} = t_b$; $t_j - t_{j-1} = h = 1/N$. Consider the sum

$$S(N) = \sum_{j=1}^{N} \left\{ y(t_j)h - D(t_j)dy(t_j, t_{j+1}) + \sum_{i=1}^{B+1} Z_i(t_j)dx_i(t_j, t_{j+1}) - \right.$$

$$\left. \sum_{i=1}^{B+1} (Z_i(t_j) - 1)x_i(t) \frac{dP_i(t_j, t_{j+1})}{P_i(t_j)} \right\} + \sum_{j=1}^{N} o(1/N) \qquad (4.16)$$

The limit exists as $N$ goes to infinity as long as the functions $y(t)$, $D(t)$, $x_i(t)$, $Z_i(t)$ and $P_i(t)$ are continuous. By theorem 4.2, $y(t)$ is continuous if $x_i$, $y_i$ are continuous. The $y_i$ are continuous by assumption. By equation 4.4, $D(t)$ is continuous if $y(t)$ and the $x_i(t)$ are continuous. The $Z_i(t)$ are continuous if the $P_i(t)$ are continuous as well as $y$ and the $y_i$. Thus, given our assumptions on the continuity of the $y_i$, all functions are continuous if the $x_i$ are continuous. This is true by assumption.

It follows that the limit of sums (equation 4.16) exists and the total continuously compounded return over the interval $t_a$, $t_b$ is

$$\frac{1}{t_b - t_a} \lim_{N \to \infty} S(N) = \frac{1}{t_b - t_a} \left\{ \int_{t_a}^{t_b} y\,dt - \int_{t_a}^{t_b} D\,dy + \sum_{i=1}^{B+1} \int_{t_a}^{t_b} \frac{P_i(y)}{P_i(y_i)} dx_i \right.$$

$$\left. - \sum_{i=1}^{B+1} \int_{t_a}^{t_b} \frac{P_i(y) - P_i(y_i)}{P_i(y_i)} x_i(y\,dt - D_i dy_i) \right\} \quad (4.17)$$

where

$$x_{B+1} = 1 - \sum_{i=1}^{B} x_i$$

$$dx_{B+1} = - \sum_{i=1}^{B} dx_i$$

### Discontinuities in Yields

Equation 4.17 gives the continuously compounded return on a portfolio assuming that security yields and asset proportions are continuous Lipschitz functions and no coupon or principal payments are received in the interval. (Under these conditions, all functions in equation 4.17 are continuous and the integral exists.) The formula must be modified to account for discontinuities in the integrand. Because we have assumed that yields on underlying securities are continuous, such discontinuities will exist, in general, when asset proportions or durations are discontinuous. Discontinuities in asset proportions can occur for several reasons. Obviously a bond maturity can (but will not necessarily) cause a discontinuity as can an instantaneous shift in preferences. Discontinuities in asset duration are caused by coupon payments. In turn, this may cause a discontinuity in asset proportions. For example, if a duration rule is being employed, a coupon receipt causes a discontinuity in the bond's duration, probably requiring a discontinuity in asset proportions to restore portfolio duration when the cash is reinvested. It is mathematically possible to have discontinuities in asset proportions that do not cause discontinuities in portfolio yields, but such events are not the rule.

To determine the impact of discontinuities in general on total return, note that the discontinuity itself occurs at a single point in time and hence does not cause an instantaneous gain or loss. Such instantaneous gains or losses occur because of discontinuities in underlying yields, which we have not assumed possible. The total return over an interval containing a single discontinuity of any kind that we have considered is thus the product of the returns over the subintervals on either side of the discontinuity. It follows at once that the continuously compounded total return over the interval $t_0$, $t_H$ containing up to a countably infinite number of discontinuities in asset proportions is given by equation 4.17, but where the region of integration excludes the set of discontinuities. Denoting the $j$th subinterval of integration (that is, a subinterval of time with closed and open left- and right-hand sides respectively) by $R_j$, the total return is given by

$$\frac{1}{t_h - t_0} \sum_j \left\{ \int_{R_j} y\,dt - \int_{R_j} D\,dy + \sum_{i=1}^{B+1} \int_{R_j} P_i(y)/P_i(y_i)\,dx_i \right.$$

$$\left. - \sum_{i=1}^{B+1} \int_{R_j} \frac{P_i(y) - P_i(y_i)}{P_i(y_i)} x_i(y_i dt - D_i dy_i) \right\} \qquad (4.18)$$

To simplify equation 4.18 somewhat, define the jump in portfolio yield associated with a discontinuity in asset duration at time $s$ as $J_{sy}$ and the jump in duration as $J_{sd}$. Define

$$I_y(t) = - \sum_{s \le t} J_{sy}, \quad I_d(t) = - \sum_{s \le t} J_{sd}$$

and define

$$y^*(t) = y(t) + I_y(t), \quad D^*(t) = D(t) + I_d(t)$$

Given these definitions, $D^*(t)$ and $y^*(t)$ are continuous functions and

$$\int_{R_j} y\,dt - \int_{R_j} D\,dy = \int_{R_j} y^*\,dt - \int_{R_j} D\,dy^* - \int_{R_j} I_y\,dt$$

because $dI_y = 0$ except at discontinuities; and

$$\int_{R_j} D\,dy^* = \int_{R_j} D^*\,dy^* - \int_{R_j} I_d\,dy^*$$

Substituting into equation 4.18, the total return is given by

$$\frac{1}{t_b - t_a} \left\{ \left( \int_{t_a}^{t_b} y^*\,dt - \int_{t_a}^{t_b} D^*\,dy^* \right) + \sum_j \left\langle \int_{R_j} I_d\,dy^* - \int_{R_j} I_y\,dt \right. \right.$$

$$\left. \left. + \sum_{i=1}^{B+1} \int_{R_j} \frac{P_i(y)}{P_i(y_i)}\,dx_i - \sum_{i=1}^{B+1} \int_{R_j} \frac{P_i(y) - P_i(y_i)}{P_i(y_i)} x_i(y_i dt - D_i dy_i) \right\rangle \right\}$$

$$(4.19)$$

Equation 4.19 gives the total return on any bond portfolio under the assumption of continuous movements in the yields on underlying securities and continuous movements in asset proportions except perhaps for a countably infinite set of jump discontinuities in asset proportions or duration. In addition, we have assumed that asset yields and asset proportions are Lipschitz functions over continuous regions.

**An Application**

An obvious application of equation 4.19 is to the case where an immunization rule is employed. Here we assume that the fund is managed over the horizon 0, $H$ in such a fashion that

$$D(t) = H - t \quad 0 \le t \le H$$

The formula for the asset proportions for which this holds is not available in a simple closed form, nor is it unique when more than two bonds are in the portfolio. It is readily shown, however, that choices for these functions exist for which the mathematical assumptions underlying equation 4.19 hold, in particular, the continuous Lipschitz assumption on the $x_i$. If the yield curve is flat initially and remains flat although at a continuously varying level, we have

$$P_i(y_i) = P_i(y)$$

for all $i$, since $y = y_i$ for all $i$ under this assumption. In this case (as is well known) we have implicitly assumed parallel shifts in forward rates and a spot rate equal to the initial yield for all maturities. Using equation 4.19, the total return reduces to

$$\frac{1}{H} \left\{ \int_0^H y\,dt - \int_0^H (H - t)\,dy \right\}$$

Hence, by equation 4.10, this reduces to $y(0)$. That is, if the yield curve is flat and remains flat, we have derived the usual immunization result for parallel shifts.

If the yield curve does not behave in this fashion, we employ equation 4.19 to find that the total return is given by

$$y(0) + \frac{1}{H}\left\{\sum_j \left(\int_{R_j} -I_y dt + \sum_{i=1}^{B+1}\int_{R_j}\frac{P_i(y)}{P_i(y_i)}dx_i\right.\right.$$

$$\left.\left.- \sum_{i=1}^{B+1}\int_{R_j}\frac{P_i(y) - P_i(y_i)}{P_i(y_i)}x_i(y_i dt - D_i dy_i)\right)\right\} \quad (4.20)$$

The total returns equals the initial yield to maturity plus several terms related to the curvature of the yield curve. Evidently, a reasonable immunization strategy is to maximize the fund in accordance with the duration rule: maximize $y(0)$ and minimize the other terms in the equation. For example, consider the simplification of equation 4.20 to the case of a portfolio consisting on two bonds. Here we have $X_2 = 1 - X_1$ and if $N_1(t)$ and $N_2(t)$ are the numbers of securities of each type held, by the definition of portfolio yield then

$$N_1 P_1(y_1) + N_2 P_2(y_2) = N_1 P_1(y) + N_2 P_2(y)$$

Defining

$$\delta_i = \frac{N_i(P_i(y) - P_i(y_i))}{N_1 P_1(y_1) + N_2 P_2(y_2)} \quad i = 1, 2$$

we have

$$\delta_1 = -\delta_2$$

Using these facts, the total return simplifies to

$$y(0) + \frac{1}{H}\sum_j \left\{\int_{R_j} -I_y dt + \int_{R_j}\frac{P_1(y)}{P_1(y_1)} - \frac{P_2(y)}{P_2(y_2)}dx_1\right.$$

$$\left.- \int_{R_j}\delta_1\left(\frac{dP_1}{P_1} - \frac{dP_2}{P_2}\right)\right\} \quad (4.21)$$

This result suggests that one way to immunize a portfolio is to select just two bonds that differ little in yield and duration. This will tend to minimize the terms on the right-hand side of expression 4.21. To test this possibility, we simulated a five-year immunization in which five- and seven-year bonds were employed. Three assumptions were made for the coupon levels of the bonds: both had 5 percent coupons, both had 7.5 percent coupons, and both had 10 percent coupons. Three assumptions were made regarding yield changes. For the five-year bond, the yield increased steadily from 10 percent to 20 percent; decreased steadily from 10 percent to 20 percent; and remained at 10 percent. The yield on the seven-year bond was assumed to fluctuate within 50 basis points of the five-year bond (although it could never have a negative yield). Initially, the yield curve was assumed flat at 10 percent so that the target return was 10 percent. An annual coupon was assumed and rebalancing was assumed to take place quarterly with any coupon income reinvested in the two bonds. Despite large fluctuations in yield, a compound return close to target was consistently provided, suggesting that investment techniques tending to minimize the terms on the right-hand side of equation 4.20 certainly exist.

As a practical matter, it is useful to have a shorthand estimate of the yield to maturity $y(0)$, which is actually the solution to a polynomial of high degree and therefore requires an iterative solution. In appendix 4A we demonstrate the following proposition.

PROPOSITION 4.1. *The yield to maturity at time t is approximately equal to*

$$y(t) \approx \sum_{i=1}^{B+1} x_i(t) \frac{D_i(t)}{\sum x_i D_i} y_i(t)$$

The proposition is made more useful by virtue of the following theorem, which is proved in appendix 4A.

THEOREM 4.4. *If for all i*

$$1 = \max_{i,t} \frac{1}{3} |y - y_i|$$

*where, for bond i, t is a payment horizon date,*

$$y(t) \geq \sum_{i=1}^{B+1} x_i(t) \frac{D_i(t)}{\sum x_i D_i} y_i(t)$$

That is, the duration- and market-weighted yield is a close lower estimate of the true yield.

## The Return to Maturity on a Bond

A second application of equation 4.19 is to the case that all funds are invested for $M$ years in a single bond with initial maturity $M$. In this case equation 4.18 reduces to

$$\frac{1}{M} \left( \int_0^M y \, dt - \int_0^M D \, dy \right)$$

where $y(t)$ is continuous and equals the yield on the one bond, and $D(t)$ is discontinuous with jumps at the points where coupons are received and reinvested. Defining

$$D^*(t) \equiv D(t) - \frac{D(0)}{M}(M - t), \quad 0 \le t \le M \tag{4.23}$$

where $D(0)$ is the initial Macaulay duration of the bond, we have the following theorem.[1]

THEOREM 4.5. *Under the conditions laid out in this section, equation 4.22 may be written*

$$\left(\frac{D(0)}{M}\right) y(0) + \left(1 - \frac{D(0)}{M}\right) \frac{1}{M} \int_0^M y\,dt - \frac{1}{M} \int_0^M D^*\,dy \tag{4.24}$$

*Proof.* See appendix 4A.

Theorem 4.5 demonstrates that the total return on a portfolio consisting of a single bond held to maturity equals the sum of three components. The sum of the first two are the weighted average of the initital yield with the average reinvestment rate, where the weighting factor is the ratio of initial duration to maturity. The third term is the mean value of the Stielties intergral of $D^*$, where $D^*$ equals the duration of actual duration from its linear trend value. $D^*$ is a piecewise continuous function with $D^*(0) = D^*(M) = 0$.

## Note

1. A similar result has been obtained by Guilford Babcox, although from a different formulation. See Guilford Babcox, "A Modified Duration Measure," University of California Working Paper (June 1976).

# Appendix 4A
## Proofs of Theorems

THEOREM 4.1. *If $y(t)$ is continuous over $0 \leq t \leq T$ and $D(t) = T - t$, then*

$$\frac{1}{T} \left\{ \int_0^T y\,dt - \int_0^T D\,dy \right\} = y(0)$$

*Proof.*

$$\frac{1}{T} \left\{ \int_0^T y\,dt - \int_0^T D\,dy \right\} = \frac{1}{T} \left\{ \int_0^T y\,dt - T\int_0^T dy + \int_0^T t\,dy \right\}$$

$$= \frac{1}{T} \left\{ \int_0^T y\,dt - T(y(T) - y(0)) + \int_0^T d(ty) - \int_0^T y\,dt \right\}$$

$$= \frac{1}{T} \left\{ T(y(0) - y(T)) + Ty(T) \right\}$$

$$= y(0)$$

THEOREM 4.2. *If over the interval $t_a \leq t \leq t_b$, the underlying asset yields and portfolio proportions, $y_i$, $x_i (i = 1, \ldots, B + 1)$ are continuous, then the portfolio yield $y(t)$ is a continuously differentiable function of the $y_i$, $x_i$, and time. Writing*

$$y = y(y_i, x_i, t; \quad i = 1, \ldots, B + 1)$$

and noting that

$$\sum_{i=1}^{B+1} x_i = 1$$

so that we may define

$$x_{B+1} = 1 - \sum_{i=1}^{B} x_i$$

we may also write

$$y = y^c(x_j, y_i, t; \quad j = 1, \ldots, B; \quad i = 1, \ldots, B + 1)$$

and

$$y_{x_i} = \frac{1}{D(t)} \frac{P_i(y)}{P_i(y_i)} \quad i = 1, \ldots, B + 1$$

$$y^c_{x_i} \equiv y_{x_i} \bigg|_{\sum x_i = 1} = \frac{1}{D(t)} \left\{ \frac{P_i(y)}{P_i(y_i)} - \frac{P_{B+1}(y)}{P_{B+1}(y_{B+1})} \right\} \quad i = 1, \ldots, B$$

and

$$dy \bigg|_{\substack{dy_i = 0 \\ dt = 0 \\ d\sum x_i = 0}} \equiv \sum_{i=1}^{B} y^c_{x_i} dx_i = \sum_{i=1}^{B+1} y_{x_i} dx_i$$

where $D(t)$ denotes portfolio Macaulay duration and $P_i(\cdot)$, ($i = 1, \ldots, B + 1$) denotes the price of bond $i$ evaluated at the given yield to maturity and where for simplicity we have abbreviated

$$P_i(y_i, t) \equiv P_i(\cdot)$$

$$D(y_i, x_i, t; \quad i = 1, \ldots, B + 1) \equiv D(t)$$

*Proof.* Letting $N_i(t)$ denote the number of units of the $i$th bond held at time $t$, equation 4.1 may be rewritten

$$V(y, N_i, t; \quad i = 1, \ldots, B + 1) = \sum_{i=1}^{B+1} N_i(t) \sum_{s \geq t} C_{i,s-t} e^{-y(s-t)} \quad (4\text{A}.1)$$

where $C_{i,s-t}$ is the cash flow from the $i$th bond at time $s - t$. Noting that the price of bond $i$ at time $t$ is

$$P_i(y_i, t) = \sum_{s \geq t} C_{i,s-t} e^{-y_i(t)(s-t)} \quad (4\text{A}.2)$$

portfolio value is defined by

$$V^*(y_i, N_i, t; \quad i = 1, \ldots, B + 1) \equiv \sum_{i=1}^{B+1} N_i(t) P_i(y_i, t) \quad (4\text{A}.3)$$

and portfolio yield is defined by

$$V(y, N_i, t; \ i = 1, \ldots, B + 1) = V^*(y_i, N_i, t; \ i = 1, \ldots, B + 1)$$
$$\text{(4A.4)}$$

where from equation 4A.1

$$V(y, N_i, t; \ i = 1, \ldots, B + 1) = \sum_{i=1}^{B+1} N_i(t) P_i(y, t)$$

Dividing equation 4A.4 by $V^*$ and noting that

$$x_i(t) = N_i(t) P_i(y_i, t) / V^*(y_i, N_i, t; \ i = 1, \ldots, B + 1) \qquad \text{(4A.5)}$$

we have

$$0 = -1 + \sum_{i=1}^{B+1} x_i P_i(y, t) / P_i(y_i, t) \qquad \text{(4A.6)}$$

The right-hand side of equation 4A.6 is a function:

$$F(y, x_i, y_i, t; \ i = 1, \ldots, B + 1)$$

and the definition of portfolio yield requires that

$$F(y, x_i, y_i, t; \ i = 1, \ldots, B + 1) = 0 \qquad \text{(4A.7)}$$

By the implicit function theorem, equation 4A.7 implies that portfolio yield may be written

$$y = y(x_i, y_i, t; \ i = 1, \ldots, B + 1)$$

and the first assertion follows.

The implicit function theorem also implies that

$$y_{x_i} = -F_{x_i}/F_y \quad i = 1, \ldots, B + 1$$

From equation 4A.6 we have

$$F_{x_i} = P_i(y, t) / P_i(y_i, t) \quad i = 1, \ldots, B + 1$$

It is also evident from equation 4A.4 that

$$F_y = \frac{-D(t) V(y, N_i, t; \ i = 1, \ldots, B + 1)}{V^*(y_i, N_i, t; \ i = 1, \ldots, B + 1)}$$

Thus when equation 4A.7 holds, $V^* = V$ so that

$$F_y = -D(t)$$

and the third assertion follows. Now, constraining equation 4A.6 by the definition

$$x_{B+1} = 1 - \sum_{i=1}^{B} x_i$$

we have

$$0 = -1 + \frac{P_{B+1}(y, t)}{P_{B+1}(y_{B+1}, t)} + \sum_{i=1}^{B+1} x_i \left( \frac{P_i(y, t)}{P_i(y_i, t)} - \frac{P_{B+1}(y, t)}{P_{B+1}(y_{B+1}, t)} \right)$$

The right-hand side of equation 4A.8 is a function

$$F^c(y, x_j, y_i, t; \quad j = 1, \ldots, B; \quad i = 1, \ldots, B + 1)$$

and the definition of portfolio yield now requires that

$$F^c(y, x_j, y_i, t; \quad j = 1, \ldots, B; \quad i = 1, \ldots, B + 1) = 0 \quad (4A.9)$$

The implicit function theorem and equation 4A.9 now imply that portfolio yield may be written

$$y = y^c(x_j, y_i, t; \ j = 1, \ldots, B; \ i = 1, \ldots, B + 1)$$

which verifies the second assertion. The fourth assertion follows by repeating the steps to $y^c$ which were applied to $y$ in proving the third assertion. The final assertion is verified by noting that

$$\sum_{i=1}^{B} y_{x_i}^c dx_i = \frac{1}{D(t)} \left\{ \left( \sum_{i=1}^{B} \frac{P_i(y, t)}{P_i(y_i, t)} dx_i \right) - \frac{P_{B+1}(y, t)}{P_{B+1}(y_{B+1}, t)} \sum_{i=1}^{B} dx_i \right\}$$

$$= \frac{1}{D(t)} \left\{ \sum_{i=1}^{B+1} \frac{P_i(y, t)}{P_i(y_i, t)} dx_i \right\}$$

$$= \sum_{i=1}^{B+1} y_{x_i} dx_i$$

assuming that

$$x_{B+1} = 1 - \sum_{i=1}^{B} x_i$$

so that

$$dx_{B+1} = -\sum_{i=1}^{B} dx_i$$

THEOREM 4.3.

$$y(t + h) - y^*(t + h) = \sum_{i=1}^{B+1} y_{x_i} dx_i(t, t + h)$$

$$- \sum_{i=1}^{B+1} \left( y_{x_i} - \frac{1}{D(t)} \right) x_i \frac{dP_i(t, t + h)}{P_i(t)} + o(h)$$

*Proof.* Define

$$x_i^*(t + h) = \frac{N_i(t)P_i(t + h)}{V(t + h)} \quad i = 1, \ldots, B + 1$$

where

$$V(t + h) = \sum_{i=1}^{B+1} N_i(t)P_i(t + h, y_i)$$

$N_i(t)$ is the number of units of bond $i$ held at time $t$ and $P_i( \cdot )$ is evaluated using $y_i( \cdot )$. If $N_i(t)$ is held fixed, the differential of $x_i(t)$ is

$$dx_i = \frac{N_i(t)dP_i}{V(t)} - \frac{N_i(t)P_i dV}{V(t)^2}$$

$$= x_i \left( \frac{dP_i}{P_i} - \frac{dV}{V} \right) \quad i = 1, \ldots, B + 1$$

Also

$$dV = \sum_{i=1}^{B+1} N_i(t)dP_i$$

$$= \sum_{i=1}^{B+1} N_i(t)P_i(dP_i/P_i)$$

so that

$$\frac{dV}{V} = \sum_{i=1}^{B+1} x_i \frac{dP_i}{P_i}$$

Hence

$$dx_i = x_i \left( \frac{dP_i}{P_i} - \sum_{i=1}^{B+1} x_i \frac{dP_i}{P_i} \right) \quad i = 1, \ldots, B + 1$$

It now follows that for small $h$

$$x_i^*(t + h) - x_i(t) = x_i(t) \left\{ \frac{dP_i(t, t + h)}{P_i(t)} - \sum_{i=1}^{B+1} x_i(t) \frac{dP_i(t, t + h)}{P_i(t)} + o(h) \right\}$$

$$(4A.10)$$

Next, observe that

$$|x_i(t + h) - x_i^*(t + h)| = |(x_i(t + h) - x_i(t)) - (x_i^*(t + h) - x_i(t))|$$

$$= K_1 h + K_2 h \quad (4A.11)$$

for $K_1$, $K_2$ independent of $t$ and $h$. The first term on the right-hand side of equation 4A.11 follows from the Lipschitz assumption on the $x_i(t)$. The second term on the right-hand side of 4A.11 follows from 4A.10 and the Lipschitz assumptions on the $y_i$. Now, using the definition of $y^*(t + h)$ and theorem 4.2, the change in portfolio yield due to rebalancing at $t + h$ is given by

$$y(t + h) - y^*(t + h) = \sum_{i=1}^{B+1} y_{x_i}^*(t + h)(x_i(t + h) - x_i^*(t + h)) + o(h)$$

$$(4A.12)$$

where $y_i^*(t + h)$ is simply the derivative in theorem 4A.2 evaluated at $t + h$ with $x_i^*(t + h)$ in place of $x_i(t + h)$. The form of the derivative in theorem 4.2 shows that, in turn, it is differentiable, so that we may write

$$y_{x_i}^*(t + h) = y_{x_i}(t) + (y_{x_i})_y(y^*(t + h) - y(t))$$

$$+ \sum_{i=1}^{B+1} (y_{x_i})_{y_i}(y_i(t + h) - y_i(t)) + (y_{x_i})_t h + o(h)$$

Again by the Lipschitz requirements, this becomes

$$y^*_{x_i}(t + h) = y_{x_i}(t) + O(h) \quad i = 1, \ldots, B + 1 \qquad (4A.13)$$

Combining equations 4A.12 and 4A.13, we may write 4A.12 as

$$y(t + h) - y^*(t + h) = \sum_{i=1}^{B+1} y_{x_i}(t)(x_i(t + h) - x^*_i(t + h)) + o(h)$$
$$(4A.14)$$

Substituting equation 4A.10 and making use of 4A.11

$$y(t + h) - y^*(t + h) = \sum_{i=1}^{B+1} y_{x_i}(x_i(t + h) - x_i(t)) - \sum_{i=1}^{B+1} y_{x_i} x_i \frac{dP_i(t, t + h)}{P_i(t)}$$

$$+ \sum_{i=1}^{B+1} y_{x_i} x_i \left( \sum_{i=1}^{B+1} x_i \frac{dP_i(t, t + h)}{P_i(t)} \right) + o(h) \quad (4A.15)$$

Finally, by theorem 4.2.

$$y_{x_i}(t) x_i(t) = \frac{1}{D(t)} \frac{P_i(y, t)}{P_i(y_i, t)} \cdot \frac{N_i(t) P_i(y_i, t)}{V(t)}$$

$$= \frac{1}{D(t)} \frac{N_i P_i(y, t)}{V(t)}$$

and hence

$$\sum_{i=1}^{B+1} y_{x_i}(t) x_i(t) = \frac{1}{D(t)}$$

by definition of $V(t)$. Substituting this into equation 4A.15

$$y(t + h) - y^*(t + h) = \sum_{i=1}^{B+1} y_{x_i} (x_i(t + h) - x_i(t))$$

$$- \sum_{i=1}^{B+1} \left( y_{x_i} - \frac{1}{D(t)} \right) x_i \frac{dP_i(t, t + h)}{P_i(t)} + o(h)$$
$$(4A.16)$$

PROPOSITION 4.1.

$$y(t) \approx \sum_{i=1}^{B+1} y_i(t) x_i(t) \frac{D_i(t)}{\sum_{i=1}^{B+1} x_i D_i} \qquad (4A.17)$$

*Proof.* $y(t)$ is defined by

$$\sum_{i=1}^{B+1} N_i P_i(y_i) = \sum_{i=1}^{B+1} N_i P_i(y) \tag{4A.18}$$

where $N_i$ is the number of bonds of type $i$ in the portfolio. We may regard the right-hand side as a function of $B + 1$ variables and write this as

$$F(y_1, \ldots, y_{B+1}) = F(y, \ldots, y) \tag{4A.19}$$

Expanding the left-hand side of equation 4A.19 in a Taylor series and substituting in 4A.18, the right-hand side of 4A.19 may be written

$$\sum_{i=1}^{B+1} N_i P_i(y) = \sum_{i=1}^{B+1} N_i P_i(y_i) + \sum_{i=1}^{B+1} N_i P_i'(y_i)(y - y_i)$$

$$+ \text{ higher-order terms}$$

or

$$0 = \sum_{i=1}^{B+1} N_i P_i'(y_i)(y - y_i) + \text{higher-order terms} \tag{4A.20}$$

Substituting $P_i' = -D_i P_i$ into equation 4A.20, dropping higher-order terms, and rearranging produces equation 4A.17.

THEOREM 4.4. *If for all i ($i = 1, \ldots, B + 1$)*

$$1 = \max_{i,t} \frac{1}{3} t \, |y - y_i|$$

where, for bond *i, t* is a payment receipt slate, then

$$y(t) \geq \sum_{i=1}^{B+1} y_i(t) x_i(t) \frac{D_i(t)}{\sum_{i=1}^{B+1} x_i D_i}$$

*Proof.* We may rearrange equation 4A.20 to find

$$y(t) = \frac{1}{-\sum_{i=1}^{B+1} N_i P_i'} \left\{ -\sum_{i=1}^{B+1} N_i P_i' y_i + \frac{1}{2} \sum_{i=1}^{B+1} N_i P_i''(y - y_i)^2 \right.$$

$$\left. + \frac{1}{6} \sum_{i=1}^{B+1} N_i P_i'''(y - y_i)^3 + \ldots \right\}$$

By direct differentiation, the terms on the right-hand side with even-order derivatives are positive while the remaining terms may be positive or negative. The condition of the theorem implies that each even-order term exceeds the term following it in absolute value. Hence

$$y(t) \geq \frac{1}{-\sum_{i=1}^{B+1} N_i P_i'} \left\{ - \sum_{i=1}^{B+1} N_i P_i' y_i \right\}$$

$$= \sum_{i=1}^{B+1} x_i(t) y_i(t) \frac{D_i(t)}{\sum_{i=1}^{B+1} x_i D_i}$$

This proves the result under continuous compounding. If discrete discounting is employed the conditions of the theorem become that for all $i$

$$1 \geq |y - y_i| / (1 + y_i)$$

and

$$1 \geq \max_{i,t} \frac{1}{3} \frac{(t + 2)}{1 + y_i} |y - y_i|$$

THEOREM 4.5. *The total compound return from investing for M years in a bond with initial maturity M equals*

$$\left( \frac{D(0)}{M} \right) y(0) + \left( 1 - \frac{D(0)}{M} \right) \frac{1}{M} \int_0^M y\, dt - \frac{1}{M} \int_0^M D^* dy \qquad (4A.21)$$

where $D^*$ is defined by equation 4.23.

*Proof.* From equation 4.22, total return equals

$$\frac{1}{M} \left\{ \int_0^M y\, dt - \int_0^M D\, dy \right\}$$

Substituting in $D^*$, this becomes

$$\frac{1}{M} \left\{ \int_0^M y\, dt - \int_0^M \frac{D(0)}{M} (M - t) dy - \int_0^M D^* dy \right\}$$

or

$$\frac{1}{M} \left\{ \frac{D(0)}{M} \left( \int_0^M y\, dt - \int_0^M (M - t) dy \right) + \left( 1 - \frac{D(0)}{M} \right) \int_0^M y\, dt - \int_0^M D^* dy \right\}$$

Applying theorem 4.1 produces equation 4A.21.

# 5

# Managing a Contingently Immunized Portfolio: A Mathematical Approach

As introduced in chapter 1, contingent immunization is the variety of immunization in which a minimum return is defined that is less than the rate which could be obtained through ordinary immunization. This difference corresponds to an excess market value equaling the actual assets less that which would be necessary to achieve, through ordinary immunization, the minimum return on the entire amount at actual rate levels. This excess implies a degree of management latitude in making interest rate forecasts. Should such forecasts be incorrect with sufficient frequency, the excess market value is driven to zero, which is the event that causes the portfolio to trigger into the immunized mode.

Although considerable work has been performed on standard immunization, relatively little has been performed on contingent immunization despite the appeal of this asset form to many investors. In part, this is because the idea is relatively new. In part, it is because contingent immunization contemplates a discontinuous change in the investment management technique. As such, it is not the sort of rule that arises out of the theories of economic behavior that economists normally ascribe to investors. When carried through to investment implications, these theories find the optimal investment technique to vary smoothly with wealth, the outlook for returns, and other factors. Hence part of the absence of academic work on contingent immunization may be a reflection of its suboptimality by this standard.

Notwithstanding this caveat, contingent immunization is readily analyzed and its return distribution may be rigorously set forth for comparison to normal immunization as well as to unconstrained management on the basis of yield forecasts. We have conducted two analyses along these lines. A simulation analysis is presented in chapter 6. That analysis considers several interest-rate forecasting abilities in increasing, stable, and decreasing yield scenarios. For each such combination we vary the two major decision variables: the floor (minimum) return relative to the immunized return and the bet "size" (see the next section). This work depicts the return distribution under various combinations of assumptions. In particular, variations in the return distribution caused by changes in the decision variables would help determine how a contingent immunization should be run in practice.

The analysis in this chapter has a similar objective but approaches the problem using methods that differ in two ways. First, the interpretation of the decision rule for bet size is somewhat different. Second, the approach is mathematical rather than empirical. That is, we mathematically derive the return distribution as opposed to deducing it through the repeated trials of a simulation. Specifically, we adopt a simple framework for how period-by-period returns are generated in a contingently immunized portfolio. We then derive, in closed form, the distribution of long-term compound return. The objective of this analysis is, again, to parameterize the return distribution in terms of the crucial contingent variables to see how such portfolios should be run in practice. Our work assumes a particular management style insofar as a particular assumption is made for how returns are generated. Nonetheless, the insights gained transcend this fact, as will be seen.

**Outline of the Analysis**

In the simulation study described in chapter 6 we analyze the performance of five-year contingently immunized portfolios under (1) three different assumptions for the secular direction of yield changes; (2) two different assumptions for yield curve volatility; (3) three different assumptions for the difference between the floor (minimum) and immunized returns; (4) five different assumptions for manager forecasting ability; and (5) four different assumptions for the bet *size*. The bet size has a subtle interpretation.

By definition, if triggering has not taken place, a contingently immunized portfolio contains a market value in excess of what would be necessary to achieve the floor return (on the original asset value) using prevailing rates. Our bet size (in the simulation) was defined as the percentage of this excess that would be lost if yields moved in the direction opposite to that forecast by one standard deviation of yield change.

The analysis in this chapter employs a similar experimental design except for three differences: (1) horizons from three to seven years are examined instead of only five years; (2) the bet size is defined in a somewhat different way; and (3) rather than employ simulation, we compute the actual probability distribution of returns. We now outline the mathematical framework for the analysis.

Let (1) $R(j)$ denote the continuously compounded return on the actual portfolio in period (quarter) $j$; (2) $I(j)$ denote the continuously compounded return on the corresponding immunized portfolio in period $j$; (3) $F$ denote the continuously compounded floor return; (4) $I^*$ denote the continuously compounded immunized return; (5) $H^*$ denote the horizon in years; (6) $V(0)$ denote the initial portfolio value. The portfolio must be triggered into the immunization mode as soon as the actual value equals the amount just sufficient to lock up the floor return (on $V(0)$) at prevailing rates. Using these definitions, this asset value at the end of period $k$ equals

$$V(0)e^{(F-I^*)H^*}e^{\sum\limits_{j=1}^{k}I(j)}$$

Thus, we must trigger at the first integer for which

$$V(0)e^{\sum\limits_{j=1}^{k}R(j)} = V(0)e^{(F-I^*)H^*}e^{\sum\limits_{j=1}^{k}I(j)}$$

Rearranging and taking logarithms, we must trigger at the first integer $k$ for which

$$\sum_{j=1}^{k}R(j) - I(j) = (F - I^*)H$$

We make the simplifying assumption that

$$R(j) - I(j)$$

can assume only the values $d$ or $-d$ for a small positive number $d$. That is, at the start of each period the manager makes an interest rate bet that will produce an actual return (in period $j$) which is related to the corresponding immunized portfolio return by

$$R(j) = I(j) \pm d$$

Suppose that in $H$ trials (periods) there are $e$ errors, or $e$ cases of $-d$ being realized and $H - e$ cases of $d$ being realized. In this case, it is simple to show that if triggering does not take place, the total return (terminal wealth divided by initial wealth) is given by

$$e^{\sum\limits_{j=1}^{H}R(j)} = e^{\sum\limits_{j=1}^{H}I(j)}e^{(H-2e)d} \tag{5.1}$$

If periods are interpreted as quarters, $H^* = H/4$; and if immunization is assumed to be perfect, by definition of $I^*$

$$e^{\sum\limits_{j=1}^{N}I(j)} = e^{I^*H/4}$$

so that expression 5.1 becomes

$$e^{\sum\limits_{j=1}^{H}R(j)} = e^{I^*H/4}e^{(H-2e)d} \tag{5.2}$$

The number $d$ reflects the degree of risk in the bets that are made; as such, it is our measurement of the bet size. It differs from the bet size employed in the simulation analysis of chapter 6 in that it assesses bet size relative to the total portfolio as opposed to only the excess market value. From $d$ we may calculate another important quantity in the analysis that (for lack of a better term) we call *degrees of freedom*. Define $N(H, I^*, F, d)$ as the greatest integer less than or equal to

$$\frac{(I^* - F)H^*}{d} \tag{5.3}$$

$N$ is the number of consecutive forecast errors that, if made at the start of the horizon, would necessitate triggering. If triggering takes place, regardless of the time of triggering, our assumptions imply that the total return is given by

$$e^{\sum_{j=1}^{H} I(j)} e^{-Nd} \tag{5.4}$$

Assuming perfect immunization, the definition of $I^*$ now implies that expression 5.4 becomes

$$e^{I^* \frac{H}{4} - Nd} \tag{5.5}$$

To complete the experimental design, we assume that correct forecasts are made with probability $p$ (and incorrect forecasts are made with probability $1 - p$). Moreover, we assume that the probability $p$ is a constant, independent of prior success or failures.

The assumptions made thus far enable a complete description of the probability distribution of return. Given an horizon of $H$ periods (quarters), consider the total compound return assuming $e$ (out of $H$) forecast errors. This number is developed from several components. Let $T(e, H, N)$ be the number of choices of $e$ errors in $H$ trials for which triggering takes place. $T$ is a function of $e$, but also of $H$ and $N$. The probability of not triggering is

$$\left\{ \binom{H}{e} - T(e,H,N) \right\} p^{H-e}(1 - p)^e$$

where $\binom{H}{e}$ is simply the number of possible ways we could have $e$ errors in $H$ trials. The probability of triggering given $e$ errors is thus

$$T(e,H,N) p^{H-e}(1 - p)^e$$

If we trigger, the total return is given by expression 5.5, and the continuously compounded return (where periods are assumed to be quarters) is thus given by

$$I^* - \frac{Nd}{H/4} \tag{5.6}$$

If we do not trigger, the continuously compounded return (from equation 5.2) is given by

$$I^* + \frac{(H - 2e)d}{H/4} \tag{5.7}$$

It follows from these results that the continuously compounded mean return given $e$ errors is

$$\frac{\left\{\left(\frac{H}{e}\right) - T(e,H,N)\right\}\left\{p^{H-e}(1 - p)^e\right\}\left\{I^* + \frac{(H - 2e)d}{H/4}\right\} + T(e,H,N)\left\{p^{H-e}(1 - p)^e\right\}\left\{I^* - \frac{Nd}{H/4}\right\}}{\left(\frac{H}{e}\right)p^{H-e}(1 - p)^e}$$

or simplifying,

$$\mu(e,H,N) \equiv I^* + \frac{4d}{H}\left\{(H - 2e) - \frac{T(e,H,N)}{\left(\frac{H}{e}\right)}(H - 2e - N)\right\} \tag{5.8}$$

Finally, the unconditional continuously compounded mean return is given by

$$\sum_{e=0}^{H} \left(\frac{H}{e}\right)p^{H-e}(1 - p)^e \mu(e,H,N) \tag{5.9}$$

These results emerge from the application of binomial probabilities. A somewhat more involved computation is required for the evaluation of $T(e, H, N)$. With some effort it may be shown that

$$T(e,H,N) \quad = \quad 0 \qquad\qquad 0 \leq e < N - 1$$

$$T(e,H,N) \quad = \quad 1 \qquad\qquad e = N$$

$$T(e,H,N) \quad = \quad \sum_{i=1}^{k+1} z(i,k) \qquad N < e < \frac{H + N}{2}$$

$$T(e,H,N) \quad = \quad \left(\frac{H}{E}\right) \qquad\qquad e \geq \frac{H + N}{2}$$

where

$$k = e - N$$

$$z(1,k) = \binom{H - N}{k}$$

$$z(i,k) = \binom{N + 2(i - 1)}{N + i - 1}\binom{H - (N + 2(i - 1))}{k - (i - 1)}$$

$$- \sum_{j=1}^{i-1} z(j,k) \frac{\binom{2(i - j)}{i - j}\binom{H - (N + 2(i - 1))}{k - (i - 1)}}{\binom{H - (N + 2(j - 1))}{k - (j - 1)}}$$

These results may be used to depict the probability distribution of return for a contingent immunization managed in the fashion described. The tables in appendix 5B show this distribution under various assumptions. In particular, we consider (1) five different horizons (from three to seven years); (2) five different manager forecasting accuracies; (3) seven different levels for floor (minimum) versus immunized return; and (4) three different bet sizes. The results are organized primarily for the purpose of identifying the effect on the return distribution of variations in the key decision variables—namely, the bet size and the difference between floor and immunized return.

**Analysis of Results**

The first twenty-five tables in appendix 5B contains results on the return distribution that are computed from the probability distribution developed in this chapter. The data across each row are as follows. First, the decision variables are: the floor (minimum) return and the leverage factor $d$. The leverage factor is measured as a number as opposed to a percent. Given these parameters as well as the immunized return (15 percent throughout), the horizon, and the forecasting accuracy (all indicated at the top of each page), the rest of the distribution is determined. Next, first the degrees of freedom are computed from equation 5.3 (that is, the number of consecutive errors that, if made at the outset of the horizon, would necessitate triggering), the probability of triggering, the probability of a continuously compounded return less than the immunized return, the expected continuously compounded return, and various return percentiles. The interpretation corresponding to, for example, the fortieth percentile is that there is at least a 40 percent chance of a continuously compounded rate below the indicated level.

The tables in appendix 5B indicate several interesting patterns. As expected, the risk-return tradeoff has a positive slope for good forecasting ability and a negative slope for poor forecasting ability. When forecasting ability is less than or equal to 50 percent, the mean return is increased (or remains constant in the case of 50 percent accuracy), while the probability of underperformance is reduced if the floor return is increased. This result holds regardless of other factors or variables. As a consequence, we shall henceforth discuss only results for forecasting accuracy in excess of 50 percent.

Holding other factors constant, increasing the horizon in cases where the probability of triggering is zero leaves the mean return the same but reduces the dispersion about the mean. The restriction to the case of a zero probability of triggering is equivalent to management solely on the basis of a yield curve outlook without regard for a floor return. It corresponds to what in practice is called *active management,* as opposed to contingent immunization. These cases occur in the analysis when the floor is so low as to represent no constraint.

Holding the same factors constant but considering cases where there is a positive probability of triggering, increasing the horizon raises the mean return and reduces the probability of underperformance. There are several cases where this pattern does not hold because the ratio in expression 5.2, which gives the maximum number of bets, is not automatically an integer and must be rounded down. The extent of rounding differs from case to case and can cause these differences.

Holding all else constant (still assuming forecasting accuracy in excess of 50 percent) and increasing the bet size increases the expected return as well as the probability of triggering and the probability of underperformance. Holding all else constant, reducing the floor return increases the mean return and even reduces the probability of underperformance as well as, of course, the probability of triggering.

The simultaneous selection of floor and bet size is subtle in that some combinations appear to dominate others. In many cases, a mean return that was as high or higher would be obtained with a reduction in the probability of underperformance if both the bet size and the floor are reduced. (Of course, a lower worst case return was possible, but this often had small probability.) This result was more prevalent the shorter the horizon and the lower the forecasting ability. In these cases, variations in floor produce variations in mean that can overcome variations in bet size. In general, bet size is a far more important determinant of risk and return than is floor level, and this dominance is highlighted for larger horizons and better forecasting ability.

The second twenty-five tables in appendix 5B are identical to the first except that data on return are replaced with data on triggering. In particular, the expected return is replaced with the mean time in years to triggering, given that triggering takes place. The return percentiles are replaced with the probability of triggering during the indicated year of the investment period, given that triggering takes place.

These results are of some interest as they depict the distribution of what is actually a probabilistic stopping time. The actual distribution conforms with expectations in that choices of decision variables that increase the probability of triggering also bring its probability distribution forward in time. In particular, the mean time to triggering (given that triggering takes place) is reduced.

## Conclusions and Extensions

The results of this study are broadly consistent with those of the simulation study described in chapter 6 despite several differences in the design of the analysis—most notably, a difference in the definition of bet size. In particular, the slope of the risk-reward frontier behaves as expected, and certain combinations of floor and bet size appear to dominate others. This latter finding is significant for the practical management of contingently immunized portfolios. A better risk-return combination often emerges for a smaller bet size combined with a lower floor. This is true especially for shorter horizons and poorer forecasting ability (but still in excess of 50 percent). This result is evidently the result of the fact that for forecasting ability over 50 percent but not high, we require many opportunities (bets) for positive ability to be evident in the results, a phenomenon related to the law of large numbers. This suggests a smaller bet size because, even with forecasting ability over 50 percent, there is a substantial probability of back-to-back errors and, if bets are large, a high probability of triggering. The decline in mean return can be compensated for by a reduction in the floor which (from formula 5.3) gives us a linear increase in degrees of freedom but without an effect on returns on any given bet.

Also, mean return generally increases and risk generally declines as the horizon increases if forecasting accuracy exceeds 50 percent and there is a positive probability of triggering. Again, this is evidently the result of the law of large numbers, allowing positive insight to be reflected. However, if the floor return is so low as to not be binding, mean returns do not increase as the horizon increases, but the dispersion about the mean declines

The results of this chapter may be extended by considering different return-generating mechanisms. So long as the structure is not radically different from the binomial process developed here, the broad conclusions will remain. However, there is some interest in examining alternative models. One form of interest is the wealth diffusion model that characterizes much of modern finance. Specifically, we may assume that the return dynamics for portfolio value are given by

$$\frac{dV(t)}{V(t)} = \frac{dB(t)}{B(t)} + u(t)dt + s(t)dz \qquad (5.10)$$

where $dV(t)/V(t)$ denotes the percentage change in portfolio value $V(t)$, which occurs over the instant $dt$; $dB(t)/B(t)$ is the percentage change in value over $dt$ of the immunized portfolio; $u(t)$ is the mean rate of return earned by the active strategy over $dt$; and $s(t)dz(t)$ is the random normal error incurred by the active strategy in achieving the mean increment over $dt(s(t)$ is the instantaneous standard deviation and $dz(t)$ is the random variable).

Equation 5.10 specifies a return dynamics that is similar to our binomial process in that the term caused by active management, $u(t)dt + s(t)dz(t)$, does not depend on performance to date. This compares with our assumption that the return differential of the immunized portfolio versus the active portfolio is plus or minus $d$. As in the binomial case, this assumption leads to a simple form for the compound return distribution. The powerful analytics made possible by a continuous time analysis allows this result even when we assume that the active component parameters $u(t)$ and $s(t)$ depend on time (as opposed to being constants) as is shown in equation 5.10. In appendix 5A we perform a mathematical analysis of this continuous time problem to develop corresponding formulas for the total compound return.

# Appendix 5A
# A Diffusion Model for
# Contingent Portfolio
# Returns

In this appendix we analyze the total compound return arising from contingent return dynamics of the form

$$\frac{dV}{V} = \frac{dB}{B} + u(t)dt + s(t)dz \qquad (5A.1)$$

where $dV/V$ is the instantaneous percentage return on the contingent portfolio; $dB/B$ is the instantaneous percentage return on the corresponding immunized portfolio; and $u(t)dt + s(t)dz$ is the contribution of active management. We shall assume that the functions $u(t)$ and $s(t)$ are only restricted so as to imply that $V(t)$ is an Ito process and that $\text{Prob}(V(t) > 0) = 1$. We shall also assume that the immunized portfolio value behaves exactly as that of a pure discount (zero coupon) bond with the same horizon $(T)$, a \$1 payoff at time $T$, and a statistically varying yield $y(t)$, which we assume to be a diffusion process. Thus we may write

$$B(t) = e^{-y(t)(T-t)} \quad 0 \le t \le T \qquad (5A.2)$$

$y(t)$ is thus the immunized target rate at time $t$ for a $T - t$ year horizon. At time 0, the contingent portfolio and the portfolio, if immunized, would have the same value, so that

$$V(0) = B(0) \qquad (5A.3)$$

We must use equation 5A.1 to develop a formula for $V(t)$. By Ito's lemma

$$\frac{dB}{B} = y(t)dt - (T - t)dy + \frac{1}{2}(T - t)^2\sigma^2(dy)\,dt \qquad (5A.4)$$

so that from equation 5A.1

$$\frac{dV}{V} = y(t)dt - (T - t)dy + \frac{1}{2}(T - t)^2\sigma^2(dy)dt + u(t)dt + s(t)dz$$

$$(5A.5)$$

Defining $W(t) = \ell n(V(t))$, Ito's lemma also implies

$$\frac{dW}{W} = \frac{dV}{V} - \tfrac{1}{2}\frac{\sigma^2(dV)}{V^2}\,dt \qquad\qquad (5A.6)$$

Evaluating $\sigma^2(dV)$

$$\sigma^2(dV) = V^2\{(T - t)^2\sigma^2(dy) + s(t)^2 - 2s(t)(T - t)\operatorname{cov}(dy,dz)\}$$

$$\qquad\qquad (5A.7)$$

Hence from equations 5A.5 and 5A.6

$$dW = y(t)dt - (T - t)dy + u(t)dt - \tfrac{1}{2}s(t)^2dt$$

$$+ s(t)(T - t)\operatorname{cov}(dy,dz) + s(t)dz \qquad (5A.8)$$

Thus

$$W(t) = \int_0^t dW$$

$$= \int_0^t y(h)dh - \int_0^t (T - h)dy(h) + \int_0^t u(h) - \tfrac{1}{2}s^2(h)$$

$$+ s(h)(T - h)\operatorname{cov}(dy,dz)dh + \int_0^t s(h)dz \qquad (5A.9)$$

Now

$$\int_0^t y(h)dh - \int_0^t (T - h)dy(h) = Ty(0) - (T - t)y(t) \qquad (5A.10)$$

so that

$$W(t) = Ty(0) - (T - t)y(t)$$

$$+ \int_0^t u(h) - \tfrac{1}{2}s^2(h) + s(t)(T - t)\operatorname{cov}(dy,dz)dh$$

$$+ \int_0^t s(h)dz \qquad\qquad (5A.11)$$

Finally, by definition of $W(t)$, we now have

$$V(t) = V(0)e^{Ty(0) - (T - t)y(t) + \int_0^t u(h) - \frac{1}{2}s(h)^2 + s(t)(T - t)\text{cov}(dy,dz)dh + \int_0^t s(h)dz}$$

$$(5A.12)$$

Formula 5A.12 provides the contingent portfolio value as of time $t$, assuming that triggering has not occurred. At the horizon date ($t = T$), we may verify several facts. First, if no active bets are taken (that is, $u(t) = s(t)) = 0$)

$$V(T) = V(0)e^{Ty(0)}$$

so that the continuously compound return equals the target rate $y(0)$. With active bets, the continuously compounded return is

$$y(0) + \left\{ \int_0^T u(h) - \frac{1}{2}s(h)^2 + s(h)(T - h)\text{cov}(dy,dz)dh + \int_0^T s(h)dz \right\}$$

$$(5A.13)$$

If parameters are set such that the probability of triggering is zero, then expression 5A.13 has mean

$$y(0) + \frac{1}{T} \left\{ \int_0^T u(h) - \frac{1}{2}s(h)^2 dh \right.$$

$$\left. + \int_0^T s(h)(T - h)E(\text{cov}(dy,dz))dh \right\} \qquad (5A.14)$$

If $\text{cov}(dy, dz)$ is a function of at most time ($\text{cov}(t)$), then expression 5A.13 has mean and variance given, respectively, by

$$y(0) + \frac{1}{T} \left\{ \int_0^T u(h) - \frac{1}{2}s(h)^2 + s(h)(T - h)\text{cov}(h)dh \right\}$$

and

$$\frac{1}{T^2} \int_0^T s^2(h)dh$$

To consider the problem when triggering is possible, assume that the minimum acceptable compound return over the horizon $T$ is given by

$y(0) - x$. Hence, the minimum acceptable terminal portfolio value is given by

$$V(0)e^{T(y(0)-x)} \tag{5A.15}$$

Because the immunized rate from $t$ to $T$ is given by $y(t)$, we must trigger at the first time $t$ for which

$$V(t) = V(0)e^{T(y(0)-x)-(T-t)y(t)} \tag{5A.16}$$

Setting equations 5A.12 and 5A.16 equal and simplifying, we must trigger at the first time, $\hat{t}$, such that

$$- Tx = \int_0^{\hat{t}} u(h) - \tfrac{1}{2}s(h)^2 + s(h)(T-h)\text{cov}(dy,dz)dh + \int_0^{\hat{t}} s(h)dz \tag{5A.17}$$

If simple forms are assumed for $u(t)$, $s(t)$, and $\text{cov}(dy, dz)$, the probability of such an event occurring (a first passage time) is readily computed. The simplest assumption would be that (1) $u(t)$ is a constant $u$; (2) $s(t)$ is a constant $s$; and that yield changes and active returns are uncorrelated $\text{cov}(dy, dz) = 0$. Then equations 5A.17 becomes[1]

$$- Tx = \int_0^{\hat{t}} u - \tfrac{1}{2}s^2 dh + \int_0^{\hat{t}} sdz \tag{5A.18}$$

or

$$- Tx = (u - \tfrac{1}{2}s^2)\hat{t} + sz(\hat{t}) \tag{5A.19}$$

**Note**

1. A similar result has been found by Oldrich Vasicek in an unpublished communication, but starting from a less general immunized return model than equation 5A.2.

# Appendix 5B
# Contingent Immunization
# Return Distributions

This appendix depicts the probability distribution of return of a contingently immunized portfolio that is mathematically derived in chapter 5. Pages 100–124 show the distribution of return, while pages 125–149 show the distribution of the time to triggering. The first row of information on each page consists of the immunized return, the horizon, and the forcasting accuracy assumed in the particular case. Horizons and forecasting accuracies vary from three to seven years and from forty percent to sixty percent respectively, while the immunized return is always fifteen percent. For subsequent rows, the first three items are the floor return, the bet size, and degrees of freedom. The bet size, which is denoted LEVERAGE FACTOR in the table, corresponds to the magnitude $d$ described in chapter 5. The degrees of freedom, denoted DEG. OF FREEDOM, refer to the number $N(H, I^*, F, d)$ and is the number of incorrect guesses that could be made in sequence at the start of the horizon before triggering would become necessary. The next three items across the page are the probability of triggering (PROBABILITY OF TRIG.), the probability of a return lower than the immunized return (PROBABILITY OF UNDER PERF.), and the expected compound return over the horizon. The remaining data are return percentiles at different probability levels.

On pages 125–149, which show the distribution of the time to triggering, the format is slightly different. The first row of data has the same format as tables 1–25 (pages 101–124), as do the first four columns of the remaining rows. However, the next item is the expected time to triggering in years, given that triggering occurs (COND. EXPECTED TRIG. TIME). The remaining items are the probabilities of triggering in each respective year of the program, given that triggering takes place (CONDITIONAL PROB. OF TRIG. IN YEAR).

IMMUNIZED RETURN: 15 PERCENT     HORIZON: 3 YEARS     FORECAST ACCURACY: 60 PERCENT

| FLOOR RETURN | LEVERAGE FACTOR | DEG. OF FREEDOM | PROBABILITY OF TRIG. | PROBABILITY OF UNDER PERF. | EXPECTED RETURN | RETURN PERCENTILES | | | | | | | | | |
|---|---|---|---|---|---|---|---|---|---|---|---|---|---|---|---|
| | | | | | | 10 | 20 | 30 | 40 | 50 | 60 | 70 | 80 | 90 | 100 |
| 8 | 0.010 | 21 | 0 | 16 | 15.80 | 14.33 | 15.00 | 15.00 | 15.67 | 15.67 | 16.33 | 16.33 | 17.00 | 17.00 | 19.00 |
| 9 | 0.010 | 18 | 0 | 16 | 15.80 | 14.33 | 15.00 | 15.00 | 15.67 | 15.67 | 16.33 | 16.33 | 17.00 | 17.00 | 19.00 |
| 10 | 0.010 | 15 | 0 | 16 | 15.80 | 14.33 | 15.00 | 15.00 | 15.67 | 15.67 | 16.33 | 16.33 | 17.00 | 17.00 | 19.00 |
| 11 | 0.010 | 12 | 0 | 16 | 15.80 | 14.33 | 15.00 | 15.00 | 15.67 | 15.67 | 16.33 | 16.33 | 17.00 | 17.00 | 19.00 |
| 12 | 0.010 | 9 | 2 | 16 | 15.80 | 14.33 | 15.00 | 15.00 | 15.67 | 15.67 | 16.33 | 16.33 | 17.00 | 17.00 | 19.00 |
| 13 | 0.010 | 6 | 2 | 16 | 15.80 | 14.33 | 15.00 | 15.00 | 15.67 | 15.67 | 16.33 | 16.33 | 17.00 | 17.00 | 19.00 |
| 14 | 0.010 | 3 | 19 | 22 | 15.72 | 14.00 | 14.33 | 15.00 | 15.67 | 15.67 | 16.33 | 16.33 | 17.00 | 17.00 | 19.00 |
| 8 | 0.020 | 10 | 0 | 16 | 16.60 | 13.67 | 15.00 | 15.00 | 16.33 | 16.33 | 17.67 | 17.67 | 19.00 | 19.00 | 23.00 |
| 9 | 0.020 | 9 | 0 | 16 | 16.60 | 13.67 | 15.00 | 15.00 | 16.33 | 16.33 | 17.67 | 17.67 | 19.00 | 19.00 | 23.00 |
| 10 | 0.020 | 7 | 1 | 16 | 16.60 | 13.67 | 15.00 | 15.00 | 16.33 | 16.33 | 17.67 | 17.67 | 19.00 | 19.00 | 23.00 |
| 11 | 0.020 | 4 | 2 | 16 | 16.59 | 13.67 | 15.00 | 15.00 | 16.33 | 16.33 | 17.67 | 17.67 | 19.00 | 19.00 | 23.00 |
| 12 | 0.020 | 4 | 10 | 17 | 16.54 | 12.33 | 15.00 | 15.00 | 16.33 | 16.33 | 17.67 | 17.67 | 19.00 | 19.00 | 23.00 |
| 13 | 0.020 | 3 | 19 | 22 | 16.45 | 13.00 | 13.67 | 15.00 | 16.33 | 16.33 | 17.67 | 17.67 | 19.00 | 19.00 | 23.00 |
| 14 | 0.020 | 1 | 60 | 60 | 15.83 | 14.33 | 14.33 | 14.33 | 14.33 | 14.33 | 14.33 | 16.33 | 17.67 | 19.00 | 23.00 |
| 8 | 0.030 | 7 | 1 | 16 | 17.40 | 13.00 | 15.00 | 15.00 | 17.00 | 17.00 | 19.00 | 19.00 | 21.00 | 21.00 | 27.00 |
| 9 | 0.030 | 6 | 2 | 16 | 17.39 | 13.00 | 15.00 | 15.00 | 17.00 | 17.00 | 19.00 | 19.00 | 21.00 | 21.00 | 27.00 |
| 10 | 0.030 | 5 | 4 | 16 | 17.36 | 13.00 | 15.00 | 15.00 | 17.00 | 17.00 | 19.00 | 19.00 | 21.00 | 21.00 | 27.00 |
| 11 | 0.030 | 4 | 10 | 17 | 17.31 | 11.00 | 15.00 | 15.00 | 17.00 | 17.00 | 19.00 | 19.00 | 21.00 | 21.00 | 27.00 |
| 12 | 0.030 | 3 | 19 | 22 | 17.17 | 12.00 | 13.00 | 15.00 | 17.00 | 17.00 | 19.00 | 19.00 | 21.00 | 21.00 | 27.00 |
| 13 | 0.030 | 2 | 35 | 35 | 16.87 | 13.00 | 13.00 | 13.00 | 15.00 | 17.00 | 19.00 | 19.00 | 21.00 | 21.00 | 27.00 |
| 14 | 0.030 | 1 | 60 | 60 | 16.24 | 14.00 | 14.00 | 14.00 | 14.00 | 14.00 | 14.00 | 17.00 | 19.00 | 21.00 | 27.00 |

IMMUNIZED RETURN: 15 PERCENT          HORIZON: 3 YEARS          FORECAST ACCURACY: 55 PERCENT

| FLOOR RETURN | LEVERAGE FACTOR | DEG. OF FREEDOM | PROBABILITY OF TRIG. | PROBABILITY UNDER PERF. | EXPECTED RETURN | RETURN PERCENTILES | | | | | | | | | |
|---|---|---|---|---|---|---|---|---|---|---|---|---|---|---|---|
| | | | | | | 10 | 20 | 30 | 40 | 50 | 60 | 70 | 80 | 90 | 100 |
| 8 | 0.010 | 21 | 0 | 26 | 15.40 | 13.67 | 14.33 | 15.00 | 15.00 | 15.67 | 15.67 | 16.33 | 16.33 | 17.00 | 19.00 |
| 9 | 0.010 | 18 | 0 | 26 | 15.40 | 13.67 | 14.33 | 15.00 | 15.00 | 15.67 | 15.67 | 16.33 | 16.33 | 17.00 | 19.00 |
| 10 | 0.010 | 15 | 0 | 26 | 15.40 | 13.67 | 14.33 | 15.00 | 15.00 | 15.67 | 15.67 | 16.33 | 16.33 | 17.00 | 19.00 |
| 11 | 0.010 | 12 | 0 | 26 | 15.40 | 13.67 | 14.33 | 15.00 | 15.00 | 15.67 | 15.67 | 16.33 | 16.33 | 17.00 | 19.00 |
| 12 | 0.010 | 9 | 0 | 26 | 15.40 | 13.67 | 14.33 | 15.00 | 15.00 | 15.67 | 15.67 | 16.33 | 16.33 | 17.00 | 19.00 |
| 13 | 0.010 | 6 | 5 | 26 | 15.40 | 13.67 | 14.33 | 15.00 | 15.00 | 15.67 | 15.67 | 16.33 | 16.33 | 17.00 | 19.00 |
| 14 | 0.010 | 3 | 28 | 33 | 15.34 | 14.00 | 14.00 | 14.33 | 15.00 | 15.67 | 15.67 | 15.67 | 16.33 | 17.00 | 19.00 |
| 8 | 0.020 | 10 | 0 | 26 | 15.80 | 12.33 | 13.67 | 15.00 | 15.00 | 16.33 | 16.33 | 17.67 | 17.67 | 19.00 | 23.00 |
| 9 | 0.020 | 9 | 0 | 26 | 15.80 | 12.33 | 13.67 | 15.00 | 15.00 | 16.33 | 16.33 | 17.67 | 17.67 | 19.00 | 23.00 |
| 10 | 0.020 | 7 | 2 | 26 | 15.80 | 12.33 | 13.67 | 15.00 | 15.00 | 16.33 | 16.33 | 17.67 | 17.67 | 19.00 | 23.00 |
| 11 | 0.020 | 6 | 5 | 26 | 15.79 | 12.33 | 13.67 | 15.00 | 15.00 | 16.33 | 16.33 | 17.67 | 17.67 | 19.00 | 23.00 |
| 12 | 0.020 | 4 | 17 | 28 | 15.75 | 12.33 | 13.67 | 15.00 | 15.00 | 16.33 | 16.33 | 17.67 | 17.67 | 19.00 | 23.00 |
| 13 | 0.020 | 3 | 28 | 33 | 15.69 | 13.00 | 13.00 | 13.67 | 15.00 | 16.33 | 16.33 | 17.67 | 17.67 | 19.00 | 23.00 |
| 14 | 0.020 | 1 | 69 | 69 | 15.36 | 14.33 | 14.33 | 14.33 | 14.33 | 14.33 | 14.33 | 15.00 | 16.33 | 17.67 | 23.00 |
| 8 | 0.030 | 7 | 2 | 26 | 16.20 | 11.00 | 13.00 | 15.00 | 15.00 | 17.00 | 17.00 | 19.00 | 19.00 | 21.00 | 27.00 |
| 9 | 0.030 | 6 | 5 | 26 | 16.19 | 11.00 | 13.00 | 15.00 | 15.00 | 17.00 | 17.00 | 19.00 | 19.00 | 21.00 | 27.00 |
| 10 | 0.030 | 5 | 8 | 26 | 16.17 | 11.00 | 13.00 | 15.00 | 15.00 | 17.00 | 17.00 | 19.00 | 19.00 | 21.00 | 27.00 |
| 11 | 0.030 | 4 | 17 | 28 | 16.12 | 11.00 | 13.00 | 15.00 | 15.00 | 17.00 | 17.00 | 19.00 | 19.00 | 21.00 | 27.00 |
| 12 | 0.030 | 3 | 28 | 33 | 16.03 | 12.00 | 12.00 | 13.00 | 15.00 | 17.00 | 17.00 | 19.00 | 19.00 | 21.00 | 27.00 |
| 13 | 0.030 | 2 | 46 | 46 | 15.86 | 13.00 | 13.00 | 13.67 | 15.00 | 15.00 | 17.00 | 17.00 | 19.00 | 21.00 | 27.00 |
| 14 | 0.030 | 1 | 69 | 69 | 15.54 | 14.00 | 14.00 | 14.00 | 14.00 | 14.00 | 14.00 | 15.00 | 17.00 | 19.00 | 27.00 |

IMMUNIZED RETURN: 15 PERCENT          HORIZON: 3 YEARS          FORECAST ACCURACY: 50 PERCENT

| FLOOR RETURN | LEVERAGE FACTOR | DEG. OF FREEDOM | PROBABILITY OF TRIG. | PROBABILITY OF UNDER PERF | EXPECTED RETURN | RETURN PERCENTILES 10 | 20 | 30 | 40 | 50 | 60 | 70 | 80 | 90 | 100 |
|---|---|---|---|---|---|---|---|---|---|---|---|---|---|---|---|
| 8 | 0.010 | 21 | 0 | 39 | 15.00 | 13.67 | 14.33 | 14.33 | 15.00 | 15.00 | 15.00 | 15.67 | 15.67 | 16.33 | 19.00 |
| 9 | 0.010 | 18 | 0 | 39 | 15.00 | 13.67 | 14.33 | 14.33 | 15.00 | 15.00 | 15.00 | 15.67 | 15.67 | 16.33 | 19.00 |
| 10 | 0.010 | 15 | 0 | 39 | 15.00 | 13.67 | 14.33 | 14.33 | 15.00 | 15.00 | 15.00 | 15.67 | 15.67 | 16.33 | 19.00 |
| 11 | 0.010 | 12 | 1 | 39 | 15.00 | 13.67 | 14.33 | 14.33 | 15.00 | 15.00 | 15.00 | 15.67 | 15.67 | 16.33 | 19.00 |
| 12 | 0.010 | 9 | 9 | 39 | 15.00 | 13.67 | 14.33 | 14.33 | 15.00 | 15.00 | 15.00 | 15.67 | 15.67 | 16.33 | 19.00 |
| 13 | 0.010 | 6 | 9 | 39 | 15.00 | 13.67 | 14.33 | 14.33 | 15.00 | 15.00 | 15.00 | 15.67 | 15.67 | 16.33 | 19.00 |
| 14 | 0.010 | 3 | 39 | 46 | 15.00 | 14.00 | 14.00 | 14.00 | 14.33 | 15.00 | 15.00 | 15.67 | 15.67 | 16.33 | 19.00 |
| 8 | 0.020 | 10 | 0 | 39 | 15.00 | 12.33 | 13.67 | 13.67 | 15.00 | 15.00 | 15.00 | 16.33 | 16.33 | 17.67 | 23.00 |
| 9 | 0.020 | 9 | 1 | 39 | 15.00 | 12.33 | 13.67 | 13.67 | 15.00 | 15.00 | 15.00 | 16.33 | 16.33 | 17.67 | 23.00 |
| 10 | 0.020 | 7 | 4 | 39 | 15.00 | 12.33 | 13.67 | 13.67 | 15.00 | 15.00 | 15.00 | 16.33 | 16.33 | 17.67 | 23.00 |
| 11 | 0.020 | 6 | 9 | 41 | 15.00 | 12.33 | 12.33 | 13.67 | 13.67 | 15.00 | 15.00 | 16.33 | 16.33 | 17.67 | 23.00 |
| 12 | 0.020 | 4 | 27 | 46 | 15.00 | 13.00 | 13.00 | 13.67 | 13.67 | 15.00 | 15.00 | 16.33 | 16.33 | 17.67 | 23.00 |
| 13 | 0.020 | 3 | 39 | 58 | 15.00 | 13.00 | 13.00 | 13.00 | 13.67 | 15.00 | 15.00 | 16.33 | 16.33 | 17.67 | 23.00 |
| 14 | 0.020 | 1 | 77 | 77 | 15.00 | 14.33 | 14.33 | 14.33 | 14.33 | 14.33 | 14.33 | 14.33 | 15.00 | 17.67 | 23.00 |
| 8 | 0.030 | 7 | 4 | 39 | 15.00 | 11.00 | 13.00 | 13.00 | 15.00 | 15.00 | 15.00 | 17.00 | 17.00 | 19.00 | 27.00 |
| 9 | 0.030 | 6 | 9 | 39 | 15.00 | 11.00 | 13.00 | 13.00 | 15.00 | 15.00 | 15.00 | 17.00 | 17.00 | 19.00 | 27.00 |
| 10 | 0.030 | 5 | 15 | 41 | 15.00 | 10.00 | 11.00 | 13.00 | 13.00 | 15.00 | 15.00 | 17.00 | 17.00 | 19.00 | 27.00 |
| 11 | 0.030 | 4 | 27 | 46 | 15.00 | 11.00 | 11.00 | 13.00 | 13.00 | 15.00 | 15.00 | 17.00 | 17.00 | 19.00 | 27.00 |
| 12 | 0.030 | 3 | 39 | 58 | 15.00 | 12.00 | 12.00 | 13.00 | 13.00 | 13.00 | 15.00 | 17.00 | 17.00 | 19.00 | 27.00 |
| 13 | 0.030 | 2 | 58 | 58 | 15.00 | 13.00 | 13.00 | 13.00 | 13.00 | 13.00 | 15.00 | 17.00 | 17.00 | 19.00 | 27.00 |
| 14 | 0.030 | 1 | 77 | 77 | 15.00 | 14.00 | 14.00 | 14.00 | 14.00 | 14.00 | 14.00 | 14.00 | 15.00 | 19.00 | 27.00 |

IMMUNIZED RETURN: 15 PERCENT          HORIZON: 3 YEARS          FORECAST ACCURACY: 45 PERCENT

| FLOOR RETURN | LEVERAGE FACTOR | DEG. OF FREEDOM | PROBABILITY OF TRIG. | PROBABILITY OF UNDER PERF. | EXPECTED RETURN | RETURN PERCENTILES | | | | | | | | | |
|---|---|---|---|---|---|---|---|---|---|---|---|---|---|---|---|
| | | | | | | 10 | 20 | 30 | 40 | 50 | 60 | 70 | 80 | 90 | 100 |
| 8 | 0.010 | 21 | 0 | 53 | 14.60 | 13.00 | 13.67 | 13.67 | 14.33 | 14.33 | 15.00 | 15.00 | 15.67 | 16.33 | 19.00 |
| 9 | 0.010 | 18 | 0 | 53 | 14.60 | 13.00 | 13.67 | 13.67 | 14.33 | 14.33 | 15.00 | 15.00 | 15.67 | 16.33 | 19.00 |
| 10 | 0.010 | 15 | 0 | 53 | 14.60 | 13.00 | 13.67 | 13.67 | 14.33 | 14.33 | 15.00 | 15.00 | 15.67 | 16.33 | 19.00 |
| 11 | 0.010 | 12 | 0 | 53 | 14.60 | 13.00 | 13.67 | 13.67 | 14.33 | 14.33 | 15.00 | 15.00 | 15.67 | 16.33 | 19.00 |
| 12 | 0.010 | 9 | 1 | 53 | 14.60 | 13.00 | 13.67 | 13.67 | 14.33 | 14.33 | 15.00 | 15.00 | 15.67 | 16.33 | 19.00 |
| 13 | 0.010 | 6 | 16 | 53 | 14.61 | 13.00 | 13.67 | 13.67 | 14.33 | 14.33 | 15.00 | 15.00 | 15.67 | 16.33 | 19.00 |
| 14 | 0.010 | 3 | 51 | 59 | 14.70 | 14.00 | 14.00 | 14.00 | 14.00 | 14.00 | 15.00 | 15.00 | 15.67 | 16.33 | 19.00 |
| 8 | 0.020 | 10 | 1 | 53 | 14.20 | 11.00 | 12.33 | 12.33 | 13.67 | 13.67 | 15.00 | 15.00 | 16.33 | 17.67 | 23.00 |
| 9 | 0.020 | 9 | 1 | 53 | 14.20 | 11.00 | 12.33 | 12.33 | 13.67 | 13.67 | 15.00 | 15.00 | 16.33 | 17.67 | 23.00 |
| 10 | 0.020 | 7 | 7 | 53 | 14.21 | 11.00 | 12.33 | 12.33 | 13.67 | 13.67 | 15.00 | 15.00 | 16.33 | 17.67 | 23.00 |
| 11 | 0.020 | 6 | 16 | 53 | 14.23 | 12.33 | 12.33 | 12.33 | 13.67 | 13.67 | 15.00 | 15.00 | 16.33 | 17.67 | 23.00 |
| 12 | 0.020 | 4 | 38 | 54 | 14.31 | 12.33 | 12.33 | 13.67 | 13.67 | 13.67 | 15.00 | 15.00 | 16.33 | 17.67 | 23.00 |
| 13 | 0.020 | 3 | 51 | 59 | 14.41 | 13.00 | 13.00 | 13.00 | 13.00 | 13.00 | 15.00 | 15.00 | 16.33 | 17.67 | 23.00 |
| 14 | 0.020 | 1 | 85 | 85 | 14.74 | 14.33 | 14.33 | 14.33 | 14.33 | 14.33 | 14.33 | 14.33 | 14.33 | 16.33 | 23.00 |
| 8 | 0.030 | 7 | 7 | 53 | 13.82 | 9.00 | 11.00 | 11.00 | 13.00 | 13.00 | 15.00 | 15.00 | 17.00 | 19.00 | 27.00 |
| 9 | 0.030 | 6 | 16 | 53 | 13.84 | 9.00 | 11.00 | 11.00 | 13.00 | 13.00 | 15.00 | 15.00 | 17.00 | 19.00 | 27.00 |
| 10 | 0.030 | 5 | 23 | 53 | 13.89 | 10.00 | 10.00 | 11.00 | 13.00 | 13.00 | 15.00 | 15.00 | 17.00 | 19.00 | 27.00 |
| 11 | 0.030 | 4 | 38 | 54 | 13.97 | 11.00 | 11.00 | 11.00 | 13.00 | 13.00 | 15.00 | 15.00 | 17.00 | 19.00 | 27.00 |
| 12 | 0.030 | 3 | 51 | 59 | 14.11 | 12.00 | 12.00 | 12.00 | 12.00 | 12.00 | 15.00 | 15.00 | 17.00 | 19.00 | 27.00 |
| 13 | 0.030 | 2 | 69 | 69 | 14.31 | 13.00 | 13.00 | 13.00 | 13.00 | 13.00 | 13.00 | 15.00 | 17.00 | 17.00 | 27.00 |
| 14 | 0.030 | 1 | 85 | 85 | 14.61 | 14.00 | 14.00 | 14.00 | 14.00 | 14.00 | 14.00 | 14.00 | 14.00 | 17.00 | 27.00 |

IMMUNIZED RETURN: 15 PERCENT      HORIZON: 3 YEARS      FORECAST ACCURACY: 40 PERCENT

| FLOOR RETURN | LEVERAGE FACTOR | DEG. OF FREEDOM | PROBABILITY OF TRIG. | PROBABILITY OF UNDER PERF. | EXPECTED RETURN | RETURN PERCENTILES | | | | | | | | | |
|---|---|---|---|---|---|---|---|---|---|---|---|---|---|---|---|
| | | | | | | 10 | 20 | 30 | 40 | 50 | 60 | 70 | 80 | 90 | 100 |
| 8 | 0.010 | 21 | 0 | 67 | 14.20 | 13.00 | 13.00 | 13.67 | 13.67 | 14.33 | 14.33 | 15.00 | 15.00 | 15.67 | 19.00 |
| 9 | 0.010 | 18 | 0 | 67 | 14.20 | 13.00 | 13.00 | 13.67 | 13.67 | 14.33 | 14.33 | 15.00 | 15.00 | 15.67 | 19.00 |
| 10 | 0.010 | 15 | 0 | 67 | 14.20 | 13.00 | 13.00 | 13.67 | 13.67 | 14.33 | 14.33 | 15.00 | 15.00 | 15.67 | 19.00 |
| 11 | 0.010 | 12 | 0 | 67 | 14.20 | 13.00 | 13.00 | 13.67 | 13.67 | 14.33 | 14.33 | 15.00 | 15.00 | 15.67 | 19.00 |
| 12 | 0.010 | 9 | 3 | 67 | 14.20 | 13.00 | 13.00 | 13.67 | 13.67 | 14.33 | 14.33 | 15.00 | 15.00 | 15.67 | 19.00 |
| 13 | 0.010 | 6 | 26 | 67 | 14.25 | 13.00 | 13.00 | 13.67 | 13.67 | 14.33 | 14.33 | 15.00 | 15.00 | 15.67 | 19.00 |
| 14 | 0.010 | 3 | 63 | 72 | 14.46 | 14.00 | 14.00 | 14.00 | 14.00 | 14.00 | 14.00 | 14.33 | 15.00 | 15.67 | 19.00 |
| 8 | 0.020 | 10 | 2 | 67 | 13.40 | 11.00 | 11.00 | 12.33 | 12.33 | 13.67 | 13.67 | 15.00 | 15.00 | 16.33 | 23.00 |
| 9 | 0.020 | 9 | 3 | 67 | 13.41 | 11.00 | 11.00 | 12.33 | 12.33 | 13.67 | 13.67 | 15.00 | 15.00 | 16.33 | 23.00 |
| 10 | 0.020 | 7 | 13 | 67 | 13.44 | 10.33 | 11.00 | 12.33 | 12.33 | 13.67 | 13.67 | 15.00 | 15.00 | 16.33 | 23.00 |
| 11 | 0.020 | 6 | 26 | 67 | 13.49 | 11.00 | 11.00 | 12.33 | 12.33 | 13.67 | 13.67 | 15.00 | 15.00 | 16.33 | 23.00 |
| 12 | 0.020 | 4 | 52 | 68 | 13.72 | 12.33 | 12.33 | 12.33 | 13.00 | 12.33 | 13.67 | 13.67 | 15.00 | 16.33 | 23.00 |
| 13 | 0.020 | 3 | 63 | 72 | 13.92 | 13.00 | 13.00 | 13.00 | 13.00 | 13.00 | 13.67 | 13.67 | 15.00 | 16.33 | 23.00 |
| 14 | 0.020 | 1 | 90 | 90 | 14.56 | 14.33 | 14.33 | 14.33 | 14.33 | 14.33 | 14.33 | 14.33 | 14.33 | 14.33 | 23.00 |
| 8 | 0.030 | 7 | 13 | 67 | 12.67 | 8.00 | 9.00 | 11.00 | 11.00 | 13.00 | 13.00 | 15.00 | 15.00 | 17.00 | 27.00 |
| 9 | 0.030 | 6 | 26 | 67 | 12.74 | 9.00 | 9.00 | 11.00 | 11.00 | 13.00 | 13.00 | 15.00 | 15.00 | 17.00 | 27.00 |
| 10 | 0.030 | 5 | 34 | 67 | 12.87 | 10.00 | 10.00 | 10.00 | 11.00 | 11.00 | 13.00 | 15.00 | 15.00 | 17.00 | 27.00 |
| 11 | 0.030 | 4 | 52 | 68 | 13.07 | 11.00 | 11.00 | 11.00 | 11.00 | 11.00 | 13.00 | 15.00 | 15.00 | 17.00 | 27.00 |
| 12 | 0.030 | 3 | 63 | 72 | 13.38 | 12.00 | 12.00 | 12.00 | 12.00 | 12.00 | 12.00 | 13.00 | 15.00 | 17.00 | 27.00 |
| 13 | 0.030 | 2 | 79 | 79 | 13.80 | 13.00 | 13.00 | 13.00 | 13.00 | 13.00 | 13.00 | 13.00 | 15.00 | 17.00 | 27.00 |
| 14 | 0.030 | 1 | 90 | 90 | 14.34 | 14.00 | 14.00 | 14.00 | 14.00 | 14.00 | 14.00 | 14.00 | 14.33 | 14.33 | 27.00 |

IMMUNIZED RETURN: 15 PERCENT          HORIZON: 4 YEARS          FORECAST ACCURACY: 60 PERCENT

| FLOOR RETURN | LEVERAGE FACTOR | DEG. OF FREEDOM | PROBABILITY OF TRIG. | PROBABILITY OF UNDER PERF. | EXPECTED RETURN | RETURN PERCENTILES | | | | | | | | | |
|---|---|---|---|---|---|---|---|---|---|---|---|---|---|---|---|
| | | | | | | 10 | 20 | 30 | 40 | 50 | 60 | 70 | 80 | 90 | 100 |
| 8 | 0.010 | 28 | 0 | 14 | 15.80 | 14.50 | 15.00 | 15.50 | 15.50 | 16.00 | 16.00 | 16.50 | 16.50 | 17.00 | 19.00 |
| 9 | 0.010 | 24 | 0 | 14 | 15.80 | 14.50 | 15.00 | 15.50 | 15.50 | 16.00 | 16.00 | 16.50 | 16.50 | 17.00 | 19.00 |
| 10 | 0.010 | 20 | 0 | 14 | 15.80 | 14.50 | 15.00 | 15.50 | 15.50 | 16.00 | 16.00 | 16.50 | 16.50 | 17.00 | 19.00 |
| 11 | 0.010 | 16 | 0 | 14 | 15.80 | 14.50 | 15.00 | 15.50 | 15.50 | 16.00 | 16.00 | 16.50 | 16.50 | 17.00 | 19.00 |
| 12 | 0.010 | 12 | 0 | 14 | 15.80 | 14.50 | 15.00 | 15.50 | 15.50 | 16.00 | 16.00 | 16.50 | 16.50 | 17.00 | 19.00 |
| 13 | 0.010 | 8 | 1 | 14 | 15.80 | 14.50 | 15.00 | 15.50 | 15.50 | 16.00 | 16.00 | 16.50 | 16.50 | 17.00 | 19.00 |
| 14 | 0.010 | 4 | 12 | 18 | 15.76 | 14.00 | 15.00 | 15.50 | 15.50 | 16.00 | 16.00 | 16.50 | 16.50 | 17.00 | 19.00 |
| 8 | 0.020 | 14 | 0 | 14 | 16.60 | 14.00 | 15.00 | 16.00 | 16.00 | 17.00 | 17.00 | 18.00 | 18.00 | 19.00 | 23.00 |
| 9 | 0.020 | 12 | 0 | 14 | 16.60 | 14.00 | 15.00 | 16.00 | 16.00 | 17.00 | 17.00 | 18.00 | 18.00 | 19.00 | 23.00 |
| 10 | 0.020 | 10 | 0 | 14 | 16.60 | 14.00 | 15.00 | 16.00 | 16.00 | 17.00 | 17.00 | 18.00 | 18.00 | 19.00 | 23.00 |
| 11 | 0.020 | 8 | 1 | 14 | 16.60 | 14.00 | 15.00 | 16.00 | 16.00 | 17.00 | 17.00 | 18.00 | 18.00 | 19.00 | 23.00 |
| 12 | 0.020 | 6 | 3 | 14 | 16.58 | 14.00 | 15.00 | 16.00 | 16.00 | 17.00 | 17.00 | 18.00 | 18.00 | 19.00 | 23.00 |
| 13 | 0.020 | 4 | 12 | 18 | 16.51 | 13.00 | 15.00 | 16.00 | 16.00 | 17.00 | 17.00 | 18.00 | 18.00 | 19.00 | 23.00 |
| 14 | 0.020 | 2 | 38 | 38 | 16.19 | 14.00 | 14.00 | 14.00 | 15.00 | 16.00 | 17.00 | 17.00 | 18.00 | 19.00 | 23.00 |
| 8 | 0.030 | 9 | 0 | 14 | 17.40 | 13.50 | 15.00 | 16.50 | 16.50 | 18.00 | 18.00 | 19.50 | 19.50 | 21.00 | 27.00 |
| 9 | 0.030 | 8 | 1 | 14 | 17.40 | 13.50 | 15.00 | 16.50 | 16.50 | 18.00 | 18.00 | 19.50 | 19.50 | 21.00 | 27.00 |
| 10 | 0.030 | 6 | 3 | 14 | 17.38 | 13.50 | 15.00 | 16.50 | 16.50 | 18.00 | 18.00 | 19.50 | 19.50 | 21.00 | 27.00 |
| 11 | 0.030 | 5 | 6 | 15 | 17.34 | 13.50 | 15.00 | 16.50 | 16.50 | 18.00 | 18.00 | 19.50 | 19.50 | 21.00 | 27.00 |
| 12 | 0.030 | 4 | 12 | 18 | 17.27 | 12.00 | 15.00 | 16.50 | 16.50 | 18.00 | 18.00 | 19.50 | 19.50 | 21.00 | 27.00 |
| 13 | 0.030 | 2 | 38 | 38 | 16.79 | 13.50 | 13.50 | 13.50 | 15.00 | 16.50 | 18.00 | 18.00 | 19.50 | 21.00 | 27.00 |
| 14 | 0.030 | 1 | 62 | 62 | 16.16 | 14.25 | 14.25 | 14.25 | 14.25 | 14.25 | 14.25 | 18.00 | 19.50 | 21.00 | 27.00 |

IMMUNIZED RETURN: 15 PERCENT          HORIZON: 4 YEARS          FORECAST ACCURACY: 55 PERCENT

| FLOOR RETURN | LEVERAGE FACTOR | DEG. OF FREEDOM | PROBABILITY OF TRIG. | PROBABILITY OF UNDER PERF. | EXPECTED RETURN | RETURN PERCENTILES | | | | | | | | | |
|---|---|---|---|---|---|---|---|---|---|---|---|---|---|---|---|
| | | | | | | 10 | 20 | 30 | 40 | 50 | 60 | 70 | 80 | 90 | 100 |
| 8 | 0.010 | 28 | 0 | 26 | 15.40 | 14.00 | 14.50 | 15.00 | 15.00 | 15.50 | 15.50 | 16.00 | 16.00 | 16.50 | 19.00 |
| 9 | 0.010 | 24 | 0 | 26 | 15.40 | 14.00 | 14.50 | 15.00 | 15.00 | 15.50 | 15.50 | 16.00 | 16.00 | 16.50 | 19.00 |
| 10 | 0.010 | 20 | 0 | 26 | 15.40 | 14.00 | 14.50 | 15.00 | 15.00 | 15.50 | 15.50 | 16.00 | 16.00 | 16.50 | 19.00 |
| 11 | 0.010 | 16 | 0 | 26 | 15.40 | 14.00 | 14.50 | 15.00 | 15.00 | 15.50 | 15.50 | 16.00 | 16.00 | 16.50 | 19.00 |
| 12 | 0.010 | 12 | 2 | 26 | 15.40 | 14.00 | 14.50 | 15.00 | 15.00 | 15.50 | 15.50 | 16.00 | 16.00 | 16.50 | 19.00 |
| 13 | 0.010 | 8 | 2 | 26 | 15.40 | 14.00 | 14.50 | 15.00 | 15.00 | 15.50 | 15.50 | 16.00 | 16.00 | 16.50 | 19.00 |
| 14 | 0.010 | 4 | 21 | 29 | 15.36 | 14.00 | 14.00 | 15.00 | 15.00 | 15.50 | 15.50 | 16.00 | 16.00 | 16.50 | 19.00 |
| 8 | 0.020 | 14 | 0 | 26 | 15.80 | 13.00 | 14.00 | 15.00 | 15.00 | 16.00 | 16.00 | 17.00 | 17.00 | 18.00 | 23.00 |
| 9 | 0.020 | 12 | 0 | 26 | 15.80 | 13.00 | 14.00 | 15.00 | 15.00 | 16.00 | 16.00 | 17.00 | 17.00 | 18.00 | 23.00 |
| 10 | 0.020 | 10 | 0 | 26 | 15.80 | 13.00 | 14.00 | 15.00 | 15.00 | 16.00 | 16.00 | 17.00 | 17.00 | 18.00 | 23.00 |
| 11 | 0.020 | 8 | 2 | 26 | 15.80 | 13.00 | 14.00 | 15.00 | 15.00 | 16.00 | 16.00 | 17.00 | 17.00 | 18.00 | 23.00 |
| 12 | 0.020 | 6 | 7 | 26 | 15.78 | 13.00 | 14.00 | 15.00 | 15.00 | 16.00 | 16.00 | 17.00 | 17.00 | 18.00 | 23.00 |
| 13 | 0.020 | 4 | 21 | 29 | 15.72 | 13.00 | 13.00 | 15.00 | 15.00 | 16.00 | 16.00 | 17.00 | 17.00 | 18.00 | 23.00 |
| 14 | 0.020 | 2 | 50 | 50 | 15.53 | 14.00 | 14.00 | 14.00 | 14.00 | 14.00 | 16.00 | 17.00 | 17.00 | 18.00 | 23.00 |
| 8 | 0.030 | 9 | 1 | 26 | 16.20 | 12.00 | 13.50 | 15.00 | 15.00 | 16.50 | 16.50 | 18.00 | 18.00 | 19.50 | 27.00 |
| 9 | 0.030 | 8 | 2 | 26 | 16.20 | 12.00 | 13.50 | 15.00 | 15.00 | 16.50 | 16.50 | 18.00 | 18.00 | 19.50 | 27.00 |
| 10 | 0.030 | 6 | 7 | 26 | 16.17 | 12.00 | 13.50 | 15.00 | 15.00 | 16.50 | 16.50 | 18.00 | 18.00 | 19.50 | 27.00 |
| 11 | 0.030 | 5 | 12 | 27 | 16.14 | 11.25 | 13.50 | 15.00 | 15.00 | 16.50 | 16.50 | 18.00 | 18.00 | 19.50 | 27.00 |
| 12 | 0.030 | 4 | 21 | 29 | 16.09 | 12.00 | 12.00 | 15.00 | 15.00 | 16.50 | 16.50 | 18.00 | 18.00 | 19.50 | 27.00 |
| 13 | 0.030 | 2 | 50 | 50 | 15.80 | 13.50 | 13.50 | 13.50 | 13.50 | 13.50 | 16.50 | 18.00 | 18.00 | 19.50 | 27.00 |
| 14 | 0.030 | 1 | 72 | 72 | 15.49 | 14.25 | 14.25 | 14.25 | 14.25 | 14.25 | 14.25 | 14.25 | 18.00 | 19.50 | 27.00 |

IMMUNIZED RETURN: 15 PERCENT    HORIZON: 4 YEARS    FORECAST ACCURACY: 50 PERCENT

| FLOOR RETURN | LEVERAGE FACTOR | DEG. OF FREEDOM | PROBABILITY OF TRIG. | PROBABILITY OF UNDER PERF. | EXPECTED RETURN | 10 | 20 | 30 | 40 | 50 | 60 | 70 | 80 | 90 | 100 |
|---|---|---|---|---|---|---|---|---|---|---|---|---|---|---|---|
| 8 | 0.010 | 28 | 0 | 40 | 15.00 | 13.50 | 14.00 | 14.50 | 14.50 | 15.00 | 15.50 | 15.50 | 16.00 | 16.50 | 19.00 |
| 9 | 0.010 | 24 | 0 | 40 | 15.00 | 13.50 | 14.00 | 14.50 | 14.50 | 15.00 | 15.50 | 15.50 | 16.00 | 16.50 | 19.00 |
| 10 | 0.010 | 20 | 0 | 40 | 15.00 | 13.50 | 14.00 | 14.50 | 14.50 | 15.00 | 15.50 | 15.50 | 16.00 | 16.50 | 19.00 |
| 11 | 0.010 | 16 | 0 | 40 | 15.00 | 13.50 | 14.00 | 14.50 | 14.50 | 15.00 | 15.50 | 15.50 | 16.00 | 16.50 | 19.00 |
| 12 | 0.010 | 12 | 0 | 40 | 15.00 | 13.50 | 14.00 | 14.50 | 14.50 | 15.00 | 15.50 | 15.50 | 16.00 | 16.50 | 19.00 |
| 13 | 0.010 | 8 | 5 | 40 | 15.00 | 13.50 | 14.00 | 14.50 | 14.50 | 15.00 | 15.50 | 15.50 | 16.00 | 16.50 | 19.00 |
| 14 | 0.010 | 4 | 33 | 44 | 15.00 | 14.00 | 14.00 | 14.00 | 14.50 | 15.00 | 15.00 | 15.50 | 16.00 | 16.50 | 19.00 |
| 8 | 0.020 | 14 | 0 | 40 | 15.00 | 12.00 | 13.00 | 14.00 | 14.00 | 15.00 | 16.00 | 16.00 | 17.00 | 18.00 | 23.00 |
| 9 | 0.020 | 12 | 0 | 40 | 15.00 | 12.00 | 13.00 | 14.00 | 14.00 | 15.00 | 16.00 | 16.00 | 17.00 | 18.00 | 23.00 |
| 10 | 0.020 | 10 | 1 | 40 | 15.00 | 12.00 | 13.00 | 14.00 | 14.00 | 15.00 | 16.00 | 16.00 | 17.00 | 18.00 | 23.00 |
| 11 | 0.020 | 8 | 5 | 40 | 15.00 | 12.00 | 13.00 | 14.00 | 14.00 | 15.00 | 16.00 | 16.00 | 17.00 | 18.00 | 23.00 |
| 12 | 0.020 | 6 | 14 | 44 | 15.00 | 12.00 | 13.00 | 14.00 | 14.00 | 15.00 | 16.00 | 16.00 | 17.00 | 18.00 | 23.00 |
| 13 | 0.020 | 4 | 33 | 44 | 15.00 | 13.00 | 13.00 | 13.00 | 14.00 | 15.00 | 15.00 | 16.00 | 17.00 | 18.00 | 23.00 |
| 14 | 0.020 | 2 | 63 | 63 | 15.00 | 14.00 | 14.00 | 14.00 | 14.00 | 14.00 | 14.00 | 15.00 | 16.00 | 17.00 | 23.00 |
| 8 | 0.030 | 9 | 2 | 40 | 15.00 | 10.50 | 12.00 | 13.50 | 13.50 | 15.00 | 16.50 | 16.50 | 18.00 | 19.50 | 27.00 |
| 9 | 0.030 | 8 | 5 | 40 | 15.00 | 10.50 | 12.00 | 13.50 | 13.50 | 15.00 | 16.50 | 16.50 | 18.00 | 19.50 | 27.00 |
| 10 | 0.030 | 6 | 14 | 41 | 15.00 | 10.50 | 12.00 | 13.50 | 13.50 | 15.00 | 16.50 | 16.50 | 18.00 | 19.50 | 27.00 |
| 11 | 0.030 | 5 | 21 | 44 | 15.00 | 11.25 | 11.25 | 13.50 | 13.50 | 15.00 | 15.00 | 16.50 | 18.00 | 19.50 | 27.00 |
| 12 | 0.030 | 3 | 33 | 44 | 15.00 | 12.00 | 12.00 | 12.00 | 13.50 | 15.00 | 15.00 | 16.00 | 18.00 | 19.50 | 27.00 |
| 13 | 0.030 | 2 | 63 | 63 | 15.00 | 13.50 | 13.50 | 13.50 | 13.50 | 15.00 | 13.50 | 15.00 | 16.50 | 18.00 | 27.00 |
| 14 | 0.030 | 1 | 80 | 80 | 15.00 | 14.25 | 14.25 | 14.25 | 14.25 | 14.25 | 14.25 | 14.25 | 14.25 | 16.00 | 27.00 |

IMMUNIZED RETURN: 15 PERCENT     HORIZON: 4 YEARS     FORECAST ACCURACY: 45 PERCENT

| FLOOR RETURN | LEVERAGE FACTOR | DEG. OF FREEDOM | PROBABILITY OF TRIG. | PROBABILITY OF UNDER PERF. | EXPECTED RETURN | RETURN PERCENTILES | | | | | | | | | |
|---|---|---|---|---|---|---|---|---|---|---|---|---|---|---|---|
| | | | | | | 10 | 20 | 30 | 40 | 50 | 60 | 70 | 80 | 90 | 100 |
| 8 | 0.010 | 28 | 0 | 56 | 14.60 | 13.50 | 14.00 | 14.00 | 14.50 | 14.50 | 15.00 | 15.00 | 15.50 | 16.00 | 19.00 |
| 9 | 0.010 | 24 | 0 | 56 | 14.60 | 13.50 | 14.00 | 14.00 | 14.50 | 14.50 | 15.00 | 15.00 | 15.50 | 16.00 | 19.00 |
| 10 | 0.010 | 20 | 0 | 56 | 14.60 | 13.50 | 14.00 | 14.00 | 14.50 | 14.50 | 15.00 | 15.00 | 15.50 | 16.00 | 19.00 |
| 11 | 0.010 | 16 | 1 | 56 | 14.60 | 13.50 | 14.00 | 14.00 | 14.50 | 14.50 | 15.00 | 15.00 | 15.50 | 16.00 | 19.00 |
| 12 | 0.010 | 12 | 1 | 56 | 14.61 | 13.50 | 14.00 | 14.00 | 14.50 | 14.50 | 15.00 | 15.00 | 15.50 | 16.00 | 19.00 |
| 13 | 0.010 | 8 | 10 | 56 | 14.61 | 13.00 | 13.50 | 14.00 | 14.50 | 14.50 | 15.00 | 15.00 | 15.50 | 16.00 | 19.00 |
| 14 | 0.010 | 4 | 47 | 60 | 14.68 | 14.00 | 14.00 | 14.00 | 14.00 | 14.50 | 15.00 | 15.00 | 15.50 | 16.00 | 19.00 |
| 8 | 0.020 | 14 | 0 | 56 | 14.20 | 12.00 | 13.00 | 13.00 | 14.00 | 14.00 | 15.00 | 15.00 | 16.00 | 17.00 | 23.00 |
| 9 | 0.020 | 12 | 1 | 56 | 14.20 | 12.00 | 13.00 | 13.00 | 14.00 | 14.00 | 15.00 | 15.00 | 16.00 | 17.00 | 23.00 |
| 10 | 0.020 | 10 | 3 | 56 | 14.20 | 12.00 | 13.00 | 13.00 | 14.00 | 14.00 | 15.00 | 15.00 | 16.00 | 17.00 | 23.00 |
| 11 | 0.020 | 8 | 10 | 56 | 14.22 | 11.00 | 12.00 | 13.00 | 14.00 | 14.00 | 15.00 | 15.00 | 16.00 | 17.00 | 23.00 |
| 12 | 0.020 | 6 | 25 | 56 | 14.26 | 12.00 | 13.00 | 13.00 | 14.00 | 14.00 | 15.00 | 15.00 | 16.00 | 17.00 | 23.00 |
| 13 | 0.020 | 4 | 47 | 60 | 14.37 | 13.00 | 13.00 | 13.00 | 13.00 | 14.00 | 15.00 | 15.00 | 16.00 | 17.00 | 23.00 |
| 14 | 0.020 | 2 | 75 | 75 | 14.60 | 14.00 | 14.00 | 14.00 | 14.00 | 14.00 | 14.00 | 14.00 | 15.00 | 17.00 | 23.00 |
| 8 | 0.030 | 9 | 5 | 56 | 13.81 | 10.50 | 12.00 | 12.00 | 13.50 | 13.50 | 15.00 | 15.00 | 16.50 | 18.00 | 27.00 |
| 9 | 0.030 | 8 | 10 | 56 | 13.82 | 9.00 | 10.50 | 12.00 | 13.50 | 13.50 | 15.00 | 15.00 | 16.50 | 18.00 | 27.00 |
| 10 | 0.030 | 6 | 25 | 57 | 13.89 | 10.50 | 10.50 | 12.00 | 13.50 | 13.50 | 15.00 | 15.00 | 16.50 | 18.00 | 27.00 |
| 11 | 0.030 | 5 | 33 | 60 | 13.95 | 11.25 | 11.25 | 11.25 | 12.00 | 13.50 | 15.00 | 15.00 | 16.50 | 18.00 | 27.00 |
| 12 | 0.030 | 4 | 47 | 60 | 14.05 | 12.00 | 12.00 | 12.00 | 13.50 | 13.50 | 15.00 | 15.00 | 16.50 | 18.00 | 27.00 |
| 13 | 0.030 | 2 | 75 | 75 | 14.40 | 13.50 | 13.50 | 13.50 | 13.50 | 13.50 | 13.50 | 13.50 | 15.00 | 18.00 | 27.00 |
| 14 | 0.030 | 1 | 88 | 88 | 14.66 | 14.25 | 14.25 | 14.25 | 14.25 | 14.25 | 14.25 | 14.25 | 14.25 | 16.50 | 27.00 |

IMMUNIZED RETURN: 15 PERCENT   HORIZON: 4 YEARS   FORECAST ACCURACY: 40 PERCENT

| FLOOR RETURN | LEVERAGE FACTOR | DEG. OF FREEDOM | PROBABILITY OF TRIG. | PROBABILITY OF UNDER PERF. | EXPECTED RETURN | RETURN PERCENTILES | | | | | | | | | |
|---|---|---|---|---|---|---|---|---|---|---|---|---|---|---|---|
| | | | | | | 10 | 20 | 30 | 40 | 50 | 60 | 70 | 80 | 90 | 100 |
| 8 | 0.010 | 28 | 0 | 72 | 14.20 | 13.00 | 13.50 | 13.50 | 14.00 | 14.00 | 14.50 | 14.50 | 15.00 | 15.50 | 19.00 |
| 9 | 0.010 | 24 | 0 | 72 | 14.20 | 13.00 | 13.50 | 13.50 | 14.00 | 14.00 | 14.50 | 14.50 | 15.00 | 15.50 | 19.00 |
| 10 | 0.010 | 20 | 0 | 72 | 14.20 | 13.00 | 13.50 | 13.50 | 14.00 | 14.00 | 14.50 | 14.50 | 15.00 | 15.50 | 19.00 |
| 11 | 0.010 | 16 | 0 | 72 | 14.20 | 13.00 | 13.50 | 13.50 | 14.00 | 14.00 | 14.50 | 14.50 | 15.00 | 15.50 | 19.00 |
| 12 | 0.010 | 12 | 2 | 72 | 14.23 | 13.00 | 13.50 | 13.50 | 14.00 | 14.00 | 14.50 | 14.50 | 15.00 | 15.50 | 19.00 |
| 13 | 0.010 | 8 | 19 | 72 | 14.23 | 13.00 | 13.50 | 13.50 | 14.00 | 14.00 | 14.50 | 14.50 | 15.00 | 15.50 | 19.00 |
| 14 | 0.010 | 4 | 62 | 74 | 14.43 | 14.00 | 14.00 | 14.00 | 14.00 | 14.00 | 14.00 | 14.50 | 15.00 | 15.50 | 19.00 |
| 8 | 0.020 | 14 | 0 | 72 | 13.40 | 11.00 | 12.00 | 12.00 | 13.00 | 13.00 | 14.00 | 14.00 | 15.00 | 16.00 | 23.00 |
| 9 | 0.020 | 12 | 2 | 72 | 13.40 | 11.00 | 12.00 | 12.00 | 13.00 | 13.00 | 14.00 | 14.00 | 15.00 | 16.00 | 23.00 |
| 10 | 0.020 | 10 | 7 | 72 | 13.41 | 11.00 | 12.00 | 12.00 | 13.00 | 13.00 | 14.00 | 14.00 | 15.00 | 16.00 | 23.00 |
| 11 | 0.020 | 8 | 19 | 72 | 13.46 | 12.00 | 12.00 | 13.00 | 13.00 | 13.00 | 14.00 | 14.00 | 15.00 | 16.00 | 23.00 |
| 12 | 0.020 | 6 | 38 | 72 | 13.59 | 12.00 | 12.00 | 13.00 | 13.00 | 13.00 | 13.00 | 14.00 | 15.00 | 16.00 | 23.00 |
| 13 | 0.020 | 4 | 62 | 74 | 13.86 | 13.00 | 13.00 | 13.00 | 13.00 | 13.00 | 13.00 | 14.00 | 15.00 | 16.00 | 23.00 |
| 14 | 0.020 | 2 | 85 | 85 | 14.32 | 14.00 | 14.00 | 14.00 | 14.00 | 14.00 | 14.00 | 14.00 | 14.00 | 15.00 | 23.00 |
| 8 | 0.030 | 9 | 10 | 72 | 12.65 | 8.25 | 10.50 | 10.50 | 12.00 | 12.00 | 13.50 | 13.50 | 15.00 | 16.50 | 27.00 |
| 9 | 0.030 | 8 | 19 | 72 | 12.69 | 9.00 | 10.50 | 10.50 | 12.00 | 12.00 | 13.50 | 13.50 | 15.00 | 16.50 | 27.00 |
| 10 | 0.030 | 6 | 38 | 72 | 12.88 | 10.50 | 10.50 | 10.50 | 12.00 | 12.00 | 13.50 | 13.50 | 15.00 | 16.50 | 27.00 |
| 11 | 0.030 | 5 | 47 | 72 | 13.05 | 11.25 | 11.25 | 11.25 | 11.75 | 12.00 | 13.50 | 13.50 | 15.00 | 16.50 | 27.00 |
| 12 | 0.030 | 4 | 62 | 74 | 13.28 | 12.00 | 12.00 | 12.00 | 12.00 | 12.00 | 12.00 | 13.50 | 15.00 | 16.50 | 27.00 |
| 13 | 0.030 | 2 | 85 | 85 | 13.98 | 13.50 | 13.50 | 13.50 | 13.50 | 13.50 | 13.50 | 13.50 | 13.50 | 15.00 | 27.00 |
| 14 | 0.030 | 1 | 93 | 93 | 14.45 | 14.25 | 14.25 | 14.25 | 14.25 | 14.25 | 14.25 | 14.25 | 14.25 | 14.25 | 27.00 |

IMMUNIZED RETURN: 15 PERCENT     HORIZON: 5 YEARS     FORECAST ACCURACY: 60 PERCENT

| FLOOR RETURN | LEVERAGE FACTOR | DEG. OF FREEDOM | PROBABILITY OF TRIG. | PROBABILITY OF UNDER PERF. | EXPECTED RETURN | RETURN PERCENTILES | | | | | | | | | |
|---|---|---|---|---|---|---|---|---|---|---|---|---|---|---|---|
| | | | | | | 10 | 20 | 30 | 40 | 50 | 60 | 70 | 80 | 90 | 100 |
| 8 | 0.010 | 35 | 0 | 13 | 15.80 | 14.60 | 15.00 | 15.40 | 15.40 | 15.80 | 16.20 | 16.20 | 16.60 | 17.00 | 19.00 |
| 9 | 0.010 | 30 | 0 | 13 | 15.80 | 14.60 | 15.00 | 15.40 | 15.40 | 15.80 | 16.20 | 16.20 | 16.60 | 17.00 | 19.00 |
| 10 | 0.010 | 25 | 0 | 13 | 15.80 | 14.60 | 15.00 | 15.40 | 15.40 | 15.80 | 16.20 | 16.20 | 16.60 | 17.00 | 19.00 |
| 11 | 0.010 | 20 | 0 | 13 | 15.80 | 14.60 | 15.00 | 15.40 | 15.40 | 15.80 | 16.20 | 16.20 | 16.60 | 17.00 | 19.00 |
| 12 | 0.010 | 15 | 0 | 13 | 15.80 | 14.60 | 15.00 | 15.40 | 15.40 | 15.80 | 16.20 | 16.20 | 16.60 | 17.00 | 19.00 |
| 13 | 0.010 | 10 | 0 | 13 | 15.80 | 14.60 | 15.00 | 15.40 | 15.40 | 15.80 | 16.20 | 16.20 | 16.60 | 17.00 | 19.00 |
| 14 | 0.010 | 5 | 8 | 14 | 15.77 | 14.60 | 15.00 | 15.40 | 15.40 | 15.80 | 16.20 | 16.20 | 16.60 | 17.00 | 19.00 |
| 8 | 0.020 | 17 | 0 | 13 | 16.60 | 14.20 | 15.00 | 15.80 | 15.80 | 16.60 | 17.40 | 17.40 | 18.20 | 19.00 | 23.00 |
| 9 | 0.020 | 15 | 0 | 13 | 16.60 | 14.20 | 15.00 | 15.80 | 15.80 | 16.60 | 17.40 | 17.40 | 18.20 | 19.00 | 23.00 |
| 10 | 0.020 | 12 | 0 | 13 | 16.60 | 14.20 | 15.00 | 15.80 | 15.80 | 16.60 | 17.40 | 17.40 | 18.20 | 19.00 | 23.00 |
| 11 | 0.020 | 10 | 2 | 13 | 16.60 | 14.20 | 15.00 | 15.80 | 15.80 | 16.60 | 17.40 | 17.40 | 18.20 | 19.00 | 23.00 |
| 12 | 0.020 | 7 | 8 | 14 | 16.59 | 14.20 | 15.00 | 15.80 | 15.80 | 16.60 | 17.40 | 17.40 | 18.20 | 19.00 | 23.00 |
| 13 | 0.020 | 5 | 8 | 14 | 16.55 | 14.20 | 15.00 | 15.80 | 15.80 | 16.60 | 17.40 | 17.40 | 18.20 | 19.00 | 23.00 |
| 14 | 0.020 | 2 | 39 | 39 | 16.15 | 14.20 | 14.20 | 14.70 | 15.00 | 15.80 | 16.60 | 17.40 | 18.20 | 19.00 | 23.00 |
| 8 | 0.030 | 11 | 0 | 13 | 17.40 | 13.80 | 15.00 | 16.20 | 16.20 | 17.40 | 18.60 | 18.60 | 19.40 | 21.00 | 27.00 |
| 9 | 0.030 | 10 | 0 | 13 | 17.40 | 13.80 | 15.00 | 16.20 | 16.20 | 17.40 | 18.60 | 18.60 | 19.40 | 21.00 | 27.00 |
| 10 | 0.030 | 8 | 1 | 13 | 17.39 | 13.80 | 15.00 | 16.20 | 16.20 | 17.40 | 18.60 | 18.60 | 19.40 | 21.00 | 27.00 |
| 11 | 0.030 | 6 | 4 | 13 | 17.36 | 13.80 | 15.00 | 16.20 | 16.20 | 17.40 | 18.60 | 18.60 | 19.40 | 21.00 | 27.00 |
| 12 | 0.030 | 5 | 8 | 14 | 17.32 | 13.80 | 15.20 | 16.20 | 16.20 | 17.40 | 18.60 | 18.60 | 19.40 | 21.00 | 27.00 |
| 13 | 0.030 | 3 | 23 | 25 | 17.06 | 13.20 | 13.20 | 15.00 | 16.20 | 17.40 | 18.60 | 18.60 | 19.40 | 21.00 | 27.00 |
| 14 | 0.030 | 1 | 63 | 63 | 16.11 | 14.40 | 14.40 | 14.40 | 14.40 | 14.40 | 14.40 | 17.40 | 18.60 | 19.80 | 27.00 |

IMMUNIZED RETURN: 15 PERCENT         HORIZON: 5 YEARS         FORECAST ACCURACY: 55 PERCENT

| FLOOR RETURN | LEVERAGE FACTOR | DEG. OF FREEDOM | PROBABILITY OF TRIG. | PROBABILITY OF UNDER PERF | EXPECTED RETURN | RETURN PERCENTILES | | | | | | | | | |
|---|---|---|---|---|---|---|---|---|---|---|---|---|---|---|---|
| | | | | | | 10 | 20 | 30 | 40 | 50 | 60 | 70 | 80 | 90 | 100 |
| 8 | 0.010 | 35 | 0 | 25 | 15.40 | 14.20 | 14.60 | 15.00 | 15.00 | 15.40 | 15.80 | 15.80 | 16.20 | 16.60 | 19.00 |
| 9 | 0.010 | 30 | 0 | 25 | 15.40 | 14.20 | 14.60 | 15.00 | 15.00 | 15.40 | 15.80 | 15.80 | 16.20 | 16.60 | 19.00 |
| 10 | 0.010 | 25 | 0 | 25 | 15.40 | 14.20 | 14.60 | 15.00 | 15.00 | 15.40 | 15.80 | 15.80 | 16.20 | 16.60 | 19.00 |
| 11 | 0.010 | 20 | 0 | 25 | 15.40 | 14.20 | 14.60 | 15.00 | 15.00 | 15.40 | 15.80 | 15.80 | 16.20 | 16.60 | 19.00 |
| 12 | 0.010 | 15 | 1 | 25 | 15.40 | 14.20 | 14.60 | 15.00 | 15.00 | 15.40 | 15.80 | 15.80 | 16.20 | 16.60 | 19.00 |
| 13 | 0.010 | 10 | 1 | 25 | 15.40 | 14.20 | 14.60 | 15.00 | 15.00 | 15.40 | 15.80 | 15.80 | 16.20 | 16.60 | 19.00 |
| 14 | 0.010 | 5 | 15 | 27 | 15.37 | 14.00 | 14.60 | 15.00 | 15.00 | 15.40 | 15.80 | 15.80 | 16.20 | 16.60 | 19.00 |
| 8 | 0.020 | 17 | 0 | 25 | 15.80 | 13.40 | 14.20 | 15.00 | 15.00 | 15.80 | 16.60 | 16.60 | 17.40 | 18.20 | 23.00 |
| 9 | 0.020 | 15 | 0 | 25 | 15.80 | 13.40 | 14.20 | 15.00 | 15.00 | 15.80 | 16.60 | 16.60 | 17.40 | 18.20 | 23.00 |
| 10 | 0.020 | 12 | 0 | 25 | 15.80 | 13.40 | 14.20 | 15.00 | 15.00 | 15.80 | 16.60 | 16.60 | 17.40 | 18.20 | 23.00 |
| 11 | 0.020 | 10 | 1 | 25 | 15.80 | 13.40 | 14.20 | 15.00 | 15.00 | 15.80 | 16.60 | 16.60 | 17.40 | 18.20 | 23.00 |
| 12 | 0.020 | 7 | 5 | 25 | 15.79 | 13.40 | 14.20 | 15.00 | 15.00 | 15.80 | 16.60 | 16.60 | 17.40 | 18.20 | 23.00 |
| 13 | 0.020 | 5 | 15 | 27 | 15.75 | 13.00 | 14.20 | 15.00 | 15.00 | 15.80 | 16.60 | 16.60 | 17.40 | 18.20 | 23.00 |
| 14 | 0.020 | 2 | 53 | 53 | 15.51 | 14.20 | 14.20 | 14.20 | 14.20 | 14.20 | 15.80 | 16.60 | 17.40 | 18.20 | 23.00 |
| 8 | 0.030 | 11 | 0 | 25 | 16.20 | 12.60 | 13.80 | 15.00 | 15.00 | 16.20 | 17.40 | 17.40 | 18.60 | 19.80 | 27.00 |
| 9 | 0.030 | 10 | 1 | 25 | 16.20 | 12.60 | 13.80 | 15.00 | 15.00 | 16.20 | 17.40 | 17.40 | 18.60 | 19.80 | 27.00 |
| 10 | 0.030 | 8 | 3 | 25 | 16.19 | 12.60 | 13.80 | 15.00 | 15.00 | 16.20 | 17.40 | 17.40 | 18.60 | 19.80 | 27.00 |
| 11 | 0.030 | 6 | 10 | 25 | 16.16 | 12.60 | 13.80 | 15.00 | 15.00 | 16.20 | 17.40 | 17.40 | 18.60 | 19.80 | 27.00 |
| 12 | 0.030 | 5 | 15 | 27 | 16.12 | 12.60 | 13.80 | 15.00 | 15.00 | 16.20 | 17.40 | 17.40 | 18.60 | 19.80 | 27.00 |
| 13 | 0.030 | 3 | 36 | 39 | 15.94 | 13.20 | 13.20 | 13.20 | 15.00 | 16.20 | 16.20 | 17.40 | 18.60 | 19.80 | 27.00 |
| 14 | 0.030 | 1 | 73 | 73 | 15.46 | 14.40 | 14.40 | 14.40 | 14.40 | 14.40 | 14.40 | 14.40 | 17.40 | 18.60 | 27.00 |

IMMUNIZED RETURN: 15 PERCENT          HORIZON: 5 YEARS          FORECAST ACCURACY: 50 PERCENT

| FLOOR RETURN | LEVERAGE FACTOR | DEG. OF FREEDOM | PROBABILITY OF TRIG. | PROBABILITY OF UNDER PERF. | EXPECTED RETURN | RETURN PERCENTILES | | | | | | | | | |
|---|---|---|---|---|---|---|---|---|---|---|---|---|---|---|---|
| | | | | | | 10 | 20 | 30 | 40 | 50 | 60 | 70 | 80 | 90 | 100 |
| 8  | 0.010 | 35 | 0  | 41 | 15.00 | 13.80 | 14.20 | 14.60 | 14.60 | 15.00 | 15.40 | 15.40 | 15.80 | 16.20 | 19.00 |
| 9  | 0.010 | 30 | 0  | 41 | 15.00 | 13.80 | 14.20 | 14.60 | 14.60 | 15.00 | 15.40 | 15.40 | 15.80 | 16.20 | 19.00 |
| 10 | 0.010 | 25 | 0  | 41 | 15.00 | 13.80 | 14.20 | 14.60 | 14.60 | 15.00 | 15.40 | 15.40 | 15.80 | 16.20 | 19.00 |
| 11 | 0.010 | 20 | 0  | 41 | 15.00 | 13.80 | 14.20 | 14.60 | 14.60 | 15.00 | 15.40 | 15.40 | 15.80 | 16.20 | 19.00 |
| 12 | 0.010 | 15 | 0  | 41 | 15.00 | 13.80 | 14.20 | 14.60 | 14.60 | 15.00 | 15.40 | 15.40 | 15.80 | 16.20 | 19.00 |
| 13 | 0.010 | 10 | 3  | 41 | 15.00 | 13.80 | 14.20 | 14.60 | 14.60 | 15.00 | 15.40 | 15.40 | 15.80 | 16.20 | 19.00 |
| 14 | 0.010 | 5  | 26 | 43 | 15.00 | 14.00 | 14.00 | 14.20 | 14.80 | 15.00 | 15.40 | 15.40 | 15.80 | 16.20 | 19.00 |
| 8  | 0.020 | 17 | 0  | 41 | 15.00 | 12.60 | 13.40 | 14.20 | 14.20 | 15.00 | 15.80 | 15.80 | 16.60 | 17.40 | 23.00 |
| 9  | 0.020 | 15 | 0  | 41 | 15.00 | 12.60 | 13.40 | 14.20 | 14.20 | 15.00 | 15.80 | 15.80 | 16.60 | 17.40 | 23.00 |
| 10 | 0.020 | 12 | 1  | 41 | 15.00 | 12.60 | 13.40 | 14.20 | 14.20 | 15.00 | 15.80 | 15.80 | 16.60 | 17.40 | 23.00 |
| 11 | 0.020 | 10 | 3  | 41 | 15.00 | 12.20 | 13.40 | 14.20 | 14.20 | 15.00 | 15.80 | 15.80 | 16.60 | 17.40 | 23.00 |
| 12 | 0.020 | 7  | 12 | 43 | 15.00 | 13.00 | 13.00 | 14.20 | 14.20 | 15.00 | 15.80 | 15.80 | 16.60 | 17.40 | 23.00 |
| 13 | 0.020 | 5  | 26 | 43 | 15.00 | 13.20 | 13.40 | 14.20 | 14.20 | 15.00 | 15.80 | 15.40 | 16.60 | 17.40 | 23.00 |
| 14 | 0.020 | 2  | 66 | 66 | 15.00 | 14.20 | 14.20 | 14.20 | 14.20 | 14.20 | 14.20 | 15.00 | 16.60 | 17.40 | 23.00 |
| 8  | 0.030 | 11 | 1  | 41 | 15.00 | 11.40 | 12.60 | 13.80 | 13.80 | 15.00 | 16.20 | 16.20 | 17.40 | 18.60 | 27.00 |
| 9  | 0.030 | 10 | 3  | 41 | 15.00 | 11.40 | 12.60 | 13.80 | 13.80 | 15.00 | 16.20 | 16.20 | 17.40 | 18.60 | 27.00 |
| 10 | 0.030 | 8  | 8  | 41 | 15.00 | 11.40 | 12.60 | 13.80 | 13.80 | 15.00 | 16.20 | 16.20 | 17.40 | 18.60 | 27.00 |
| 11 | 0.030 | 6  | 19 | 42 | 15.00 | 11.40 | 12.60 | 13.80 | 13.80 | 15.00 | 16.20 | 16.20 | 17.40 | 18.60 | 27.00 |
| 12 | 0.030 | 5  | 26 | 43 | 15.00 | 12.00 | 12.00 | 12.60 | 13.80 | 15.00 | 16.20 | 16.20 | 17.40 | 18.60 | 27.00 |
| 13 | 0.030 | 3  | 50 | 54 | 15.00 | 13.20 | 13.20 | 13.20 | 13.20 | 13.20 | 15.00 | 16.20 | 17.40 | 18.60 | 27.00 |
| 14 | 0.030 | 1  | 82 | 82 | 15.00 | 14.40 | 14.40 | 14.40 | 14.40 | 14.40 | 14.40 | 14.40 | 14.40 | 17.00 | 27.00 |

IMMUNIZED RETURN: 15 PERCENT          HORIZON: 5 YEARS          FORECAST ACCURACY: 45 PERCENT

| FLOOR RETURN | LEVERAGE FACTOR | DEG. OF FREEDOM | PROBABILITY OF TRIG. | PROBABILITY OF UNDER PERF. | EXPECTED RETURN | RETURN PERCENTILES | | | | | | | | | |
|---|---|---|---|---|---|---|---|---|---|---|---|---|---|---|---|
| | | | | | | 10 | 20 | 30 | 40 | 50 | 60 | 70 | 80 | 90 | 100 |
| 8 | 0.010 | 35 | 0 | 59 | 14.60 | 13.40 | 13.80 | 14.20 | 14.20 | 14.60 | 15.00 | 15.00 | 15.40 | 15.80 | 19.00 |
| 9 | 0.010 | 30 | 0 | 59 | 14.60 | 13.40 | 13.80 | 14.20 | 14.20 | 14.60 | 15.00 | 15.00 | 15.40 | 15.80 | 19.00 |
| 10 | 0.010 | 25 | 0 | 59 | 14.60 | 13.40 | 13.80 | 14.20 | 14.20 | 14.60 | 15.00 | 15.00 | 15.40 | 15.80 | 19.00 |
| 11 | 0.010 | 20 | 0 | 59 | 14.60 | 13.40 | 13.80 | 14.20 | 14.20 | 14.60 | 15.00 | 15.00 | 15.40 | 15.80 | 19.00 |
| 12 | 0.010 | 15 | 0 | 59 | 14.60 | 13.40 | 13.80 | 14.20 | 14.20 | 14.60 | 15.00 | 15.00 | 15.40 | 15.80 | 19.00 |
| 13 | 0.010 | 10 | 7 | 59 | 14.60 | 13.60 | 13.80 | 14.20 | 14.20 | 14.60 | 15.00 | 15.00 | 15.40 | 15.80 | 19.00 |
| 14 | 0.010 | 5 | 41 | 61 | 14.67 | 14.00 | 14.00 | 14.00 | 14.00 | 14.60 | 14.60 | 15.00 | 15.40 | 15.80 | 19.00 |
| 8 | 0.020 | 17 | 0 | 59 | 14.20 | 11.80 | 12.60 | 13.40 | 13.40 | 14.20 | 15.00 | 15.00 | 15.80 | 16.60 | 23.00 |
| 9 | 0.020 | 15 | 0 | 59 | 14.20 | 11.80 | 12.60 | 13.40 | 13.40 | 14.20 | 15.00 | 15.00 | 15.80 | 16.60 | 23.00 |
| 10 | 0.020 | 12 | 2 | 59 | 14.20 | 11.80 | 12.60 | 13.40 | 13.40 | 14.20 | 15.00 | 15.00 | 15.80 | 16.60 | 23.00 |
| 11 | 0.020 | 10 | 7 | 59 | 14.21 | 11.80 | 12.60 | 13.40 | 13.40 | 14.20 | 15.00 | 15.00 | 15.80 | 16.60 | 23.00 |
| 12 | 0.020 | 7 | 22 | 59 | 14.25 | 12.20 | 13.00 | 13.40 | 13.40 | 14.20 | 15.00 | 15.00 | 15.80 | 16.60 | 23.00 |
| 13 | 0.020 | 5 | 41 | 61 | 14.34 | 13.00 | 13.20 | 13.40 | 13.40 | 14.20 | 14.20 | 15.00 | 15.80 | 16.60 | 23.00 |
| 14 | 0.020 | 2 | 79 | 79 | 14.64 | 14.20 | 14.20 | 14.00 | 14.00 | 14.20 | 14.20 | 14.20 | 15.00 | 15.80 | 23.00 |
| 8 | 0.030 | 11 | 3 | 59 | 13.81 | 10.20 | 11.40 | 12.60 | 12.60 | 13.80 | 15.00 | 15.00 | 16.20 | 17.40 | 27.00 |
| 9 | 0.030 | 10 | 7 | 59 | 13.81 | 10.20 | 11.40 | 12.60 | 12.60 | 13.80 | 15.00 | 15.00 | 16.20 | 17.40 | 27.00 |
| 10 | 0.030 | 8 | 16 | 59 | 13.85 | 10.20 | 11.40 | 12.60 | 12.60 | 13.80 | 15.00 | 15.00 | 16.20 | 17.40 | 27.00 |
| 11 | 0.030 | 6 | 32 | 61 | 13.93 | 11.40 | 11.40 | 11.40 | 12.60 | 13.80 | 13.80 | 15.00 | 16.20 | 17.40 | 27.00 |
| 12 | 0.030 | 5 | 41 | 70 | 14.01 | 12.00 | 12.00 | 12.00 | 12.00 | 13.80 | 13.20 | 15.00 | 16.20 | 17.40 | 27.00 |
| 13 | 0.030 | 3 | 65 | 90 | 14.27 | 13.20 | 13.20 | 13.20 | 13.20 | 13.20 | 13.20 | 14.40 | 16.20 | 17.40 | 27.00 |
| 14 | 0.030 | 1 | 90 | 90 | 14.70 | 14.40 | 14.20 | 14.40 | 14.40 | 14.40 | 14.40 | 14.40 | 14.40 | 15.00 | 27.00 |

IMMUNIZED RETURN: 15 PERCENT　　　　　HORIZON: 5 YEARS　　　　　FORECAST ACCURACY: 40 PERCENT

| FLOOR RETURN | LEVERAGE FACTOR | DEG. OF FREEDOM | PROBABILITY OF TRIG. | PROBABILITY OF UNDER PERF. | EXPECTED RETURN | 10 | 20 | 30 | 40 | 50 | 60 | 70 | 80 | 90 | 100 |
|---|---|---|---|---|---|---|---|---|---|---|---|---|---|---|---|
| | | | | | | | | | RETURN PERCENTILES | | | | | | |
| 8 | 0.010 | 35 | 0 | 76 | 14.20 | 13.00 | 13.40 | 13.80 | 13.80 | 14.20 | 14.60 | 14.00 | 15.00 | 15.40 | 19.00 |
| 9 | 0.010 | 30 | 0 | 76 | 14.20 | 13.00 | 13.40 | 13.80 | 13.80 | 14.20 | 14.60 | 14.00 | 15.00 | 15.40 | 19.00 |
| 10 | 0.010 | 25 | 0 | 76 | 14.20 | 13.00 | 13.40 | 13.80 | 13.80 | 14.20 | 14.60 | 14.00 | 15.00 | 15.40 | 19.00 |
| 11 | 0.010 | 20 | 0 | 76 | 14.20 | 13.00 | 13.40 | 13.80 | 13.80 | 14.20 | 14.60 | 14.60 | 15.00 | 15.40 | 19.00 |
| 12 | 0.010 | 15 | 1 | 76 | 14.20 | 13.00 | 13.40 | 13.80 | 13.80 | 14.20 | 14.60 | 14.60 | 15.00 | 15.40 | 19.00 |
| 13 | 0.010 | 10 | 14 | 76 | 14.22 | 13.00 | 13.40 | 13.80 | 13.80 | 14.20 | 14.60 | 14.60 | 15.00 | 15.40 | 19.00 |
| 14 | 0.010 | 5 | 58 | 77 | 14.40 | 14.00 | 14.00 | 14.00 | 14.00 | 14.00 | 14.20 | 14.60 | 15.00 | 15.40 | 19.00 |
| 8 | 0.020 | 17 | 0 | 76 | 13.40 | 11.00 | 11.80 | 12.60 | 12.60 | 13.40 | 14.20 | 14.20 | 15.00 | 15.80 | 23.00 |
| 9 | 0.020 | 15 | 1 | 76 | 13.40 | 11.00 | 11.80 | 12.60 | 12.60 | 13.40 | 14.20 | 14.20 | 15.00 | 15.80 | 23.00 |
| 10 | 0.020 | 12 | 6 | 76 | 13.41 | 11.00 | 11.80 | 12.60 | 12.60 | 13.40 | 14.60 | 14.20 | 15.00 | 15.80 | 23.00 |
| 11 | 0.020 | 10 | 14 | 76 | 13.44 | 11.00 | 11.80 | 12.60 | 12.60 | 13.40 | 14.20 | 14.20 | 15.00 | 15.80 | 23.00 |
| 12 | 0.020 | 7 | 36 | 76 | 13.59 | 12.20 | 12.20 | 12.60 | 12.60 | 13.40 | 14.20 | 14.20 | 15.00 | 15.80 | 23.00 |
| 13 | 0.020 | 5 | 58 | 77 | 13.81 | 13.00 | 13.00 | 13.00 | 13.00 | 13.00 | 13.40 | 14.20 | 15.00 | 15.80 | 23.00 |
| 14 | 0.020 | 2 | 88 | 88 | 14.41 | 14.20 | 14.20 | 14.20 | 14.20 | 14.20 | 14.20 | 14.20 | 14.20 | 15.00 | 23.00 |
| 8 | 0.030 | 11 | 8 | 76 | 12.63 | 9.00 | 10.20 | 11.40 | 11.40 | 12.60 | 13.80 | 13.80 | 15.00 | 16.20 | 27.00 |
| 9 | 0.030 | 10 | 14 | 76 | 12.66 | 9.00 | 10.20 | 11.40 | 11.40 | 12.60 | 13.80 | 13.80 | 15.00 | 16.20 | 27.00 |
| 10 | 0.030 | 8 | 29 | 76 | 12.78 | 10.20 | 10.20 | 11.40 | 11.40 | 12.60 | 13.80 | 13.80 | 15.00 | 16.20 | 27.00 |
| 11 | 0.030 | 6 | 49 | 77 | 13.02 | 11.40 | 11.40 | 11.40 | 11.40 | 12.60 | 12.60 | 13.80 | 15.00 | 16.20 | 27.00 |
| 12 | 0.030 | 5 | 58 | 77 | 13.21 | 12.00 | 12.00 | 12.00 | 12.00 | 12.60 | 12.60 | 13.80 | 15.00 | 16.20 | 27.00 |
| 13 | 0.030 | 3 | 79 | 83 | 13.76 | 13.20 | 13.20 | 13.20 | 13.20 | 13.20 | 13.20 | 13.20 | 13.80 | 16.20 | 27.00 |
| 14 | 0.030 | 1 | 95 | 95 | 14.53 | 14.40 | 14.40 | 14.40 | 14.40 | 14.40 | 14.40 | 14.40 | 14.40 | 14.40 | 27.00 |

IMMUNIZED RETURN: 15 PERCENT  HORIZON: 6 YEARS  FORECAST ACCURACY: 60 PERCENT

| FLOOR RETURN | LEVERAGE FACTOR | DEG. OF FREEDOM | PROBABILITY OF TRIG. | PROBABILITY OF UNDER PERF. | EXPECTED RETURN | RETURN PERCENTILES | | | | | | | | | |
|---|---|---|---|---|---|---|---|---|---|---|---|---|---|---|---|
| | | | | | | 10 | 20 | 30 | 40 | 50 | 60 | 70 | 80 | 90 | 100 |
| 8 | 0.010 | 42 | 0 | 11 | 15.80 | 14.67 | 15.00 | 15.33 | 15.67 | 15.67 | 16.00 | 16.33 | 16.33 | 16.67 | 19.00 |
| 9 | 0.010 | 36 | 0 | 11 | 15.80 | 14.67 | 15.00 | 15.33 | 15.67 | 15.67 | 16.00 | 16.33 | 16.33 | 16.67 | 19.00 |
| 10 | 0.010 | 30 | 0 | 11 | 15.80 | 14.67 | 15.00 | 15.33 | 15.67 | 15.67 | 16.00 | 16.33 | 16.33 | 16.67 | 19.00 |
| 11 | 0.010 | 24 | 0 | 11 | 15.80 | 14.67 | 15.00 | 15.33 | 15.67 | 15.67 | 16.00 | 16.33 | 16.33 | 16.67 | 19.00 |
| 12 | 0.010 | 18 | 0 | 11 | 15.80 | 14.67 | 15.00 | 15.33 | 15.67 | 15.67 | 16.00 | 16.33 | 16.33 | 16.67 | 19.00 |
| 13 | 0.010 | 12 | 0 | 11 | 15.80 | 14.67 | 15.00 | 15.33 | 15.67 | 15.67 | 16.00 | 16.33 | 16.33 | 16.67 | 19.00 |
| 14 | 0.010 | 6 | 5 | 12 | 15.78 | 14.67 | 15.00 | 15.67 | 15.67 | 15.67 | 16.00 | 16.33 | 16.33 | 16.67 | 19.00 |
| 8 | 0.020 | 21 | 0 | 11 | 16.60 | 14.33 | 15.00 | 15.67 | 16.33 | 16.33 | 17.00 | 17.67 | 17.67 | 18.33 | 23.00 |
| 9 | 0.020 | 18 | 0 | 11 | 16.60 | 14.33 | 15.00 | 15.67 | 16.33 | 16.33 | 17.00 | 17.67 | 17.67 | 18.33 | 23.00 |
| 10 | 0.020 | 15 | 0 | 11 | 16.60 | 14.33 | 15.00 | 15.67 | 16.33 | 16.33 | 17.00 | 17.67 | 17.67 | 18.33 | 23.00 |
| 11 | 0.020 | 12 | 0 | 11 | 16.60 | 14.33 | 15.00 | 15.67 | 16.33 | 16.33 | 17.00 | 17.67 | 17.67 | 18.33 | 23.00 |
| 12 | 0.020 | 9 | 1 | 11 | 16.60 | 14.33 | 15.00 | 15.67 | 16.33 | 16.33 | 17.00 | 17.67 | 17.67 | 18.33 | 23.00 |
| 13 | 0.020 | 6 | 5 | 12 | 16.57 | 14.33 | 15.00 | 15.67 | 16.33 | 16.33 | 17.00 | 17.67 | 17.67 | 18.33 | 23.00 |
| 14 | 0.020 | 3 | 25 | 26 | 16.35 | 14.00 | 14.00 | 15.00 | 15.67 | 16.33 | 17.00 | 17.67 | 17.67 | 18.33 | 23.00 |
| 8 | 0.030 | 14 | 0 | 11 | 17.40 | 14.00 | 15.00 | 16.00 | 17.00 | 17.00 | 18.00 | 19.00 | 19.00 | 20.00 | 27.00 |
| 9 | 0.030 | 12 | 0 | 11 | 17.40 | 14.00 | 15.00 | 16.00 | 17.00 | 17.00 | 18.00 | 19.00 | 19.00 | 20.00 | 27.00 |
| 10 | 0.030 | 10 | 0 | 11 | 17.40 | 14.00 | 15.00 | 16.00 | 17.00 | 17.00 | 18.00 | 19.00 | 19.00 | 20.00 | 27.00 |
| 11 | 0.030 | 8 | 1 | 11 | 17.39 | 14.00 | 15.00 | 16.00 | 17.00 | 17.00 | 18.00 | 19.00 | 19.00 | 20.00 | 27.00 |
| 12 | 0.030 | 6 | 5 | 12 | 17.35 | 14.00 | 15.00 | 16.00 | 17.00 | 17.00 | 18.00 | 19.00 | 19.00 | 20.00 | 27.00 |
| 13 | 0.030 | 4 | 15 | 18 | 17.20 | 14.00 | 15.00 | 16.00 | 17.00 | 17.00 | 18.00 | 19.00 | 19.00 | 20.00 | 27.00 |
| 14 | 0.030 | 2 | 40 | 40 | 16.68 | 13.00 | 14.00 | 14.00 | 14.00 | 17.00 | 18.00 | 19.00 | 19.00 | 20.00 | 27.00 |

IMMUNIZED RETURN: 15 PERCENT            HORIZON: 6 YEARS            FORECAST ACCURACY: 55 PERCENT

| FLOOR RETURN | LEVERAGE FACTOR | DEG. OF FREEDOM | PROBABILITY OF TRIG. | PROBABILITY OF UNDER PERF. | EXPECTED RETURN | RETURN PERCENTILES | | | | | | | | | |
|---|---|---|---|---|---|---|---|---|---|---|---|---|---|---|---|
| | | | | | | 10 | 20 | 30 | 40 | 50 | 60 | 70 | 80 | 90 | 100 |
| 8 | 0.010 | 42 | 0 | 24 | 15.40 | 14.33 | 14.67 | 15.00 | 15.33 | 15.33 | 15.67 | 15.67 | 16.00 | 16.33 | 19.00 |
| 9 | 0.010 | 36 | 0 | 24 | 15.40 | 14.33 | 14.67 | 15.00 | 15.33 | 15.33 | 15.67 | 15.67 | 16.00 | 16.33 | 19.00 |
| 10 | 0.010 | 30 | 0 | 24 | 15.40 | 14.33 | 14.67 | 15.00 | 15.33 | 15.33 | 15.67 | 15.67 | 16.00 | 16.33 | 19.00 |
| 11 | 0.010 | 24 | 0 | 24 | 15.40 | 14.33 | 14.67 | 15.00 | 15.33 | 15.33 | 15.67 | 15.67 | 16.00 | 16.33 | 19.00 |
| 12 | 0.010 | 18 | 0 | 24 | 15.40 | 14.33 | 14.67 | 15.00 | 15.33 | 15.33 | 15.67 | 15.67 | 16.00 | 16.33 | 19.00 |
| 13 | 0.010 | 12 | 0 | 24 | 15.40 | 14.33 | 14.67 | 15.00 | 15.33 | 15.33 | 15.67 | 15.67 | 16.00 | 16.33 | 19.00 |
| 14 | 0.010 | 6 | 12 | 25 | 15.38 | 14.00 | 14.67 | 15.00 | 15.33 | 15.33 | 15.67 | 15.67 | 16.00 | 16.33 | 19.00 |
| 8 | 0.020 | 21 | 0 | 24 | 15.80 | 13.67 | 14.33 | 15.00 | 15.67 | 15.67 | 16.33 | 16.33 | 17.00 | 17.67 | 23.00 |
| 9 | 0.020 | 18 | 0 | 24 | 15.80 | 13.67 | 14.33 | 15.00 | 15.67 | 15.67 | 16.33 | 16.33 | 17.00 | 17.67 | 23.00 |
| 10 | 0.020 | 15 | 0 | 24 | 15.80 | 13.67 | 14.33 | 15.00 | 15.67 | 15.67 | 16.33 | 16.33 | 17.00 | 17.67 | 23.00 |
| 11 | 0.020 | 12 | 0 | 24 | 15.80 | 13.67 | 14.33 | 15.00 | 15.67 | 15.67 | 16.33 | 16.33 | 17.00 | 17.67 | 23.00 |
| 12 | 0.020 | 9 | 2 | 24 | 15.80 | 13.67 | 14.33 | 15.00 | 15.67 | 15.67 | 16.33 | 16.33 | 17.00 | 17.67 | 23.00 |
| 13 | 0.020 | 6 | 12 | 25 | 15.76 | 13.00 | 14.33 | 15.00 | 15.67 | 15.67 | 16.33 | 16.33 | 17.00 | 17.67 | 23.00 |
| 14 | 0.020 | 3 | 38 | 41 | 15.61 | 14.00 | 14.00 | 14.00 | 14.33 | 15.33 | 16.33 | 16.33 | 17.00 | 17.67 | 23.00 |
| 8 | 0.030 | 14 | 0 | 24 | 16.20 | 13.00 | 14.00 | 15.00 | 16.00 | 16.00 | 17.00 | 17.00 | 18.00 | 19.00 | 27.00 |
| 9 | 0.030 | 12 | 0 | 24 | 16.20 | 13.00 | 14.00 | 15.00 | 16.00 | 16.00 | 17.00 | 17.00 | 18.00 | 19.00 | 27.00 |
| 10 | 0.030 | 10 | 1 | 24 | 16.20 | 13.00 | 14.00 | 15.00 | 16.00 | 16.00 | 17.00 | 17.00 | 18.00 | 19.00 | 27.00 |
| 11 | 0.030 | 8 | 4 | 24 | 16.19 | 13.00 | 14.00 | 15.00 | 16.00 | 16.00 | 17.00 | 17.00 | 18.00 | 19.00 | 27.00 |
| 12 | 0.030 | 6 | 12 | 25 | 16.15 | 12.00 | 14.00 | 15.00 | 15.00 | 16.00 | 17.00 | 17.00 | 18.00 | 19.00 | 27.00 |
| 13 | 0.030 | 4 | 27 | 32 | 16.03 | 13.00 | 13.00 | 14.00 | 15.00 | 16.00 | 16.00 | 17.00 | 18.00 | 19.00 | 27.00 |
| 14 | 0.030 | 2 | 55 | 55 | 15.73 | 14.00 | 14.00 | 14.00 | 14.00 | 14.00 | 16.00 | 17.00 | 18.00 | 19.00 | 27.00 |

IMMUNIZED RETURN: 15 PERCENT     HORIZON: 6 YEARS     FORECAST ACCURACY: 50 PERCENT

| FLOOR RETURN | LEVERAGE FACTOR | DEG. OF FREEDOM | PROBABILITY OF TRIG. | PROBABILITY OF UNDER PERF. | EXPECTED RETURN | RETURN PERCENTILES | | | | | | | | | |
|---|---|---|---|---|---|---|---|---|---|---|---|---|---|---|---|
| | | | | | | 10 | 20 | 30 | 40 | 50 | 60 | 70 | 80 | 90 | 100 |
| 8 | 0.010 | 42 | 0 | 42 | 15.00 | 14.00 | 14.33 | 14.67 | 14.67 | 15.00 | 15.33 | 15.33 | 15.67 | 16.00 | 19.00 |
| 9 | 0.010 | 36 | 0 | 42 | 15.00 | 14.00 | 14.33 | 14.67 | 14.67 | 15.00 | 15.33 | 15.33 | 15.67 | 16.00 | 19.00 |
| 10 | 0.010 | 30 | 0 | 42 | 15.00 | 14.00 | 14.33 | 14.67 | 14.67 | 15.00 | 15.33 | 15.33 | 15.67 | 16.00 | 19.00 |
| 11 | 0.010 | 24 | 0 | 42 | 15.00 | 14.00 | 14.33 | 14.67 | 14.67 | 15.00 | 15.33 | 15.33 | 15.67 | 16.00 | 19.00 |
| 12 | 0.010 | 18 | 0 | 42 | 15.00 | 14.00 | 14.33 | 14.67 | 14.67 | 15.00 | 15.33 | 15.33 | 15.67 | 16.00 | 19.00 |
| 13 | 0.010 | 12 | 1 | 42 | 15.00 | 14.00 | 14.33 | 14.67 | 14.67 | 15.00 | 15.33 | 15.33 | 15.67 | 16.00 | 19.00 |
| 14 | 0.010 | 6 | 23 | 43 | 15.00 | 14.00 | 14.00 | 14.33 | 14.67 | 15.00 | 15.33 | 15.33 | 15.67 | 16.00 | 19.00 |
| 8 | 0.020 | 21 | 0 | 42 | 15.00 | 13.00 | 13.67 | 14.33 | 14.33 | 15.00 | 15.67 | 15.67 | 16.33 | 17.00 | 23.00 |
| 9 | 0.020 | 18 | 0 | 42 | 15.00 | 13.00 | 13.67 | 14.33 | 14.33 | 15.00 | 15.67 | 15.67 | 16.33 | 17.00 | 23.00 |
| 10 | 0.020 | 15 | 0 | 42 | 15.00 | 13.00 | 13.67 | 14.33 | 14.33 | 15.00 | 15.67 | 15.67 | 16.33 | 17.00 | 23.00 |
| 11 | 0.020 | 12 | 1 | 42 | 15.00 | 13.00 | 13.67 | 14.33 | 14.33 | 15.00 | 15.67 | 15.67 | 16.33 | 17.00 | 23.00 |
| 12 | 0.020 | 9 | 6 | 42 | 15.00 | 13.00 | 13.00 | 14.33 | 14.33 | 15.00 | 15.67 | 15.67 | 16.33 | 17.00 | 23.00 |
| 13 | 0.020 | 6 | 23 | 43 | 15.00 | 13.00 | 13.00 | 13.67 | 14.33 | 15.00 | 15.67 | 15.67 | 16.33 | 17.00 | 23.00 |
| 14 | 0.020 | 3 | 54 | 57 | 15.00 | 14.00 | 14.00 | 14.00 | 14.00 | 15.00 | 15.00 | 15.67 | 16.33 | 17.00 | 23.00 |
| 8 | 0.030 | 14 | 0 | 42 | 15.00 | 12.00 | 13.00 | 14.00 | 14.00 | 15.00 | 16.00 | 16.00 | 17.00 | 18.00 | 27.00 |
| 9 | 0.030 | 12 | 1 | 42 | 15.00 | 12.00 | 13.00 | 14.00 | 14.00 | 15.00 | 16.00 | 16.00 | 17.00 | 18.00 | 27.00 |
| 10 | 0.030 | 10 | 4 | 42 | 15.00 | 12.00 | 13.00 | 14.00 | 14.00 | 15.00 | 16.00 | 16.00 | 17.00 | 18.00 | 27.00 |
| 11 | 0.030 | 8 | 11 | 42 | 15.00 | 11.00 | 13.00 | 14.00 | 14.00 | 15.00 | 16.00 | 16.00 | 17.00 | 18.00 | 27.00 |
| 12 | 0.030 | 6 | 23 | 43 | 15.00 | 12.00 | 12.00 | 13.00 | 14.00 | 15.00 | 16.00 | 16.00 | 17.00 | 18.00 | 27.00 |
| 13 | 0.030 | 4 | 42 | 50 | 15.00 | 13.00 | 13.00 | 13.00 | 13.00 | 15.00 | 15.00 | 16.00 | 17.00 | 18.00 | 27.00 |
| 14 | 0.030 | 2 | 69 | 69 | 15.00 | 14.00 | 14.00 | 14.00 | 14.00 | 14.00 | 14.00 | 15.00 | 16.00 | 18.00 | 27.00 |

IMMUNIZED RETURN: 15 PERCENT                HORIZON: 6 YEARS                FORECAST ACCURACY: 45 PERCENT

| FLOOR RETURN | LEVERAGE FACTOR | DEG. OF FREEDOM | PROBABILITY OF TRIG. | PROBABILITY OF UNDER PERF. | EXPECTED RETURN | RETURN PERCENTILES | | | | | | | | | |
|---|---|---|---|---|---|---|---|---|---|---|---|---|---|---|---|
| | | | | | | 10 | 20 | 30 | 40 | 50 | 60 | 70 | 80 | 90 | 100 |
| 8 | 0.010 | 42 | 0 | 62 | 14.60 | 13.67 | 14.00 | 14.33 | 14.33 | 14.67 | 14.67 | 15.00 | 15.33 | 15.67 | 19.00 |
| 9 | 0.010 | 36 | 0 | 62 | 14.60 | 13.67 | 14.00 | 14.33 | 14.33 | 14.67 | 14.67 | 15.00 | 15.33 | 15.67 | 19.00 |
| 10 | 0.010 | 30 | 0 | 62 | 14.60 | 13.67 | 14.00 | 14.33 | 14.33 | 14.67 | 14.67 | 15.00 | 15.33 | 15.67 | 19.00 |
| 11 | 0.010 | 24 | 0 | 62 | 14.60 | 13.67 | 14.00 | 14.33 | 14.33 | 14.67 | 14.67 | 15.00 | 15.33 | 15.67 | 19.00 |
| 12 | 0.010 | 18 | 0 | 62 | 14.60 | 13.67 | 14.00 | 14.33 | 14.33 | 14.67 | 14.67 | 15.00 | 15.33 | 15.67 | 19.00 |
| 13 | 0.010 | 12 | 4 | 62 | 14.60 | 13.67 | 14.00 | 14.33 | 14.33 | 14.67 | 14.67 | 15.00 | 15.33 | 15.67 | 19.00 |
| 14 | 0.010 | 6 | 39 | 62 | 14.66 | 14.00 | 14.00 | 14.00 | 14.33 | 14.67 | 14.67 | 15.00 | 15.33 | 15.67 | 19.00 |
| 8 | 0.020 | 21 | 0 | 62 | 14.20 | 13.00 | 13.00 | 13.67 | 13.67 | 14.33 | 14.33 | 15.00 | 15.67 | 16.33 | 23.00 |
| 9 | 0.020 | 18 | 0 | 62 | 14.20 | 13.00 | 13.00 | 13.67 | 13.67 | 14.33 | 14.33 | 15.00 | 15.67 | 16.33 | 23.00 |
| 10 | 0.020 | 15 | 1 | 62 | 14.20 | 13.00 | 13.00 | 13.67 | 13.67 | 14.33 | 14.33 | 15.00 | 15.67 | 16.33 | 23.00 |
| 11 | 0.020 | 12 | 4 | 62 | 14.21 | 13.00 | 13.00 | 13.67 | 13.67 | 14.33 | 14.33 | 15.00 | 15.67 | 16.33 | 23.00 |
| 12 | 0.020 | 9 | 14 | 62 | 14.23 | 13.00 | 13.00 | 13.00 | 13.67 | 14.33 | 14.33 | 15.00 | 15.67 | 16.33 | 23.00 |
| 13 | 0.020 | 6 | 39 | 62 | 14.32 | 13.00 | 13.00 | 13.00 | 13.67 | 14.33 | 14.33 | 15.00 | 15.67 | 16.33 | 23.00 |
| 14 | 0.020 | 3 | 70 | 73 | 14.55 | 14.00 | 14.00 | 14.00 | 14.00 | 14.00 | 14.00 | 14.33 | 15.00 | 16.33 | 23.00 |
| 8 | 0.030 | 14 | 1 | 62 | 13.80 | 11.00 | 12.00 | 13.00 | 13.00 | 14.00 | 14.00 | 15.00 | 16.00 | 17.00 | 27.00 |
| 9 | 0.030 | 12 | 4 | 62 | 13.81 | 11.00 | 12.00 | 13.00 | 13.00 | 14.00 | 14.00 | 15.00 | 16.00 | 17.00 | 27.00 |
| 10 | 0.030 | 10 | 11 | 62 | 13.83 | 10.00 | 11.00 | 12.00 | 13.00 | 14.00 | 14.00 | 15.00 | 16.00 | 17.00 | 27.00 |
| 11 | 0.030 | 8 | 22 | 62 | 13.87 | 11.00 | 12.00 | 12.00 | 13.00 | 14.00 | 14.00 | 15.00 | 16.00 | 17.00 | 27.00 |
| 12 | 0.030 | 6 | 39 | 62 | 13.98 | 12.00 | 12.00 | 12.00 | 13.00 | 13.00 | 14.00 | 15.00 | 16.00 | 17.00 | 27.00 |
| 13 | 0.030 | 4 | 68 | 68 | 14.18 | 13.00 | 13.00 | 13.00 | 13.00 | 13.00 | 14.00 | 15.00 | 16.00 | 17.00 | 27.00 |
| 14 | 0.030 | 2 | 82 | 82 | 14.51 | 14.00 | 14.00 | 14.00 | 14.00 | 14.00 | 14.00 | 14.00 | 14.00 | 16.00 | 27.00 |

IMMUNIZED RETURN: 15 PERCENT    HORIZON: 6 YEARS    FORECAST ACCURACY: 40 PERCENT

| FLOOR RETURN | LEVERAGE FACTOR | DEG. OF FREEDOM | PROBABILITY OF TRIG. | PROBABILITY OF UNDER PERF. | EXPECTED RETURN | RETURN PERCENTILES | | | | | | | | | |
|---|---|---|---|---|---|---|---|---|---|---|---|---|---|---|---|
| | | | | | | 10 | 20 | 30 | 40 | 50 | 60 | 70 | 80 | 90 | 100 |
| 8 | 0.010 | 42 | 0 | 79 | 14.20 | 13.33 | 13.67 | 13.67 | 14.00 | 14.33 | 14.33 | 14.67 | 15.00 | 15.33 | 19.00 |
| 9 | 0.010 | 36 | 0 | 79 | 14.20 | 13.33 | 13.67 | 13.67 | 14.00 | 14.33 | 14.33 | 14.67 | 15.00 | 15.33 | 19.00 |
| 10 | 0.010 | 30 | 0 | 79 | 14.20 | 13.33 | 13.67 | 13.67 | 14.00 | 14.33 | 14.33 | 14.67 | 15.00 | 15.33 | 19.00 |
| 11 | 0.010 | 24 | 0 | 79 | 14.20 | 13.33 | 13.67 | 13.67 | 14.00 | 14.33 | 14.33 | 14.67 | 15.00 | 15.33 | 19.00 |
| 12 | 0.010 | 18 | 0 | 79 | 14.20 | 13.33 | 13.67 | 13.67 | 14.00 | 14.33 | 14.33 | 14.67 | 15.00 | 15.33 | 19.00 |
| 13 | 0.010 | 12 | 11 | 79 | 14.21 | 13.00 | 13.67 | 13.67 | 14.00 | 14.33 | 14.33 | 14.67 | 15.00 | 15.33 | 19.00 |
| 14 | 0.010 | 6 | 57 | 79 | 14.39 | 14.00 | 14.00 | 14.00 | 14.00 | 14.00 | 14.33 | 14.67 | 15.00 | 15.33 | 19.00 |
| 8 | 0.020 | 21 | 0 | 79 | 13.40 | 11.67 | 12.33 | 12.33 | 13.00 | 13.67 | 13.67 | 14.33 | 15.00 | 15.67 | 23.00 |
| 9 | 0.020 | 18 | 0 | 79 | 13.40 | 11.67 | 12.33 | 12.33 | 13.00 | 13.67 | 13.67 | 14.33 | 15.00 | 15.67 | 23.00 |
| 10 | 0.020 | 15 | 2 | 79 | 13.40 | 11.67 | 12.33 | 12.33 | 13.00 | 13.67 | 13.67 | 14.33 | 15.00 | 15.67 | 23.00 |
| 11 | 0.020 | 12 | 11 | 79 | 13.43 | 11.00 | 12.00 | 12.33 | 13.00 | 13.67 | 13.67 | 14.33 | 15.00 | 15.67 | 23.00 |
| 12 | 0.020 | 9 | 28 | 79 | 13.52 | 12.00 | 12.00 | 12.33 | 13.00 | 13.67 | 13.67 | 14.33 | 15.00 | 15.67 | 23.00 |
| 13 | 0.020 | 6 | 57 | 79 | 13.77 | 13.00 | 13.00 | 13.00 | 13.00 | 13.00 | 13.67 | 14.33 | 15.00 | 15.67 | 23.00 |
| 14 | 0.020 | 3 | 83 | 86 | 14.26 | 14.00 | 14.00 | 14.00 | 14.00 | 14.00 | 14.00 | 14.00 | 14.00 | 15.00 | 23.00 |
| 8 | 0.030 | 14 | 5 | 79 | 12.61 | 10.00 | 11.00 | 11.00 | 12.00 | 13.00 | 13.00 | 14.00 | 15.00 | 16.00 | 27.00 |
| 9 | 0.030 | 12 | 11 | 79 | 12.64 | 9.00 | 11.00 | 11.00 | 12.00 | 13.00 | 13.00 | 14.00 | 15.00 | 16.00 | 27.00 |
| 10 | 0.030 | 10 | 22 | 79 | 12.72 | 10.00 | 10.00 | 11.00 | 12.00 | 13.00 | 13.00 | 14.00 | 15.00 | 16.00 | 27.00 |
| 11 | 0.030 | 8 | 38 | 79 | 12.87 | 11.00 | 11.00 | 11.00 | 12.00 | 13.00 | 13.00 | 14.00 | 15.00 | 16.00 | 27.00 |
| 12 | 0.030 | 6 | 57 | 82 | 13.16 | 12.00 | 12.00 | 12.00 | 12.00 | 13.00 | 13.00 | 14.00 | 15.00 | 16.00 | 27.00 |
| 13 | 0.030 | 4 | 76 | 82 | 13.60 | 13.00 | 13.00 | 13.00 | 13.00 | 13.00 | 13.00 | 14.00 | 15.00 | 16.00 | 27.00 |
| 14 | 0.030 | 2 | 91 | 91 | 14.22 | 14.00 | 14.00 | 14.00 | 14.00 | 14.00 | 14.00 | 14.00 | 14.00 | 14.00 | 27.00 |

IMMUNIZED RETURN: 15 PERCENT  HORIZON: 7 YEARS  FORECAST ACCURACY: 60 PERCENT

| FLOOR RETURN | LEVERAGE FACTOR | DEG. OF FREEDOM | PROBABILITY OF TRIG. | PROBABILITY OF UNDER PERF. | EXPECTED RETURN | RETURN PERCENTILES | | | | | | | | | |
|---|---|---|---|---|---|---|---|---|---|---|---|---|---|---|---|
| | | | | | | 10 | 20 | 30 | 40 | 50 | 60 | 70 | 80 | 90 | 100 |
| 8 | 0.010 | 49 | 0 | 10 | 15.80 | 14.71 | 15.29 | 15.29 | 15.57 | 15.86 | 15.86 | 16.14 | 16.43 | 16.71 | 19.00 |
| 9 | 0.010 | 42 | 0 | 10 | 15.80 | 14.71 | 15.29 | 15.29 | 15.57 | 15.86 | 15.86 | 16.14 | 16.43 | 16.71 | 19.00 |
| 10 | 0.010 | 35 | 0 | 10 | 15.80 | 14.71 | 15.29 | 15.29 | 15.57 | 15.86 | 15.86 | 16.14 | 16.43 | 16.71 | 19.00 |
| 11 | 0.010 | 28 | 0 | 10 | 15.80 | 14.71 | 15.29 | 15.29 | 15.57 | 15.86 | 15.86 | 16.14 | 16.43 | 16.71 | 19.00 |
| 12 | 0.010 | 21 | 0 | 10 | 15.80 | 14.71 | 15.29 | 15.29 | 15.57 | 15.86 | 15.86 | 16.14 | 16.43 | 16.71 | 19.00 |
| 13 | 0.010 | 14 | 0 | 10 | 15.80 | 14.71 | 15.29 | 15.29 | 15.57 | 15.86 | 15.86 | 16.14 | 16.43 | 16.71 | 19.00 |
| 14 | 0.010 | 7 | 3 | 11 | 15.79 | 14.71 | 15.29 | 15.29 | 15.57 | 15.86 | 15.86 | 16.14 | 16.43 | 16.71 | 19.00 |
| 8 | 0.020 | 24 | 0 | 10 | 16.60 | 14.43 | 15.57 | 15.57 | 16.14 | 16.71 | 16.71 | 17.29 | 17.86 | 18.43 | 23.00 |
| 9 | 0.020 | 21 | 0 | 10 | 16.60 | 14.43 | 15.57 | 15.57 | 16.14 | 16.71 | 16.71 | 17.29 | 17.86 | 18.43 | 23.00 |
| 10 | 0.020 | 17 | 0 | 10 | 16.60 | 14.43 | 15.57 | 15.57 | 16.14 | 16.71 | 16.71 | 17.29 | 17.86 | 18.43 | 23.00 |
| 11 | 0.020 | 14 | 0 | 10 | 16.60 | 14.43 | 15.57 | 15.57 | 16.14 | 16.71 | 16.71 | 17.29 | 17.86 | 18.43 | 23.00 |
| 12 | 0.020 | 10 | 1 | 10 | 16.60 | 14.43 | 15.57 | 15.57 | 16.14 | 16.71 | 16.71 | 17.29 | 17.86 | 18.43 | 23.00 |
| 13 | 0.020 | 7 | 3 | 11 | 16.58 | 14.43 | 15.57 | 15.57 | 16.14 | 16.71 | 16.71 | 17.29 | 17.86 | 18.43 | 23.00 |
| 14 | 0.020 | 3 | 26 | 27 | 16.32 | 14.14 | 14.14 | 15.00 | 14.14 | 16.71 | 16.71 | 17.29 | 17.86 | 18.43 | 23.00 |
| 8 | 0.030 | 16 | 0 | 10 | 17.40 | 14.14 | 15.86 | 15.86 | 16.71 | 17.57 | 17.57 | 18.43 | 19.29 | 20.14 | 27.00 |
| 9 | 0.030 | 14 | 0 | 10 | 17.40 | 14.14 | 15.86 | 15.86 | 16.71 | 17.57 | 17.57 | 18.43 | 19.29 | 20.14 | 27.00 |
| 10 | 0.030 | 11 | 0 | 10 | 17.40 | 14.14 | 15.86 | 15.86 | 16.71 | 17.57 | 17.57 | 18.43 | 19.29 | 20.14 | 27.00 |
| 11 | 0.030 | 9 | 1 | 10 | 17.39 | 14.14 | 15.86 | 15.86 | 16.71 | 17.57 | 17.57 | 18.43 | 19.29 | 20.14 | 27.00 |
| 12 | 0.030 | 7 | 3 | 11 | 17.37 | 14.14 | 15.86 | 15.86 | 16.71 | 17.57 | 17.57 | 18.43 | 19.29 | 20.14 | 27.00 |
| 13 | 0.030 | 4 | 16 | 18 | 17.18 | 13.29 | 15.00 | 15.86 | 16.71 | 17.57 | 17.57 | 18.43 | 19.29 | 20.14 | 27.00 |
| 14 | 0.030 | 2 | 41 | 41 | 16.64 | 14.14 | 14.14 | 14.14 | 14.14 | 16.71 | 17.57 | 18.43 | 19.29 | 20.14 | 27.00 |

IMMUNIZED RETURN: 15 PERCENT  HORIZON: 7 YEARS  FORECAST ACCURACY: 55 PERCENT

| FLOOR RETURN | LEVERAGE FACTOR | DEG. OF FREEDOM | PROBABILITY OF TRIG. | PROBABILITY OF UNDER PERF. | EXPECTED RETURN | RETURN PERCENTILES | | | | | | | | | |
|---|---|---|---|---|---|---|---|---|---|---|---|---|---|---|---|
| | | | | | | 10 | 20 | 30 | 40 | 50 | 60 | 70 | 80 | 90 | 100 |
| 8  | 0.010 | 49 | 0 | 23 | 15.40 | 14.43 | 14.71 | 15.00 | 15.29 | 15.29 | 15.57 | 15.86 | 16.14 | 16.43 | 19.00 |
| 9  | 0.010 | 42 | 0 | 23 | 15.40 | 14.43 | 14.71 | 15.00 | 15.29 | 15.29 | 15.57 | 15.86 | 16.14 | 16.43 | 19.00 |
| 10 | 0.010 | 35 | 0 | 23 | 15.40 | 14.43 | 14.71 | 15.00 | 15.29 | 15.29 | 15.57 | 15.86 | 16.14 | 16.43 | 19.00 |
| 11 | 0.010 | 28 | 0 | 23 | 15.40 | 14.43 | 14.71 | 15.00 | 15.29 | 15.29 | 15.57 | 15.86 | 16.14 | 16.43 | 19.00 |
| 12 | 0.010 | 21 | 0 | 23 | 15.40 | 14.43 | 14.71 | 15.00 | 15.29 | 15.29 | 15.57 | 15.86 | 16.14 | 16.43 | 19.00 |
| 13 | 0.010 | 14 | 0 | 23 | 15.40 | 14.43 | 14.71 | 15.00 | 15.29 | 15.29 | 15.57 | 15.86 | 16.14 | 16.43 | 19.00 |
| 14 | 0.010 | 7  | 8 | 24 | 15.39 | 14.43 | 14.71 | 15.00 | 15.29 | 15.29 | 15.57 | 15.86 | 16.14 | 16.43 | 19.00 |
| 8  | 0.020 | 24 | 0  | 23 | 15.80 | 13.86 | 14.43 | 15.00 | 15.57 | 15.57 | 16.14 | 16.71 | 17.29 | 17.86 | 23.00 |
| 9  | 0.020 | 21 | 0  | 23 | 15.80 | 13.86 | 14.43 | 15.00 | 15.57 | 15.57 | 16.14 | 16.71 | 17.29 | 17.86 | 23.00 |
| 10 | 0.020 | 17 | 0  | 23 | 15.80 | 13.86 | 14.43 | 15.00 | 15.57 | 15.57 | 16.14 | 16.71 | 17.29 | 17.86 | 23.00 |
| 11 | 0.020 | 14 | 0  | 23 | 15.80 | 13.86 | 14.43 | 15.00 | 15.57 | 15.57 | 16.14 | 16.71 | 17.29 | 17.86 | 23.00 |
| 12 | 0.020 | 10 | 2  | 23 | 15.80 | 13.86 | 14.43 | 15.00 | 15.57 | 15.57 | 16.14 | 16.71 | 17.29 | 17.86 | 23.00 |
| 13 | 0.020 | 7  | 8  | 24 | 15.77 | 13.86 | 14.43 | 15.00 | 15.57 | 15.57 | 16.14 | 16.71 | 17.29 | 17.86 | 23.00 |
| 14 | 0.020 | 3  | 40 | 42 | 15.59 | 14.14 | 14.14 | 14.14 | 14.14 | 15.57 | 16.14 | 16.71 | 17.29 | 17.86 | 23.00 |
| 8  | 0.030 | 16 | 0  | 23 | 16.20 | 13.29 | 14.14 | 15.00 | 15.86 | 15.86 | 16.71 | 17.57 | 18.43 | 19.29 | 27.00 |
| 9  | 0.030 | 14 | 0  | 23 | 16.20 | 13.29 | 14.14 | 15.00 | 15.86 | 15.86 | 16.71 | 17.57 | 18.43 | 19.29 | 27.00 |
| 10 | 0.030 | 11 | 1  | 23 | 16.20 | 13.29 | 14.14 | 15.00 | 15.86 | 15.86 | 16.71 | 17.57 | 18.43 | 19.29 | 27.00 |
| 11 | 0.030 | 9  | 3  | 24 | 16.19 | 13.29 | 14.14 | 15.00 | 15.86 | 15.86 | 16.71 | 17.57 | 18.43 | 19.29 | 27.00 |
| 12 | 0.030 | 7  | 8  | 24 | 16.16 | 13.29 | 14.14 | 15.00 | 15.86 | 15.86 | 16.71 | 17.57 | 18.43 | 19.29 | 27.00 |
| 13 | 0.030 | 4  | 29 | 33 | 16.01 | 13.29 | 14.14 | 14.14 | 15.00 | 15.86 | 16.71 | 17.57 | 18.43 | 19.29 | 27.00 |
| 14 | 0.030 | 2  | 56 | 56 | 15.70 | 14.14 | 14.14 | 14.14 | 14.14 | 14.14 | 15.86 | 16.71 | 17.57 | 19.29 | 27.00 |

IMMUNIZED RETURN: 15 PERCENT          HORIZON: 7 YEARS                    FORECAST ACCURACY: 50 PERCENT

| FLOOR RETURN | LEVERAGE FACTOR | DEG. OF FREEDOM | PROBABILITY OF TRIG. | PROBABILITY OF UNDER PERF. | EXPECTED RETURN | RETURN PERCENTILES | | | | | | | | | |
|---|---|---|---|---|---|---|---|---|---|---|---|---|---|---|---|
| | | | | | | 10 | 20 | 30 | 40 | 50 | 60 | 70 | 80 | 90 | 100 |
| 8 | 0.010 | 49 | 0 | 43 | 15.00 | 14.14 | 14.43 | 14.71 | 14.71 | 15.00 | 15.29 | 15.29 | 15.57 | 15.86 | 19.00 |
| 9 | 0.010 | 42 | 0 | 43 | 15.00 | 14.14 | 14.43 | 14.71 | 14.71 | 15.00 | 15.29 | 15.29 | 15.57 | 15.86 | 19.00 |
| 10 | 0.010 | 35 | 0 | 43 | 15.00 | 14.14 | 14.43 | 14.71 | 14.71 | 15.00 | 15.29 | 15.29 | 15.57 | 15.86 | 19.00 |
| 11 | 0.010 | 28 | 0 | 43 | 15.00 | 14.14 | 14.43 | 14.71 | 14.71 | 15.00 | 15.29 | 15.29 | 15.57 | 15.86 | 19.00 |
| 12 | 0.010 | 21 | 0 | 43 | 15.00 | 14.14 | 14.43 | 14.71 | 14.71 | 15.00 | 15.29 | 15.29 | 15.57 | 15.86 | 19.00 |
| 13 | 0.010 | 14 | 1 | 43 | 15.00 | 14.14 | 14.43 | 14.71 | 14.71 | 15.00 | 15.29 | 15.29 | 15.57 | 15.86 | 19.00 |
| 14 | 0.010 | 7 | 18 | 43 | 15.00 | 14.00 | 14.14 | 14.43 | 14.71 | 15.00 | 15.29 | 15.29 | 15.57 | 15.86 | 19.00 |
| 8 | 0.020 | 24 | 0 | 43 | 15.00 | 13.29 | 13.86 | 14.43 | 14.43 | 15.00 | 15.57 | 15.57 | 16.14 | 16.71 | 23.00 |
| 9 | 0.020 | 21 | 0 | 43 | 15.00 | 13.29 | 13.86 | 14.43 | 14.43 | 15.00 | 15.57 | 15.57 | 16.14 | 16.71 | 23.00 |
| 10 | 0.020 | 17 | 0 | 43 | 15.00 | 13.29 | 13.86 | 14.43 | 14.43 | 15.00 | 15.57 | 15.57 | 16.14 | 16.71 | 23.00 |
| 11 | 0.020 | 14 | 1 | 43 | 15.00 | 13.29 | 13.86 | 14.43 | 14.43 | 15.00 | 15.57 | 15.57 | 16.14 | 16.71 | 23.00 |
| 12 | 0.020 | 10 | 6 | 43 | 15.00 | 13.29 | 13.86 | 14.43 | 14.43 | 15.00 | 15.57 | 15.57 | 16.14 | 16.71 | 23.00 |
| 13 | 0.020 | 7 | 18 | 43 | 15.00 | 13.00 | 13.29 | 13.86 | 14.43 | 15.00 | 15.57 | 15.57 | 16.14 | 16.71 | 23.00 |
| 14 | 0.020 | 3 | 57 | 60 | 15.00 | 14.14 | 14.14 | 14.14 | 14.14 | 14.14 | 15.00 | 15.57 | 16.14 | 16.71 | 23.00 |
| 8 | 0.030 | 16 | 0 | 43 | 15.00 | 12.43 | 13.29 | 14.14 | 14.14 | 15.00 | 15.86 | 15.86 | 16.71 | 17.57 | 27.00 |
| 9 | 0.030 | 14 | 1 | 43 | 15.00 | 12.43 | 13.29 | 14.14 | 14.14 | 15.00 | 15.86 | 15.86 | 16.71 | 17.57 | 27.00 |
| 10 | 0.030 | 11 | 4 | 43 | 15.00 | 12.43 | 13.29 | 14.14 | 14.14 | 15.00 | 15.86 | 15.86 | 16.71 | 17.57 | 27.00 |
| 11 | 0.030 | 9 | 9 | 43 | 15.00 | 11.57 | 13.29 | 14.14 | 14.14 | 15.00 | 15.86 | 15.86 | 16.71 | 17.57 | 27.00 |
| 12 | 0.030 | 7 | 18 | 43 | 15.00 | 12.00 | 12.43 | 13.29 | 14.14 | 15.00 | 15.86 | 15.86 | 16.71 | 17.57 | 27.00 |
| 13 | 0.030 | 4 | 46 | 52 | 15.00 | 13.29 | 13.29 | 13.29 | 13.29 | 14.14 | 15.00 | 15.86 | 16.71 | 17.57 | 27.00 |
| 14 | 0.030 | 2 | 71 | 71 | 15.00 | 14.14 | 14.14 | 14.14 | 14.14 | 14.14 | 14.14 | 14.14 | 15.86 | 17.57 | 27.00 |

IMMUNIZED RETURN: 15 PERCENT          HORIZON: 7 YEARS          FORECAST ACCURACY: 45 PERCENT

| FLOOR RETURN | LEVERAGE FACTOR | DEG. OF FREEDOM | PROBABILITY OF TRIG. | PROBABILITY OF UNDER PERF. | EXPECTED RETURN | RETURN PERCENTILES | | | | | | | | | |
|---|---|---|---|---|---|---|---|---|---|---|---|---|---|---|---|
| | | | | | | 10 | 20 | 30 | 40 | 50 | 60 | 70 | 80 | 90 | 100 |
| 8 | 0.010 | 49 | 0 | 64 | 14.60 | 13.57 | 13.86 | 14.14 | 14.43 | 14.71 | 14.71 | 15.00 | 15.29 | 15.57 | 19.00 |
| 9 | 0.010 | 42 | 0 | 64 | 14.60 | 13.57 | 13.86 | 14.14 | 14.43 | 14.71 | 14.71 | 15.00 | 15.29 | 15.57 | 19.00 |
| 10 | 0.010 | 35 | 0 | 64 | 14.60 | 13.57 | 13.86 | 14.14 | 14.43 | 14.71 | 14.71 | 15.00 | 15.29 | 15.57 | 19.00 |
| 11 | 0.010 | 28 | 0 | 64 | 14.60 | 13.57 | 13.86 | 14.14 | 14.43 | 14.71 | 14.71 | 15.00 | 15.29 | 15.57 | 19.00 |
| 12 | 0.010 | 21 | 0 | 64 | 14.60 | 13.57 | 13.86 | 14.14 | 14.43 | 14.71 | 14.71 | 15.00 | 15.29 | 15.57 | 19.00 |
| 13 | 0.010 | 14 | 3 | 64 | 14.60 | 13.57 | 13.86 | 14.14 | 14.43 | 14.71 | 14.71 | 15.00 | 15.29 | 15.57 | 19.00 |
| 14 | 0.010 | 7 | 34 | 64 | 14.65 | 14.00 | 14.00 | 14.00 | 14.43 | 14.71 | 14.71 | 15.00 | 15.29 | 15.57 | 19.00 |
| 8 | 0.020 | 24 | 0 | 64 | 14.20 | 12.14 | 12.71 | 13.29 | 13.86 | 14.43 | 14.43 | 15.00 | 15.57 | 16.14 | 23.00 |
| 9 | 0.020 | 21 | 0 | 64 | 14.20 | 12.14 | 12.71 | 13.29 | 13.86 | 14.43 | 14.43 | 15.00 | 15.57 | 16.14 | 23.00 |
| 10 | 0.020 | 17 | 0 | 64 | 14.20 | 12.14 | 12.71 | 13.29 | 13.86 | 14.43 | 14.43 | 15.00 | 15.57 | 16.14 | 23.00 |
| 11 | 0.020 | 14 | 3 | 64 | 14.20 | 12.14 | 12.71 | 13.29 | 13.86 | 14.43 | 14.43 | 15.00 | 15.57 | 16.14 | 23.00 |
| 12 | 0.020 | 10 | 15 | 64 | 14.23 | 12.14 | 12.71 | 13.29 | 13.86 | 14.43 | 14.43 | 15.00 | 15.57 | 16.14 | 23.00 |
| 13 | 0.020 | 7 | 34 | 64 | 14.30 | 13.00 | 13.00 | 13.00 | 13.86 | 13.86 | 13.86 | 15.00 | 15.57 | 16.14 | 23.00 |
| 14 | 0.020 | 3 | 73 | 76 | 14.58 | 14.14 | 14.14 | 14.14 | 14.14 | 14.14 | 14.14 | 14.14 | 15.00 | 16.14 | 23.00 |
| 8 | 0.030 | 16 | 1 | 64 | 13.80 | 10.71 | 11.57 | 12.43 | 13.29 | 14.14 | 14.14 | 15.00 | 15.86 | 16.71 | 27.00 |
| 9 | 0.030 | 14 | 3 | 64 | 13.80 | 10.71 | 11.57 | 12.43 | 13.29 | 14.14 | 14.14 | 15.00 | 15.86 | 16.71 | 27.00 |
| 10 | 0.030 | 11 | 10 | 64 | 13.83 | 10.71 | 11.57 | 12.43 | 13.29 | 14.14 | 14.14 | 15.00 | 15.86 | 16.71 | 27.00 |
| 11 | 0.030 | 9 | 19 | 64 | 13.87 | 11.14 | 11.57 | 12.43 | 13.29 | 14.14 | 14.14 | 15.00 | 15.86 | 16.71 | 27.00 |
| 12 | 0.030 | 7 | 34 | 64 | 13.95 | 12.00 | 12.00 | 12.43 | 13.29 | 14.14 | 14.14 | 15.00 | 15.86 | 16.71 | 27.00 |
| 13 | 0.030 | 4 | 64 | 71 | 14.23 | 13.29 | 13.29 | 13.29 | 13.29 | 13.29 | 13.29 | 14.14 | 15.86 | 16.71 | 27.00 |
| 14 | 0.030 | 2 | 84 | 84 | 14.55 | 14.14 | 14.14 | 14.14 | 14.14 | 14.14 | 14.14 | 14.14 | 14.14 | 15.86 | 27.00 |

IMMUNIZED RETURN: 15 PERCENT                HORIZON: 7 YEARS                FORECAST ACCURACY: 40 PERCENT

| FLOOR RETURN | LEVERAGE FACTOR | DEG. OF FREEDOM | PROBABILITY OF TRIG. | PROBABILITY OF UNDER PERF. | EXPECTED RETURN | RETURN PERCENTILES | | | | | | | | | |
|---|---|---|---|---|---|---|---|---|---|---|---|---|---|---|---|
| | | | | | | 10 | 20 | 30 | 40 | 50 | 60 | 70 | 80 | 90 | 100 |
| 8 | 0.010 | 49 | 0 | 81 | 14.20 | 13.29 | 13.57 | 13.86 | 14.14 | 14.14 | 14.43 | 14.71 | 14.71 | 15.29 | 19.00 |
| 9 | 0.010 | 42 | 0 | 81 | 14.20 | 13.29 | 13.57 | 13.86 | 14.14 | 14.14 | 14.43 | 14.71 | 14.71 | 15.29 | 19.00 |
| 10 | 0.010 | 35 | 0 | 81 | 14.20 | 13.29 | 13.57 | 13.86 | 14.14 | 14.14 | 14.43 | 14.71 | 14.71 | 15.29 | 19.00 |
| 11 | 0.010 | 28 | 0 | 81 | 14.20 | 13.29 | 13.57 | 13.86 | 14.14 | 14.14 | 14.43 | 14.71 | 14.71 | 15.29 | 19.00 |
| 12 | 0.010 | 21 | 0 | 81 | 14.20 | 13.29 | 13.57 | 13.86 | 14.14 | 14.14 | 14.43 | 14.71 | 14.71 | 15.29 | 19.00 |
| 13 | 0.010 | 14 | 8 | 81 | 14.21 | 13.29 | 13.57 | 13.86 | 14.14 | 14.14 | 14.43 | 14.71 | 14.71 | 15.29 | 19.00 |
| 14 | 0.010 | 7 | 54 | 82 | 14.37 | 14.00 | 14.00 | 14.00 | 14.00 | 14.00 | 14.43 | 14.43 | 14.71 | 15.29 | 19.00 |
| 8 | 0.020 | 24 | 0 | 81 | 13.40 | 11.57 | 12.14 | 12.71 | 13.29 | 13.29 | 13.86 | 14.43 | 14.43 | 15.57 | 23.00 |
| 9 | 0.020 | 21 | 0 | 81 | 13.40 | 11.57 | 12.14 | 12.71 | 13.29 | 13.29 | 13.86 | 14.43 | 14.43 | 15.57 | 23.00 |
| 10 | 0.020 | 17 | 2 | 81 | 13.40 | 11.57 | 12.14 | 12.71 | 13.29 | 13.29 | 13.86 | 14.43 | 14.43 | 15.57 | 23.00 |
| 11 | 0.020 | 14 | 8 | 81 | 13.42 | 11.57 | 12.14 | 12.71 | 13.29 | 13.29 | 13.86 | 14.43 | 14.43 | 15.57 | 23.00 |
| 12 | 0.020 | 10 | 30 | 81 | 13.52 | 12.14 | 12.14 | 12.71 | 13.29 | 13.29 | 13.86 | 14.43 | 14.43 | 15.57 | 23.00 |
| 13 | 0.020 | 7 | 54 | 82 | 13.74 | 13.00 | 13.00 | 13.00 | 13.00 | 13.00 | 13.86 | 13.86 | 14.43 | 15.57 | 23.00 |
| 14 | 0.020 | 3 | 86 | 89 | 14.33 | 14.14 | 14.14 | 14.14 | 14.14 | 14.14 | 14.14 | 14.14 | 14.14 | 15.00 | 23.00 |
| 8 | 0.030 | 16 | 4 | 81 | 12.61 | 9.86 | 10.71 | 11.57 | 12.43 | 12.43 | 13.29 | 14.14 | 14.14 | 15.86 | 27.00 |
| 9 | 0.030 | 14 | 8 | 81 | 12.63 | 9.86 | 10.71 | 11.57 | 12.43 | 12.43 | 13.29 | 14.14 | 14.14 | 15.86 | 27.00 |
| 10 | 0.030 | 11 | 21 | 81 | 12.72 | 10.29 | 10.29 | 11.57 | 12.43 | 12.43 | 13.29 | 14.14 | 14.14 | 15.86 | 27.00 |
| 11 | 0.030 | 9 | 36 | 81 | 12.87 | 11.14 | 11.14 | 11.14 | 11.57 | 12.43 | 13.29 | 14.14 | 14.14 | 15.86 | 27.00 |
| 12 | 0.030 | 7 | 54 | 82 | 13.11 | 12.00 | 12.00 | 11.14 | 12.00 | 12.00 | 13.29 | 14.14 | 13.29 | 15.86 | 27.00 |
| 13 | 0.030 | 4 | 80 | 85 | 13.72 | 13.29 | 13.29 | 13.29 | 13.29 | 13.29 | 13.29 | 13.29 | 13.29 | 15.00 | 27.00 |
| 14 | 0.030 | 2 | 93 | 93 | 14.30 | 14.14 | 14.14 | 14.14 | 14.14 | 14.14 | 14.14 | 14.14 | 14.14 | 14.14 | 27.00 |

IMMUNIZED RETURN: 15 PERCENT     HORIZON: 3 YEARS     FORECAST ACCURACY: 60 PERCENT

| FLOOR RETURN | LEVERAGE FACTOR | DEG. OF FREEDOM | PROBABILITY OF TRIG. | COND. EXPECTED TRIG. TIME | CONDITIONAL PROB. OF TRIG. IN YEAR 1 | 2 | 3 |
|---|---|---|---|---|---|---|---|
| 8  | 0.010 | 21 | 0.00  | 0.00 | 0.00  | 0.00  | 0.00   |
| 9  | 0.010 | 18 | 0.00  | 0.00 | 0.00  | 0.00  | 0.00   |
| 10 | 0.010 | 15 | 0.00  | 0.00 | 0.00  | 0.00  | 0.00   |
| 11 | 0.010 | 12 | 0.00  | 3.00 | 0.00  | 0.00  | 100.00 |
| 12 | 0.010 | 9  | 0.08  | 2.59 | 0.00  | 0.00  | 100.00 |
| 13 | 0.010 | 6  | 2.26  | 2.33 | 0.00  | 44.24 | 55.76  |
| 14 | 0.010 | 3  | 18.71 | 1.45 | 34.20 | 42.35 | 23.45  |
| 8  | 0.020 | 10 | 0.04  | 2.85 | 0.00  | 0.00  | 100.00 |
| 9  | 0.020 | 9  | 0.08  | 2.59 | 0.00  | 0.00  | 100.00 |
| 10 | 0.020 | 7  | 0.77  | 2.36 | 0.00  | 21.29 | 78.71  |
| 11 | 0.020 | 6  | 2.26  | 2.33 | 0.00  | 44.24 | 55.76  |
| 12 | 0.020 | 4  | 10.18 | 1.65 | 25.14 | 44.41 | 30.45  |
| 13 | 0.020 | 3  | 18.71 | 1.45 | 34.20 | 42.35 | 23.45  |
| 14 | 0.020 | 1  | 60.17 | 0.59 | 82.44 | 12.25 | 5.31   |
| 8  | 0.030 | 7  | 0.77  | 2.36 | 0.00  | 21.29 | 78.71  |
| 9  | 0.030 | 6  | 2.26  | 2.33 | 0.00  | 44.24 | 55.76  |
| 10 | 0.030 | 5  | 4.49  | 2.00 | 0.00  | 50.13 | 49.87  |
| 11 | 0.030 | 4  | 10.18 | 1.65 | 25.14 | 44.41 | 30.45  |
| 12 | 0.030 | 3  | 18.71 | 1.45 | 34.20 | 42.35 | 23.45  |
| 13 | 0.030 | 2  | 35.30 | 1.12 | 67.09 | 21.83 | 11.08  |
| 14 | 0.030 | 1  | 60.17 | 0.59 | 82.44 | 12.25 | 5.31   |

IMMUNIZED RETURN: 15 PERCENT          HORIZON: 3 YEARS          FORECAST ACCURACY: 55 PERCENT

| FLOOR RETURN | LEVERAGE FACTOR | DEG. OF FREEDOM | PROBABILITY OF TRIG. | COND. EXPECTED TRIG. TIME | CONDITIONAL PROB. OF TRIG. IN YEAR 1 | 2 | 3 |
|---|---|---|---|---|---|---|---|
| 8  | 0.010 | 21 | 0.00  | 0.00 | 0.00  | 0.00  | 0.00   |
| 9  | 0.010 | 18 | 0.00  | 0.00 | 0.00  | 0.00  | 0.00   |
| 10 | 0.010 | 15 | 0.00  | 0.00 | 0.00  | 0.00  | 0.00   |
| 11 | 0.010 | 12 | 0.01  | 3.00 | 0.00  | 0.00  | 100.00 |
| 12 | 0.010 | 9  | 0.24  | 2.60 | 0.00  | 0.00  | 100.00 |
| 13 | 0.010 | 6  | 4.82  | 2.34 | 0.00  | 42.80 | 57.20  |
| 14 | 0.010 | 3  | 27.85 | 1.48 | 32.72 | 42.34 | 24.94  |
| 8  | 0.020 | 10 | 0.12  | 2.86 | 0.00  | 0.00  | 100.00 |
| 9  | 0.020 | 9  | 0.24  | 2.60 | 0.00  | 0.00  | 100.00 |
| 10 | 0.020 | 7  | 1.82  | 2.37 | 0.00  | 20.51 | 79.49  |
| 11 | 0.020 | 6  | 4.82  | 2.34 | 0.00  | 42.80 | 57.20  |
| 12 | 0.020 | 4  | 17.20 | 1.88 | 23.84 | 44.05 | 32.11  |
| 13 | 0.020 | 3  | 27.85 | 1.48 | 32.72 | 42.34 | 24.94  |
| 14 | 0.020 | 1  | 69.18 | 0.62 | 81.15 | 12.90 | 5.95   |
| 8  | 0.030 | 7  | 1.82  | 2.37 | 0.00  | 20.51 | 79.49  |
| 9  | 0.030 | 6  | 4.82  | 2.34 | 0.00  | 42.80 | 57.20  |
| 10 | 0.030 | 5  | 8.49  | 2.02 | 0.00  | 48.64 | 51.36  |
| 11 | 0.030 | 4  | 17.20 | 1.88 | 23.84 | 44.05 | 32.11  |
| 12 | 0.030 | 3  | 27.85 | 1.48 | 32.72 | 42.34 | 24.94  |
| 13 | 0.030 | 2  | 46.45 | 1.15 | 65.18 | 22.61 | 12.22  |
| 14 | 0.030 | 1  | 69.18 | 0.62 | 81.15 | 12.90 | 5.95   |

IMMUNIZED RETURN: 15 PERCENT   HORIZON: 3 YEARS   FORECAST ACCURACY: 50 PERCENT

| FLOOR RETURN | LEVERAGE FACTOR | DEG. OF FREEDOM | PROBABILITY OF TRIG. | COND. EXPECTED TRIG. TIME | CONDITIONAL PROB. OF TRIG. IN YEAR | | |
|---|---|---|---|---|---|---|---|
| | | | | | 1 | 2 | 3 |
| 8 | 0.010 | 21 | 0.00 | 0.00 | 0.00 | 0.00 | 0.00 |
| 9 | 0.010 | 18 | 0.00 | 0.00 | 0.00 | 0.00 | 0.00 |
| 10 | 0.010 | 15 | 0.00 | 0.00 | 0.00 | 0.00 | 0.00 |
| 11 | 0.010 | 12 | 0.02 | 3.00 | 0.00 | 0.00 | 100.00 |
| 12 | 0.010 | 9 | 0.63 | 2.60 | 0.00 | 0.00 | 100.00 |
| 13 | 0.010 | 6 | 9.23 | 2.35 | 0.00 | 42.33 | 57.67 |
| 14 | 0.010 | 3 | 38.77 | 1.49 | 32.24 | 42.32 | 25.44 |
| 8 | 0.020 | 10 | 0.34 | 2.86 | 0.00 | 0.00 | 100.00 |
| 9 | 0.020 | 9 | 0.63 | 2.60 | 0.00 | 0.00 | 100.00 |
| 10 | 0.020 | 7 | 3.86 | 2.37 | 0.00 | 20.25 | 79.75 |
| 11 | 0.020 | 6 | 9.23 | 2.35 | 0.00 | 42.33 | 57.67 |
| 12 | 0.020 | 4 | 26.68 | 1.89 | 23.42 | 43.92 | 32.66 |
| 13 | 0.020 | 3 | 38.77 | 1.49 | 32.24 | 42.32 | 25.44 |
| 14 | 0.020 | 1 | 77.44 | 0.62 | 80.71 | 13.11 | 6.18 |
| 8 | 0.030 | 7 | 3.06 | 2.37 | 0.00 | 20.25 | 79.75 |
| 9 | 0.030 | 6 | 9.23 | 2.35 | 0.00 | 42.33 | 57.67 |
| 10 | 0.030 | 5 | 14.60 | 2.03 | 0.00 | 46.16 | 51.84 |
| 11 | 0.030 | 4 | 26.68 | 1.89 | 23.42 | 43.92 | 32.66 |
| 12 | 0.030 | 3 | 38.77 | 1.49 | 32.24 | 42.32 | 25.44 |
| 13 | 0.030 | 2 | 58.11 | 1.16 | 64.54 | 22.86 | 12.61 |
| 14 | 0.030 | 1 | 77.44 | 0.62 | 80.71 | 13.11 | 6.18 |

IMMUNIZED RETURN: 15 PERCENT　　　　　HORIZON: 3 YEARS　　　　　FORECAST ACCURACY: 45 PERCENT

| FLOOR RETURN | LEVERAGE FACTOR | DEG. OF FREEDOM | PROBABILITY OF TRIG. | COND. EXPECTED TRIG. TIME | CONDITIONAL PROB. OF TRIG. IN YEAR | | |
|---|---|---|---|---|---|---|---|
| | | | | | 1 | 2 | 3 |
| 8 | 0.010 | 21 | 0.00 | 0.00 | 0.00 | 0.00 | 0.00 |
| 9 | 0.010 | 18 | 0.00 | 0.00 | 0.00 | 0.00 | 0.00 |
| 10 | 0.010 | 15 | 0.00 | 0.00 | 0.00 | 0.00 | 0.00 |
| 11 | 0.010 | 12 | 0.08 | 3.00 | 0.00 | 0.00 | 100.00 |
| 12 | 0.010 | 9 | 1.49 | 2.60 | 0.00 | 0.00 | 100.00 |
| 13 | 0.010 | 6 | 16.07 | 2.34 | 0.00 | 42.80 | 57.20 |
| 14 | 0.010 | 3 | 50.84 | 1.48 | 32.72 | 42.34 | 24.94 |
| 8 | 0.020 | 10 | 0.88 | 2.86 | 0.00 | 0.00 | 100.00 |
| 9 | 0.020 | 9 | 1.49 | 2.60 | 0.00 | 0.00 | 100.00 |
| 10 | 0.020 | 7 | 7.42 | 2.37 | 0.00 | 20.51 | 79.49 |
| 11 | 0.020 | 6 | 16.07 | 2.34 | 0.00 | 42.80 | 57.20 |
| 12 | 0.020 | 4 | 38.38 | 1.88 | 23.84 | 44.05 | 32.11 |
| 13 | 0.020 | 3 | 50.84 | 1.48 | 32.72 | 42.34 | 24.94 |
| 14 | 0.020 | 1 | 84.55 | 0.62 | 81.15 | 12.90 | 5.95 |
| 8 | 0.030 | 7 | 7.42 | 2.37 | 0.00 | 20.51 | 79.49 |
| 9 | 0.030 | 6 | 16.07 | 2.34 | 0.00 | 42.80 | 57.20 |
| 10 | 0.030 | 5 | 23.15 | 2.02 | 0.00 | 48.64 | 51.36 |
| 11 | 0.030 | 4 | 38.38 | 1.88 | 23.84 | 44.05 | 32.11 |
| 12 | 0.030 | 3 | 50.84 | 1.48 | 32.72 | 42.34 | 24.94 |
| 13 | 0.030 | 2 | 69.39 | 1.15 | 65.18 | 22.61 | 12.22 |
| 14 | 0.030 | 1 | 84.55 | 0.62 | 81.15 | 12.90 | 5.95 |

IMMUNIZED RETURN: 15 PERCENT                HORIZON: 3 YEARS                    FORECAST ACCURACY: 40 PERCENT

| FLOOR RETURN | LEVERAGE FACTOR | DEG. OF FREEDOM | PROBABILITY OF TRIG. | COND. EXPECTED TRIG. TIME | CONDITIONAL PROB. OF TRIG. IN YEAR | | |
|---|---|---|---|---|---|---|---|
| | | | | | 1 | 2 | 3 |
| 8 | 0.010 | 21 | 0.00 | 0.00 | 0.00 | 0.00 | 0.00 |
| 9 | 0.010 | 18 | 0.00 | 0.00 | 0.00 | 0.00 | 0.00 |
| 10 | 0.010 | 15 | 0.00 | 0.00 | 0.00 | 0.00 | 0.00 |
| 11 | 0.010 | 12 | 0.22 | 3.00 | 0.00 | 0.00 | 100.00 |
| 12 | 0.010 | 9 | 3.18 | 2.59 | 0.00 | 0.00 | 100.00 |
| 13 | 0.010 | 6 | 25.73 | 2.33 | 0.00 | 44.24 | 55.76 |
| 14 | 0.010 | 3 | 63.16 | 1.45 | 34.20 | 42.35 | 23.45 |
| 8 | 0.020 | 10 | 2.06 | 2.85 | 0.00 | 0.00 | 100.00 |
| 9 | 0.020 | 9 | 3.18 | 2.59 | 0.00 | 0.00 | 100.00 |
| 10 | 0.020 | 7 | 13.15 | 2.36 | 0.00 | 21.29 | 78.71 |
| 11 | 0.020 | 6 | 25.73 | 2.33 | 0.00 | 44.24 | 55.76 |
| 12 | 0.020 | 4 | 51.55 | 1.85 | 25.14 | 44.41 | 30.45 |
| 13 | 0.020 | 3 | 63.16 | 1.45 | 34.20 | 42.35 | 23.45 |
| 14 | 0.020 | 1 | 90.25 | 0.59 | 82.44 | 12.25 | 5.31 |
| 8 | 0.030 | 7 | 13.15 | 2.36 | 0.00 | 21.29 | 78.71 |
| 9 | 0.030 | 6 | 25.73 | 2.33 | 0.00 | 44.24 | 55.76 |
| 10 | 0.030 | 5 | 34.13 | 2.00 | 0.00 | 50.13 | 49.87 |
| 11 | 0.030 | 4 | 51.55 | 1.85 | 25.14 | 44.41 | 30.45 |
| 12 | 0.030 | 3 | 63.16 | 1.45 | 34.20 | 42.35 | 23.45 |
| 13 | 0.030 | 2 | 79.42 | 1.12 | 67.09 | 21.83 | 11.08 |
| 14 | 0.030 | 1 | 90.25 | 0.59 | 82.44 | 12.25 | 5.31 |

IMMUNIZED RETURN: 15 PERCENT     HORIZON: 4 YEARS     FORECAST ACCURACY: 60 PERCENT

| FLOUR RETURN | LEVERAGE FACTOR | DEG. OF FREEDOM | PROBABILITY OF TRIG. | COND. EXPECTED TRIG. TIME | CONDITIONAL PROB. OF TRIG. IN YEAR | | | |
|---|---|---|---|---|---|---|---|---|
| | | | | | 1 | 2 | 3 | 4 |
| 8 | 0.010 | 28 | 0.00 | 0.00 | 0.00 | 0.00 | 0.00 | 0.00 |
| 9 | 0.010 | 24 | 0.00 | 0.00 | 0.00 | 0.00 | 0.00 | 0.00 |
| 10 | 0.010 | 20 | 0.00 | 0.00 | 0.00 | 0.00 | 0.00 | 0.00 |
| 11 | 0.010 | 16 | 0.00 | 4.00 | 0.00 | 0.00 | 0.00 | 100.00 |
| 12 | 0.010 | 12 | 0.02 | 3.73 | 0.00 | 0.00 | 11.03 | 88.97 |
| 13 | 0.010 | 8 | 0.74 | 3.22 | 0.00 | 8.81 | 39.25 | 51.94 |
| 14 | 0.010 | 4 | 12.33 | 2.18 | 20.77 | 36.68 | 25.15 | 17.40 |
| 8 | 0.020 | 14 | 0.00 | 3.89 | 0.00 | 0.00 | 0.00 | 100.00 |
| 9 | 0.020 | 12 | 0.02 | 3.73 | 0.00 | 0.00 | 11.03 | 86.97 |
| 10 | 0.020 | 10 | 0.13 | 3.52 | 0.00 | 0.00 | 28.37 | 71.63 |
| 11 | 0.020 | 8 | 0.74 | 3.22 | 0.00 | 8.81 | 39.25 | 51.94 |
| 12 | 0.020 | 6 | 3.38 | 2.79 | 0.00 | 29.60 | 37.31 | 33.09 |
| 13 | 0.020 | 4 | 12.33 | 2.18 | 20.77 | 36.68 | 25.15 | 17.40 |
| 14 | 0.020 | 2 | 37.66 | 1.28 | 62.88 | 20.46 | 10.39 | 6.27 |
| 8 | 0.030 | 9 | 0.26 | 3.23 | 0.00 | 0.00 | 31.46 | 68.54 |
| 9 | 0.030 | 8 | 0.74 | 3.22 | 0.00 | 8.81 | 39.25 | 51.94 |
| 10 | 0.030 | 6 | 3.38 | 2.79 | 0.00 | 29.60 | 37.31 | 33.09 |
| 11 | 0.030 | 4 | 6.24 | 2.42 | 0.00 | 36.08 | 35.89 | 28.03 |
| 12 | 0.030 | 4 | 12.33 | 2.18 | 20.77 | 36.68 | 25.15 | 17.40 |
| 13 | 0.030 | 2 | 37.66 | 1.28 | 62.88 | 20.46 | 10.39 | 6.27 |
| 14 | 0.030 | 1 | 61.96 | 0.68 | 80.05 | 11.90 | 5.16 | 2.90 |

IMMUNIZED RETURN: 15 PERCENT          HORIZON: 4 YEARS          FORECAST ACCURACY: 55 PERCENT

| FLOOR RETURN | LEVERAGE FACTOR | DEG. OF FREEDOM | PROBABILITY OF TRIG. | COND. EXPECTED TRIG. TIME | CONDITIONAL PROB. OF TRIG. IN YEAR | | | |
|---|---|---|---|---|---|---|---|---|
| | | | | | 1 | 2 | 3 | 4 |
| 8 | 0.010 | 28 | 0.00 | 0.00 | 0.00 | 0.00 | 0.00 | 0.00 |
| 9 | 0.010 | 24 | 0.00 | 0.00 | 0.00 | 0.00 | 0.00 | 0.00 |
| 10 | 0.010 | 20 | 0.00 | 0.00 | 0.00 | 0.00 | 0.00 | 0.00 |
| 11 | 0.010 | 16 | 0.00 | 4.00 | 0.00 | 0.00 | 0.00 | 100.00 |
| 12 | 0.010 | 12 | 0.07 | 3.74 | 0.00 | 0.00 | 10.55 | 89.45 |
| 13 | 0.010 | 8 | 2.06 | 3.25 | 0.00 | 8.17 | 38.19 | 53.65 |
| 14 | 0.010 | 4 | 21.27 | 2.23 | 19.28 | 35.63 | 25.97 | 19.12 |
| 8 | 0.020 | 14 | 0.01 | 3.89 | 0.00 | 0.00 | 0.00 | 100.00 |
| 9 | 0.020 | 12 | 0.07 | 3.74 | 0.00 | 0.00 | 10.55 | 89.45 |
| 10 | 0.020 | 10 | 0.43 | 3.53 | 0.00 | 0.00 | 27.23 | 72.77 |
| 11 | 0.020 | 8 | 2.06 | 3.25 | 0.00 | 8.17 | 38.19 | 53.65 |
| 12 | 0.020 | 6 | 7.42 | 2.83 | 0.00 | 27.80 | 37.16 | 35.03 |
| 13 | 0.020 | 4 | 21.27 | 2.23 | 19.28 | 35.63 | 25.97 | 19.12 |
| 14 | 0.020 | 2 | 50.09 | 1.34 | 60.44 | 20.96 | 11.33 | 7.27 |
| 8 | 0.030 | 9 | 0.81 | 3.25 | 0.00 | 0.00 | 30.24 | 69.76 |
| 9 | 0.030 | 8 | 2.06 | 3.25 | 0.00 | 8.17 | 38.19 | 53.65 |
| 10 | 0.030 | 6 | 7.42 | 2.83 | 0.00 | 27.80 | 37.16 | 35.03 |
| 11 | 0.030 | 5 | 12.11 | 2.46 | 0.00 | 34.10 | 36.00 | 29.90 |
| 12 | 0.030 | 4 | 21.27 | 2.23 | 19.28 | 35.63 | 25.97 | 19.12 |
| 13 | 0.030 | 2 | 50.09 | 1.34 | 60.44 | 20.96 | 11.33 | 7.27 |
| 14 | 0.030 | 1 | 71.64 | 0.71 | 78.36 | 12.46 | 5.75 | 3.44 |

IMMUNIZED RETURN: 15 PERCENT     HORIZON: 4 YEARS     FORECAST ACCURACY: 50 PERCENT

| FLOOR RETURN | LEVERAGE FACTOR | DEG. OF FREEDOM | PROBABILITY OF TRIG. | COND. EXPECTED TRIG. TIME | CONDITIONAL PROB. OF TRIG. IN YEAR | | | |
|---|---|---|---|---|---|---|---|---|
| | | | | | 1 | 2 | 3 | 4 |
| 8  | 0.010 | 28 | 0.00  | 0.00 | 0.00  | 0.00  | 0.00  | 0.00   |
| 9  | 0.010 | 24 | 0.00  | 0.00 | 0.00  | 0.00  | 0.00  | 0.00   |
| 10 | 0.010 | 20 | 0.00  | 0.00 | 0.00  | 0.00  | 0.00  | 0.00   |
| 11 | 0.010 | 16 | 0.00  | 4.00 | 0.00  | 0.00  | 0.00  | 100.00 |
| 12 | 0.010 | 12 | 0.23  | 3.74 | 0.00  | 0.00  | 10.39 | 89.61  |
| 13 | 0.010 | 8  | 4.90  | 3.25 | 0.00  | 7.97  | 37.83 | 54.20  |
| 14 | 0.010 | 4  | 33.23 | 2.25 | 18.81 | 35.26 | 26.23 | 19.70  |
| 8  | 0.020 | 14 | 0.03  | 3.89 | 0.00  | 0.00  | 0.00  | 100.00 |
| 9  | 0.020 | 12 | 0.23  | 3.74 | 0.00  | 0.00  | 10.39 | 89.61  |
| 10 | 0.020 | 10 | 1.27  | 3.54 | 0.00  | 0.00  | 26.86 | 73.14  |
| 11 | 0.020 | 8  | 4.90  | 3.25 | 0.00  | 7.97  | 37.83 | 54.20  |
| 12 | 0.020 | 6  | 14.35 | 2.85 | 0.00  | 27.23 | 37.10 | 35.67  |
| 13 | 0.020 | 4  | 33.23 | 2.25 | 18.81 | 35.26 | 26.23 | 19.70  |
| 14 | 0.020 | 2  | 62.91 | 1.36 | 59.61 | 21.11 | 11.64 | 7.63   |
| 8  | 0.030 | 9  | 2.13  | 3.25 | 0.00  | 0.00  | 29.84 | 70.16  |
| 9  | 0.030 | 8  | 4.90  | 3.25 | 0.00  | 7.97  | 37.83 | 54.20  |
| 10 | 0.030 | 6  | 14.35 | 2.85 | 0.00  | 27.23 | 37.10 | 35.67  |
| 11 | 0.030 | 5  | 21.01 | 2.47 | 0.00  | 33.46 | 36.02 | 30.52  |
| 12 | 0.030 | 4  | 33.23 | 2.25 | 18.81 | 35.26 | 26.23 | 19.70  |
| 13 | 0.030 | 2  | 62.91 | 1.36 | 59.61 | 21.11 | 11.64 | 7.63   |
| 14 | 0.030 | 1  | 80.36 | 0.73 | 77.77 | 12.64 | 5.95  | 3.63   |

IMMUNIZED RETURN: 15 PERCENT          HORIZON: 4 YEARS          FORECAST ACCURACY: 45 PERCENT

| FLOOR RETURN | LEVERAGE FACTOR | DEG. OF FREEDOM | PROBABILITY OF TRIG. | COND. EXPECTED TRIG. TIME | CONDITIONAL PROB. OF TRIG. IN YEAR | | | |
|---|---|---|---|---|---|---|---|---|
| | | | | | 1 | 2 | 3 | 4 |
| 8 | 0.010 | 28 | 0.00 | 0.00 | 0.00 | 0.00 | 0.00 | 0.00 |
| 9 | 0.010 | 24 | 0.00 | 0.00 | 0.00 | 0.00 | 0.00 | 0.00 |
| 10 | 0.010 | 20 | 0.00 | 0.00 | 0.00 | 0.00 | 0.00 | 0.00 |
| 11 | 0.010 | 16 | 0.01 | 4.00 | 0.00 | 0.00 | 0.00 | 100.00 |
| 12 | 0.010 | 12 | 0.73 | 3.74 | 0.00 | 0.00 | 10.55 | 89.45 |
| 13 | 0.010 | 8 | 10.25 | 3.25 | 0.00 | 8.17 | 38.19 | 53.65 |
| 14 | 0.010 | 4 | 47.45 | 2.23 | 19.28 | 35.63 | 25.97 | 19.12 |
| 8 | 0.020 | 14 | 0.10 | 3.89 | 0.00 | 0.00 | 0.00 | 100.00 |
| 9 | 0.020 | 12 | 0.73 | 3.74 | 0.00 | 0.00 | 10.55 | 89.45 |
| 10 | 0.020 | 10 | 3.23 | 3.53 | 0.00 | 0.00 | 27.23 | 72.77 |
| 11 | 0.020 | 8 | 10.25 | 3.25 | 0.00 | 8.17 | 38.19 | 53.65 |
| 12 | 0.020 | 6 | 24.74 | 2.83 | 0.00 | 27.80 | 37.16 | 35.03 |
| 13 | 0.020 | 4 | 47.45 | 2.23 | 19.28 | 35.63 | 25.97 | 19.12 |
| 14 | 0.020 | 2 | 74.83 | 1.34 | 60.44 | 20.96 | 11.33 | 7.27 |
| 8 | 0.030 | 9 | 4.92 | 3.25 | 0.00 | 0.00 | 30.24 | 69.76 |
| 9 | 0.030 | 8 | 10.25 | 3.25 | 0.00 | 8.17 | 38.19 | 53.65 |
| 10 | 0.030 | 6 | 24.74 | 2.83 | 0.00 | 27.80 | 37.16 | 35.03 |
| 11 | 0.030 | 5 | 33.02 | 2.46 | 0.00 | 34.10 | 36.00 | 29.90 |
| 12 | 0.030 | 4 | 47.45 | 2.23 | 19.28 | 35.63 | 25.97 | 19.12 |
| 13 | 0.030 | 2 | 74.63 | 1.34 | 60.44 | 20.96 | 11.33 | 7.27 |
| 14 | 0.030 | 1 | 87.57 | 0.71 | 78.36 | 12.46 | 5.75 | 3.44 |

IMMUNIZED RETURN: 15 PERCENT      HORIZON: 4 YEARS      FORECAST ACCURACY: 40 PERCENT

| FLOOR RETURN | LEVERAGE FACTOR | DEG. OF FREEDOM | PROBABILITY OF TRIG. | COND. EXPECTED TRIG. TIME | CONDITIONAL PROB. OF TRIG. IN YEAR | | | |
|---|---|---|---|---|---|---|---|---|
| | | | | | 1 | 2 | 3 | 4 |
| 8  | 0.010 | 28 | 0.00  | 0.00 | 0.00  | 0.00  | 0.00  | 0.00   |
| 9  | 0.010 | 24 | 0.00  | 0.00 | 0.00  | 0.00  | 0.00  | 0.00   |
| 10 | 0.010 | 20 | 0.00  | 0.00 | 0.00  | 0.00  | 0.00  | 0.00   |
| 11 | 0.010 | 16 | 0.03  | 4.00 | 0.00  | 0.00  | 0.00  | 100.00 |
| 12 | 0.010 | 12 | 1.97  | 3.73 | 0.00  | 0.00  | 11.03 | 88.97  |
| 13 | 0.010 | 8  | 19.06 | 3.22 | 0.00  | 8.81  | 39.25 | 51.94  |
| 14 | 0.010 | 4  | 62.41 | 2.18 | 20.77 | 36.68 | 25.15 | 17.40  |
| 8  | 0.020 | 14 | 0.34  | 3.89 | 0.00  | 0.00  | 0.00  | 100.00 |
| 9  | 0.020 | 12 | 1.97  | 3.73 | 0.00  | 0.00  | 11.03 | 88.97  |
| 10 | 0.020 | 10 | 7.25  | 3.52 | 0.00  | 0.00  | 28.37 | 71.63  |
| 11 | 0.020 | 8  | 19.06 | 3.22 | 0.00  | 8.81  | 39.25 | 51.94  |
| 12 | 0.020 | 6  | 38.46 | 2.79 | 0.00  | 29.60 | 37.31 | 33.09  |
| 13 | 0.020 | 4  | 62.41 | 2.18 | 20.77 | 36.68 | 25.15 | 17.40  |
| 14 | 0.020 | 2  | 84.73 | 1.28 | 62.88 | 20.46 | 10.39 | 6.27   |
| 8  | 0.030 | 9  | 10.12 | 3.23 | 0.00  | 0.00  | 31.46 | 68.54  |
| 9  | 0.030 | 8  | 19.06 | 3.22 | 0.00  | 8.81  | 39.25 | 51.94  |
| 10 | 0.030 | 6  | 38.46 | 2.79 | 0.00  | 29.60 | 37.31 | 33.09  |
| 11 | 0.030 | 5  | 47.42 | 2.42 | 0.00  | 36.08 | 35.89 | 28.03  |
| 12 | 0.030 | 4  | 62.41 | 2.18 | 20.77 | 36.68 | 25.15 | 17.40  |
| 13 | 0.030 | 2  | 84.73 | 1.28 | 62.88 | 20.46 | 10.39 | 6.27   |
| 14 | 0.030 | 1  | 92.95 | 0.68 | 80.05 | 11.90 | 5.16  | 2.90   |

IMMUNIZED RETURN: 15 PERCENT          HORIZON: 5 YEARS          FORECAST ACCURACY: 60 PERCENT

| FLOOR RETURN | LEVERAGE FACTOR | DEG. OF FREEDOM | PROBABILITY OF TRIG. | COND. EXPECTED TRIG. TIME | CONDITIONAL PROB. OF TRIG. IN YEAR | | | | |
|---|---|---|---|---|---|---|---|---|---|
| | | | | | 1 | 2 | 3 | 4 | 5 |
| 8  | 0.010 | 35 | 0.00  | 0.00 | 0.00  | 0.00  | 0.00  | 0.00  | 0.00   |
| 9  | 0.010 | 30 | 0.00  | 0.00 | 0.00  | 0.00  | 0.00  | 0.00  | 0.00   |
| 10 | 0.010 | 25 | 0.00  | 0.00 | 0.00  | 0.00  | 0.00  | 0.00  | 0.00   |
| 11 | 0.010 | 20 | 0.00  | 5.00 | 0.00  | 0.00  | 0.00  | 0.00  | 100.00 |
| 12 | 0.010 | 15 | 0.00  | 4.52 | 0.00  | 0.00  | 0.00  | 8.08  | 91.92  |
| 13 | 0.010 | 10 | 0.25  | 4.14 | 0.00  | 0.00  | 14.29 | 36.07 | 49.64  |
| 14 | 0.010 | 5  | 7.58  | 2.78 | 0.00  | 29.72 | 29.57 | 23.09 | 17.61  |
| 8  | 0.020 | 17 | 0.00  | 4.65 | 0.00  | 0.00  | 0.00  | 0.00  | 100.00 |
| 9  | 0.020 | 15 | 0.00  | 4.52 | 0.00  | 0.00  | 0.00  | 8.08  | 91.92  |
| 10 | 0.020 | 12 | 0.04  | 4.42 | 0.00  | 0.00  | 3.81  | 30.74 | 65.44  |
| 11 | 0.020 | 10 | 0.25  | 4.14 | 0.00  | 0.00  | 14.29 | 36.07 | 49.64  |
| 12 | 0.020 | 7  | 2.11  | 3.39 | 0.00  | 7.77  | 26.70 | 32.94 | 30.59  |
| 13 | 0.020 | 5  | 7.58  | 2.78 | 0.00  | 29.72 | 29.57 | 23.09 | 17.61  |
| 14 | 0.020 | 2  | 39.22 | 1.42 | 60.37 | 19.64 | 9.97  | 6.02  | 3.99   |
| 8  | 0.030 | 11 | 0.69  | 4.13 | 0.00  | 0.00  | 4.63  | 32.75 | 62.62  |
| 9  | 0.030 | 10 | 0.25  | 4.14 | 0.00  | 0.00  | 14.29 | 36.07 | 49.64  |
| 10 | 0.030 | 8  | 1.14  | 3.75 | 0.00  | 5.77  | 25.68 | 33.99 | 34.57  |
| 11 | 0.030 | 6  | 4.30  | 3.21 | 0.00  | 23.25 | 29.31 | 26.00 | 21.44  |
| 12 | 0.030 | 5  | 7.58  | 2.78 | 0.00  | 29.72 | 29.57 | 23.09 | 17.61  |
| 13 | 0.030 | 3  | 23.30 | 1.93 | 27.47 | 34.02 | 18.83 | 11.75 | 7.93   |
| 14 | 0.030 | 1  | 43.11 | 0.74 | 78.60 | 11.68 | 5.06  | 2.85  | 1.81   |

Bond Portfolio Immunization

IMMUNIZED RETURN: 15 PERCENT     HORIZON: 5 YEARS     FORECAST ACCURACY: 55 PERCENT

| FLOOR RETURN | LEVERAGE FACTOR | DEG. OF FREEDOM | PROBABILITY OF TRIG. | COND. EXPECTED TRIG. TIME | CONDITIONAL PROB. OF TRIG. IN YEAR 1 | 2 | 3 | 4 | 5 |
|---|---|---|---|---|---|---|---|---|---|
| 8  | 0.010 | 35 | 0.00  | 0.00 | 0.00  | 0.00  | 0.00  | 0.00  | 0.00   |
| 9  | 0.010 | 30 | 0.00  | 0.00 | 0.00  | 0.00  | 0.00  | 0.00  | 0.00   |
| 10 | 0.010 | 25 | 0.00  | 0.00 | 0.00  | 0.00  | 0.00  | 0.00  | 0.00   |
| 11 | 0.010 | 20 | 0.00  | 5.00 | 0.00  | 0.00  | 0.00  | 0.00  | 100.00 |
| 12 | 0.010 | 15 | 0.01  | 4.53 | 0.00  | 0.00  | 0.00  | 7.70  | 92.30  |
| 13 | 0.010 | 10 | 0.90  | 4.17 | 0.00  | 0.00  | 13.19 | 35.26 | 51.55  |
| 14 | 0.010 | 5  | 15.04 | 2.86 | 0.00  | 27.45 | 28.98 | 24.06 | 19.52  |
| 8  | 0.020 | 17 | 0.00  | 4.65 | 0.00  | 0.00  | 0.00  | 0.00  | 100.00 |
| 9  | 0.020 | 15 | 0.01  | 4.53 | 0.00  | 0.00  | 0.00  | 7.70  | 92.30  |
| 10 | 0.020 | 12 | 0.20  | 4.44 | 0.00  | 0.00  | 3.49  | 29.62 | 66.89  |
| 11 | 0.020 | 10 | 0.90  | 4.17 | 0.00  | 0.00  | 13.19 | 35.26 | 51.55  |
| 12 | 0.020 | 7  | 5.33  | 3.44 | 0.00  | 7.01  | 27.17 | 33.12 | 32.69  |
| 13 | 0.020 | 5  | 15.04 | 2.86 | 0.00  | 27.45 | 28.98 | 24.06 | 19.52  |
| 14 | 0.020 | 2  | 52.66 | 1.50 | 57.49 | 19.94 | 10.77 | 6.92  | 4.88   |
| 8  | 0.030 | 11 | 0.36  | 4.15 | 0.00  | 0.00  | 4.25  | 31.62 | 64.13  |
| 9  | 0.030 | 10 | 0.90  | 4.17 | 0.00  | 0.00  | 13.19 | 35.26 | 51.55  |
| 10 | 0.030 | 8  | 3.25  | 3.80 | 0.00  | 5.17  | 24.17 | 33.96 | 36.71  |
| 11 | 0.030 | 6  | 9.70  | 3.28 | 0.00  | 21.27 | 28.43 | 26.80 | 23.50  |
| 12 | 0.030 | 5  | 15.04 | 2.86 | 25.48 | 27.45 | 28.98 | 24.06 | 19.52  |
| 13 | 0.030 | 3  | 35.77 | 2.02 | 76.57 | 32.96 | 19.42 | 12.89 | 9.25   |
| 14 | 0.030 | 1  | 73.31 | 0.80 |       | 12.17 | 5.62  | 3.36  | 2.28   |

IMMUNIZED RETURN: 15 PERCENT     HORIZON: 5 YEARS     FORECAST ACCURACY: 50 PERCENT

| FLOOR RETURN | LEVERAGE FACTOR | DEG. OF FREEDOM | PROBABILITY OF TRIG. | COND. EXPECTED TRIG. TIME | CONDITIONAL PROB. OF TRIG. IN YEAR 1 | 2 | 3 | 4 | 5 |
|---|---|---|---|---|---|---|---|---|---|
| 8 | 0.010 | 35 | 0.00 | 0.00 | 0.00 | 0.00 | 0.00 | 0.00 | 0.00 |
| 9 | 0.010 | 30 | 0.00 | 0.00 | 0.00 | 0.00 | 0.00 | 0.00 | 0.00 |
| 10 | 0.010 | 25 | 0.00 | 0.00 | 0.00 | 0.00 | 0.00 | 0.00 | 0.00 |
| 11 | 0.010 | 20 | 0.00 | 5.00 | 0.00 | 0.00 | 0.00 | 0.00 | 100.00 |
| 12 | 0.010 | 15 | 0.04 | 4.53 | 0.00 | 0.00 | 0.00 | 7.58 | 92.42 |
| 13 | 0.010 | 10 | 2.66 | 4.18 | 0.00 | 0.00 | 12.85 | 34.99 | 52.17 |
| 14 | 0.010 | 5 | 26.32 | 2.88 | 0.00 | 26.72 | 28.76 | 24.36 | 20.16 |
| 8 | 0.020 | 17 | 0.00 | 4.65 | 0.00 | 0.00 | 0.00 | 0.00 | 100.00 |
| 9 | 0.020 | 15 | 0.04 | 4.53 | 0.00 | 0.00 | 0.00 | 7.58 | 92.42 |
| 10 | 0.020 | 12 | 0.72 | 4.44 | 0.00 | 0.00 | 3.39 | 29.26 | 67.35 |
| 11 | 0.020 | 10 | 2.66 | 4.18 | 0.00 | 0.00 | 12.85 | 34.99 | 52.17 |
| 12 | 0.020 | 7 | 11.53 | 3.46 | 0.00 | 6.77 | 26.68 | 33.16 | 33.39 |
| 13 | 0.020 | 5 | 26.32 | 2.88 | 0.00 | 26.72 | 28.76 | 24.36 | 20.16 |
| 14 | 0.020 | 2 | 66.36 | 1.53 | 56.51 | 20.01 | 11.04 | 7.23 | 5.21 |
| 8 | 0.030 | 11 | 1.18 | 4.16 | 0.00 | 0.00 | 4.13 | 31.25 | 64.62 |
| 9 | 0.030 | 10 | 2.66 | 4.18 | 0.00 | 0.00 | 12.85 | 34.99 | 52.17 |
| 10 | 0.030 | 8 | 7.84 | 3.81 | 0.00 | 4.99 | 23.68 | 33.92 | 37.41 |
| 11 | 0.030 | 6 | 18.92 | 3.31 | 0.00 | 20.64 | 28.12 | 27.04 | 24.19 |
| 12 | 0.030 | 5 | 26.32 | 2.88 | 0.00 | 26.72 | 28.76 | 24.36 | 20.16 |
| 13 | 0.030 | 3 | 50.34 | 2.05 | 24.83 | 32.59 | 19.59 | 13.27 | 9.72 |
| 14 | 0.030 | 1 | 82.38 | 0.82 | 75.87 | 12.33 | 5.81 | 3.55 | 2.45 |

IMMUNIZED RETURN: 15 PERCENT          HORIZON: 5 YEARS          FORECAST ACCURACY: 45 PERCENT

| FLOOR RETURN | LEVERAGE FACTOR | DEG. OF FREEDOM | PROBABILITY OF TRIG. | COND. EXPECTED TRIG. TIME | CONDITIONAL PROB. OF TRIG, IN YEAR | | | | |
|---|---|---|---|---|---|---|---|---|---|
| | | | | | 1 | 2 | 3 | 4 | 5 |
| 8 | 0.010 | 35 | 0.00 | 0.00 | 0.00 | 0.00 | 0.00 | 0.00 | 0.00 |
| 9 | 0.010 | 30 | 0.00 | 0.00 | 0.00 | 0.00 | 0.00 | 0.00 | 0.00 |
| 10 | 0.010 | 25 | 0.00 | 0.00 | 0.00 | 0.00 | 0.00 | 0.00 | 0.00 |
| 11 | 0.010 | 20 | 0.00 | 5.00 | 0.00 | 0.00 | 0.00 | 0.00 | 100.00 |
| 12 | 0.010 | 15 | 0.17 | 4.53 | 0.00 | 0.00 | 0.00 | 7.70 | 92.30 |
| 13 | 0.010 | 10 | 6.67 | 4.17 | 0.00 | 0.00 | 13.19 | 35.26 | 51.55 |
| 14 | 0.010 | 5 | 41.03 | 2.86 | 0.00 | 27.45 | 28.98 | 24.06 | 19.52 |
| 8 | 0.020 | 17 | 0.02 | 4.65 | 0.00 | 0.00 | 0.00 | 0.00 | 100.00 |
| 9 | 0.020 | 15 | 0.17 | 4.53 | 0.00 | 0.00 | 0.00 | 7.70 | 92.30 |
| 10 | 0.020 | 12 | 2.19 | 4.44 | 0.00 | 0.00 | 3.49 | 29.62 | 66.89 |
| 11 | 0.020 | 10 | 6.67 | 4.17 | 0.00 | 0.00 | 13.19 | 35.26 | 51.55 |
| 12 | 0.020 | 7 | 21.72 | 3.44 | 0.00 | 7.01 | 27.17 | 33.12 | 32.69 |
| 13 | 0.020 | 5 | 41.03 | 2.86 | 0.00 | 27.45 | 28.98 | 24.06 | 19.52 |
| 14 | 0.020 | 2 | 78.67 | 1.50 | 57.49 | 19.94 | 10.77 | 6.92 | 4.88 |
| 8 | 0.030 | 11 | 3.28 | 4.15 | 0.00 | 0.00 | 4.25 | 31.62 | 64.13 |
| 9 | 0.030 | 10 | 6.67 | 4.17 | 0.00 | 0.00 | 13.19 | 35.26 | 51.55 |
| 10 | 0.030 | 8 | 16.20 | 3.80 | 0.00 | 5.17 | 24.17 | 33.96 | 36.71 |
| 11 | 0.030 | 6 | 32.34 | 3.28 | 0.00 | 21.27 | 26.43 | 26.80 | 23.50 |
| 12 | 0.030 | 5 | 41.03 | 2.86 | 0.00 | 27.45 | 26.98 | 24.06 | 19.52 |
| 13 | 0.030 | 3 | 65.31 | 2.02 | 25.48 | 32.96 | 19.42 | 12.89 | 9.25 |
| 14 | 0.030 | 1 | 89.60 | 0.80 | 76.57 | 12.17 | 5.62 | 3.36 | 2.28 |

IMMUNIZED RETURN: 15 PERCENT          HORIZON: 5 YEARS          FORECAST ACCURACY: 40 PERCENT

| FLOOR RETURN | LEVERAGE FACTOR | DEG. OF FREEDOM | PROBABILITY OF TRIG. | COND. EXPECTED TRIG. TIME | CONDITIONAL PROB. OF TRIG. IN YEAR | | | | |
|---|---|---|---|---|---|---|---|---|---|
| | | | | | 1 | 2 | 3 | 4 | 5 |
| 8  | 0.010 | 35 | 0.00  | 0.00 | 0.00  | 0.00  | 0.00  | 0.00  | 0.00   |
| 9  | 0.010 | 30 | 0.00  | 0.00 | 0.00  | 0.00  | 0.00  | 0.00  | 0.00   |
| 10 | 0.010 | 25 | 0.00  | 0.00 | 0.00  | 0.00  | 0.00  | 0.00  | 0.00   |
| 11 | 0.010 | 20 | 0.00  | 5.00 | 0.00  | 0.00  | 0.00  | 0.00  | 100.00 |
| 12 | 0.010 | 15 | 0.58  | 4.52 | 0.00  | 0.00  | 0.00  | 8.08  | 91.92  |
| 13 | 0.010 | 10 | 14.39 | 4.14 | 0.00  | 0.00  | 14.29 | 36.07 | 49.64  |
| 14 | 0.010 | 5  | 57.56 | 2.78 | 0.00  | 29.72 | 29.57 | 23.09 | 17.61  |
| 8  | 0.020 | 17 | 0.09  | 4.65 | 0.00  | 0.00  | 0.00  | 0.00  | 100.00 |
| 9  | 0.020 | 15 | 0.58  | 4.52 | 0.00  | 0.00  | 0.00  | 8.08  | 91.92  |
| 10 | 0.020 | 12 | 5.71  | 4.42 | 0.00  | 0.00  | 3.81  | 30.74 | 65.44  |
| 11 | 0.020 | 10 | 14.39 | 4.14 | 0.00  | 0.00  | 14.29 | 36.07 | 49.64  |
| 12 | 0.020 | 7  | 36.05 | 3.39 | 0.00  | 7.77  | 28.70 | 32.94 | 30.59  |
| 13 | 0.020 | 5  | 57.56 | 2.78 | 0.00  | 29.72 | 29.57 | 23.09 | 17.61  |
| 14 | 0.020 | 2  | 88.25 | 1.42 | 60.37 | 19.64 | 9.97  | 6.02  | 3.99   |
| 8  | 0.030 | 11 | 7.84  | 4.13 | 0.00  | 0.00  | 4.63  | 32.75 | 62.62  |
| 9  | 0.030 | 10 | 14.39 | 4.14 | 0.00  | 0.00  | 14.29 | 36.07 | 49.64  |
| 10 | 0.030 | 8  | 29.13 | 3.75 | 0.00  | 5.77  | 25.68 | 33.99 | 34.57  |
| 11 | 0.030 | 6  | 48.95 | 3.21 | 0.00  | 23.25 | 29.31 | 26.00 | 21.44  |
| 12 | 0.030 | 5  | 57.56 | 2.78 | 0.00  | 29.72 | 29.57 | 23.09 | 17.61  |
| 13 | 0.030 | 3  | 78.64 | 1.93 | 27.47 | 34.02 | 18.83 | 11.75 | 7.93   |
| 14 | 0.030 | 1  | 94.66 | 0.74 | 78.60 | 11.68 | 5.06  | 2.85  | 1.81   |

IMMUNIZED RETURN: 15 PERCENT          HORIZON: 6 YEARS          FORECAST ACCURACY: 60 PERCENT

| FLOOR RETURN | LEVERAGE FACTOR | DEG. OF FREEDOM | PROBABILITY OF TRIG. | COND. EXPECTED TRIG. TIME | CONDITIONAL PROB. OF TRIG. IN YEAR | | | | | |
|---|---|---|---|---|---|---|---|---|---|---|
| | | | | | 1 | 2 | 3 | 4 | 5 | 6 |
| 8 | 0.010 | 42 | 0.00 | 0.00 | 0.00 | 0.00 | 0.00 | 0.00 | 0.00 | 0.00 |
| 9 | 0.010 | 36 | 0.00 | 0.00 | 0.00 | 0.00 | 0.00 | 0.00 | 0.00 | 0.00 |
| 10 | 0.010 | 30 | 0.00 | 0.00 | 0.00 | 0.00 | 0.00 | 0.00 | 0.00 | 0.00 |
| 11 | 0.010 | 24 | 0.00 | 6.00 | 0.00 | 0.00 | 0.00 | 0.00 | 0.00 | 100.00 |
| 12 | 0.010 | 18 | 0.00 | 5.70 | 0.00 | 0.00 | 0.00 | 0.00 | 14.30 | 85.70 |
| 13 | 0.010 | 12 | 0.08 | 5.07 | 0.00 | 0.00 | 1.98 | 15.96 | 33.97 | 48.09 |
| 14 | 0.010 | 6 | 5.04 | 3.58 | 0.00 | 19.81 | 24.97 | 22.15 | 18.26 | 14.81 |
| 8 | 0.020 | 21 | 0.00 | 5.67 | 0.00 | 0.00 | 0.00 | 0.00 | 0.00 | 100.00 |
| 9 | 0.020 | 18 | 0.00 | 5.70 | 0.00 | 0.00 | 0.00 | 0.00 | 14.30 | 85.70 |
| 10 | 0.020 | 15 | 0.00 | 5.26 | 0.00 | 0.00 | 0.00 | 2.24 | 25.47 | 72.29 |
| 11 | 0.020 | 12 | 0.08 | 5.07 | 0.00 | 0.00 | 1.98 | 15.96 | 33.97 | 48.09 |
| 12 | 0.020 | 9 | 0.72 | 4.36 | 0.00 | 0.00 | 11.51 | 25.08 | 31.20 | 32.21 |
| 13 | 0.020 | 6 | 5.04 | 3.58 | 0.00 | 19.81 | 24.97 | 22.15 | 18.26 | 14.81 |
| 14 | 0.020 | 3 | 24.62 | 2.12 | 26.00 | 32.20 | 17.83 | 11.12 | 7.51 | 5.34 |
| 8 | 0.030 | 14 | 0.02 | 5.33 | 0.00 | 0.00 | 0.00 | 7.59 | 31.14 | 61.27 |
| 9 | 0.030 | 12 | 0.08 | 5.07 | 0.00 | 0.00 | 1.98 | 15.96 | 33.97 | 48.09 |
| 10 | 0.030 | 10 | 0.39 | 4.71 | 0.00 | 0.00 | 9.22 | 23.26 | 32.02 | 35.50 |
| 11 | 0.030 | 8 | 1.50 | 4.23 | 0.00 | 4.37 | 19.46 | 25.76 | 26.19 | 24.22 |
| 12 | 0.030 | 6 | 5.04 | 3.58 | 0.00 | 19.81 | 24.97 | 22.15 | 18.26 | 14.81 |
| 13 | 0.030 | 4 | 15.01 | 2.71 | 17.06 | 30.13 | 20.65 | 14.29 | 10.26 | 7.61 |
| 14 | 0.030 | 2 | 40.33 | 1.54 | 58.72 | 19.11 | 9.70 | 5.86 | 3.88 | 2.73 |

IMMUNIZED RETURN: 15 PERCENT        HORIZON: 6 YEARS        FORECAST ACCURACY: 55 PERCENT

| FLOOR RETURN | LEVERAGE FACTOR | DEG. OF FREEDOM | PROBABILITY OF TRIG. | COND. EXPECTED TRIG. TIME | CONDITIONAL PROB. OF TRIG. IN YEAR | | | | | |
|---|---|---|---|---|---|---|---|---|---|---|
| | | | | | 1 | 2 | 3 | 4 | 5 | 6 |
| 8  | 0.010 | 42 | 0.00  | 0.00 | 0.00  | 0.00  | 0.00  | 0.00  | 0.00  | 0.00   |
| 9  | 0.010 | 36 | 0.00  | 0.00 | 0.00  | 0.00  | 0.00  | 0.00  | 0.00  | 0.00   |
| 10 | 0.010 | 30 | 0.00  | 0.00 | 0.00  | 0.00  | 0.00  | 0.00  | 0.00  | 0.00   |
| 11 | 0.010 | 24 | 0.00  | 6.00 | 0.00  | 0.00  | 0.00  | 0.00  | 0.00  | 100.00 |
| 12 | 0.010 | 18 | 0.00  | 5.71 | 0.00  | 0.00  | 0.00  | 0.00  | 13.62 | 86.38  |
| 13 | 0.010 | 12 | 0.40  | 5.11 | 0.00  | 0.00  | 1.74  | 14.77 | 33.34 | 50.15  |
| 14 | 0.010 | 6  | 11.67 | 3.70 | 0.00  | 17.69 | 23.64 | 22.28 | 19.54 | 16.85  |
| 8  | 0.020 | 21 | 0.00  | 5.67 | 0.00  | 0.00  | 0.00  | 0.00  | 0.00  | 100.00 |
| 9  | 0.020 | 18 | 0.00  | 5.71 | 0.00  | 0.00  | 0.00  | 0.00  | 13.62 | 86.38  |
| 10 | 0.020 | 15 | 0.03  | 5.28 | 0.00  | 0.00  | 0.00  | 2.04  | 24.43 | 73.54  |
| 11 | 0.020 | 12 | 0.40  | 5.11 | 0.00  | 0.00  | 1.74  | 14.77 | 33.34 | 50.15  |
| 12 | 0.020 | 9  | 2.37  | 4.42 | 0.00  | 0.00  | 10.30 | 23.78 | 31.43 | 34.49  |
| 13 | 0.020 | 6  | 11.67 | 3.70 | 0.00  | 17.69 | 23.64 | 22.28 | 19.54 | 16.85  |
| 14 | 0.020 | 3  | 38.27 | 2.24 | 23.81 | 30.80 | 18.15 | 12.04 | 8.65  | 6.55   |
| 8  | 0.030 | 14 | 0.09  | 5.36 | 0.00  | 0.00  | 0.00  | 6.94  | 30.13 | 62.93  |
| 9  | 0.030 | 12 | 0.40  | 5.11 | 0.00  | 0.00  | 1.74  | 14.77 | 33.34 | 50.15  |
| 10 | 0.030 | 10 | 1.44  | 4.77 | 0.00  | 0.00  | 8.21  | 21.94 | 32.07 | 37.79  |
| 11 | 0.030 | 8  | 4.43  | 4.31 | 0.00  | 3.80  | 17.76 | 24.95 | 26.97 | 26.52  |
| 12 | 0.030 | 6  | 11.67 | 3.70 | 0.00  | 17.69 | 23.64 | 22.28 | 19.54 | 16.85  |
| 13 | 0.030 | 4  | 26.82 | 2.84 | 15.29 | 28.25 | 20.59 | 15.16 | 11.58 | 9.13   |
| 14 | 0.030 | 2  | 54.59 | 1.65 | 55.46 | 19.24 | 10.39 | 6.68  | 4.71  | 3.53   |

IMMUNIZED RETURN: 15 PERCENT          HORIZON: 6 YEARS          FORECAST ACCURACY: 50 PERCENT

| FLOOR RETURN | LEVERAGE FACTOR | DEG. OF FREEDOM | PROBABILITY OF TRIG. | COND. EXPECTED TRIG. TIME | CONDITIONAL PROB. OF TRIG. IN YEAR | | | | | |
|---|---|---|---|---|---|---|---|---|---|---|
| | | | | | 1 | 2 | 3 | 4 | 5 | 6 |
| 8  | 0.010 | 42 | 0.00  | 0.00 | 0.00  | 0.00  | 0.00  | 0.00  | 0.00  | 0.00   |
| 9  | 0.010 | 36 | 0.00  | 0.00 | 0.00  | 0.00  | 0.00  | 0.00  | 0.00  | 0.00   |
| 10 | 0.010 | 30 | 0.00  | 0.00 | 0.00  | 0.00  | 0.00  | 0.00  | 0.00  | 0.00   |
| 11 | 0.010 | 24 | 0.00  | 6.00 | 0.00  | 0.00  | 0.00  | 0.00  | 0.00  | 100.00 |
| 12 | 0.010 | 18 | 0.02  | 5.71 | 0.00  | 0.00  | 0.00  | 0.00  | 13.40 | 86.60  |
| 13 | 0.010 | 12 | 1.46  | 5.12 | 0.00  | 0.00  | 1.67  | 14.39 | 33.13 | 50.82  |
| 14 | 0.010 | 6  | 22.95 | 3.73 | 0.00  | 17.02 | 23.19 | 22.30 | 19.95 | 17.55  |
| 8  | 0.020 | 21 | 0.00  | 5.67 | 0.00  | 0.00  | 0.00  | 0.00  | 0.00  | 100.00 |
| 9  | 0.020 | 18 | 0.02  | 5.71 | 0.00  | 0.00  | 0.00  | 0.00  | 13.40 | 86.60  |
| 10 | 0.020 | 15 | 0.15  | 5.29 | 0.00  | 0.00  | 0.00  | 1.98  | 24.09 | 73.93  |
| 11 | 0.020 | 12 | 1.46  | 5.12 | 0.00  | 0.00  | 1.67  | 14.39 | 33.13 | 50.82  |
| 12 | 0.020 | 9  | 6.39  | 4.44 | 0.00  | 0.00  | 9.93  | 23.35 | 31.48 | 35.24  |
| 13 | 0.020 | 6  | 22.95 | 3.73 | 0.00  | 17.02 | 23.19 | 22.30 | 19.95 | 17.55  |
| 14 | 0.020 | 3  | 54.13 | 2.29 | 23.09 | 30.31 | 18.22 | 12.34 | 9.04  | 6.99   |
| 8  | 0.030 | 14 | 0.41  | 5.37 | 0.00  | 0.00  | 0.00  | 6.74  | 29.80 | 63.47  |
| 9  | 0.030 | 12 | 1.46  | 5.12 | 0.00  | 0.00  | 1.67  | 14.39 | 33.13 | 50.82  |
| 10 | 0.030 | 10 | 4.33  | 4.79 | 0.00  | 0.00  | 7.90  | 21.50 | 32.06 | 38.54  |
| 11 | 0.030 | 8  | 10.78 | 4.34 | 0.00  | 3.63  | 17.22 | 24.67 | 27.20 | 27.28  |
| 12 | 0.030 | 6  | 22.95 | 3.73 | 0.00  | 17.02 | 23.19 | 22.30 | 19.95 | 17.55  |
| 13 | 0.030 | 4  | 42.44 | 2.89 | 14.73 | 27.62 | 20.54 | 15.43 | 12.02 | 9.67   |
| 14 | 0.030 | 2  | 69.00 | 1.70 | 54.34 | 19.25 | 10.61 | 6.96  | 5.01  | 3.83   |

IMMUNIZED RETURN: 15 PERCENT          HORIZON: 6 YEARS          FORECAST ACCURACY: 45 PERCENT

| FLOOR RETURN | LEVERAGE FACTOR | DEG. OF FREEDOM | PROBABILITY OF TRIG. | COND. EXPECTED TRIG. TIME | CONDITIONAL PROB. OF TRIG. IN YEAR | | | | | |
|---|---|---|---|---|---|---|---|---|---|---|
| | | | | | 1 | 2 | 3 | 4 | 5 | 6 |
| 8 | 0.010 | 42 | 0.00 | 0.00 | 0.00 | 0.00 | 0.00 | 0.00 | 0.00 | 0.00 |
| 9 | 0.010 | 36 | 0.00 | 0.00 | 0.00 | 0.00 | 0.00 | 0.00 | 0.00 | 0.00 |
| 10 | 0.010 | 30 | 0.00 | 0.00 | 0.00 | 0.00 | 0.00 | 0.00 | 0.00 | 0.00 |
| 11 | 0.010 | 24 | 0.00 | 6.00 | 0.00 | 0.00 | 0.00 | 0.00 | 0.00 | 100.00 |
| 12 | 0.010 | 18 | 0.08 | 5.71 | 0.00 | 0.00 | 0.00 | 0.00 | 13.62 | 86.38 |
| 13 | 0.010 | 12 | 4.40 | 5.11 | 0.00 | 0.00 | 1.74 | 14.77 | 33.34 | 50.15 |
| 14 | 0.010 | 6 | 36.89 | 3.70 | 0.00 | 17.69 | 23.64 | 22.28 | 19.54 | 16.85 |
| 8 | 0.020 | 21 | 0.00 | 5.67 | 0.00 | 0.00 | 0.00 | 0.00 | 0.00 | 100.00 |
| 9 | 0.020 | 18 | 0.08 | 5.71 | 0.00 | 0.00 | 0.00 | 0.00 | 13.62 | 86.38 |
| 10 | 0.020 | 15 | 0.63 | 5.28 | 0.00 | 0.00 | 0.00 | 2.04 | 24.43 | 73.54 |
| 11 | 0.020 | 12 | 4.40 | 5.11 | 0.00 | 0.00 | 1.74 | 14.77 | 33.34 | 50.15 |
| 12 | 0.020 | 9 | 14.42 | 4.42 | 0.00 | 0.00 | 10.30 | 23.78 | 31.43 | 34.49 |
| 13 | 0.020 | 6 | 38.89 | 3.70 | 0.00 | 17.69 | 23.64 | 22.28 | 19.54 | 16.85 |
| 14 | 0.020 | 3 | 69.88 | 2.24 | 23.81 | 30.80 | 18.15 | 12.04 | 8.65 | 6.55 |
| 8 | 0.030 | 14 | 1.49 | 5.36 | 0.00 | 0.00 | 0.00 | 6.94 | 30.13 | 62.93 |
| 9 | 0.030 | 12 | 4.40 | 5.11 | 0.00 | 0.00 | 1.74 | 14.77 | 33.34 | 50.15 |
| 10 | 0.030 | 10 | 10.72 | 4.77 | 0.00 | 0.00 | 8.21 | 21.94 | 32.07 | 37.79 |
| 11 | 0.030 | 8 | 22.04 | 4.31 | 0.00 | 3.80 | 17.76 | 24.95 | 26.97 | 26.52 |
| 12 | 0.030 | 6 | 38.89 | 3.70 | 0.00 | 17.69 | 23.64 | 22.28 | 19.54 | 16.85 |
| 13 | 0.030 | 4 | 59.84 | 2.84 | 15.29 | 28.25 | 20.59 | 15.16 | 11.58 | 9.13 |
| 14 | 0.030 | 2 | 81.55 | 1.65 | 55.46 | 19.24 | 10.39 | 6.68 | 4.71 | 3.53 |

IMMUNIZED RETURN: 15 PERCENT                  HORIZON: 6 YEARS                          FORECAST ACCURACY: 40 PERCENT

| FLOOR RETURN | LEVERAGE FACTOR | DEG. OF FREEDOM | PROBABILITY OF TRIG. | COND. EXPECTED TRIG. TIME | CONDITIONAL PROB. OF TRIG. IN YEAR | | | | | |
|---|---|---|---|---|---|---|---|---|---|---|
| | | | | | 1 | 2 | 3 | 4 | 5 | 6 |
| 8 | 0.010 | 42 | 0.00 | 0.00 | 0.00 | 0.00 | 0.00 | 0.00 | 0.00 | 0.00 |
| 9 | 0.010 | 36 | 0.00 | 0.00 | 0.00 | 0.00 | 0.00 | 0.00 | 0.00 | 0.00 |
| 10 | 0.010 | 30 | 0.00 | 0.00 | 0.00 | 0.00 | 0.00 | 0.00 | 0.00 | 0.00 |
| 11 | 0.010 | 24 | 0.00 | 6.00 | 0.00 | 0.00 | 0.00 | 0.00 | 0.00 | 100.00 |
| 12 | 0.010 | 18 | 0.38 | 5.70 | 0.00 | 0.00 | 0.00 | 0.00 | 14.30 | 85.70 |
| 13 | 0.010 | 12 | 11.00 | 5.07 | 0.00 | 0.00 | 1.98 | 15.96 | 33.97 | 48.09 |
| 14 | 0.010 | 6 | 57.46 | 3.58 | 0.00 | 19.81 | 24.97 | 22.15 | 18.26 | 14.81 |
| 8 | 0.020 | 21 | 0.01 | 5.67 | 0.00 | 0.00 | 0.00 | 0.00 | 0.00 | 100.00 |
| 9 | 0.020 | 18 | 0.38 | 5.70 | 0.00 | 0.00 | 0.00 | 0.00 | 14.30 | 85.70 |
| 10 | 0.020 | 15 | 2.10 | 5.26 | 0.00 | 0.00 | 0.00 | 2.24 | 25.47 | 72.29 |
| 11 | 0.020 | 12 | 11.00 | 5.07 | 0.00 | 0.00 | 1.98 | 15.96 | 33.97 | 48.09 |
| 12 | 0.020 | 9 | 27.67 | 4.36 | 0.00 | 0.00 | 11.51 | 25.08 | 31.20 | 32.21 |
| 13 | 0.020 | 6 | 57.46 | 3.58 | 0.00 | 19.81 | 24.97 | 22.15 | 18.26 | 14.81 |
| 14 | 0.020 | 3 | 83.08 | 2.12 | 26.00 | 32.20 | 17.83 | 11.12 | 7.51 | 5.34 |
| 8 | 0.030 | 14 | 4.50 | 5.33 | 0.00 | 0.00 | 0.00 | 7.59 | 31.14 | 61.27 |
| 9 | 0.030 | 12 | 11.00 | 5.07 | 0.00 | 0.00 | 1.98 | 15.96 | 33.97 | 48.09 |
| 10 | 0.030 | 10 | 22.31 | 4.71 | 0.00 | 0.00 | 9.22 | 23.26 | 32.02 | 35.50 |
| 11 | 0.030 | 8 | 38.44 | 4.23 | 0.00 | 4.37 | 19.46 | 25.76 | 26.19 | 24.22 |
| 12 | 0.030 | 6 | 57.46 | 3.58 | 0.00 | 19.81 | 24.97 | 22.15 | 18.26 | 14.81 |
| 13 | 0.030 | 4 | 75.99 | 2.71 | 17.06 | 30.13 | 20.65 | 14.29 | 10.26 | 7.61 |
| 14 | 0.030 | 2 | 90.73 | 1.54 | 58.72 | 19.11 | 9.70 | 5.86 | 3.88 | 2.73 |

IMMUNIZED RETURN: 15 PERCENT  HORIZON: 7 YEARS  FORECAST ACCURACY: 60 PERCENT

| FLOOR RETURN | LEVERAGE FACTOR | DEG. OF FREEDOM | PROBABILITY OF TRIG. | COND. EXPECTED TRIG. TIME | CONDITIONAL PROB. OF TRIG. IN YEAR | | | | | | |
|---|---|---|---|---|---|---|---|---|---|---|---|
| | | | | | 1 | 2 | 3 | 4 | 5 | 6 | 7 |
| 8 | 0.010 | 49 | 0.00 | 0.00 | 0.00 | 0.00 | 0.00 | 0.00 | 0.00 | 0.00 | 0.00 |
| 9 | 0.010 | 42 | 0.00 | 0.00 | 0.00 | 0.00 | 0.00 | 0.00 | 0.00 | 0.00 | 0.00 |
| 10 | 0.010 | 35 | 0.00 | 0.00 | 0.00 | 0.00 | 0.00 | 0.00 | 0.00 | 0.00 | 0.00 |
| 11 | 0.010 | 28 | 0.00 | 7.00 | 0.00 | 0.00 | 0.00 | 0.00 | 0.00 | 0.00 | 100.00 |
| 12 | 0.010 | 21 | 0.03 | 6.48 | 0.00 | 0.00 | 0.00 | 0.00 | 0.00 | 11.61 | 88.39 |
| 13 | 0.010 | 14 | 0.03 | 6.01 | 0.00 | 0.00 | 0.00 | 4.03 | 16.52 | 32.50 | 46.96 |
| 14 | 0.010 | 7 | 3.15 | 4.23 | 0.00 | 5.21 | 19.25 | 22.10 | 20.52 | 17.82 | 15.10 |
| 8 | 0.020 | 24 | 0.00 | 6.85 | 0.00 | 0.00 | 0.00 | 0.00 | 0.00 | 3.93 | 96.07 |
| 9 | 0.020 | 21 | 0.00 | 6.48 | 0.00 | 0.00 | 0.00 | 0.00 | 0.00 | 11.61 | 88.39 |
| 10 | 0.020 | 17 | 0.00 | 6.18 | 0.00 | 0.00 | 0.00 | 0.00 | 4.98 | 27.35 | 67.67 |
| 11 | 0.020 | 14 | 0.03 | 6.01 | 0.00 | 0.00 | 0.00 | 4.03 | 16.52 | 32.50 | 46.96 |
| 12 | 0.020 | 10 | 0.52 | 5.24 | 0.00 | 0.00 | 6.80 | 17.16 | 23.62 | 26.18 | 26.25 |
| 13 | 0.020 | 7 | 3.15 | 4.23 | 0.00 | 5.21 | 19.25 | 22.10 | 20.52 | 17.82 | 15.10 |
| 14 | 0.020 | 3 | 25.59 | 2.29 | 25.01 | 30.97 | 17.15 | 10.70 | 7.22 | 5.14 | 3.80 |
| 8 | 0.030 | 16 | 0.01 | 6.26 | 0.00 | 0.00 | 0.00 | 0.79 | 10.00 | 30.95 | 58.25 |
| 9 | 0.030 | 14 | 0.03 | 6.01 | 0.00 | 0.00 | 0.00 | 4.03 | 16.52 | 32.50 | 46.96 |
| 10 | 0.030 | 11 | 0.25 | 5.33 | 0.00 | 0.00 | 1.70 | 12.00 | 22.94 | 30.04 | 33.33 |
| 11 | 0.030 | 9 | 0.94 | 4.86 | 0.00 | 0.00 | 8.81 | 19.19 | 23.88 | 24.66 | 21.46 |
| 12 | 0.030 | 7 | 3.15 | 4.23 | 0.00 | 5.21 | 19.25 | 22.10 | 20.52 | 17.82 | 15.10 |
| 13 | 0.030 | 4 | 15.88 | 2.93 | 16.12 | 28.48 | 19.52 | 13.51 | 9.70 | 7.19 | 5.47 |
| 14 | 0.030 | 2 | 41.14 | 1.64 | 57.57 | 18.73 | 9.51 | 5.74 | 3.81 | 2.68 | 1.97 |

IMMUNIZED RETURN: 15 PERCENT          HORIZON: 7 YEARS          FORECAST ACCURACY: 55 PERCENT

| FLOOR RETURN | LEVERAGE FACTOR | DEG. OF FREEDOM | PROBABILITY OF TRIG. | COND. EXPECTED TRIG. TIME | CONDITIONAL PROB. OF TRIG. IN YEAR | | | | | | |
|---|---|---|---|---|---|---|---|---|---|---|---|
| | | | | | 1 | 2 | 3 | 4 | 5 | 6 | 7 |
| 8 | 0.010 | 49 | 0.00 | 0.00 | 0.00 | 0.00 | 0.00 | 0.00 | 0.00 | 0.00 | 0.00 |
| 9 | 0.010 | 42 | 0.00 | 0.00 | 0.00 | 0.00 | 0.00 | 0.00 | 0.00 | 0.00 | 0.00 |
| 10 | 0.010 | 35 | 0.00 | 0.00 | 0.00 | 0.00 | 0.00 | 0.00 | 0.00 | 0.00 | 0.00 |
| 11 | 0.010 | 28 | 0.00 | 7.00 | 0.00 | 0.00 | 0.00 | 0.00 | 0.00 | 0.00 | 100.00 |
| 12 | 0.010 | 21 | 0.00 | 6.49 | 0.00 | 0.00 | 0.00 | 0.00 | 0.00 | 11.04 | 88.96 |
| 13 | 0.010 | 14 | 0.18 | 6.05 | 0.00 | 0.00 | 0.00 | 3.53 | 15.32 | 32.01 | 49.14 |
| 14 | 0.010 | 7 | 8.39 | 4.36 | 0.00 | 4.45 | 17.27 | 21.05 | 20.77 | 19.18 | 17.28 |
| 8 | 0.020 | 24 | 0.00 | 6.85 | 0.00 | 0.00 | 0.00 | 0.00 | 0.00 | 3.73 | 96.27 |
| 9 | 0.020 | 21 | 0.00 | 6.49 | 0.00 | 0.00 | 0.00 | 0.00 | 0.00 | 11.04 | 88.96 |
| 10 | 0.020 | 17 | 0.01 | 6.21 | 0.00 | 0.00 | 0.00 | 0.00 | 4.53 | 26.32 | 69.15 |
| 11 | 0.020 | 14 | 0.18 | 6.05 | 0.00 | 0.00 | 0.00 | 3.53 | 15.32 | 32.01 | 49.14 |
| 12 | 0.020 | 10 | 2.02 | 5.34 | 0.00 | 0.00 | 5.85 | 15.64 | 22.86 | 26.94 | 28.72 |
| 13 | 0.020 | 7 | 8.39 | 4.36 | 0.00 | 4.45 | 17.27 | 21.05 | 20.77 | 19.18 | 17.28 |
| 14 | 0.020 | 3 | 40.25 | 2.45 | 22.64 | 29.30 | 17.26 | 11.46 | 8.23 | 6.23 | 4.90 |
| 8 | 0.030 | 16 | 0.04 | 6.29 | 0.00 | 0.00 | 0.00 | 0.69 | 9.16 | 30.06 | 60.09 |
| 9 | 0.030 | 14 | 0.18 | 6.05 | 0.00 | 0.00 | 0.00 | 3.53 | 15.32 | 32.01 | 49.14 |
| 10 | 0.030 | 11 | 1.06 | 5.41 | 0.00 | 0.00 | 1.44 | 10.74 | 21.78 | 30.30 | 35.74 |
| 11 | 0.030 | 9 | 3.20 | 4.96 | 0.00 | 0.00 | 7.64 | 17.63 | 23.30 | 25.57 | 25.86 |
| 12 | 0.030 | 7 | 8.39 | 4.36 | 0.00 | 4.45 | 17.27 | 21.05 | 20.77 | 19.18 | 17.28 |
| 13 | 0.030 | 4 | 28.80 | 3.11 | 14.24 | 26.31 | 19.18 | 14.12 | 10.78 | 8.50 | 6.88 |
| 14 | 0.030 | 2 | 56.09 | 1.79 | 53.97 | 18.72 | 10.12 | 6.50 | 4.58 | 3.43 | 2.68 |

IMMUNIZED RETURN: 15 PERCENT  HORIZON: 7 YEARS  FORECAST ACCURACY: 50 PERCENT

| FLOOR RETURN | LEVERAGE FACTOR | DEG. OF FREEDOM | PROBABILITY OF TRIG. | COND. EXPECTED TRIG. TIME | CONDITIONAL PROB. OF TRIG. IN YEAR | | | | | | |
|---|---|---|---|---|---|---|---|---|---|---|---|
| | | | | | 1 | 2 | 3 | 4 | 5 | 6 | 7 |
| 8 | 0.010 | 49 | 0.00 | 0.00 | 0.00 | 0.00 | 0.00 | 0.00 | 0.00 | 0.00 | 0.00 |
| 9 | 0.010 | 42 | 0.00 | 0.00 | 0.00 | 0.00 | 0.00 | 0.00 | 0.00 | 0.00 | 0.00 |
| 10 | 0.010 | 35 | 0.00 | 0.00 | 0.00 | 0.00 | 0.00 | 0.00 | 0.00 | 0.00 | 0.00 |
| 11 | 0.010 | 28 | 0.00 | 7.00 | 0.00 | 0.00 | 0.00 | 0.00 | 0.00 | 0.00 | 100.00 |
| 12 | 0.010 | 21 | 0.00 | 6.50 | 0.00 | 0.00 | 0.00 | 0.00 | 0.00 | 10.86 | 89.14 |
| 13 | 0.010 | 14 | 0.81 | 6.07 | 0.00 | 0.00 | 0.00 | 3.38 | 14.94 | 31.83 | 49.85 |
| 14 | 0.010 | 7 | 18.49 | 4.40 | 0.00 | 4.22 | 16.63 | 20.68 | 20.82 | 19.61 | 18.03 |
| 8 | 0.020 | 24 | 0.00 | 6.85 | 0.00 | 0.00 | 0.00 | 0.00 | 0.00 | 3.67 | 96.33 |
| 9 | 0.020 | 21 | 0.00 | 6.50 | 0.00 | 0.00 | 0.00 | 0.00 | 0.00 | 10.86 | 89.14 |
| 10 | 0.020 | 17 | 0.09 | 6.21 | 0.00 | 0.00 | 0.00 | 0.00 | 4.39 | 25.99 | 69.62 |
| 11 | 0.020 | 14 | 0.81 | 6.07 | 0.00 | 0.00 | 0.00 | 3.38 | 14.94 | 31.83 | 49.85 |
| 12 | 0.020 | 10 | 6.14 | 5.37 | 0.00 | 0.00 | 5.56 | 15.15 | 22.59 | 27.16 | 29.54 |
| 13 | 0.020 | 7 | 18.49 | 4.40 | 0.00 | 4.22 | 16.63 | 20.68 | 20.82 | 19.61 | 18.03 |
| 14 | 0.020 | 3 | 57.16 | 2.51 | 21.87 | 28.70 | 17.26 | 11.69 | 8.56 | 6.62 | 5.31 |
| 8 | 0.030 | 16 | 0.23 | 6.30 | 0.00 | 0.00 | 0.00 | 0.66 | 8.90 | 29.76 | 60.68 |
| 9 | 0.030 | 14 | 0.81 | 6.07 | 0.00 | 0.00 | 0.00 | 3.38 | 14.94 | 31.83 | 49.85 |
| 10 | 0.030 | 11 | 3.57 | 5.43 | 0.00 | 0.00 | 1.37 | 10.34 | 21.39 | 30.36 | 36.53 |
| 11 | 0.030 | 9 | 8.72 | 4.99 | 0.00 | 0.00 | 7.28 | 17.12 | 23.08 | 25.84 | 26.67 |
| 12 | 0.030 | 7 | 18.49 | 4.40 | 0.00 | 4.22 | 16.63 | 20.68 | 20.82 | 19.61 | 18.03 |
| 13 | 0.030 | 4 | 45.63 | 3.17 | 13.64 | 25.57 | 19.02 | 14.28 | 11.13 | 8.96 | 7.40 |
| 14 | 0.030 | 2 | 71.11 | 1.84 | 52.74 | 18.68 | 10.30 | 6.75 | 4.86 | 3.71 | 2.96 |

IMMUNIZED RETURN: 15 PERCENT      HORIZON: 7 YEARS      FORECAST ACCURACY: 45 PERCENT

| FLOOR RETURN | LEVERAGE FACTOR | DEG. OF FREEDOM | PROBABILITY OF TRIG. | COND. EXPECTED TRIG. TIME | CONDITIONAL PROB. OF TRIG. IN YEAR | | | | | | |
|---|---|---|---|---|---|---|---|---|---|---|---|
| | | | | | 1 | 2 | 3 | 4 | 5 | 6 | 7 |
| 8 | 0.010 | 49 | 0.00 | 0.00 | 0.00 | 0.00 | 0.00 | 0.00 | 0.00 | 0.00 | 0.00 |
| 9 | 0.010 | 42 | 0.00 | 0.00 | 0.00 | 0.00 | 0.00 | 0.00 | 0.00 | 0.00 | 0.00 |
| 10 | 0.010 | 35 | 0.00 | 0.00 | 0.00 | 0.00 | 0.00 | 0.00 | 0.00 | 0.00 | 0.00 |
| 11 | 0.010 | 28 | 0.00 | 7.00 | 0.00 | 0.00 | 0.00 | 0.00 | 0.00 | 0.00 | 100.00 |
| 12 | 0.010 | 21 | 0.02 | 6.49 | 0.00 | 0.00 | 0.00 | 0.00 | 0.00 | 11.04 | 88.96 |
| 13 | 0.010 | 14 | 2.93 | 6.05 | 0.00 | 0.00 | 0.00 | 3.53 | 15.32 | 32.01 | 49.14 |
| 14 | 0.010 | 7 | 34.18 | 4.36 | 0.00 | 4.45 | 17.27 | 21.05 | 20.77 | 19.18 | 17.28 |
| 8 | 0.020 | 24 | 0.00 | 6.85 | 0.00 | 0.00 | 0.00 | 0.00 | 0.00 | 3.73 | 96.27 |
| 9 | 0.020 | 21 | 0.02 | 6.49 | 0.00 | 0.00 | 0.00 | 0.00 | 0.00 | 11.04 | 88.96 |
| 10 | 0.020 | 17 | 0.44 | 6.21 | 0.00 | 0.00 | 0.00 | 0.00 | 4.53 | 26.32 | 69.15 |
| 11 | 0.020 | 14 | 2.93 | 6.05 | 0.00 | 0.00 | 0.00 | 3.53 | 15.32 | 32.01 | 49.14 |
| 12 | 0.020 | 10 | 15.04 | 5.34 | 0.00 | 0.00 | 5.85 | 15.64 | 22.86 | 26.94 | 28.72 |
| 13 | 0.020 | 7 | 34.18 | 4.36 | 0.00 | 4.45 | 17.27 | 21.05 | 20.77 | 19.18 | 17.28 |
| 14 | 0.020 | 3 | 73.48 | 2.45 | 22.64 | 29.30 | 17.26 | 11.46 | 8.23 | 6.23 | 4.90 |
| 8 | 0.030 | 16 | 1.02 | 6.29 | 0.00 | 0.00 | 0.00 | 0.69 | 9.16 | 30.06 | 60.09 |
| 9 | 0.030 | 14 | 2.93 | 6.05 | 0.00 | 0.00 | 0.00 | 3.53 | 15.32 | 32.01 | 49.14 |
| 10 | 0.030 | 11 | 9.65 | 5.41 | 0.00 | 0.00 | 1.44 | 10.74 | 21.78 | 30.30 | 35.74 |
| 11 | 0.030 | 9 | 19.46 | 4.96 | 0.00 | 0.00 | 7.64 | 17.63 | 23.30 | 25.57 | 25.86 |
| 12 | 0.030 | 7 | 34.18 | 4.36 | 0.00 | 4.45 | 17.27 | 21.05 | 20.77 | 19.18 | 17.28 |
| 13 | 0.030 | 4 | 64.27 | 3.11 | 14.24 | 26.31 | 19.18 | 14.12 | 10.78 | 8.50 | 6.88 |
| 14 | 0.030 | 2 | 83.79 | 1.79 | 53.97 | 18.72 | 10.12 | 6.50 | 4.58 | 3.43 | 2.68 |

IMMUNIZED RETURN: 15 PERCENT        HORIZON: 7 YEARS        FORECAST ACCURACY: 40 PERCENT

| FLOOR RETURN | LEVERAGE FACTOR | DEG. OF FREEDOM | PROBABILITY OF TRIG. | COND. EXPECTED TRIG. TIME | CONDITIONAL PROB. OF TRIG. IN YEAR | | | | | | |
|---|---|---|---|---|---|---|---|---|---|---|---|
| | | | | | 1 | 2 | 3 | 4 | 5 | 6 | 7 |
| 8 | 0.010 | 49 | 0.00 | 0.00 | 0.00 | 0.00 | 0.00 | 0.00 | 0.00 | 0.00 | 0.00 |
| 9 | 0.010 | 42 | 0.00 | 0.00 | 0.00 | 0.00 | 0.00 | 0.00 | 0.00 | 0.00 | 0.00 |
| 10 | 0.010 | 35 | 0.00 | 0.00 | 0.00 | 0.00 | 0.00 | 0.00 | 0.00 | 0.00 | 0.00 |
| 11 | 0.010 | 28 | 0.00 | 7.00 | 0.00 | 0.00 | 0.00 | 0.00 | 0.00 | 0.00 | 100.00 |
| 12 | 0.010 | 21 | 0.11 | 6.48 | 0.00 | 0.00 | 0.00 | 0.00 | 0.00 | 11.61 | 88.39 |
| 13 | 0.010 | 14 | 8.48 | 6.01 | 0.00 | 0.00 | 0.00 | 4.03 | 16.52 | 32.50 | 46.96 |
| 14 | 0.010 | 7 | 53.74 | 4.23 | 0.00 | 5.21 | 19.25 | 22.10 | 20.52 | 17.82 | 15.10 |
| 8 | 0.020 | 24 | 0.01 | 6.85 | 0.00 | 0.00 | 0.00 | 0.00 | 0.00 | 3.93 | 96.07 |
| 9 | 0.020 | 21 | 0.11 | 6.48 | 0.00 | 0.00 | 0.00 | 0.00 | 0.00 | 11.61 | 88.39 |
| 10 | 0.020 | 17 | 1.73 | 6.18 | 0.00 | 0.00 | 0.00 | 0.00 | 4.98 | 27.35 | 67.67 |
| 11 | 0.020 | 14 | 8.48 | 6.01 | 0.00 | 0.00 | 0.00 | 4.03 | 16.52 | 32.50 | 46.96 |
| 12 | 0.020 | 10 | 30.25 | 5.24 | 0.00 | 0.00 | 6.80 | 17.16 | 23.62 | 26.18 | 26.25 |
| 13 | 0.020 | 7 | 53.74 | 4.23 | 0.00 | 5.21 | 19.25 | 22.10 | 20.52 | 17.82 | 15.10 |
| 14 | 0.020 | 3 | 86.36 | 2.29 | 25.01 | 30.97 | 17.15 | 10.70 | 7.22 | 5.14 | 3.80 |
| 8 | 0.030 | 16 | 3.55 | 6.26 | 0.00 | 0.00 | 0.00 | 0.79 | 10.00 | 30.95 | 58.25 |
| 9 | 0.030 | 14 | 8.48 | 6.01 | 0.00 | 0.00 | 0.00 | 4.03 | 16.52 | 32.50 | 46.96 |
| 10 | 0.030 | 11 | 21.40 | 5.33 | 0.00 | 0.00 | 1.70 | 12.00 | 22.94 | 30.04 | 33.33 |
| 11 | 0.030 | 9 | 36.15 | 4.86 | 0.00 | 0.00 | 8.81 | 19.19 | 23.88 | 24.66 | 23.46 |
| 12 | 0.030 | 7 | 53.74 | 4.23 | 0.00 | 5.21 | 19.25 | 22.10 | 20.52 | 17.82 | 15.10 |
| 13 | 0.030 | 4 | 80.39 | 2.93 | 16.12 | 28.48 | 19.52 | 13.51 | 9.70 | 7.19 | 5.47 |
| 14 | 0.030 | 2 | 92.55 | 1.64 | 57.57 | 16.73 | 9.51 | 5.74 | 3.81 | 2.68 | 1.97 |

# 6 Managing a Contingently Immunized Portfolio: A Simulation Approach

Chapter 5 provides a mathematical analysis of contingent immunization. The purpose of that analysis was to produce insights regarding how a contingent program should be run in practice. Specifically, we developed a model for how returns are generated relative to the returns on a bullet immunization. This assumption allowed us to derive the distribution of total compound return mathematically. In turn, this distribution was parameterized in terms of the important contingent parameters: bet size, probability of an accurate rate forecast, horizon, and floor (or minimum acceptable rate). The tables in appendix 5B—that is, the return distribution for different parameter settings—illustrate various conclusions of the analysis. Most important, we found that large bets should not be made when forecasting accuracy is not significantly greater than 50 percent. This phenomenon was related to the law of large numbers. A large number of trials would allow true insight to be reflected in expected return. Too large a bet size raised the probability of triggering to the point that the law of large numbers, in effect, did not have a chance to work. This work was predicated on a particular assumption regarding how contingent returns are generated. Although the specific assumption was quite representative, many other assumptions could have been made. However, the analysis revealed an important statistical structure of returns that we believe is quite robust with respect to plausible variations in assumptions.

This chapter presents a simulation approach to the same problem. The investment paradigm is somewhat different in the case we have modeled versus the purely mathematical case described in chapter 5. However, the major decision variables (bet size and differential between immunized return and floor) remain. The objective continues to be a depiction of the risk-reward tradeoff as it is affected by changes in the decision variables or other critical parameters, such as the probability of correct yield curve change forecasts. As in the purely mathematical case, we adopt a plausible framework for managing such a portfolio and examine changes in results caused by controlled changes in the critical parameters. Moreover, certain simplifying assumptions have been made that are intended to isolate the impact of the contingent parameters. For example (as discussed in this chapter), we have assumed a flat yield curve that shifts in an unpredictable manner but that remains flat.

Our broad objective is to begin with a representative hypothesis for how a contingent immunization is run in practice (for example, fixed bet size as a percentage of portfolio value) and to measure the affect on the return distribution (for example, mean return, probability of triggering, standard deviation, or probability of underperforming the immunized return) of four parameters: size of bet, difference between immunized return and floor, forecasting accuracy, and yield volatility. Although the method of return generation is different than that assumed in chapter 5, the broad conclusions are similar.

## Design of the Study

Our starting point was a simulation of yields. We assumed a yield curve that was initially flat at 15 percent and that remained flat although at a stochastically varying level. We considered three scenarios: yields secularly decline from 15 percent to 12 percent, yields remain stable near 15 percent, and yields secularly increase from 15 percent to 18 percent. Yield change volatility was assumed to have two possible values: a period-to-period standard deviation of either 100 or 200 basis points. All of our results are generated first under the 100 basis point assumption and then under the 200 basis point assumption. Quarter-to-quarter yield changes were generated by a simple model with an autoregressive mean component plus an independent unit normal variable times a standard deviation that was proportional to a yield level measure.

We then simulated the management process. A five-year contingent immunization was assumed in which the manager made twenty interest rate bets in all (four per quarter times five years). We developed all results under varying assumptions regarding yield forecasting ability. In particular, we generated all results under assumption of a 40 percent accuracy (an average of eight correct forecasts out of twenty) through a 60 percent accuracy (an average of twelve correct forecasts out of twenty). A forecast is simply a forecast of the direction of change in the yield curve.

For each choice of interest rate scenario, yield volatility, and forecasting ability, we varied two additional parameters: (1) the level of the floor return versus the immunized return, and (2) the bet size made at each quarter. Because the yield curve was initially flat at 15 percent, the immunized rate available was 15 percent in every case. We generated all results under the assumption of floor returns of 12 percent, 13 percent, and 14 percent. The bet size assumed four possible values. Interpretation of the bet size requires some explanation.

Unless triggering takes place, a contingent immunization will contain market value in excess of what is necessary to achieve the floor return at the immunized rate currently available. It is this excess that gives the manager latitude for making interest rate bets. In our analysis we define the bet size as the percentage of this excess that would be lost if interest rates went in the wrong direction (the direction opposite to that which was forecast) by an amount equal to one standard deviation. This method of defining the bet conforms with the widespread investor behavior of proportional asset allocation. That is, there is a strong investor preference toward allocating (risking) funds as a proportion of the total as opposed to an allocation in terms of dollar amounts. This technique differs from that adopted in chapter 5 where it was assumed that the contingent rate of return equaled the immunized return plus (with probability $p$) or minus (with probability $1 - p$) a fixed amount.

To summarize the experimental design, we generated all of our results under a variety of assumptions: (1) three yield change scenarios; (2) two yield volatility scenarios; (3) five manager forecasting accuracies; (4) three levels of floor relative to immunized level; and (5) four bet size assumptions. For each combination, 500 simulated five-year contingent portfolios were run. The results of the analysis, which are discussed in the next section, depict the return distributions under this variety of assumptions. As an operational matter, we hope to gain from this analysis some insight about running a contingent immunization—that is, the bet size and floor level versus immunized rate that offer the most attractive return profile to different investors.

## Simulation Results

Tables 6A–1 to 6A–30 in appendix 6A contain the simulated return results. Each table includes the yield scenario (represented by the difference between the equilibrium yield and the initial yield level, where the equilibrium yield refers to the mean yield level to which rates are moving), the yield volatility, the forecasting accuracy, and various return statistics for different floor levels and bet sizes. The immunized yield was 15 percent in every case because the initial yield curve was assumed to be flat at 15 percent.

In each row of each table the first two numbers reflect values of the decision variables. The first is the bet size measured as a percentage. The second is the floor return. Bet sizes range from 25 percent to 100 percent. For example, a 25 percent bet means that at each period 25 percent of the excess market value would be lost if the yield curve moved in the direction opposite to that forecast by one standard deviation. (The standard deviation is given by the volatility indicated at the top of each table.) The excess market value is the market value of the portfolio over that necessary to hit the floor return at prevailing yield levels. Floor returns of 12 percent through 14 percent are considered. Data across each row are five-year compound return confidence levels, mean and standard deviation of five-year compound returns, the lowest returns (that is, the minimum order statistic or the lowest simulated return out of 500 trials), and the percentage of returns that were at the floor. This final column may be interpreted as the probability of triggering.

The tables generally yield results that were expected; however, some results are surprising. Generally, larger bet sizes produced greater return volatility (other things being equal) as did a larger difference between floor and immunized return. When forecasting accuracy is poor, better results were generally obtained for smaller bet sizes and higher floor returns regardless of the direction of change in yields or yield volatility; mean returns were higher and standard deviations lower. In particular, mean returns were always below the immunized return for less than a 50 percent forecasting accuracy.

When forecasting accuracy exceeded 50 percent, a positive risk-reward tradeoff emerged. That is, a tradeoff emerged where increases in risk produced increases in expected return. Regardless of the direction of yield change or yield volatility, a larger bet size or a lower floor increased both the mean return and standard deviation. Holding all else constant, either increasing the bet size or reducing the floor would also increase the probability of triggering.

The most important observation that the analysis permits is that, given a particular yield volatility and forecasting ability, there is more than one way to produce a given mean return. Consider table 6A–9, page 166. With a 100 basis point volatility and a 55 percent forecasting accuracy, a 16.54 percent mean five-year compound return is produced by a floor of 13 percent and a bet size of 50 percent. Nearly this same mean is produced by a floor of 12 percent and a bet size of 25 percent but with a smaller standard deviation and a smaller probability of triggering. Analogous assumptions considered in tables 6A–4 and 6A–14 on pages 161 and 171 (but with declining yields and increasing yields respectively) show a similar pattern. Using a different example on page 166, under a 100 basis point volatility, a bet size of 25 percent and floor of 13 percent always has roughly the same mean return, significantly lower standard deviation, and lower probability of triggering than a 50 percent bet size with a 14 percent floor, and with only a 25 percent chance (roughly) of a return less than 14 percent. This result appears to have its origin in the fact that even with forecasting accuracy normally viewed as representing market insight (55 percent to 60 percent), there is still a substantial probability of back-to-back errors. When the bet size is large, the probability of triggering is thus high and a good forecasting ability is prevented from having as favorable an effect as is possible.

For several reasons, the simulated mean returns can also behave in a slightly unpredictable manner. We developed the simulation so that across the 500 iterations, forecasting accuracy would average 40 percent, 45 percent, 50 percent, 55 percent, and 60 percent, respectively, in the different cases. The return-generating process was constructed in such a way that at a 50 percent accuracy, mean returns should equal the immunized target. Although close (especially when the equilibrium yield was also the starting value), means deviated from the anticipated value in this case for two reasons. First, the standard deviation of simulated returns is often quite large so that the significance of the difference is extremely low.

Second, and more important, in simulating the bet size we had to place restrictions on the magnitude of portfolio duration because, when unconstrained, durations often assumed extreme and unrealistic levels. Thus, we constrained duration to lie between plus or minus ten years of the immunized duration. A symmetrical range about the target duration was necessary to avoid giving a bias to results for increasing versus decreasing yield scenarios. The implicit allowance of negative durations implies the existence of a futures market in which securities can be shorted. Although the allowed range seems wide compared with actual portfolios, it is small compared with the durations that would have resulted in the large bet cases if duration was not constrained. Thus, although any constraint implies some bias, the selection made was believed to be a good choice in terms of reasonableness and symmetrical unbias across yield scenarios, although the higher-risk strategies are affected more. Interestingly, the effect of the constraint in cases of 50 percent forecasting accuracy was to cause simulated means to be slightly above 15 percent for high-risk strategies and slightly below for low-risk strategies, although neither difference was statistically significant, and the action of the constraint was more detrimental to the high-risk strategies for more extreme forecasting abilities.

## Conclusions

Our results provide some interesting perspectives on how to manage a contingent immunization that are similar to those in chapter 5 despite a difference in assumption regarding how contingent returns are generated. Contrary to the belief of many, it does not appear optimal to make large bets. This approach causes a significant probability of triggering and a significant probability of a return less than the immunized level—even if forecasting accuracy is good. This is evidently the result of the fact that, even with good forecasting ability, the probability of back-to-back errors is sufficiently large so that triggering has high probability and the law of large numbers does not have a chance to work. A better approach is to make smaller bets. This permits a larger number of opportunities for a forecasting accuracy in excess of 50 percent to have a positive effect. As a consequence, there is a significant decrease in standard deviation and a large decrease in the probability of triggering without as large a decline in expected return. If desired, a decline in expected return can be compensated for by a reduction in the floor, thus permitting smaller bets with a larger amount and hence higher mean returns. With sufficient forecasting accuracy the probability of falling between the initial and lowered floor may actually be quite small.

# Appendix 6A
# Simulated Contingent
# Immunization Return
# Distributions

This appendix depicts the simulated return distribution of a contingently immunized portfolio managed according to the procedures described in chapter 6. On each page, the first four lines of data show: (1) the yield volatility in basis points denoted (*bp*); (2) the initial yield level, which is also the immunized target return; (3) the equilibrium yield, which is the average level of yields that will exist at the end of the horizon of five years (which was common to all pages); and (4) the accuracy of the interest rate forecasts, represented as the average number of correct directional forecasts out of twenty. The volatility level corresponds to the standard deviation of the quarterly change in the yield level.

Going across the subsequent columns, the first two items are the bet size and floor. The bet size (denoted MAX. LOSS PERCENT) is the percentage loss of the excess market value which would be incurred by an adverse move in rates of one standard deviation. The next five items are return confidence intervals at various percentages. The next two items are the mean and standard deviation of total compound return (denoted MEAN and STD DEV). The final two items provide the lowest simulated return in each case and the percentage of simulated returns that were at the floor return. Pages 158–172 cover an assumed volatility of 100 basis points, while pages 173–187 are otherwise identical but assume a 200 basis point volatility.

YIELD VOLATILITY(HP): 100

INITIAL YIELD LEVEL: 15

IMMUNIZED RETURN: 15

EQUILIBRIUM YIELD: 12

ACCURATE FORECASTS (OUT OF 20): 8

| MAX. LOSS PER- CENT | FLOOR | RETURN CONFIDENCE INTERVALS | | | | | MEAN | STD DEV | LOWEST RETURN | PERCENT AT FLOOR |
|---|---|---|---|---|---|---|---|---|---|---|
| | | 5 | 25 | 50 | 75 | 95 | | | | |
| 25 | 12 | 12.05 | 12.22 | 12.58 | 13.43 | 17.61 | 13.37 | 2.15 | 12.00 | 0.40 |
| 25 | 13 | 13.03 | 13.14 | 13.37 | 13.92 | 16.49 | 13.89 | 1.40 | 13.00 | 0.40 |
| 25 | 14 | 14.02 | 14.07 | 14.18 | 14.45 | 15.73 | 14.43 | 0.70 | 14.00 | 0.40 |
| 50 | 12 | 12.00 | 12.00 | 12.00 | 12.12 | 20.67 | 13.12 | 3.29 | 12.00 | 46.40 |
| 50 | 13 | 13.00 | 13.00 | 13.00 | 13.04 | 17.66 | 13.65 | 2.32 | 13.00 | 49.60 |
| 50 | 14 | 14.00 | 14.00 | 14.00 | 14.02 | 14.95 | 14.24 | 1.15 | 14.00 | 51.40 |
| 75 | 12 | 12.00 | 12.00 | 12.00 | 12.00 | 22.80 | 13.22 | 3.64 | 12.00 | 78.80 |
| 75 | 13 | 13.00 | 13.00 | 13.00 | 13.00 | 18.94 | 13.72 | 2.73 | 13.00 | 83.20 |
| 75 | 14 | 14.00 | 14.00 | 14.00 | 14.00 | 14.76 | 14.30 | 1.60 | 14.00 | 88.60 |
| 100 | 12 | 12.00 | 12.00 | 12.00 | 12.00 | 22.78 | 13.28 | 3.78 | 12.00 | 84.40 |
| 100 | 13 | 13.00 | 13.00 | 13.00 | 13.00 | 19.73 | 13.78 | 2.90 | 13.00 | 90.00 |
| 100 | 14 | 14.00 | 14.00 | 14.00 | 14.00 | 14.27 | 14.37 | 1.90 | 14.00 | 94.60 |

YIELD VOLATILITY(BP): 100

INITIAL YIELD LEVEL: 15

IMMUNIZED RETURN: 15

EQUILIBRIUM YIELD: 12

ACCURATE FORECASTS (OUT OF 20): 9

| MAX. LOSS PER- CENT | FLOOR | RETURN CONFIDENCE INTERVALS | | | | | MEAN | STD DEV | LOWEST RETURN | PERCENT AT FLOOR |
|---|---|---|---|---|---|---|---|---|---|---|
| | | 5 | 25 | 50 | 75 | 95 | | | | |
| 25 | 12 | 12.09 | 12.36 | 12.99 | 14.54 | 20.42 | 14.07 | 2.87 | 12.00 | 0.20 |
| 25 | 13 | 13.06 | 13.23 | 13.63 | 14.65 | 18.59 | 14.36 | 1.96 | 13.00 | 0.20 |
| 25 | 14 | 14.03 | 14.11 | 14.31 | 14.80 | 16.77 | 14.67 | 1.02 | 14.00 | 0.20 |
| 50 | 12 | 12.00 | 12.00 | 12.00 | 12.78 | 25.98 | 13.92 | 4.41 | 12.00 | 43.40 |
| 50 | 13 | 13.00 | 13.00 | 13.00 | 13.20 | 22.26 | 14.19 | 3.34 | 13.00 | 46.60 |
| 50 | 14 | 14.00 | 14.00 | 14.00 | 14.04 | 16.62 | 14.56 | 2.11 | 14.00 | 49.60 |
| 75 | 12 | 12.00 | 12.00 | 12.00 | 12.04 | 25.57 | 14.05 | 4.75 | 12.00 | 71.60 |
| 75 | 13 | 13.00 | 13.00 | 13.00 | 13.00 | 24.10 | 14.38 | 3.93 | 13.00 | 76.80 |
| 75 | 14 | 14.00 | 14.00 | 14.00 | 14.00 | 19.21 | 14.65 | 2.64 | 14.00 | 84.00 |
| 100 | 12 | 12.00 | 12.00 | 12.00 | 12.00 | 26.27 | 14.06 | 4.81 | 12.00 | 76.60 |
| 100 | 13 | 13.00 | 13.00 | 13.00 | 13.00 | 24.55 | 14.51 | 4.16 | 13.00 | 82.20 |
| 100 | 14 | 14.00 | 14.00 | 14.00 | 14.00 | 20.83 | 14.75 | 2.98 | 14.00 | 90.20 |

YIELD VOLATILITY(BP): 100

INITIAL YIELD LEVEL: 15

IMMUNIZED RETURN: 15

EQUILIBRIUM YIELD: 12

ACCURATE FORECASTS (OUT OF 20): 10

| MAX. LOSS PER- CENT | FLOOR | RETURN CONFIDENCE INTERVALS | | | | | MEAN | STD DEV | LOWEST RETURN | PERCENT AT FLOOR |
|---|---|---|---|---|---|---|---|---|---|---|
| | | 5 | 25 | 50 | 75 | 95 | | | | |
| 25 | 12 | 12.16 | 12.58 | 13.38 | 15.61 | 23.20 | 14.93 | 3.90 | 12.00 | 0.20 |
| 25 | 13 | 13.10 | 13.38 | 13.89 | 15.32 | 20.27 | 14.96 | 2.85 | 13.00 | 0.20 |
| 25 | 14 | 14.05 | 14.18 | 14.42 | 15.13 | 17.66 | 14.98 | 1.52 | 14.00 | 0.20 |
| 50 | 12 | 12.00 | 12.00 | 12.04 | 14.80 | 27.93 | 14.98 | 5.76 | 12.00 | 35.40 |
| 50 | 13 | 13.00 | 13.00 | 13.01 | 13.85 | 26.47 | 15.09 | 4.77 | 13.00 | 39.80 |
| 50 | 14 | 14.00 | 14.00 | 14.00 | 14.19 | 20.96 | 15.07 | 3.27 | 14.00 | 42.00 |
| 75 | 12 | 12.00 | 12.00 | 12.00 | 15.08 | 28.73 | 15.16 | 6.11 | 12.00 | 65.40 |
| 75 | 13 | 13.00 | 13.00 | 13.00 | 13.01 | 26.95 | 15.22 | 5.23 | 13.00 | 73.40 |
| 75 | 14 | 14.00 | 14.00 | 14.00 | 15.96 | 24.14 | 15.29 | 4.03 | 14.00 | 79.80 |
| 100 | 12 | 12.00 | 12.00 | 12.00 | 15.96 | 29.21 | 15.23 | 6.20 | 12.00 | 69.60 |
| 100 | 13 | 13.00 | 13.00 | 13.00 | 13.00 | 27.01 | 15.28 | 5.38 | 13.00 | 77.40 |
| 100 | 14 | 14.00 | 14.00 | 14.00 | 14.00 | 24.64 | 15.43 | 4.35 | 14.00 | 84.40 |

YIELD VOLATILITY(BP): 100

INITIAL YIELD LEVEL: 15

IMMUNIZED RETURN: 15

EQUILIBRIUM YIELD: 12

ACCURATE FORECASTS (OUT OF 20): 11

| MAX. LOSS PER- CENT | FLOOR | RETURN CONFIDENCE INTERVALS | | | | | MEAN | STD DEV | LOWEST RETURN | PERCENT AT FLOOR |
|---|---|---|---|---|---|---|---|---|---|---|
| | | 5 | 25 | 50 | 75 | 95 | | | | |
| 25 | 12 | 12.24 | 13.10 | 14.56 | 18.04 | 28.07 | 16.49 | 5.02 | 12.01 | 0.00 |
| 25 | 13 | 13.15 | 13.71 | 14.65 | 16.72 | 24.74 | 16.05 | 3.71 | 13.01 | 0.00 |
| 25 | 14 | 14.07 | 14.33 | 14.79 | 15.81 | 19.85 | 15.54 | 2.01 | 14.00 | 0.20 |
| 50 | 12 | 12.00 | 12.00 | 12.32 | 21.55 | 33.67 | 17.13 | 7.49 | 12.00 | 31.20 |
| 50 | 13 | 13.00 | 13.00 | 13.09 | 17.99 | 31.75 | 16.73 | 6.36 | 13.00 | 35.00 |
| 50 | 14 | 14.00 | 14.00 | 14.02 | 14.88 | 28.12 | 16.06 | 4.60 | 14.00 | 40.40 |
| 75 | 12 | 12.00 | 12.00 | 12.00 | 22.72 | 34.49 | 17.36 | 7.96 | 12.00 | 54.60 |
| 75 | 13 | 13.00 | 13.00 | 13.00 | 19.82 | 33.41 | 17.10 | 7.08 | 13.00 | 63.00 |
| 75 | 14 | 14.00 | 14.00 | 14.00 | 14.09 | 30.37 | 16.52 | 5.55 | 14.00 | 70.60 |
| 100 | 12 | 12.00 | 12.00 | 12.00 | 23.17 | 34.61 | 17.41 | 8.03 | 12.00 | 58.40 |
| 100 | 13 | 13.00 | 13.00 | 13.00 | 21.03 | 34.21 | 17.43 | 7.42 | 13.00 | 64.80 |
| 100 | 14 | 14.00 | 14.00 | 14.00 | 14.00 | 32.14 | 16.77 | 5.94 | 14.00 | 74.60 |

YIELD VOLATILITY(BP): 100

INITIAL YIELD LEVEL: 15

IMMUNIZED RETURN: 15

EQUILIBRIUM YIELD: 12

ACCURATE FORECASTS (OUT OF 20): 12

| MAX. LOSS PER- CENT | FLOOR | RETURN CONFIDENCE INTERVALS | | | | | MEAN | STD DEV | LOWEST RETURN | PERCENT AT FLOOR |
|---|---|---|---|---|---|---|---|---|---|---|
| | | 5 | 25 | 50 | 75 | 95 | | | | |
| 25 | 12 | 12.36 | 13.44 | 15.55 | 20.89 | 31.39 | 18.05 | 6.42 | 12.02 | 0.00 |
| 25 | 13 | 13.23 | 13.92 | 15.28 | 18.58 | 28.34 | 17.26 | 5.10 | 13.02 | 0.00 |
| 25 | 14 | 14.11 | 14.44 | 15.10 | 16.76 | 22.86 | 16.28 | 3.22 | 14.01 | 0.00 |
| 50 | 12 | 12.00 | 12.00 | 13.44 | 25.90 | 35.84 | 19.20 | 9.01 | 12.00 | 27.60 |
| 50 | 13 | 13.00 | 13.00 | 13.44 | 23.48 | 34.18 | 18.50 | 7.99 | 13.00 | 31.20 |
| 50 | 14 | 14.00 | 14.00 | 14.09 | 17.86 | 30.96 | 17.40 | 6.28 | 14.00 | 35.80 |
| 75 | 12 | 12.00 | 12.00 | 12.68 | 26.50 | 36.58 | 19.52 | 9.42 | 12.00 | 44.40 |
| 75 | 13 | 13.00 | 13.00 | 13.00 | 25.27 | 35.94 | 19.07 | 8.71 | 13.00 | 53.80 |
| 75 | 14 | 14.00 | 14.00 | 14.00 | 20.36 | 33.80 | 17.98 | 7.29 | 14.00 | 64.20 |
| 100 | 12 | 12.00 | 12.00 | 12.34 | 27.10 | 36.58 | 19.61 | 9.46 | 12.00 | 48.40 |
| 100 | 13 | 13.00 | 13.00 | 13.00 | 25.98 | 36.58 | 19.33 | 9.02 | 13.00 | 57.00 |
| 100 | 14 | 14.00 | 14.00 | 14.00 | 21.59 | 34.58 | 18.42 | 7.84 | 14.00 | 68.80 |

YIELD VOLATILITY(BP): 100

INITIAL YIELD LEVEL: 15

IMMUNIZED RETURN: 15

EQUILIBRIUM YIELD: 15

ACCURATE FORECASTS (OUT OF 20): 8

| MAX. LOSS PER- CENT | FLOOR | RETURN CONFIDENCE INTERVALS | | | | | MEAN | STD DEV | LOWEST RETURN | PERCENT AT FLOOR |
|---|---|---|---|---|---|---|---|---|---|---|
| | | 5 | 25 | 50 | 75 | 95 | | | | |
| 25 | 12 | 12.07 | 12.30 | 12.67 | 13.59 | 17.25 | 13.43 | 2.08 | 12.00 | 0.20 |
| 25 | 13 | 13.05 | 13.19 | 13.43 | 14.04 | 16.50 | 13.93 | 1.37 | 13.00 | 0.20 |
| 25 | 14 | 14.02 | 14.09 | 14.21 | 14.51 | 15.75 | 14.46 | 0.69 | 14.00 | 0.20 |
| 50 | 12 | 12.00 | 12.00 | 12.00 | 12.21 | 20.87 | 13.09 | 3.16 | 12.00 | 36.80 |
| 50 | 13 | 13.00 | 13.00 | 13.00 | 13.08 | 18.09 | 13.65 | 2.18 | 13.00 | 39.60 |
| 50 | 14 | 14.00 | 14.00 | 14.00 | 14.03 | 15.21 | 14.26 | 1.14 | 14.00 | 41.40 |
| 75 | 12 | 12.00 | 12.00 | 12.00 | 12.00 | 21.29 | 13.09 | 3.41 | 12.00 | 78.00 |
| 75 | 13 | 13.00 | 13.00 | 13.00 | 13.00 | 18.99 | 13.69 | 2.70 | 13.00 | 82.40 |
| 75 | 14 | 14.00 | 14.00 | 14.00 | 14.00 | 14.45 | 14.25 | 1.38 | 14.00 | 86.80 |
| 100 | 12 | 12.00 | 12.00 | 12.00 | 12.00 | 22.49 | 13.15 | 3.54 | 12.00 | 84.40 |
| 100 | 13 | 13.00 | 13.00 | 13.00 | 13.00 | 19.92 | 13.73 | 2.86 | 13.00 | 89.80 |
| 100 | 14 | 14.00 | 14.00 | 14.00 | 14.00 | 14.00 | 14.29 | 1.71 | 14.00 | 95.00 |

YIELD VOLATILITY(BP): 100

INITIAL YIELD LEVEL: 15

IMMUNIZED RETURN: 15

EQUILIBRIUM YIELD: 15

ACCURATE FORECASTS (OUT OF 20): 9

| MAX. LOSS PER- CENT | FLOOR | RETURN CONFIDENCE INTERVALS | | | | | MEAN | STD DEV | LOWEST RETURN | PERCENT AT FLOOR |
|---|---|---|---|---|---|---|---|---|---|---|
| | | 5 | 25 | 50 | 75 | 95 | | | | |
| 25 | 12 | 12.11 | 12.46 | 13.13 | 14.47 | 19.86 | 14.12 | 2.78 | 12.02 | 0.00 |
| 25 | 13 | 13.07 | 13.29 | 13.73 | 14.61 | 18.10 | 14.40 | 1.92 | 13.01 | 0.00 |
| 25 | 14 | 14.03 | 14.14 | 14.35 | 14.78 | 16.55 | 14.69 | 1.01 | 14.01 | 0.00 |
| 50 | 12 | 12.00 | 12.00 | 12.02 | 12.80 | 25.00 | 13.85 | 4.22 | 12.00 | 34.00 |
| 50 | 13 | 13.00 | 13.00 | 13.01 | 13.28 | 23.29 | 14.21 | 3.31 | 13.00 | 36.80 |
| 50 | 14 | 14.00 | 14.00 | 14.00 | 14.08 | 16.74 | 14.57 | 2.04 | 14.00 | 39.00 |
| 75 | 12 | 12.00 | 12.00 | 12.00 | 12.11 | 25.43 | 13.94 | 4.56 | 12.00 | 67.80 |
| 75 | 13 | 13.00 | 13.00 | 13.00 | 13.00 | 24.54 | 14.26 | 3.76 | 13.00 | 75.80 |
| 75 | 14 | 14.00 | 14.00 | 14.00 | 14.00 | 20.49 | 14.67 | 2.61 | 14.00 | 81.40 |
| 100 | 12 | 12.00 | 12.00 | 12.00 | 12.00 | 25.63 | 14.03 | 4.67 | 12.00 | 75.60 |
| 100 | 13 | 13.00 | 13.00 | 13.00 | 13.00 | 23.81 | 14.39 | 3.94 | 13.00 | 82.60 |
| 100 | 14 | 14.00 | 14.00 | 14.00 | 14.00 | 21.54 | 14.78 | 2.98 | 14.00 | 89.20 |

YIELD VOLATILITY(BP): 100

INITIAL YIELD LEVEL: 15

IMMUNIZED RETURN: 15

EQUILIBRIUM YIELD: 15

ACCURATE FORECASTS (OUT OF 20): 10

| MAX. LOSS PER- CENT | FLOOR | RETURN CONFIDENCE INTERVALS | | | | | MEAN | STD DEV | LOWEST RETURN | PERCENT AT FLOOR |
|---|---|---|---|---|---|---|---|---|---|---|
| | | 5 | 25 | 50 | 75 | 95 | | | | |
| 25 | 12 | 12.21 | 12.73 | 13.52 | 15.51 | 22.44 | 14.91 | 3.63 | 12.02 | 0.00 |
| 25 | 13 | 13.14 | 13.47 | 13.98 | 15.30 | 20.12 | 14.95 | 2.64 | 13.01 | 0.00 |
| 25 | 14 | 14.06 | 14.23 | 14.48 | 15.13 | 17.64 | 14.98 | 1.42 | 14.01 | 0.00 |
| 50 | 12 | 12.00 | 12.00 | 12.09 | 15.44 | 26.65 | 14.95 | 5.45 | 12.00 | 26.20 |
| 50 | 13 | 13.00 | 13.00 | 13.04 | 14.01 | 25.33 | 14.98 | 4.46 | 13.00 | 28.20 |
| 50 | 14 | 14.00 | 14.00 | 14.01 | 14.20 | 20.02 | 15.00 | 3.00 | 14.00 | 30.80 |
| 75 | 12 | 12.00 | 12.00 | 12.00 | 16.76 | 27.31 | 15.15 | 5.82 | 12.00 | 61.00 |
| 75 | 13 | 13.00 | 13.00 | 13.00 | 13.08 | 26.47 | 15.09 | 4.97 | 13.00 | 70.00 |
| 75 | 14 | 14.00 | 14.00 | 14.00 | 14.00 | 22.98 | 15.18 | 3.73 | 14.00 | 78.40 |
| 100 | 12 | 12.00 | 12.00 | 12.00 | 17.16 | 28.68 | 15.23 | 5.95 | 12.00 | 67.40 |
| 100 | 13 | 13.00 | 13.00 | 13.00 | 13.00 | 27.11 | 15.27 | 5.14 | 13.00 | 76.40 |
| 100 | 14 | 14.00 | 14.00 | 14.00 | 14.00 | 25.23 | 15.34 | 4.11 | 14.00 | 84.20 |

YIELD VOLATILITY(BP): 100

INITIAL YIELD LEVEL: 15

IMMUNIZED RETURN: 15

EQUILIBRIUM YIELD: 15

ACCURATE FORECASTS (OUT OF 20): 11

| MAX. LOSS PER- CENT | FLOOR | RETURN CONFIDENCE INTERVALS | | | | | MEAN | STD DEV | LOWEST RETURN | PERCENT AT FLOOR |
|---|---|---|---|---|---|---|---|---|---|---|
| | | 5 | 25 | 50 | 75 | 95 | | | | |
| 25 | 12 | 12.31 | 13.25 | 14.64 | 17.88 | 27.76 | 16.41 | 4.65 | 12.03 | 0.00 |
| 25 | 13 | 13.20 | 13.81 | 14.71 | 16.75 | 24.26 | 15.97 | 3.39 | 13.02 | 0.00 |
| 25 | 14 | 14.09 | 14.39 | 14.83 | 15.84 | 19.52 | 15.50 | 1.80 | 14.01 | 0.00 |
| 50 | 12 | 12.00 | 12.00 | 12.58 | 21.47 | 32.56 | 16.98 | 7.01 | 12.00 | 23.20 |
| 50 | 13 | 13.00 | 13.00 | 13.27 | 17.74 | 31.17 | 16.54 | 5.94 | 13.00 | 27.00 |
| 50 | 14 | 14.00 | 14.00 | 14.07 | 14.96 | 27.44 | 15.97 | 4.29 | 14.00 | 30.40 |
| 75 | 12 | 12.00 | 12.00 | 12.00 | 22.01 | 33.37 | 17.20 | 7.51 | 12.00 | 50.20 |
| 75 | 13 | 13.00 | 13.00 | 13.00 | 20.08 | 32.57 | 16.95 | 6.73 | 13.00 | 59.80 |
| 75 | 14 | 14.00 | 14.00 | 14.00 | 14.09 | 29.89 | 16.33 | 5.20 | 14.00 | 69.40 |
| 100 | 12 | 12.00 | 12.00 | 12.00 | 22.41 | 33.39 | 17.33 | 7.57 | 12.00 | 55.00 |
| 100 | 13 | 13.00 | 13.00 | 13.00 | 20.74 | 33.17 | 17.25 | 7.05 | 13.00 | 63.40 |
| 100 | 14 | 14.00 | 14.00 | 14.00 | 14.00 | 30.10 | 16.58 | 5.59 | 14.00 | 74.80 |

YIELD VOLATILITY(BP): 100

INITIAL YIELD LEVEL: 15

IMMUNIZED RETURN: 15

EQUILIBRIUM YIELD: 15

ACCURATE FORECASTS (OUT OF 20): 12

| MAX. LOSS PER-CENT | FLOOR | RETURN CONFIDENCE INTERVALS | | | | | MEAN | STD DEV | LOWEST RETURN | PERCENT AT FLOOR |
|---|---|---|---|---|---|---|---|---|---|---|
| | | 5 | 25 | 50 | 75 | 95 | | | | |
| 25 | 12 | 12.47 | 13.66 | 15.64 | 20.22 | 30.79 | 17.92 | 6.02 | 12.03 | 0.00 |
| 25 | 13 | 13.29 | 14.07 | 15.32 | 18.34 | 27.70 | 17.14 | 4.75 | 13.02 | 0.00 |
| 25 | 14 | 14.14 | 14.52 | 15.12 | 16.71 | 22.18 | 16.20 | 2.96 | 14.01 | 0.00 |
| 50 | 12 | 12.00 | 12.01 | 14.29 | 25.10 | 35.89 | 19.04 | 8.55 | 12.00 | 20.60 |
| 50 | 13 | 13.00 | 13.00 | 13.72 | 23.19 | 34.66 | 18.37 | 7.64 | 13.00 | 24.80 |
| 50 | 14 | 14.00 | 14.00 | 14.17 | 17.57 | 30.80 | 17.31 | 5.94 | 14.00 | 27.80 |
| 75 | 12 | 12.00 | 12.00 | 14.25 | 26.30 | 36.41 | 19.42 | 8.98 | 12.00 | 41.60 |
| 75 | 13 | 13.00 | 13.00 | 13.00 | 24.93 | 36.02 | 18.88 | 8.33 | 13.00 | 50.60 |
| 75 | 14 | 14.00 | 14.00 | 14.00 | 20.25 | 33.51 | 17.90 | 7.01 | 14.00 | 61.60 |
| 100 | 12 | 12.00 | 12.00 | 15.26 | 26.41 | 36.41 | 19.60 | 9.00 | 12.00 | 43.80 |
| 100 | 13 | 13.00 | 13.00 | 13.00 | 25.27 | 36.41 | 19.07 | 8.58 | 13.00 | 55.80 |
| 100 | 14 | 14.00 | 14.00 | 14.00 | 20.66 | 35.27 | 18.20 | 7.50 | 14.00 | 67.80 |

YIELD VOLATILITY(BP): 100

INITIAL YIELD LEVEL: 15

IMMUNIZED RETURN: 15

EQUILIBRIUM YIELD: 18

ACCURATE FORECASTS (OUT OF 20): 8

| MAX. LOSS PER-CENT | FLOOR | RETURN CONFIDENCE INTERVALS | | | | | MEAN | STD DEV | LOWEST RETURN | PERCENT AT FLOOR |
|---|---|---|---|---|---|---|---|---|---|---|
| | | 5 | 25 | 50 | 75 | 95 | | | | |
| 25 | 12 | 12.09 | 12.32 | 12.69 | 13.66 | 17.51 | 13.43 | 2.02 | 12.00 | 0.20 |
| 25 | 13 | 13.06 | 13.21 | 13.45 | 14.07 | 16.66 | 13.94 | 1.35 | 13.00 | 0.20 |
| 25 | 14 | 14.03 | 14.10 | 14.22 | 14.52 | 15.81 | 14.46 | 0.68 | 14.00 | 0.20 |
| 50 | 12 | 12.00 | 12.00 | 12.01 | 12.23 | 20.09 | 13.02 | 3.03 | 12.00 | 33.40 |
| 50 | 13 | 13.00 | 13.00 | 13.00 | 13.10 | 16.53 | 13.62 | 2.16 | 13.00 | 36.60 |
| 50 | 14 | 14.00 | 14.00 | 14.00 | 14.04 | 15.24 | 14.28 | 1.18 | 14.00 | 38.20 |
| 75 | 12 | 12.00 | 12.00 | 12.00 | 12.00 | 20.46 | 13.03 | 3.25 | 12.00 | 76.20 |
| 75 | 13 | 13.00 | 13.00 | 13.00 | 13.00 | 17.18 | 13.59 | 2.46 | 13.00 | 82.60 |
| 75 | 14 | 14.00 | 14.00 | 14.00 | 14.00 | 14.16 | 14.26 | 1.49 | 14.00 | 87.40 |
| 100 | 12 | 12.00 | 12.00 | 12.00 | 12.00 | 20.80 | 13.09 | 3.42 | 12.00 | 83.60 |
| 100 | 13 | 13.00 | 13.00 | 13.00 | 13.00 | 16.22 | 13.57 | 2.53 | 13.00 | 90.00 |
| 100 | 14 | 14.00 | 14.00 | 14.00 | 14.00 | 14.00 | 14.28 | 1.71 | 14.00 | 95.20 |

YIELD VOLATILITY(BP): 100

INITIAL YIELD LEVEL: 15

IMMUNIZED RETURN: 15

EQUILIBRIUM YIELD: 18

ACCURATE FORECASTS (OUT OF 20): 9

| MAX. LOSS PER- CENT | FLOOR | RETURN CONFIDENCE INTERVALS | | | | | MEAN | STD DEV | LOWEST RETURN | PERCENT AT FLOOR |
|---|---|---|---|---|---|---|---|---|---|---|
| | | 5 | 25 | 50 | 75 | 95 | | | | |
| 25 | 12 | 12.15 | 12.49 | 13.17 | 14.56 | 19.74 | 14.16 | 2.80 | 12.03 | 0.00 |
| 25 | 13 | 13.08 | 13.32 | 13.76 | 14.66 | 18.00 | 14.43 | 1.95 | 13.02 | 0.00 |
| 25 | 14 | 14.04 | 14.15 | 14.37 | 14.79 | 16.52 | 14.71 | 1.03 | 14.01 | 0.00 |
| 50 | 12 | 12.00 | 12.00 | 12.03 | 12.84 | 24.45 | 13.85 | 4.18 | 12.00 | 30.20 |
| 50 | 13 | 13.00 | 13.00 | 13.02 | 13.29 | 22.11 | 14.25 | 3.34 | 13.00 | 32.20 |
| 50 | 14 | 14.00 | 14.00 | 14.01 | 14.11 | 17.93 | 14.62 | 2.12 | 14.00 | 34.60 |
| 75 | 12 | 12.00 | 12.00 | 12.00 | 12.20 | 25.53 | 13.92 | 4.51 | 12.00 | 65.00 |
| 75 | 13 | 13.00 | 13.00 | 13.00 | 13.00 | 23.53 | 14.27 | 3.73 | 13.00 | 73.60 |
| 75 | 14 | 14.00 | 14.00 | 14.00 | 14.00 | 19.74 | 14.70 | 2.70 | 14.00 | 79.00 |
| 100 | 12 | 12.00 | 12.00 | 12.00 | 12.01 | 26.04 | 14.03 | 4.63 | 12.00 | 73.40 |
| 100 | 13 | 13.00 | 13.00 | 13.00 | 13.00 | 24.27 | 14.38 | 3.96 | 13.00 | 83.40 |
| 100 | 14 | 14.00 | 14.00 | 14.00 | 14.00 | 21.13 | 14.81 | 3.03 | 14.00 | 89.00 |

YIELD VOLATILITY(BP): 100

INITIAL YIELD LEVEL: 15

IMMUNIZED RETURN: 15

EQUILIBRIUM YIELD: 18

ACCURATE FORECASTS (OUT OF 20): 10

| MAX. LOSS PER- CENT | FLOOR | RETURN CONFIDENCE INTERVALS | | | | | MEAN | STD DEV | LOWEST RETURN | PERCENT AT FLOOR |
|---|---|---|---|---|---|---|---|---|---|---|
| | | 5 | 25 | 50 | 75 | 95 | | | | |
| 25 | 12 | 12.22 | 12.75 | 13.62 | 15.36 | 22.39 | 14.91 | 3.56 | 12.02 | 0.00 |
| 25 | 13 | 13.14 | 13.49 | 14.05 | 15.19 | 19.59 | 14.95 | 2.57 | 13.01 | 0.00 |
| 25 | 14 | 14.07 | 14.24 | 14.51 | 15.07 | 17.37 | 14.98 | 1.39 | 14.01 | 0.00 |
| 50 | 12 | 12.00 | 12.00 | 12.13 | 14.84 | 27.03 | 14.91 | 5.41 | 12.00 | 23.40 |
| 50 | 13 | 13.00 | 13.00 | 13.05 | 13.82 | 25.03 | 15.00 | 4.42 | 13.00 | 26.40 |
| 50 | 14 | 14.00 | 14.00 | 14.02 | 14.22 | 20.68 | 15.00 | 2.92 | 14.00 | 28.60 |
| 75 | 12 | 12.00 | 12.00 | 12.00 | 15.83 | 28.07 | 15.13 | 5.82 | 12.00 | 59.80 |
| 75 | 13 | 13.00 | 13.00 | 13.00 | 13.08 | 26.64 | 15.19 | 4.98 | 13.00 | 70.20 |
| 75 | 14 | 14.00 | 14.00 | 14.00 | 14.00 | 22.77 | 15.21 | 3.64 | 14.00 | 77.20 |
| 100 | 12 | 12.00 | 12.00 | 12.00 | 16.58 | 28.33 | 15.22 | 5.89 | 12.00 | 67.00 |
| 100 | 13 | 13.00 | 13.00 | 13.00 | 13.08 | 27.21 | 15.34 | 5.14 | 13.00 | 74.20 |
| 100 | 14 | 14.00 | 14.00 | 14.00 | 14.00 | 24.58 | 15.33 | 3.96 | 14.00 | 85.20 |

YIELD VOLATILITY(BP): 100

INITIAL YIELD LEVEL: 15

IMMUNIZED RETURN: 15

EQUILIBRIUM YIELD: 18

ACCURATE FORECASTS (OUT OF 20): 11

| MAX. LOSS PER-CENT | FLOOR | RETURN CONFIDENCE INTERVALS | | | | | MEAN | STD DEV | LOWEST RETURN | PERCENT AT FLOOR |
|---|---|---|---|---|---|---|---|---|---|---|
| | | 5 | 25 | 50 | 75 | 95 | | | | |
| 25 | 12 | 12.34 | 13.25 | 14.67 | 17.96 | 27.17 | 16.40 | 4.53 | 12.05 | 0.00 |
| 25 | 13 | 13.22 | 13.81 | 14.75 | 16.88 | 23.79 | 15.96 | 3.29 | 13.03 | 0.00 |
| 25 | 14 | 14.11 | 14.39 | 14.85 | 15.91 | 19.61 | 15.49 | 1.74 | 14.01 | 0.00 |
| 50 | 12 | 12.00 | 12.01 | 12.79 | 20.63 | 31.71 | 16.90 | 6.80 | 12.00 | 21.20 |
| 50 | 13 | 13.00 | 13.00 | 13.32 | 17.53 | 30.55 | 16.52 | 5.84 | 13.00 | 24.00 |
| 50 | 14 | 14.00 | 14.00 | 14.12 | 15.42 | 26.91 | 16.01 | 4.21 | 14.00 | 27.60 |
| 75 | 12 | 12.00 | 12.00 | 12.02 | 21.72 | 32.76 | 17.02 | 7.29 | 12.00 | 48.40 |
| 75 | 13 | 13.00 | 13.00 | 13.00 | 18.32 | 31.57 | 16.72 | 6.49 | 13.00 | 57.40 |
| 75 | 14 | 14.00 | 14.00 | 14.00 | 14.06 | 29.63 | 16.37 | 5.21 | 14.00 | 69.20 |
| 100 | 12 | 12.00 | 12.00 | 12.00 | 22.35 | 33.32 | 17.25 | 7.34 | 12.00 | 52.80 |
| 100 | 13 | 13.00 | 13.00 | 13.00 | 20.36 | 32.40 | 17.03 | 6.81 | 13.00 | 64.40 |
| 100 | 14 | 14.00 | 14.00 | 14.00 | 14.00 | 30.26 | 16.58 | 5.54 | 14.00 | 76.00 |

YIELD VOLATILITY(BP): 100

INITIAL YIELD LEVEL: 15

IMMUNIZED RETURN: 15

EQUILIBRIUM YIELD: 18

ACCURATE FORECASTS (OUT OF 20): 12

| MAX. LOSS PER-CENT | FLOOR | RETURN CONFIDENCE INTERVALS | | | | | MEAN | STD DEV | LOWEST RETURN | PERCENT AT FLOOR |
|---|---|---|---|---|---|---|---|---|---|---|
| | | 5 | 25 | 50 | 75 | 95 | | | | |
| 25 | 12 | 12.49 | 13.67 | 15.66 | 19.99 | 30.74 | 17.86 | 5.87 | 12.03 | 0.00 |
| 25 | 13 | 13.32 | 14.09 | 15.40 | 18.29 | 27.82 | 17.10 | 4.63 | 13.02 | 0.00 |
| 25 | 14 | 14.15 | 14.52 | 15.17 | 16.64 | 22.10 | 16.18 | 2.89 | 14.01 | 0.00 |
| 50 | 12 | 12.00 | 12.05 | 14.65 | 24.81 | 36.36 | 19.02 | 8.33 | 12.00 | 17.20 |
| 50 | 13 | 13.01 | 13.01 | 13.95 | 22.09 | 34.90 | 18.32 | 7.44 | 13.00 | 20.20 |
| 50 | 14 | 14.00 | 14.00 | 14.23 | 17.39 | 32.24 | 17.26 | 5.85 | 14.00 | 22.60 |
| 75 | 12 | 12.00 | 12.00 | 14.20 | 25.65 | 37.02 | 19.26 | 8.83 | 12.00 | 40.80 |
| 75 | 13 | 13.00 | 13.00 | 13.00 | 23.94 | 36.39 | 18.87 | 8.18 | 13.00 | 48.80 |
| 75 | 14 | 14.00 | 14.00 | 14.00 | 19.68 | 34.47 | 17.84 | 6.89 | 14.00 | 60.00 |
| 100 | 12 | 12.00 | 12.00 | 14.52 | 25.60 | 37.12 | 19.32 | 8.87 | 12.00 | 46.00 |
| 100 | 13 | 13.00 | 13.00 | 13.00 | 24.77 | 36.92 | 19.15 | 8.47 | 13.00 | 54.80 |
| 100 | 14 | 14.00 | 14.00 | 14.00 | 20.65 | 35.37 | 18.24 | 7.33 | 14.00 | 65.20 |

YIELD VOLATILITY(BP): 200

INITIAL YIELD LEVEL: 15

IMMUNIZED RETURN: 15

EQUILIBRIUM YIELD: 12

ACCURATE FORECASTS (OUT OF 20): 8

| MAX. LOSS PER- CENT | FLOOR | 5 | 25 | 50 | 75 | 95 | MEAN | STD DEV | LOWEST RETURN | PERCENT AT FLOOR |
|---|---|---|---|---|---|---|---|---|---|---|
| | | | | RETURN CONFIDENCE INTERVALS | | | | | | |
| 25 | 12 | 12.05 | 12.24 | 12.57 | 13.46 | 17.43 | 13.38 | 2.09 | 12.00 | 0.40 |
| 25 | 13 | 13.03 | 13.15 | 13.37 | 13.95 | 16.62 | 13.90 | 1.40 | 13.00 | 0.40 |
| 25 | 14 | 14.01 | 14.07 | 14.18 | 14.46 | 15.81 | 14.44 | 0.70 | 14.00 | 0.40 |
| 50 | 12 | 12.00 | 12.00 | 12.00 | 12.09 | 16.58 | 12.87 | 3.29 | 12.00 | 50.40 |
| 50 | 13 | 13.00 | 13.00 | 13.00 | 13.05 | 15.37 | 13.53 | 2.36 | 13.00 | 50.60 |
| 50 | 14 | 14.00 | 14.00 | 14.00 | 14.02 | 14.79 | 14.20 | 0.88 | 14.00 | 52.00 |
| 75 | 12 | 12.00 | 12.00 | 12.00 | 12.00 | 20.91 | 13.08 | 4.58 | 12.00 | 84.40 |
| 75 | 13 | 13.00 | 13.00 | 13.00 | 13.00 | 14.04 | 13.57 | 3.06 | 13.00 | 87.00 |
| 75 | 14 | 14.00 | 14.00 | 14.00 | 14.00 | 14.07 | 14.21 | 1.77 | 14.00 | 89.00 |
| 100 | 12 | 12.00 | 12.00 | 12.00 | 12.00 | 21.50 | 13.19 | 5.17 | 12.00 | 91.80 |
| 100 | 13 | 13.00 | 13.00 | 13.00 | 13.00 | 13.35 | 13.80 | 3.95 | 13.00 | 93.60 |
| 100 | 14 | 14.00 | 14.00 | 14.00 | 14.00 | 14.00 | 14.22 | 1.93 | 14.00 | 96.20 |

YIELD VOLATILITY(BP): 200

INITIAL YIELD LEVEL: 15

IMMUNIZED RETURN: 15

EQUILIBRIUM YIELD: 12

ACCURATE FORECASTS (OUT OF 20): 9

| MAX. LOSS PER- CENT | FLOOR | RETURN CONFIDENCE INTERVALS | | | | | MEAN | STD DEV | LOWEST RETURN | PERCENT AT FLOOR |
|---|---|---|---|---|---|---|---|---|---|---|
| | | 5 | 25 | 50 | 75 | 95 | | | | |
| 25 | 12 | 12.09 | 12.38 | 13.05 | 14.50 | 19.90 | 14.07 | 2.96 | 12.00 | 0.20 |
| 25 | 13 | 13.06 | 13.24 | 13.68 | 14.62 | 18.32 | 14.37 | 2.04 | 13.00 | 0.20 |
| 25 | 14 | 14.03 | 14.11 | 14.33 | 14.78 | 16.67 | 14.68 | 1.07 | 14.00 | 0.20 |
| 50 | 12 | 12.00 | 12.00 | 12.00 | 12.28 | 25.57 | 13.77 | 5.53 | 12.00 | 44.20 |
| 50 | 13 | 13.00 | 13.00 | 13.00 | 13.14 | 19.00 | 14.13 | 4.19 | 13.00 | 45.60 |
| 50 | 14 | 14.00 | 14.00 | 14.00 | 14.06 | 16.38 | 14.54 | 2.53 | 14.00 | 47.60 |
| 75 | 12 | 12.00 | 12.00 | 12.00 | 12.00 | 30.80 | 13.86 | 6.66 | 12.00 | 80.00 |
| 75 | 13 | 13.00 | 13.00 | 13.00 | 13.00 | 24.43 | 14.33 | 5.37 | 13.00 | 83.40 |
| 75 | 14 | 14.00 | 14.00 | 14.00 | 14.00 | 14.89 | 14.67 | 3.63 | 14.00 | 85.80 |
| 100 | 12 | 12.00 | 12.00 | 12.00 | 12.00 | 31.44 | 14.14 | 7.24 | 12.00 | 85.60 |
| 100 | 13 | 13.00 | 13.00 | 13.00 | 13.00 | 26.36 | 14.51 | 6.09 | 13.00 | 90.20 |
| 100 | 14 | 14.00 | 14.00 | 14.00 | 14.00 | 14.89 | 14.77 | 3.80 | 14.00 | 92.80 |

YIELD VOLATILITY(BP): 200

INITIAL YIELD LEVEL: 15

IMMUNIZED RETURN: 15

EQUILIBRIUM YIELD: 12

ACCURATE FORECASTS (OUT OF 20): 10

| MAX. LOSS PER- CENT | FLOOR | RETURN CONFIDENCE INTERVALS | | | | | MEAN | STD DEV | LOWEST RETURN | PERCENT AT FLOOR |
|---|---|---|---|---|---|---|---|---|---|---|
| | | 5 | 25 | 50 | 75 | 95 | | | | |
| 25 | 12 | 12.15 | 12.61 | 13.44 | 15.48 | 22.90 | 14.91 | 3.98 | 12.00 | 0.20 |
| 25 | 13 | 13.09 | 13.38 | 13.93 | 15.28 | 20.43 | 14.94 | 2.79 | 13.00 | 0.20 |
| 25 | 14 | 14.04 | 14.18 | 14.45 | 15.13 | 17.78 | 14.97 | 1.48 | 14.00 | 0.20 |
| 50 | 12 | 12.00 | 12.00 | 12.02 | 13.14 | 32.86 | 15.07 | 7.89 | 12.00 | 39.00 |
| 50 | 13 | 13.00 | 13.00 | 13.01 | 13.46 | 26.95 | 15.03 | 6.18 | 13.00 | 40.80 |
| 50 | 14 | 14.00 | 14.00 | 14.00 | 14.17 | 18.51 | 15.01 | 3.91 | 14.00 | 42.80 |
| 75 | 12 | 12.00 | 12.00 | 12.00 | 12.00 | 37.02 | 15.41 | 9.20 | 12.00 | 74.40 |
| 75 | 13 | 13.00 | 13.00 | 13.00 | 13.00 | 33.52 | 15.46 | 7.83 | 13.00 | 78.60 |
| 75 | 14 | 14.00 | 14.00 | 14.00 | 14.00 | 22.04 | 15.31 | 5.53 | 14.00 | 83.60 |
| 100 | 12 | 12.00 | 12.00 | 12.00 | 12.00 | 36.93 | 15.64 | 9.55 | 12.00 | 81.20 |
| 100 | 13 | 13.00 | 13.00 | 13.00 | 13.00 | 34.25 | 15.76 | 8.44 | 13.00 | 84.60 |
| 100 | 14 | 14.00 | 14.00 | 14.00 | 14.00 | 26.16 | 15.55 | 6.32 | 14.00 | 89.60 |

Bond Portfolio Immunization

YIELD VOLATILITY(BP): 200

INITIAL YIELD LEVEL: 15

IMMUNIZED RETURN: 15

EQUILIBRIUM YIELD: 12

ACCURATE FORECASTS (OUT OF 20): 11

| MAX. LOSS PER-CENT | FLOOR | RETURN CONFIDENCE INTERVALS | | | | | MEAN | STD DEV | LOWEST RETURN | PERCENT AT FLOOR |
|---|---|---|---|---|---|---|---|---|---|---|
| | | 5 | 25 | 50 | 75 | 95 | | | | |
| 25 | 12 | 12.25 | 13.16 | 14.56 | 17.72 | 28.48 | 16.48 | 5.26 | 12.00 | 0.20 |
| 25 | 13 | 13.16 | 13.74 | 14.66 | 16.75 | 24.46 | 16.02 | 3.72 | 13.00 | 0.20 |
| 25 | 14 | 14.07 | 14.35 | 14.79 | 15.85 | 19.97 | 15.52 | 1.98 | 14.00 | 0.20 |
| 50 | 12 | 12.00 | 12.00 | 12.20 | 16.51 | 44.72 | 17.72 | 10.91 | 12.00 | 33.80 |
| 50 | 13 | 13.00 | 13.00 | 13.09 | 14.95 | 40.94 | 17.05 | 8.96 | 13.00 | 36.80 |
| 50 | 14 | 14.00 | 14.00 | 14.03 | 14.58 | 31.35 | 16.29 | 6.26 | 14.00 | 39.60 |
| 75 | 12 | 12.00 | 12.00 | 12.00 | 20.89 | 49.54 | 18.73 | 12.66 | 12.00 | 65.20 |
| 75 | 13 | 13.00 | 13.00 | 13.00 | 13.10 | 43.20 | 17.69 | 10.72 | 13.00 | 71.20 |
| 75 | 14 | 14.00 | 14.00 | 14.00 | 14.00 | 37.53 | 16.92 | 8.32 | 14.00 | 76.20 |
| 100 | 12 | 12.00 | 12.00 | 12.00 | 24.05 | 51.72 | 19.32 | 13.51 | 12.00 | 69.20 |
| 100 | 13 | 13.00 | 13.00 | 13.00 | 13.00 | 49.39 | 18.39 | 11.75 | 13.00 | 74.60 |
| 100 | 14 | 14.00 | 14.00 | 14.00 | 14.00 | 40.66 | 17.37 | 9.36 | 14.00 | 82.80 |

YIELD VOLATILITY(BP): 200

INITIAL YIELD LEVEL: 15

IMMUNIZED RETURN: 15

EQUILIBRIUM YIELD: 12

ACCURATE FORECASTS (OUT OF 20): 12

| MAX. LOSS PER- CENT | FLOOR | RETURN CONFIDENCE INTERVALS | | | | | MEAN | STD DEV | LOWEST RETURN | PERCENT AT FLOOR |
|---|---|---|---|---|---|---|---|---|---|---|
| | | 5 | 25 | 50 | 75 | 95 | | | | |
| 25 | 12 | 12.38 | 13.53 | 15.54 | 20.10 | 34.15 | 18.34 | 7.81 | 12.03 | 0.00 |
| 25 | 13 | 13.24 | 13.95 | 15.33 | 18.42 | 29.03 | 17.40 | 5.94 | 13.02 | 0.00 |
| 25 | 14 | 14.11 | 14.46 | 15.10 | 16.67 | 22.79 | 16.31 | 3.49 | 14.01 | 0.00 |
| 50 | 12 | 12.00 | 12.00 | 12.59 | 27.41 | 52.06 | 20.95 | 14.39 | 12.00 | 29.80 |
| 50 | 13 | 13.00 | 13.00 | 13.25 | 20.58 | 47.15 | 19.74 | 12.38 | 13.00 | 32.40 |
| 50 | 14 | 14.00 | 14.00 | 14.09 | 15.79 | 39.49 | 17.97 | 9.13 | 14.00 | 35.00 |
| 75 | 12 | 12.00 | 12.00 | 12.00 | 30.55 | 56.13 | 22.11 | 16.30 | 12.00 | 56.80 |
| 75 | 13 | 13.00 | 13.00 | 13.00 | 24.50 | 53.89 | 20.88 | 14.60 | 13.00 | 63.60 |
| 75 | 14 | 14.00 | 14.00 | 14.00 | 14.08 | 46.64 | 19.09 | 11.82 | 14.00 | 71.00 |
| 100 | 12 | 12.00 | 12.00 | 12.00 | 33.42 | 57.68 | 22.92 | 17.01 | 12.00 | 60.80 |
| 100 | 13 | 13.00 | 13.00 | 13.00 | 27.51 | 56.03 | 21.86 | 15.77 | 13.00 | 68.40 |
| 100 | 14 | 14.00 | 14.00 | 14.00 | 14.00 | 49.93 | 20.01 | 13.08 | 14.00 | 76.00 |

YIELD VOLATILITY(BP): 200

INITIAL YIELD LEVEL: 15

IMMUNIZED RETURN: 15

EQUILIBRIUM YIELD: 15

ACCURATE FORECASTS (OUT OF 20): 8

| MAX. LOSS PER- CENT | FLOOR | RETURN CONFIDENCE INTERVALS | | | | | MEAN | STD DEV | LOWEST RETURN | PERCENT AT FLOOR |
|---|---|---|---|---|---|---|---|---|---|---|
| | | 5 | 25 | 50 | 75 | 95 | | | | |
| 25 | 12 | 12.07 | 12.30 | 12.67 | 13.55 | 17.45 | 13.42 | 2.04 | 12.00 | 0.20 |
| 25 | 13 | 13.04 | 13.19 | 13.43 | 14.01 | 16.60 | 13.93 | 1.37 | 13.00 | 0.40 |
| 25 | 14 | 14.02 | 14.09 | 14.21 | 14.49 | 15.78 | 14.46 | 0.69 | 14.00 | 0.40 |
| 50 | 12 | 12.00 | 12.00 | 12.00 | 12.14 | 16.47 | 12.88 | 3.18 | 12.00 | 39.40 |
| 50 | 13 | 13.00 | 13.00 | 13.00 | 13.08 | 15.50 | 13.55 | 2.31 | 13.00 | 40.60 |
| 50 | 14 | 14.00 | 14.00 | 14.00 | 14.03 | 15.08 | 14.22 | 0.87 | 14.00 | 41.80 |
| 75 | 12 | 12.00 | 12.00 | 12.00 | 12.00 | 19.22 | 13.03 | 4.39 | 12.00 | 85.00 |
| 75 | 13 | 13.00 | 13.00 | 13.00 | 13.00 | 14.13 | 13.53 | 2.87 | 13.00 | 85.00 |
| 75 | 14 | 14.00 | 14.00 | 14.00 | 14.00 | 14.10 | 14.22 | 1.80 | 14.00 | 87.40 |
| 100 | 12 | 12.00 | 12.00 | 12.00 | 12.00 | 21.50 | 13.14 | 4.96 | 12.00 | 91.00 |
| 100 | 13 | 13.00 | 13.00 | 13.00 | 13.00 | 15.03 | 13.64 | 3.52 | 13.00 | 94.00 |
| 100 | 14 | 14.00 | 14.00 | 14.00 | 14.00 | 14.00 | 14.24 | 2.04 | 14.00 | 96.60 |

YIELD VOLATILITY(BP): 200

INITIAL YIELD LEVEL: 15

IMMUNIZED RETURN: 15

EQUILIBRIUM YIELD: 15

ACCURATE FORECASTS (OUT OF 20): 9

| MAX. LOSS PER- CENT | FLOOR | RETURN CONFIDENCE INTERVALS | | | | | MEAN | STD DEV | LOWEST RETURN | PERCENT AT FLOOR |
|---|---|---|---|---|---|---|---|---|---|---|
| | | 5 | 25 | 50 | 75 | 95 | | | | |
| 25 | 12 | 12.11 | 12.46 | 13.16 | 14.51 | 19.65 | 14.12 | 2.86 | 12.00 | 0.20 |
| 25 | 13 | 13.07 | 13.30 | 13.74 | 14.63 | 18.15 | 14.40 | 1.98 | 13.00 | 0.20 |
| 25 | 14 | 14.04 | 14.14 | 14.36 | 14.79 | 16.58 | 14.70 | 1.03 | 14.00 | 0.20 |
| 50 | 12 | 12.00 | 12.00 | 12.01 | 12.37 | 27.12 | 13.81 | 5.40 | 12.00 | 36.60 |
| 50 | 13 | 13.00 | 13.00 | 13.01 | 13.22 | 19.19 | 14.16 | 4.06 | 13.00 | 37.80 |
| 50 | 14 | 14.00 | 14.00 | 14.00 | 14.10 | 16.38 | 14.56 | 2.46 | 14.00 | 38.40 |
| 75 | 12 | 12.00 | 12.00 | 12.00 | 12.00 | 32.12 | 13.91 | 6.56 | 12.00 | 77.60 |
| 75 | 13 | 13.00 | 13.00 | 13.00 | 13.00 | 25.35 | 14.33 | 5.22 | 13.00 | 80.80 |
| 75 | 14 | 14.00 | 14.00 | 14.00 | 14.00 | 15.17 | 14.63 | 3.45 | 14.00 | 82.80 |
| 100 | 12 | 12.00 | 12.00 | 12.00 | 12.00 | 30.75 | 14.09 | 6.99 | 12.00 | 85.80 |
| 100 | 13 | 13.00 | 13.00 | 13.00 | 13.00 | 25.77 | 14.51 | 5.89 | 13.00 | 89.60 |
| 100 | 14 | 14.00 | 14.00 | 14.00 | 14.00 | 17.48 | 14.75 | 3.68 | 14.00 | 92.00 |

YIELD VOLATILITY(BP): 200

INITIAL YIELD LEVEL: 15

IMMUNIZED RETURN: 15

EQUILIBRIUM YIELD: 15

ACCURATE FORECASTS (OUT OF 20): 10

| MAX. LOSS PER- CENT | FLOOR | RETURN CONFIDENCE INTERVALS | | | | | MEAN | STD DEV | LOWEST RETURN | PERCENT AT FLOOR |
|---|---|---|---|---|---|---|---|---|---|---|
| | | 5 | 25 | 50 | 75 | 95 | | | | |
| 25 | 12 | 12.19 | 12.72 | 13.56 | 15.48 | 22.60 | 14.91 | 3.76 | 12.00 | 0.20 |
| 25 | 13 | 13.12 | 13.46 | 14.00 | 15.27 | 20.16 | 14.94 | 2.63 | 13.00 | 0.20 |
| 25 | 14 | 14.06 | 14.22 | 14.49 | 15.12 | 17.61 | 14.97 | 1.39 | 14.00 | 0.20 |
| 50 | 12 | 12.00 | 12.00 | 12.05 | 13.14 | 31.34 | 14.98 | 7.46 | 12.00 | 29.40 |
| 50 | 13 | 13.00 | 13.00 | 13.03 | 13.53 | 25.27 | 14.99 | 5.80 | 13.00 | 31.40 |
| 50 | 14 | 14.00 | 14.00 | 14.01 | 14.19 | 18.48 | 15.00 | 3.70 | 14.00 | 33.40 |
| 75 | 12 | 12.00 | 12.00 | 12.00 | 12.01 | 36.55 | 15.23 | 8.78 | 12.00 | 71.60 |
| 75 | 13 | 13.00 | 13.00 | 13.00 | 13.00 | 30.83 | 15.33 | 7.36 | 13.00 | 75.40 |
| 75 | 14 | 14.00 | 14.00 | 14.00 | 14.00 | 22.35 | 15.23 | 5.16 | 14.00 | 80.20 |
| 100 | 12 | 12.00 | 12.00 | 12.00 | 12.00 | 38.28 | 15.67 | 9.30 | 12.00 | 79.20 |
| 100 | 13 | 13.00 | 13.00 | 13.00 | 13.00 | 35.06 | 15.65 | 8.13 | 13.00 | 84.40 |
| 100 | 14 | 14.00 | 14.00 | 14.00 | 14.00 | 27.16 | 15.48 | 5.95 | 14.00 | 89.80 |

YIELD VOLATILITY(BP): 200

INITIAL YIELD LEVEL: 15

IMMUNIZED RETURN: 15

EQUILIBRIUM YIELD: 15

ACCURATE FORECASTS (OUT OF 20): 11

| MAX. LOSS PER-CENT | FLOOR | RETURN CONFIDENCE INTERVALS | | | | | MEAN | STD DEV | LOWEST RETURN | PERCENT AT FLOOR |
|---|---|---|---|---|---|---|---|---|---|---|
| | | 5 | 25 | 50 | 75 | 95 | | | | |
| 25 | 12 | 12.30 | 13.28 | 14.68 | 17.64 | 27.51 | 16.40 | 4.84 | 12.01 | 0.00 |
| 25 | 13 | 13.20 | 13.82 | 14.74 | 16.73 | 23.80 | 15.96 | 3.41 | 13.00 | 0.00 |
| 25 | 14 | 14.09 | 14.40 | 14.84 | 15.83 | 19.64 | 15.49 | 1.80 | 14.00 | 0.20 |
| 50 | 12 | 12.00 | 12.00 | 12.40 | 17.15 | 43.06 | 17.56 | 10.33 | 12.00 | 27.20 |
| 50 | 13 | 13.00 | 15.00 | 13.19 | 15.27 | 39.62 | 16.90 | 8.40 | 13.00 | 29.60 |
| 50 | 14 | 14.00 | 14.00 | 14.06 | 14.83 | 31.93 | 16.15 | 5.72 | 14.00 | 32.80 |
| 75 | 12 | 12.00 | 12.00 | 12.00 | 17.87 | 47.05 | 18.35 | 12.02 | 12.00 | 63.20 |
| 75 | 13 | 13.00 | 13.00 | 13.00 | 13.19 | 43.83 | 17.63 | 10.35 | 13.00 | 69.00 |
| 75 | 14 | 14.00 | 14.00 | 14.00 | 14.00 | 38.43 | 16.81 | 7.88 | 14.00 | 73.20 |
| 100 | 12 | 12.00 | 12.00 | 12.00 | 21.55 | 48.75 | 18.95 | 12.82 | 12.00 | 68.60 |
| 100 | 13 | 13.00 | 13.00 | 13.00 | 13.00 | 46.02 | 18.12 | 11.10 | 13.00 | 74.60 |
| 100 | 14 | 14.00 | 14.00 | 14.00 | 14.00 | 40.00 | 17.21 | 8.86 | 14.00 | 82.40 |

YIELD VOLATILITY(BP): 200

INITIAL YIELD LEVEL: 15

IMMUNIZED RETURN: 15

EQUILIBRIUM YIELD: 15

ACCURATE FORECASTS (OUT OF 20): 12

| MAX. LOSS PER-CENT | FLOOR | RETURN CONFIDENCE INTERVALS | | | | | MEAN | STD DEV | LOWEST RETURN | PERCENT AT FLOOR |
|---|---|---|---|---|---|---|---|---|---|---|
| | | 5 | 25 | 50 | 75 | 95 | | | | |
| 25 | 12 | 12.47 | 13.70 | 15.59 | 19.59 | 32.82 | 18.16 | 7.21 | 12.03 | 0.00 |
| 25 | 13 | 13.30 | 14.11 | 15.31 | 18.03 | 27.76 | 17.26 | 5.44 | 13.02 | 0.00 |
| 25 | 14 | 14.14 | 14.52 | 15.14 | 16.52 | 21.72 | 16.22 | 3.15 | 14.01 | 0.00 |
| 50 | 12 | 12.00 | 12.00 | 12.92 | 26.99 | 50.00 | 20.71 | 13.70 | 12.00 | 25.00 |
| 50 | 13 | 13.00 | 13.00 | 13.45 | 20.77 | 46.34 | 19.54 | 11.69 | 13.00 | 26.80 |
| 50 | 14 | 14.00 | 14.00 | 14.15 | 16.01 | 37.53 | 17.88 | 8.63 | 14.00 | 29.20 |
| 75 | 12 | 12.00 | 12.00 | 12.00 | 30.23 | 54.31 | 21.86 | 15.57 | 12.00 | 54.80 |
| 75 | 13 | 13.00 | 13.00 | 13.00 | 25.19 | 51.83 | 20.73 | 13.98 | 13.00 | 60.20 |
| 75 | 14 | 14.00 | 14.00 | 14.00 | 14.42 | 43.89 | 18.94 | 11.16 | 14.00 | 68.00 |
| 100 | 12 | 12.00 | 12.00 | 12.00 | 33.01 | 56.02 | 22.58 | 16.24 | 12.00 | 59.60 |
| 100 | 13 | 13.00 | 13.00 | 13.00 | 26.51 | 54.18 | 21.40 | 15.03 | 13.00 | 66.60 |
| 100 | 14 | 14.00 | 14.00 | 14.00 | 14.00 | 49.92 | 19.65 | 12.41 | 14.00 | 75.40 |

YIELD VOLATILITY(BP): 200

INITIAL YIELD LEVEL: 15

IMMUNIZED RETURN: 15

EQUILIBRIUM YIELD: 18

ACCURATE FORECASTS (OUT OF 20): 8

| MAX. LOSS PER- CENT | FLOOR | RETURN CONFIDENCE INTERVALS | | | | | MEAN | STD DEV | LOWEST RETURN | PERCENT AT FLOOR |
|---|---|---|---|---|---|---|---|---|---|---|
| | | 5 | 25 | 50 | 75 | 95 | | | | |
| 25 | 12 | 12.08 | 12.33 | 12.73 | 13.67 | 17.40 | 13.45 | 2.00 | 12.00 | 0.20 |
| 25 | 13 | 13.05 | 13.22 | 13.47 | 14.09 | 16.59 | 13.95 | 1.34 | 13.00 | 0.20 |
| 25 | 14 | 14.02 | 14.10 | 14.23 | 14.53 | 15.78 | 14.47 | 0.68 | 14.00 | 0.20 |
| 50 | 12 | 12.00 | 12.00 | 12.01 | 12.18 | 16.92 | 12.93 | 3.32 | 12.00 | 33.20 |
| 50 | 13 | 13.00 | 13.00 | 13.00 | 13.10 | 15.85 | 13.59 | 2.33 | 13.00 | 34.20 |
| 50 | 14 | 14.00 | 14.00 | 14.00 | 14.05 | 15.32 | 14.23 | 0.89 | 14.00 | 35.20 |
| 75 | 12 | 12.00 | 12.00 | 12.00 | 12.00 | 15.98 | 12.91 | 4.12 | 12.00 | 82.80 |
| 75 | 13 | 13.00 | 13.03 | 13.00 | 13.00 | 13.89 | 13.53 | 2.92 | 13.00 | 84.80 |
| 75 | 14 | 14.00 | 14.00 | 14.00 | 14.00 | 14.10 | 14.22 | 1.77 | 14.00 | 87.20 |
| 100 | 12 | 12.00 | 12.00 | 12.00 | 12.00 | 14.54 | 12.93 | 4.57 | 12.00 | 91.60 |
| 100 | 13 | 13.00 | 13.00 | 13.00 | 13.00 | 13.00 | 13.54 | 3.34 | 13.00 | 94.00 |
| 100 | 14 | 14.00 | 14.00 | 14.00 | 14.00 | 14.00 | 14.26 | 2.10 | 14.00 | 96.40 |

YIELD VOLATILITY(BP): 200

INITIAL YIELD LEVEL: 15

IMMUNIZED RETURN: 15

EQUILIBRIUM YIELD: 18

ACCURATE FORECASTS (OUT OF 20): 9

| MAX. LOSS PER-CENT | FLOOR | RETURN CONFIDENCE INTERVALS | | | | | MEAN | STD DEV | LOWEST RETURN | PERCENT AT FLOOR |
|---|---|---|---|---|---|---|---|---|---|---|
| | | 5 | 25 | 50 | 75 | 95 | | | | |
| 25 | 12 | 12.14 | 12.49 | 13.21 | 14.63 | 19.04 | 14.16 | 2.82 | 12.00 | 0.20 |
| 25 | 13 | 13.08 | 13.32 | 13.79 | 14.71 | 17.74 | 14.43 | 1.95 | 13.00 | 0.20 |
| 25 | 14 | 14.04 | 14.15 | 14.38 | 14.83 | 16.39 | 14.71 | 1.02 | 14.00 | 0.20 |
| 50 | 12 | 12.00 | 12.00 | 12.03 | 12.40 | 25.21 | 13.83 | 5.36 | 12.00 | 31.40 |
| 50 | 13 | 13.00 | 13.00 | 13.02 | 13.24 | 19.04 | 14.20 | 4.05 | 13.00 | 32.20 |
| 50 | 14 | 14.00 | 14.00 | 14.01 | 14.11 | 16.52 | 14.58 | 2.46 | 14.00 | 33.00 |
| 75 | 12 | 12.00 | 12.00 | 12.00 | 12.00 | 29.60 | 13.92 | 6.49 | 12.00 | 76.80 |
| 75 | 13 | 13.00 | 13.00 | 13.00 | 13.00 | 24.21 | 14.38 | 5.26 | 13.00 | 78.40 |
| 75 | 14 | 14.00 | 14.00 | 14.00 | 14.00 | 15.79 | 14.67 | 3.44 | 14.00 | 80.80 |
| 100 | 12 | 12.00 | 12.00 | 12.00 | 12.00 | 29.60 | 14.02 | 6.87 | 12.00 | 86.80 |
| 100 | 13 | 13.00 | 13.00 | 13.00 | 13.00 | 26.18 | 14.54 | 5.88 | 13.00 | 88.60 |
| 100 | 14 | 14.00 | 14.00 | 14.00 | 14.00 | 15.66 | 14.82 | 4.00 | 14.00 | 92.20 |

YIELD VOLATILITY(BP): 200

INITIAL YIELD LEVEL: 15

IMMUNIZED RETURN: 15

EQUILIBRIUM YIELD: 18

ACCURATE FORECASTS (OUT OF 20): 10

| MAX. LOSS PER- CENT | FLOOR | RETURN CONFIDENCE INTERVALS | | | | | MEAN | STD DEV | LOWEST RETURN | PERCENT AT FLOOR |
|---|---|---|---|---|---|---|---|---|---|---|
| | | 5 | 25 | 50 | 75 | 95 | | | | |
| 25 | 12 | 12.24 | 12.80 | 13.64 | 15.41 | 22.93 | 14.92 | 3.63 | 12.01 | 0.00 |
| 25 | 13 | 13.15 | 13.51 | 14.05 | 15.23 | 20.48 | 14.95 | 2.53 | 13.00 | 0.20 |
| 25 | 14 | 14.07 | 14.25 | 14.51 | 15.09 | 17.81 | 14.97 | 1.34 | 14.00 | 0.20 |
| 50 | 12 | 12.00 | 12.00 | 12.09 | 13.19 | 33.52 | 14.97 | 7.28 | 12.00 | 25.80 |
| 50 | 13 | 13.00 | 13.00 | 13.05 | 13.59 | 26.09 | 14.96 | 5.57 | 13.00 | 27.40 |
| 50 | 14 | 14.00 | 14.00 | 14.00 | 14.22 | 19.16 | 15.02 | 3.63 | 14.00 | 28.40 |
| 75 | 12 | 12.00 | 12.00 | 12.00 | 12.02 | 34.56 | 15.33 | 8.63 | 12.00 | 69.40 |
| 75 | 13 | 13.00 | 13.00 | 13.00 | 13.00 | 31.39 | 15.34 | 7.19 | 13.00 | 72.80 |
| 75 | 14 | 14.00 | 14.00 | 14.00 | 14.00 | 19.93 | 15.13 | 4.82 | 14.00 | 77.60 |
| 100 | 12 | 12.00 | 12.00 | 12.00 | 12.00 | 37.69 | 15.54 | 9.04 | 12.00 | 79.80 |
| 100 | 13 | 13.00 | 13.00 | 13.00 | 13.00 | 34.31 | 15.63 | 7.81 | 13.00 | 83.40 |
| 100 | 14 | 14.00 | 14.00 | 14.00 | 14.00 | 24.83 | 15.35 | 5.63 | 14.00 | 89.80 |

YIELD VOLATILITY(BP): 200

INITIAL YIELD LEVEL: 15

IMMUNIZED RETURN: 15

EQUILIBRIUM YIELD: 18

ACCURATE FORECASTS (OUT OF 20): 11

| MAX. LOSS PER- CENT | FLOOR | RETURN CONFIDENCE INTERVALS | | | | | MEAN | STD DEV | LOWEST RETURN | PERCENT AT FLOOR |
|---|---|---|---|---|---|---|---|---|---|---|
| | | 5 | 25 | 50 | 75 | 95 | | | | |
| 25 | 12 | 12.38 | 13.29 | 14.70 | 17.75 | 27.08 | 16.36 | 4.61 | 12.02 | 0.00 |
| 25 | 13 | 13.23 | 13.82 | 14.74 | 16.81 | 23.46 | 15.93 | 3.24 | 13.01 | 0.00 |
| 25 | 14 | 14.11 | 14.40 | 14.85 | 15.90 | 19.48 | 15.48 | 1.71 | 14.01 | 0.00 |
| 50 | 12 | 12.00 | 12.00 | 12.51 | 17.82 | 42.81 | 17.54 | 10.03 | 12.00 | 23.00 |
| 50 | 13 | 13.00 | 13.00 | 13.27 | 16.09 | 38.54 | 16.89 | 8.09 | 13.00 | 24.00 |
| 50 | 14 | 14.00 | 14.00 | 14.10 | 14.93 | 29.31 | 16.07 | 5.42 | 14.00 | 27.60 |
| 75 | 12 | 12.00 | 12.00 | 12.00 | 16.73 | 46.95 | 18.07 | 11.70 | 12.00 | 60.20 |
| 75 | 13 | 13.00 | 13.00 | 13.00 | 13.24 | 45.02 | 17.60 | 10.21 | 13.00 | 65.80 |
| 75 | 14 | 14.00 | 14.00 | 14.00 | 14.01 | 36.70 | 16.74 | 7.62 | 14.00 | 69.80 |
| 100 | 12 | 12.00 | 12.00 | 12.00 | 21.77 | 47.85 | 18.62 | 12.37 | 12.00 | 69.40 |
| 100 | 13 | 13.00 | 13.00 | 13.00 | 13.00 | 45.42 | 18.08 | 10.93 | 13.00 | 75.20 |
| 100 | 14 | 14.00 | 14.00 | 14.00 | 14.00 | 39.97 | 17.26 | 8.79 | 14.00 | 81.60 |

YIELD VOLATILITY(BP): 200

INITIAL YIELD LEVEL: 15

IMMUNIZED RETURN: 15

EQUILIBRIUM YIELD: 18

ACCURATE FORECASTS (OUT OF 20): 12

| MAX. LOSS PER-CENT | FLOOR | RETURN CONFIDENCE INTERVALS | | | | | MEAN | STD DEV | LOWEST RETURN | PERCENT AT FLOOR |
|---|---|---|---|---|---|---|---|---|---|---|
| | | 5 | 25 | 50 | 75 | 95 | | | | |
| 25 | 12 | 12.53 | 13.75 | 15.71 | 19.66 | 31.69 | 18.06 | 6.88 | 12.03 | 0.00 |
| 25 | 13 | 13.34 | 14.14 | 15.41 | 18.13 | 27.10 | 17.17 | 5.15 | 13.02 | 0.00 |
| 25 | 14 | 14.16 | 14.55 | 15.18 | 16.57 | 21.63 | 16.17 | 2.96 | 14.01 | 0.00 |
| 50 | 12 | 12.00 | 12.02 | 13.30 | 25.58 | 50.41 | 20.58 | 13.25 | 12.00 | 19.60 |
| 50 | 13 | 13.00 | 13.01 | 13.66 | 19.71 | 44.53 | 19.38 | 11.33 | 13.00 | 20.60 |
| 50 | 14 | 14.00 | 14.00 | 14.19 | 16.00 | 35.60 | 17.80 | 8.32 | 14.00 | 23.60 |
| 75 | 12 | 12.00 | 12.00 | 12.00 | 29.85 | 55.44 | 21.72 | 15.14 | 12.00 | 54.80 |
| 75 | 13 | 13.00 | 13.00 | 13.00 | 24.47 | 51.15 | 20.56 | 13.56 | 13.00 | 58.60 |
| 75 | 14 | 14.00 | 14.00 | 14.00 | 14.37 | 44.92 | 18.79 | 10.77 | 14.00 | 67.60 |
| 100 | 12 | 12.00 | 12.00 | 12.00 | 32.12 | 56.80 | 22.42 | 15.79 | 12.00 | 59.40 |
| 100 | 13 | 13.00 | 13.00 | 13.00 | 27.67 | 54.94 | 21.40 | 14.58 | 13.00 | 65.40 |
| 100 | 14 | 14.00 | 14.00 | 14.00 | 14.00 | 47.60 | 19.53 | 12.07 | 14.00 | 75.00 |

# 7 Dedicated Bond Portfolios

Chapter 1 gave a detailed summary of the concept and the decision to dedicate a portfolio. This chapter goes into considerable depth on the main issues connected with dedication. The first section defines the related concepts of dedication. Second, we provide a detailed treatment of the decision to dedicate. Third, we consider the advantages to managing a dedicated portfolio actively as opposed to treating it as a passive vehicle. Finally, we treat various technical questions involved in dedicating. Most of the technical discussion involving the actual implementation of a dedicated portfolio concerns the more popular cash matching variety, as opposed to variations on duration matching, the alternative to cash matching. However, we explain the duration match alternatives and provide a theoretical analysis of them in chapter 9. (See also the summary of this chapter in chapter 1.)

## Definition

The dedicated portfolio is the simplest type of immunization. One starts with a set of estimated payments to be made in future years, which may be set at annual, quarterly, or other intervals. Then a universe of bonds is selected that has coupon and principal payment dates near the payment dates of the liabilities. An analytical procedure is then used that selects the appropriate number of bonds in each maturity so that the cash flow schedule (principal plus coupon) of the overall portfolio matches the liability. The resulting portfolio would be called a *dedicated portfolio*. Generally, more than one combination of bonds exists that will match the liabilities so that the best portfolio is not obvious. In these cases, one usually selects the least expensive portfolio, which would be called the *optimal dedicated portfolio*.

This gives the general idea. We must now be more precise about several factors. First, what does one really mean by a match of a particular liability with income and/or principal receipt? Second, how is the universe chosen and how are other portfolio characteristics (such as credit quality) controlled, in addition to the total cost or cash flow profile? Third, how are the computations actually made?

These questions are best answered by considering the computational aspects first. Because of the complexities that may be involved, as well as the restrictions that one may wish to place on other portfolio characteristics, a computer-based mathematical technique called *linear programming* is normally employed. Using this method, the computer is ordinarily programmed to minimize portfolio cost subject to certain restrictions—that is, the liabilities must be matched, together with any other constraints which we may wish to specify. Typically these other restrictions include the requirement that (1) a maximum of, say, 10 percent of the portfolio be in any one issue and that a maximum of, say, 5 percent be in any single issue; (2) a maximum of, say, 20 percent be in Yankee bonds; (3) no single issue with less than a single A credit be accepted; and (4) the average credit quality of the overall portfolio be, say, AA + or better.

Although every conceivable portfolio restriction cannot necessarily be digested by the typical linear programming computer code, virtually all restrictions of practical interest are possible. In fact, it is common to find the same kind of constraints used in many different programs, with only the specific parameters varying from case to case.

Having said this much, it is apparent that one controls the portfolio characteristics other than cash flow and cost through the specification of constraints. An additional way of controlling issue and issuer constraints is through specification of the universe of bonds from which the computer initially selects the optimal portfolio. Obviously, leaving a bond out of the universe is equivalent to leaving it in, along with the restriction that no percentage of the portfolio be held in that bond. Undesirable credits are screened out this way.

More generally, the selection of the universe is one of the key human (and often underrated) inputs in what would seem in general to be a rather mechanical process. The overall quality of the results is critically dependent on the appropriateness of the securities included, given the liability stream at hand and the expectations for rebalancing. Moreover, the accurate pricing of the universe is essential. If purchases are made on the basis of unrealistic prices, the chosen portfolio will be dedicated but suboptimal. The trading expertise of the manager also is critical because of the need to recognize, in the universe and its pricing, bonds in which there may be short-term special factors in the market causing them to be particularly available or unavailable, cheap or expensive.

We are left with the problem of what we mean by the restriction that the cash flow from the portfolio match each liability. Different interpretations are possible, depending on the degree of safety one requires; as might be expected, greater precision in matching the amounts and timing of cash flows with liabilities generally entails a higher portfolio cost. At one extreme we have what is conventionally called a *cash match,* in which cash flows from the portfolio closely precede the liability payments and are sufficient to meet them, even with a very low assumed reinvestment rate. At the other extreme, immunization theory suggests that we need merely maintain through time the equality of the duration of assets and the duration of the liabilities. This would give us greater flexibility in the choice of investments and thus produce a higher financing rate and greater potential return from swap activity in the future. The problem with duration matching is that it is subject to some risk in perfomance because of nonparallel shifts in yields, just as in bullet immunization. To remedy this, one can identify theoretical measurements of the difference between the time profile of the liabilities and that of the portfolio, and these measurements can be constrained in the process of creating the duration match to minimize the risk. An explicit analysis along these lines is provided in chapter 9 and summarized in chapter 1. We also provide a more elementary discussion later in this chapter that motivates the concept behind duration matching. For the balance of our present discussion, we will contrast cash matching with a single intuitive version of duration matching that does not require mathematical analysis.

On one hand, we could specify a monthly liability stream and require that for each such payment, the cash flow (interest plus principal) must arrive on or before the payment date. Cash flows arriving early (as will undoubtedly exist) are assumed to be reinvested at what is usually a conservative rate (6 percent to 8 percent). We contrast this with one version of duration matching (as opposed to cash matching). The version discussed is the closest relative of cash matching within the duration matching family. In this case, we require that the total cash flow within each year equal the total liability to be paid during the year, with the understanding that the universe be prescreened so that there will be a distribution of maturity dates throughout the year with the average maturity near or slightly ahead of mid-year. In the former safe case, there is little reinvestment rate risk (so long as the assumed reinvestment rate is low enough) so that the safety level is high; with the exception of default, there will be cash on hand to pay each liability. But there will be a potentially appreciable difference between the yield on the basic portfolio and the estimated financing rate on the liabilities because of the dilution of the yield on the portfolio by the lower assumed reinvestment rate. In contrast, in the duration-matching case much less dilution takes place because net reinvestment is near zero. If short rates are low, the low rate on maturing cash at mid-year is balanced by the fact that fewer bonds are sold early in the year to pay liabilities. Conversely, if short rates turn out to be high that year, more bonds must be sold early in the year but reinvestment will take place at higher rates.

To summarize, in the safe case, the portfolio yield is diluted by a low reinvestment rate. In the alternative case, bonds are chosen so that on average, net reinvestment is zero (hedging occurs year by year with equal and offsetting effects resulting from capital gain or loss versus reinvestment), no dilution takes place, and the yield is higher—although not as safe because the law of averages still must work in one's favor. Which extreme an investor opts for is critical to overall performance and depends on the specific requirements of the case at hand, the availability of interim financing for evening out cash flows if the hedges do not work perfectly, and so on.

**The Decision to Dedicate**

Any institution possessing a future liability faces an array of options pertaining to the funding decision. Remarkably, the issues are sometimes more divisive when all or part of the dollar amount of the liability is known than when it is uncertain. This is because a surgical elimination of this part of the liability becomes possible via the bond or insurance markets at rates that are occasionally quite high. This is attractive to many; but many others are naturally suspicious. Adding to the confusion is the fact that pros and cons of the different approaches are often described in detailed actuarial terms, suggesting to the layman that an explanation which is both simple and correct is unavailable.

In fact, there are two main bodies of analysis in whose terms these thoughts may be developed: actuarial science and financial theory. In this section we shall not delve into the deep actuarial consequences of locking up liabilities as they pertain to future funding ratios, normal costs, and so forth. Instead we shall examine the consequences for contributions and the asset mix in a financial context. This will involve the familiar concepts of present value and capital budgeting that lie at the heart of the financial valuation of the firm. Insofar as the funding decision involves allocating assets of the firm and influences income and share prices, we believe that this is the appropriate framework for decision making.

The following discussion considers the decision to dedicate from several points of view. We first outline a theoretical role for dedicated portfolios as a normal portion of a pension fund. Next, we discuss the effect of dedication on contributions. In this connection, the interpretation of a dedicated fund as a simple bond portfolio is made.

*A Theoretical Role for Dedication*

Analysis of the asset mix considerations involved in dedication is quite subtle given the firm valuation perspective that we have adopted. The reason is that rigorous financial theory implies that, in the main, the value of the firm does not depend on the allocation of assets in the pension fund. This counterintuitive result follows from a line of reasoning similar to that employed by Modigliani and Miller in deducing that, under perfect capital market conditions, the value of the firm does not depend upon how it is financed.[1] One argument is simply that if it did, and if a firm adopted a financing mix producing a low market value, another firm would buy it up and reissue equity and debt in the preferred (higher market value) mix and keep the arbitrage profit. A pension fund's asset mix is just as malleable as its owner's liability structure. Hence, if some suboptimal asset mix existed, another firm could take it over, adjust the asset mix, and keep the arbitrage profit. A different way of looking at the same issue is to observe that the value of the firm equals (in a sense to be slightly qualified later) the present value of the net aftertax cash flows from operations excluding pension costs, plus the market value of pension assets $(M)$ minus the present value of aftertax pension benefits payable $(L)$. (The component of firm value $M - L$—or its negative $L - M$)—is a critical concept, as shall be seen later.) Because the market value of pension assets at any time does not depend on the asset mix at that same time (just on the total value), the value of the firm cannot depend on the mix.

This rather strong position must be softened somewhat in a way that increases the usefulness of the financial perspective but that still fails to elevate the asset mix decision to a level commensurate with the attention paid to it. Unless the plan is terminated and the excess assets extracted, pension market value in excess of the present value of benefits payable does not contribute to the value of the firm. An immediate corollary is that a well-funded plan should not take a high-risk–high expected return posture because there is downside risk to the value of the firm butlittle (or less) upside potential. This implies a risk preference that is inversely related to the funding level.

Aside from this relationship, it is evident that strong preference for one asset mix over another must arise from factors other than financial valuation—in particular, management preference and pension law. These effects induce asset mix patterns that imply, as a rule, preference for underfunded plans to become fully funded over some horizon.

As a backdrop to our analysis, the near-universal reaction to the prospect of dedicating a portfolio is that more risk should be taken elsewhere in the portfolio, evidently to keep the general level of aggressiveness the same. If the existing asset mix is regarded as correct and if dedication entails an increased commitment to lower-risk securities, this reaction is correct. One might say that the universal reaction gives the prior funding approach the benefit of the doubt. If on the other hand (still assuming the existing allocation to be optimal), we merely reallocate fixed income assets, not appreciably changing duration or our attitude toward the risk of the portfolio, the reaction is mistaken—no change is warranted insofar as the risk concept to which these sentiments appeal has not been changed.

Actually adjusting a portfolio to have the same degree of aggressiveness is not so refined a procedure as the volume of discussion in its favor would suggest. A duration change within the rest of the bond portfolio opposite in direction to the change caused by the dedication is appropriate. Among equities, a change in beta may be appropriate or, more closely correlated, the corresponding change in the interest sensitive sector. Clearly, whatever offsetting changes are made, they should be reversed as the dedicated fund matures and declines as a portion of the fund. This assumes no change in the preferred aggressiveness resulting from any change in the overall funding level of the total portfolio over this same period.

In contrast, it will normally be incorrect to dedicate without regarding this as an element in the overall optimal risk-reward posture of the fund, taking into account both asset returns and plan status. That is, it will normally be suboptimal to regard the dedicated portion as just a component of the bond fund. On the actuarial side, the economic characteristics of the remaining liabilities will be quite different if the frequent practice of carving out the dedicated portion is undertaken. On the asset side, the long-run horizon and risk control attributes of the dedicated assets makes it inappropriate to compare them with or substitute them for other assets with short-run risk-return objectives or expectations.

To begin with, dedication may often attend a change in the overall aggressiveness of the fund. This may take place as a consequence of discovering that prior actuarial assumptions failed to reflect market rates properly. By far the most important circumstance leading to this result is the improvement in the overall funding level of the pension fund, or perhaps the discovery that the funding level exceeds what had been believed to be the case. A less aggressive posture is appropriate for a higher funding level for reasons laid out at the start of this section. The value of the firm is not increased by pension fund assets in excess of the present value of future benefits. Thus a highly funded plan cannot make full use of the high rewards associated with a high-risk strategy. As the funding level increases, successive reductions in the risk level are appropriate. This is analogous to the observed behavior of individuals. A person with $1,000 in assets may put it all in stock options; that same person with $10,000,000 is more likely to buy municipals. This general phenomenon relates naturally to the role of dedicated bond portfolios as a dynamically changing, indeed, increasing portion of the total fund.

To further appreciate the logic of reduced risk as the funding level increases, as well as to see the potential ongoing role of dedicated bonds in a portfolio, we examine a simple but important concept of funding. For a given firm, consider the present value of all future benefit payments $L$. $L$

includes not only accrued but also unaccrued benefits. (It even includes benefits payable to those who have not even been hired yet!) Subtract from $L$ the market value of the pension fund $M$. The quantity $L - M$ is a measure of how well funded the plan is in an absolute sense. It is also the same (major) component of firm value discussed at the start of this section on asset mix. A plan that is fully funded according to this concept (that is, $L - M = $ O) is far better funded than what actuaries typically call *fully funded* because this latter condition refers to the case where contributions are still being made to cover benefits currently accrued. Such contributions are called *normal costs.* According to the $L - M$ concept, the plan is fully funded when no contributions are made. As a final step divide $L - M$ by $M$ to obtain the ratio $(L - M)/M$. Call this $F$. This standardizes the unfunded portion by showing it as a percentage of $M$.

The ratio $F$ is a highly useful measure for understanding how pension risk-taking behaves in practice and for estimating how much risk the pension fund should take. According to the normal actuarial concept of full funding (where normal costs are still paid and hence $F$ exceeds zero), the firm may wish to take some risk in its pension plans so that large investment gains may reduce future contributions. By the present definition, full funding implies that $F = 0$ and no such risk should be taken. The reason is that if $F = 0$, then $L - M = 0$, or $L = M$. Thus the fund has the assets to finance the liabilities fully. Additional assets do not help whereas investment losses hurt.

Intuitively, it seems clear that as $F$ decreases (if it decreases) the risk level in the fund should decline. To see this, consider the consequence of $F$ remaining constant ($F = $ constant). This means that the true unfunded portion bears a constant relationship to fund market value ($L - M = $ constant $\times M$). Thus an extra 1 percent return on the fund would always have the same percentage effect on $L - M$, which, it should be recalled, is a crucial element in the valuation of the firm. Moreover, our standard risk-return measures (mean and standard deviation of return) are expressed in percentages that are now convertible into mean and standard deviations for percentage changes in $L - M$ (and hence $M - L$). This constitutes compelling support for the prospect that if $F$ is a constant, to maintain a stable risk-return posture for $L - M$, the firm must keep a stable risk-return posture for $M$—that is, a stable, effective asset mix.

We have suggested that if $F$ is zero, risk should be low, and if $F$ is stable, risk should be stable (at least according to the logic of our approach). It seems clear that if $F$ is declining through time, the pension plan is becoming ever better funded and the rewards to risk-taking are becoming progressively smaller (and conversely if $F$ is increasing). In the case of $F$ declining, what does this mean for the role of dedicated portfolios?

To answer this question, we must first ask what $F = 0$ really means. The condition $L = M$ does not necessarily mean that the assets are guaranteed to finance the liabilities. This is because the discount rate for computing the present value of the liabilities is the assumed actuarial rate that reflects returns on equity as well as bonds. Thus some risk may remain in the portfolio, even if $F = 0$, insofar as the asset mix merely reflects the assumed equity exposure underlying actuarial assumptions. It is critical to recognize, however, the implications for funding of the theoretically optimal behavior of anyone having to finance a single payment in the future, as his risk aversion increases. The optimal behavior is to go from a risky posture for low levels of risk aversion to a locked-up posture for high levels of risk aversion, even if a riskier managment of the same instruments is attractive to others. This implies that a bias toward dedicating assets is possible. Insofar as actuarially assumed rates are in part jointly determined with the firm's investment activities, this also implies an inclination toward specifying the assumed rate as equal to the immunized rate as this component becomes more important.

To summarize, our analysis consists of two strong statements. Given a bias toward increasing the funding level, financial theory warrants reduced risk insofar as the upside potential resulting from higher risk does not reward the firm. This statement is coupled with the statement that as risk aversion increases, there is an increased inclination toward not only lower risk assets but toward locking up rates. These facts imply an ongoing role for dedicated portfolios as funding levels improve. They naturally suggest a stable funding plan in which fixed income securities are used to lock up liabilities over a variable horizon, with riskier securities (equities and active bond management for instance) targeting more distinct liabilities. The mix of dedicated and nondedicated would depend on the funding level of the plan and the attractiveness of immunized rates relative to expected risky asset returns and relative to the actuarial rate used in computing the present value of the liabilities. This general approach has the affect of deemphasizing the short-term risk-reward posture of the fund in favor of the long-term risk-reward posture. Assets are explicitly targeted toward the horizons for which they are most appropriate. Dedicated assets provide financing rates over maturity horizons for which they totally manage risk. Equity and other riskier assets are targeted toward horizons over which (through time diversification) their compound returns are more certain. These remarks underscore the observation that a dedicated bond portfolio is more than just another bond portfolio when its long-run risk control elements are recognized and factored into an overall funding decision.

The impact of dedication on contributions has not yet entered the analysis because we have addressed the investment merits of dedicating, leaving to the next section the evaluation of dedication as a tool for affecting contributions. This does not mean that contributions should not be affected if we dedicate for sound investment reasons. Indeed, it would not be surprising to find that they typically drop (rise) as the dedicated portion rises (falls). But this result is treated here as an outcome rather than an objective.

## The Effect of Dedicating on Contributions

*Optimal Adjustments to Contributions.* The foregoing section considered the investment merits of bond dedication. As such, the effect on contribution was treated as an output rather than as a motivating factor. The widespread use of dedication as a vehicle for reducing contributions, however, has created the cynical perception that dedication has no other investment merit than being a device for directly or indirectly raising the assumed rate, thus allowing contributions to decline. The dedicated portfolio is treated in this sense as just another bond portfolio and its long-run risk-control attributes are ignored.

On the contrary, the asset mix, actuarial rate, and contribution rate should in theory be jointly optimized. Hence we should not be surprised to see a change in contribution and actuarial rate attend a change in the dedicated portion of a fund. Moreover, there is no necessary presumption that contributions should be reduced or actuarial rate increased when an increase in the dedicated portion occurs. An increase in the dedicated portion could occur solely for risk (as opposed to return) considerations so that no change in actuarial rate or contribution is warranted. Alternatively, if market rates rose (other things being equal) an increase in the actuarial rate would be warranted with no change or even an increase in contribution. To see this latter possibility, it must be recognized that the contribution rate involves a business decision concerning the horizon over which the plan attains its target funding status. If rates rise (other things being equal), the firm can (1) reduce contributions and hit its target over the same time; (2) leave contributions unchanged and hit the target sooner; or (3) advance the contribution rate and hit the target much sooner. Preference may depend on such factors as the period of time over which the higher rates are expected to prevail, as well as which management generation should be the beneficiary of the high rates.

By late 1982, most of the firms (although not all) that have dedicated have increased their effective actuarial rate and have reduced contributions. Although this seems self-serving at a time of low corporate profits, several factors suggest that this correlation of low profits and high rates may have been an added incentive for firms to reduce contributions but that suboptimal funding policies may not have emerged. In particular, record high interest rates and changed perceptions about the rate of inflation (and hence the growth of salaries and wages) may have caused actuarial assumptions to be out of line with current conditions and pension plans to be appreciably better funded than had been believed. This is the sort of environment in which dedicating and reducing contributions would be expected. As a general matter, however, extreme caution must be employed before jumping to the conclusion that even a major increase in rates warrants either an increased actuarial rate or a reduction in contribution or both.

To appreciate this caveat, keep several factors in mind. First, an increase in rates may occur for only a relatively small period compared to the life of the pension plan. Any increase in actuarial rate must reflect this. Second, the increase in rates may be the result of an increase in inflation, which may imply an analogous change in salary growth rates. Third, a common technique for adjusting the assumed rate is to value the liabilities that are being financed by the dedicated portfolio at the cost of that portfolio. The present value of total liability is adjusted by this amount. The new effective actuarial rate is then found by computing the rate that sets the present value of the total liability stream equal to the new adjusted total present value. Contributions are now computed using the new rate, or the adjusted total present value.

This approach seems reasonable insofar as the component of liability being singled out for special treatment is indeed being financed at the internal rate of return defined by setting the present value of this liability stream equal to the cost of the dedicated portfolio. However, once we take this step, we should recognize that we are changing the actuarial rate on the basis of having carved out a particular liability stream from the total and having analyzed it separately. To the extent possible, a similar exercise should be made for other components of the liability stream. Normally, the dedicated portion is all or part of the nominally fixed component of total liabilities; an increase in bond yields clearly improves the financing of such liabilities. If we carve out other components of liability along economic rather than actuarial lines in the same way, we may find that expected rates of return on asset categories financing these streams have fallen just as fixed income rates have risen! Thus, for example, one component of total liability may be that component which is highly sensitive to inflation. As interest rates rise, we may find that expected return on inflation hedge assets has declined, so that no change (or even a reduction) in the actuarial rate is warranted.

*Suboptimal Adjustment to Contributions.* The previous section discussed optimal modifications to the contribution rate given the asset mix decision. In particular, we argued that the act of dedicating may involve recognition of such changes as market rates or funding levels that imply that a reduction in contribution is appropriate. This, of course, implies that the funding policy (such as contribution rate or asset mix) that existed prior to dedicating is now viewed as suboptimal. It is quite possible, however, that dedication is performed solely to reduce contributions. That is, dedication is performed to reduce contribution either by an increase in the overall assumed rate or by carving out particular liabilities (leaving the assumed rate for remaining liabilities the same), when in fact the prior pension funding policy is correct in the following sense. The assumed rate results in a contribution level that will eliminate the unfunded liability over the expected horizon. In particular, overfunding is not expected to take place, the existing asset mix is deemed correct, and actuarial assumptions correctly reflect risk-adjusted expected returns. In this case, one popular attitude toward dedication is correct—a reduction in contribution today must be met with an increase in the future.

Although such a scheme is not normally regarded as prudent from a pension point of view, there may be a positive effect on the firm from a financial point of view. To analyze this, we make the assumption that whatever sense of optimality existed prior to the dedication also exists afterward. Thus to the extent of any portfolio shift, an offsetting change must be made elsewhere. Both the short- and long-run total portfolio profiles must be the same before and after, which implies that any long-run risk control element in the dedicated portfolio must be ignored or reversed elsewhere. This is more critical on the actuarial side where the analysis of liabilities should not be affected by the change (or else more is changed than simply the current contribution rate). We make these optimality assumptions regarding funding policy before the dedication because otherwise there would be no sound basis for comparison. We assume that the effective asset mix remains optimal after the change (as well as before) because we are seeking to isolate the effects of a change in contributions. Otherwise we would have to add to this the costs of going to a suboptimal asset mix; these costs are quite difficult to quantify.

*The Capital Budgeting Problem.* Under these conditions, a current reduction in contribution by any means including dedication necessitates an expected increase in contributions in future years. Such a reduction will be beneficial if the current aftertax savings, when reinvested at the appropriate opportunity cost, generate enough return to replenish the fund (with appropriate interest) and still leave an excess return available for shareholders. This is a capital budgeting problem. There are two computational approaches.

The simplest approach is to view the pension fund as an alternative source of funds. That is, we borrow from the pension fund as if it were a bank or any other source of capital. To set up the capital budgeting problem, we estimate the pretax cash flows associated with the project into which the current savings are to be invested. We then compute the present value using the estimated earnings rate on the assets in the fund as the discount rate. That is, the discount rate should be the earning rate on the assets that would have been purchased had the full contribution been made.

If the present value has the appropriate sign, the value of shareholder interest will be increased by accepting the project and financing in this way. This approach may be generalized to the case where borrowings from the pension fund are included with other sources of capital and a weighted-average discount rate is used, as is the normal practice. This overall method of computation is the present value counterpart of the rule to accept a project as long as the marginal return on capital exceeds the marginal cost of capital.

The second approach to the problem disregards the specific cash flows of the project to be undertaken. Instead, it discounts the aftertax change in contributions (now and in the future) at the rate representing the marginal aftertax investment rate for the firm. After some reflection, it is apparent that this will produce the same answer as the first approach if the discount rate used in the second approach is the same as rate of return on the project considered. That is, the approaches are mathematically equivalent. Contributions should be reduced if the marginal aftertax return exceeds the earning rate on assets in the pension fund.

Although these approaches are conceptually simple, applying them can be difficult because of problems in estimating the various inputs. Moreover, there are pitfalls which must be avoided when doing any capital budgeting analysis. We mention several of the more significant problems.

First, even if the present value computation suggests that shareholder interests are improved by undertaking a project financed through reduced current contributions, it may be suboptimal to do so if a cheaper source of financing exists. This is merely a reaffirmation of the financial management rule that we should always finance projects at the lowest marginal cost of capital. Thus all cheaper forms of financing should be exhausted before borrowing from the pension fund.

Second, in specifying cash flows or discount rates, appropriate risk adjustments must be made. As an example of the subtleties here, consider the second approach where instead of reinvesting the saved contribution, the firm distributes it to shareholders and reduces future income to replenish the fund. The appropriate discount rate is then the aftertax cost of equity. (This is similar to the firm investing in equity of other firms rather than giving it to shareholders.) The earning rate on the assets in the fund is likely to be a weighted average of expected returns from stocks and bonds. This is likely to be smaller than the firm's aftertax cost of equity. This implies that the firm would always reduce current contributions according to the present value rule. The fallacy is that the pure equity return is riskier than the fund return. Hence, the equity discount rate must be risk-adjusted prior to computing present values to represent the same degree of risk as that of the assets in the fund. Similarly, when we use the first approach and discount cash flows at the fund earning rate, the cash flows must be adjusted to represent the same risk level as that of the earning rate.

A third consideration is the tax treatment of cash flows. When discounting the net change in contributions at the marginal aftertax rate of return, due to recognition must be given to two facts: (1) taxes are paid on current increases in income resulting from reduced contribution; and (2) taxes are reduced in future years as income is reduced through higher contribution.

Such problems are representative of the kinds of numerical and conceptual difficulties that often arise in any capital budgeting problem. They reflect the fact that the decision to dedicate a portfolio is as sophisticated as it is interesting. The most competent applications of the concepts discussed here are likely to be computations made from several points of view. Simulation analysis may be warranted. Hybrid techniques can be developed. One such simple technique is to adopt the first approach of forecasting cash flows, but simply to net out repayments to the pension plans from future flows rather than to discount at any earnings rate. The net flow is then a measurement of the future dollar returns to shareholders obtained through current contribution reduction. If after simulation this number is reliably expected to be positive, current contribution reduction is supported. Other hybrid approaches are possible.

*Practical Implications of the Capital Budgeting Analysis.* It is apparent that the analysis of the benefits of reducing contributions does not depend on the specific liabilities being analyzed. This implies two things. First, arriving at reduced contribution through a dedicated bond portfolio is no different than arriving at the same result through simply a higher assumed actuarial rate, unless the asset mix is altered in such a fashion that a higher overall return is expected to be earned. (But if a higher return is expected to be earned, we are contradicting our initial assumption that the asset mix was deemed correct with expected returns correctly reflected in actuarial assumptions.) The second implication is that when dedicating a portfolio to a particular set of liabilities, it does not matter whether these are retired lives' liabilities or not. The analysis is cleaner using retiree benefits to the extent that they are more easily estimated. Also, the practice of segmenting and separately valuing these liabilities (at a higher rate) for the purpose of determining the reduction in contributions is more practical than an analogous process for other liabilities. But nothing says that an estimated nominal benefit stream could not simply be carved out of the total liability stream and dedicated.

The obvious question now is: How likely is it that the present value computation will favor reduced contribution today? To answer this question, we shall assume the framework of the second approach to the dedication decision. We shall visualize borrowing from the pension plan as simply another source of capital, contributing to (in principle) an upward-sloping marginal cost of capital curve. The firm continues to invest (using cheap financing first) up to the point where the marginal aftertax return on capital equals the marginal aftertax cost. We anticipate that the long-run marginal aftertax cost of funds equals the weighted average aftertax cost of capital normally identified in financial analysis. Moreover, we expect that firms gradually take on all investments up to this point or generally maintain a hurdle rate bearing a fixed relationship to this rate.

Under these conditions, it is unlikely that a firm would find reduced contribution optimal. This is because the earning rate on marginal assets in the pension fund is in general a weighted average of the market equity yield and the market bond yield. The marginal aftertax cost of capital is a weighted average of this same equity return with an aftertax bond yield. Thus we know that either (1) the marginal aftertax return on investment equals the aftertax weighted average cost of capital, which is likely to be less than the cost of borrowing from the pension fund; or (2) the hurdle rate exceeds the cost of borrowing from the pension fund, but a still lower cost of financing is available (the weighted aftertax cost of capital). These remarks substantiate our doubt that reducing current contributions should be a frequent activity. Nevertheless, special factors may reverse this from time to time.

First, economic fluctuations may cause the tax rate to be temporarily depressed. This may influence the aftertax discount rate over the near term. More important, the current savings may be much larger. For example, if a firm loses money now but expects to make profits in the future, increased income through reduced contribution today is not taxed while repayments to the fund in the future are on an aftertax basis.

Second, temporary shortages of capital can lead to rationing of the available supply so that the aftertax return on marginal investment exceeds both the normal weighted-average aftertax cost of capital as well as the earning rate on the pension fund. The firm may then look to alternative sources of funds, such as reduced contribution. Although such rationing may even take place in good economic times among some firms, it is more common when capital is scarce, economy wide, and interest rates are high.

Third, it is generally not safe to assume one earnings rate on the fund and one discount rate. For example, the relationship between expected stock and bond returns may change if bond yields fall to more normal levels and the risk in bonds is reduced. These factors are enormously difficult to incorporate into estimates of future discount and earnings rates. Yet some effort along these lines is essential.

Finally, both the pension earnings rate and the normal cost of capital are weighted rates. But, obviously, the weights may differ so as to emphasize or deemphasize the different treatment of the cost of debt in each case.

## Rewards to Activeness

Conventional wisdom views a cash matched bond portfolio as passive insofar as a properly chosen set of bonds with no credit risk will finance the liabilities (that is, it will accomplish the basic objective of the program) without additional trades. Even duration matched portfolios, which clearly require rebalancing, are often viewed as passive vehicles where sector or yield curve shape bets are considered as forms of activeness because the duration is constrained. If there were only default-free bonds in existence and if they were available in every maturity, we would probably find more investors taking on the bond selection and custody tasks themselves rather than hiring an external manager (although many would retain managers to assist in the original portfolio construction). However, in a world where substantial and variable yield premiums are available for incurring credit risk, the complexities of the selection and review process are magnified. Up to 75 to 150 basis points of return can be added by reducing the overall credit level of the portfolio, while still adhering to investment grade securities. Prudence or fiduciary responsibility requires constant evaluation of the securities. The vast majority of investors find the costs of retaining a manager to evaluate such credits to be far less than the increase in return. That is, a cost-benefit evaluation warrants hiring the manager. At this point there is a tendency to believe that the management fee is an insurance premium necessary for identifying the bad credit that could arise, albeit rarely. In fact, there are many other opportunities to add value to a dedicated bond portfolio through more active, indeed, regular trading.

First, and perhaps most significant, relative values among the various sectors in the bond market change over time. Because of changing conditions in the market relating to economic activity, security supply, or other factors, the least expensive bond (satisfying credit requirements) used to finance a particular segment of the liability at one point in time may not be the least expensive six to twelve months later. Such rotation in the bond market may make it desirable to totally reoptimize the portfolio on a periodic basis. The reoptimization would only take place if and when an appreciable savings can be generated—savings that would, at the very least, be guaranteed to cover the transaction costs incurred in rebalancing the portfolio. The frequency of such opportunities are difficult to predict, but they inevitably occur because relative values (spreads off Treasury securities) of different sectors are dynamic. Therefore, the original cost of the portfolio should represent the maximum expected but not necessarily the final cost. This is not a suggestion that there is a free lunch. It is merely a proposal that if, for example, the original portfolio contains more issues that improve in credit quality on a relative basis than deteriorate (which would occur if a manager's credit judgments prove superior), the account could recognize the net gain. This is accomplished through reoptimizing (arriving at a new lower-cost portfolio that finances the liabilities) and realizing the difference in cash.

Another opportunity for active management is the filling in of maturity sectors. As an example, the maturity range 1995 to 1999 currently contains very few issues with coupons over 8 percent but below 10 percent. Deeper discount bonds are available but are expensive on a relative basis and difficult to accumulate. Such a condition makes it more difficult to fund liabilities maturing during that period. However, a volume of 10-year note issuance in 1985 will fill in the 1995 maturity. As a result, original funding will be easier and swap opportunities will be more plentiful for existing portfolios. Thus, a 7 percent coupon issue could be swapped into a smaller amount of higher-coupon higher-yielding bonds with the shortfall of principal made up through the purchase of a zero coupon bond (and vice versa over time). Or perhaps an original issue 7 percent bond could be swapped for an existing 7 percent bond to pick up yield and take out cash. Potentially as important as direct swap opportunities using the newly issued bonds is the increase in activity in existing issues that is encouraged by the sale of new bonds. This occurs as brokerage firms seek to create swaps for clients out of similar issues to place the new securities.

The third approach pertains to changing conditions in specific bonds. For technical reasons, a specific issue may be offered relatively cheaply by one or more dealers or may be sought (bid for) very aggressively by one or more dealers. The consequent variation in yield relative to the average yield for bonds with similar credit quality, coupon, and maturity can be sizable, often 25 to 40 basis points or more. Such events take place for a variety of reasons, such as the pricing of a new issue at a yield premium so that it will be absorbed by the market; the impact of such primary market activity on existing bonds for the same issuer in the market, making the entire credit appear "cheap"; or the unwinding of large dealer positions in a specific issue. Typically these conditions, when they exist, are shortlived. If a money manager has an active trading desk, such situations are recognized and can represent attractive swap opportunities for a dedicated portfolio.

Typically, a bond with a similar or superior credit rating but higher yield is substituted for one with the same (or lower) coupon and the same (or later) maturity. Either the proceeds of the sale of the existing bond are used in full to buy the new bond (resulting in overfunding at some point in the future), or the proceeds are not used in full, resulting in a possible cash withdrawal. If only four such trades were done each year (one per quarter), each trade involving 5 percent of the total fund at an average improvement of 25 basis points in yield, the net effect on the overall portfolio would be roughly 5 basis points—a sizable amount relative to the typical fee for such an account. Moreover, given our experience, that example is conservative. It is very common in practice to see a trade frequency closer to one per month. Under the same assumptions this produces a gain of 15 basis points! Therefore, it may well be worth paying a somewhat higher management fee for an active trading desk.

Finally, the maturing process of the dedicated portfolio often gives rise to a predictable pattern of profitable trades, as the following examples indicate. First, unwary managers often establish dedicated portfolios with the desired average credit rating but with the early maturities having a much higher rating than the intermediate or long sectors. This implies that the portfolio will have a deteriorating credit exposure as time passes and the high-grade short-dated bonds mature. This should not be allowed. A more uniform distribution of credit should be required with, if anything, a bias toward improving credit in distant years. As maturity approaches, selective and prudent downgrading of credit can be made (for example, from U.S. Treasury to AAA corporate, or from AAA corporate to AA corporate) as the payoffs from these bonds are now influenced by events in the foreseeable rather than unforeseeable future and the insurance of an extra layer of credit is no longer necessary.

Second, call protection is often obtained in dedicated portfolios through purchase of noncallable or deep discount bonds. A ten-year 6 percent discount bond purchased five years ago for a dedicated program may now, with yields much higher, be prudently traded for a higher coupon bond at a higher yield, as the high degree of protection is no longer required. Thus we may utilize the full proceeds and overfund or to take some cash out. This example would be less extreme if yields declined rather than rose, but the point is that, as a rule, less call protection in the form of lower-yielding discount bonds is less necessary for nearby maturities than for distant maturities. This gives rise to a pattern of selling lower coupon issues as they approach maturity and replacing them with higher-yielding but still call-protected bonds.

Third, the bond market sector that is most attractive for financing-say, the 1995-2000 liabilities today—may not be the most attractive in five to ten years because different categories of issues may become available in the ten- to fifteen-year maturity range that were not available in the fifteen- to twenty-year range.

To assess the overall importance of the various swap and general portfolio restructuring methods that we have discussed, suppose that the total effect is just 10 basis points per year. Consider the case of a liability stream that declines linearly from $2 million to $0 over thirty years. If the yield on the portfolio is initially 15 percent, the initial cost of the cash matched portfolio is $11,168,972. If the yield remains at 15 percent over the life of the portfolio, we may compute the year-by-year dollar value of the portfolio and the year-by-year savings resulting from swap activity. At 15 percent, this savings has a present value of $57,242. If this is netted out against the original cost of the portfolio, the going-in financing rate is computed to be 15.12 percent—a 12 basis point pickup. Viewed differently, we may net the 10 basis point savings against the fee. Thus if the fee is 15 basis points, it becomes a new 5 basis points! Alternatively, the present value $57,242 equals the present value of the full fee over the first 5.4 years.

**Technical Analysis**

This section on technical matters is somewhat less structured than foregoing sections. By far the most important issue (involving the definition of the asset or liability) is taken up first. After discussing liability updating and call risk, the nature of the cash match is taken up again in connection with the rewards of rebalancing the portfolio. Finally, some aspects of the choice of reinvestment rate are considered.

*Different Concepts of Asset-Liability Match*

To set the framework, a typical investor with a system of liability payments will treat, say, the $1 million payment in 1990 as follows. Recognizing a gradual payoff during the year, a $250,000 liability will be assumed to be paid on the first day of each quarter of the year: 1/1/90, 4/1/90, 7/1/90, 10/1/90. Requiring payment at the start of the quarter is a safety measure. (Some would do it monthly rather than quarterly.) Then this investor would request the manager to select the lowest cost portfolio so that at least $250,000 in cash is available on each of these dates. A usually conservative reinvestment rate is also specified that is to be applied to funds maturing before the payment date.

This seems rather an innocuous approach and, indeed, is probably about as close as one could get to the industry norm. Bearing in mind that for similar credit restrictions, trading capacity, and so on, the variation in performance among dedicated funds depends in part on the degree of departure from these assumptions, we will examine such differences in some detail. In particular, this cash match method implies that the duration of the inflows equals the duration of the outflows (or is slightly shorter). As long as a conservative reinvestment assumption is made, there is no downside risk as a practical matter. (As a theoretical matter, some downside risk remains as long as any funds are reinvested at a positive rate to the liability payment date.) But does this standard approach really make sense, and did we pay too much for the safety it provides us?

There are several aspects to this question—some involving the assets and some involving the liabilities. As long as a conservative reinvestment rate was assumed, the overall portfolio yield was surely diluted through the action of reinvesting funds at this low rate. Presumably this could be avoided by buying bonds that mature very close to the liability dates. But in the end, as much and probably more would be paid for this program because of the costs of finding these bonds. Notwithstanding these observations, the dilution problem usually takes a back seat to the example of the bond maturing one day after the due date for the liability and yielding 100 basis points more than the selected bond that matured on the due date. The former bond would clearly be disregarded in the standard bond selection process.

On the liability side, we have committed several acts that, if not well justified, are questionable. First, requiring cash flows at the start of the quarter as opposed to, say, midway through the quarter, is another layer of safety that has not, evidently, provoked relaxation of constraints on the other side in any conscious way. Excess cash flows will necessarily develop through reinvestment of funds during the quarter. Unless care is exercised, it may be difficult to distinguish this cash from that earned through favorable swaps.

Second, the act of dividing the liabilities into four equal amounts is a standard practice that is known to be, strictly speaking, inaccurate (a declining scale is correct), but is justified on the basis of the imprecision of the estimated overall annual liability and the difficulty in coming up with the precise decrement factor. We submit that the predictable affects of this error alone can, in certain cases, dwarf the well-intended conservative reinvestment rate effect. Moreover, it is not at all obvious that the within-year slope is inherently more difficult to forecast than the level of liability payments for a given year.

Finally, the admission of imprecision in liability estimates should give considerable reason for questioning the logic of diluting the basic portfolio yield (through a low reinvestment rate or lower yielding bonds with maturities exactly corresponding to liability dates) to exactly finance a set of payments that we know will not be the actual payments.

It may well be that the problem solution that was criticized in the foregoing section is well understood and that the high level of safety is demanded. But the problems outlined may arise out of too stringent a concept of what a cash match should be. Often they arise out of the ignorance of alternative problem specifications. To the extent that too rigid a cash match is required, further rebalancing in the form of swaps outlined in an earlier section (for example) is to this extent limited. The total cost of too stringent a cash match is the initial cost measured in yield given up, plus the present value of all lost swap opportunities. This total could easily be sizable.

Alternatives to the typical problem specifications involve changing both the liability payment dates as well as the timing of bond maturities. As a conceptual framework for their description we will discuss the duration matching approach that provides maximum flexibility. One of the insights coming out of general immunization analysis is that a stream of liabilities may be financed through management of a bond portfolio according to fairly simple rules. We know that the immunization rule for a single lump sum payment in the future is to manage a portfolio in such a way that its duration always equals the time remaining until the payment. Quite obviously, if we have a stream of, say, forty payments, we may construct forty such portfolios. The weight of any one portfolio within the overall portfolio will clearly equal the present value of its intended liability relative to the present value of the entire liability stream. Thus the duration of the overall portfolio (measured as the weighted average of the durations of the individual portfolios) is simply the weighted average of the horizons of the individual liabilities, where the weights are simply the present value of the respective future payment relative to the total present value. But this merely amounts to saying that the duration of the overall portfolio equals the duration of the liabilities. Thus one way to finance the liabilities is to duration match rather than to cash match. That is, choose a portfolio whose duration equals the duration of the liabilities and maintain this match through any necessary periodic rebalancing. This provides a maximum of flexibility in choosing the portfolio.

Although duration matching is an extremely interesting approach for certain cases, a problem ordinarily emerges because of the associated imprecision in overall performance. Because of nonparallel movements in certain important yield curve concepts (forward rates), each of the individual immunizations within the duration match may underperform (or overperform) by as much as 15 to 25 basis points even under the best of circumstances where this risk is individually minimized for each of the immunizations. This may be a small cost compared to the increased flexibility it allows. But this comparison must be made on a case-by-case basis. Moreover, tolerance of the risks often depends on the financial characteristics of the plan sponsor, its cash flow into the pension fund, and so on. Although there are a whole range of interesting options between strict duration matching and strict cash matching (see the first section of this chapter and chapter 9), the following discussion focuses on one approach that involves the duration matching concept but that is close enough to cash matching to be considered a reasonable alternative by most firms who may wish to dedicate a portfolio.

Suppose that we again focus on only the 1990 liability. If this were the entire problem and if it were now January 1, 1990, immunization theory would tell us that we will finance the payment with minimal reinvestment rate risk if the present value of the assets equals the present value of the liabilities and if the duration of the assets equals the duration of the liabilities (where duration is a measure of maturity). Thus, if the duration of the liability in 1990 is, say, five months (starting from January 1), this could be financed by the proper number of bonds maturing on June 1, 1990. We would sell bonds ahead of time to make payments in January, February, and so on; then when the rest of the money matures, we would reinvest and slowly draw down the balance as we pay monthly liabilities occuring after June 1. If interest rates are high during the year, we sell more bonds during the first half of the year but make it up on the higher reinvestment rate during the second half. If rates are low, we sell fewer bonds in the first half but reinvest at a lower rate in the second half. Immunization theory suggests that if we do our analysis correctly at the outset, whether rates are high or low during the year is immaterial; in either case, we will have just about the right amount of assets to pay the full liability. That is, reinvestment rate risk will be small.

These remarks indicate that through use of a simple problem formulation we may simultaneously increase the flexibility in our choice of bonds (for example, we avoid the problem of the high yielding bond maturing one day after the payment is due), and make a more realistic estimate of the actual liability payment date. We simply make sure that the present values and durations of the assets and liabilities match year by year. (In a sense, the typical technique attempts to do this quarter by quarter or month by month with several additional problems of nonflexibility overlaid.) This lets us choose the most attractive bonds within a given year, thus avoiding some of the timing problems, but still imposes a maturity discipline that minimizes reinvestment rate risk. This new approach to the cash match portfolio is very attractive in the case where the investor tolerates some (if small) reinvestment risk. Generally, higher-yielding portfolios result that can ordinarily take greater advantage of future swap opportunities because of their inherently greater flexibility.

Implementing this approach is not quite as easy as the standard approach. The residual reinvestment risk is larger, although still small. Year by year, it is expected that the results would tend to average out so that the net requirement would be for the program sponsor to make available a small pool of liquid assets in the future that would be drawn on and replenished over time, with a small net withdrawal possible if a larger than average share of the annual risks go negative. This is ordinarily not a problem for most corporations, which maintain such pools anyway. Nor can it be concluded that this asset pool should be added to the asset base in computing the financing rate, because the temporary use of the pools would be balanced by reimbursement.

A different problem involves the computation of within-year duration and present value. In particular, present value and durations should be equal when evaluated at the interest rates that will prevail in the year in question. This is not a problem if cash flows and liabilities are perfectly matched, because these durations and present values are equal at any interest rate. (But, in part, this is the requirement we are seeking to avoid!) It turns out that over a single year, the relative duration of assets and liabilities will not be greatly affected by the interest rate so that using some reasonable reinvestment rate for the year in question will satisfy this requirement. Relative present values will be more affected by the difference in realized versus predicted discount rates. But here we merely wish to make sure that whatever the rate turns out to be, the present value of the assets is at least as large as the present value of the liabilities. To guarantee this, we simply discount the liabilities using the same rate as in the duration calculation and discount the assets at a slightly higher rate. If this is done, when we choose enough bonds in each year to match annual present values at the assumed reinvestment rate, we will still have enough present value in each year even if the actual rate comes in appreciably different. Strictly speaking, we discount the liabilities to that point in the year equal to the horizon or duration of the liabilities. This is done by reinvesting payments before this date to it, and discounting payments after this date forward to it. Similarly, bond payments are adjusted by reinvesting payments before the duration of the liabilities to that date and discounting payments after that date back to it at the slightly higher rate. This technique amounts to a general safety measure for protection against reinvestment rate risk.

Although solutions to these difficulties are fairly simple, a manager may wish to obtain some of the advantages of this technique without departing entirely from the standard solution that we have criticized. Several intermediate steps are available, involving both assets and liabilities, that cause the solution to approach that of the flexible technique while using the standard methodology.

On the liability side, one may partition the payment intervals differently—for example, go from monthly to quarterly or quarterly to semiannually. Then, choose the date of the payment as the duration of the payments within the interval rather than the first day of the period. Finally, the level of the payment on this date should be such that its present value at the start of the period equals the present value of the actual anticipated monthly stream, both present values computed using a conservative rate. (A conservative rate is necessary here because, if the actual rate turned out lower than that used to compute the present values, the actual present value of the stream would exceed the actual present value of the lump sum. This conservative rate does not imply overfunding because it is applied to both liability concepts.)

So far, application of the standard technique now implies a solution such that in each period the duration of the assets equals the duration of the liabilities. If a conservative reinvestment rate is used, the present value of the assets within each period will also be at least as large as the present value of the liabilities. Hence, this still entails probable overfunding and does not allow maturities after the duration date—that is, the within-year immunization concept is still not used. Approaches to correct this lead to other changes in assumed payment, such as assuming payment at the end of the period rather than at the duration date where the assumed payment is appropriately increased by compounding the original level by a reinvestment rate through the end of the period. (That is, this now implies the eligibility of bonds with cash flows after the duration date.) But this soon becomes a quagmire as other constraints now become necessary to control duration and present value. By far the more ingenious approach is modification on the asset side rather than the liability side.

For each payment made by each bond in the universe, we know the corresponding liability duration date. Adjust each such payment to an equivalent payment on the liability date and optimize exactly as before but use a universe of adjusted bonds. Payments will be reinvested or discounted back to the proper date. In cases where a bond could go in either direction, it could be entered twice in the universe with the same price but different cash flows. This general approach solves the problem of allowing maturities after the duration date but does not imply that duration and present values are equal. If we force duration to be equal (that is, the proper balance of actual cash maturation before and after the duration date), we need not assume a conservative low reinvestment rate for early maturities and a high discount rate for late maturities. The reason is that we are hedged—immunization theory shows our actual investment risk to be small so that we need not penalize ourselves with over conservatism. We may use the same rate for both reinvestment and discounting so that the effect of its level is a wash. This rate should be the same as was used in computing the present value of the liability for this period. If it is felt that securities are discounted or sold at higher yields than those at which reinvestment takes place because of differences in the type of securities involved, a differential between investment and discount rates is warranted. Otherwise, a differential would be used only as an added safety measure over the effect of being immunized within the period. If we do not force durations to be equal, we have not hedged the reinvestment risk. We must then assume a conservative reinvestment rate and a high discount rate to guarantee sufficient present value on the duration date.

These remarks illustrate the general steps one may take in correcting some of the problems underlying the standard approach by using the duration based techniques that provide greater flexibility. Although we will not delve into the numerous variations that follow from these approaches, we will consider one additional related topic: the role of borrowing and lending in the cash-matched portfolio.

A common provision in a cash matched optimization is the allowance or prohibition of borrowing or lending. *Lending* refers to the practice of overfunding prior to a particular payment date, reinvesting these funds through to the next payment date or beyond. Thus a 12/89 maturity is used to fund not only the 1/90 liability but the 4/90 liability as well. The overfunding is usually assumed to be reinvested at a conservative rate. This circumstance arises when the 12/89 maturity with reinvestment still provides a better yield than anything maturing during the first quarter of 1990. Because these conditions often arise, most investors find this to be quite an acceptable practice as long as credit and issuer constraints are met and a conservative rate is used. This lending is distinctly different than the within-period reinvestment discussed in connection with the standard versus duration-based optimization. It refers only to reinvestment across a period boundary and does not imply the use of a duration-based technique for avoiding the necessity of the conservative rate assumption (although presumably something could be developed with enough ingenuity).

*Borrowing* refers to the case where a liability payment is paid in part through funds borrowed from an overfunded position in a future period. For example, the 1/90 liability is financed through borrowing from the 4/90 overfunded position. If such borrowing is permitted, the optimization will call for it if there is a security maturing between 1/90 and 4/90, which, after discounting back at the discount rate, produces a higher yield than securities maturing before 1/90. When such borrowing is allowed, a high discount or borrowing rate is usually assumed.

Even assuming a low lending rate and a high borrowing rate, allowance of such activities can add appreciably to the overall portfolio yield. This results from unevenness in yields along the yield curve implicit in securities in any likely universe. The greater the allowable position in individual securities, the greater the contribution to yield, as would be expected. Allowance of lending is common. Allowance of borrowing is rare, often because funds tend to be borrowed over several periods. This is viewed as riskier than lending over several periods. The actual meaning of borrowing should be kept in mind before making this conclusion, however. Although the computer literally computes the quantities as if money were actually borrowed from a future period, this corresponds in practice to the sale of securities that produce the future overfunded position. The high borrowing rate corresponds to the highest yield at which the securities might be sold. That is, so long as the borrowing rate exceeds this level, the sale of securities creating the overfunding position will supply the borrowed funds with no adverse surprises. Of course, we could accomplish the same thing through literal borrowing from a short-term pool and replenish this pool with interest when the overfunded position matures. It should also be apparent that this type of borrowing eliminates one of the problems of the standard optimization method discussed previously by allowing the use of securities maturing after the liability payment date. In our earlier discussion of this problem, we proposed setting the liability payment date within the interval rather than at its beginning and selecting bonds that mature before and after this date but that were still contained within the interval. Along with this was a duration matching technique that kept us from having to make extreme lending and borrowing rate assumptions within the interval. As with the across-period lending discussed previously, we offer no technique for avoiding an extreme rate assumption for across-period borrowing. Without a corresponding duration matching rule, there is no guarantee that across-period lending and across-period borrowing will net out in a hedged position.

*Updating Liabilities*

In most cases the manifest characteristic of the optimal cash-matched portfolio is its application of a very precise model to a very imprecise set of numbers. When the liability to be financed is a stream of future pension benefit payments, actual future experience will normally differ from initial predictions, giving rise to an updated liability stream. As a general rule, when the existing cash flow stream is confronted with this new liability, a pattern of over and under funding appears.

There are two general solutions to this problem. One approach is to reoptimize the fund totally with the possibility of additional cash over existing market value being necessary if acturial experience is adverse, and cash withdrawal possible if experience is favorable. In this reoptimization, all, some, or perhaps none of the existing holdings will be maintained depending on the degree of the change in liabilities and the degree of change in relative values (and security supply in different sectors) in the bond market. The greater the elapsed time from portfolio inception, the greater the likelihood of a substantial change on rebalancing.

The notion that a substantial change is optimal is counterintuitive to many who reason that transaction costs may be large if this is done. They may be right. Transaction costs may be large. But if appropriate bid-ask spreads are included in the analysis, as they should be, and if a substantial restructuring still emerges as optimal, the benefits of a large change simply exceed the transaction costs and restructuring should take place.

The second general solution is that which conforms to the intuition of the skeptics. The liability-cash flow mismatch may be small enough, the transaction costs large enough, and changes in relative values in the market small enough so that a trained eye can see that reoptimization is not warranted, but that instead a simple set of trades (purchases and sales) will eliminate the mismatch. This approach is normally taken when the gains from a complete reoptimization are small relative to possible errors in estimating the transaction costs that go into the optimization model. Intuition would also suggest that the match resulting from manual rebalancing may be less precise than that resulting from a full optimization. This may or may not be true. In either case the investor normally has at this point a greater tolerance for minor mismatch, having discovered its inevitability. If a precise match were obtained initially at some cost to overall yield, it has now become apparent that the added expense may not have been worth it and will not now be worth it for the same reason.

These general remarks apply with equal force to rebalancing pursuant to liability updates resulting from the additions of a new liability stream to the old. Typically, in the case of retirees in a pension plan, the experience with respect to prior retirees is reflected in an update to the old liability stream and a new liability stream for recent or upcoming retirees is added to it. The net liability stream to be funded is normally positive in each future year, but is often not a smoothly declining stream. This new liability stream may be funded through an optimization procedure identical to the original funding and without regard for the existing portfolio. A match may be obtained using any of the techniques described earlier in this report. An exact match may not be possible if the stream is sufficiently irregular. In this case, overfunding is normally prescribed if the original portfolio is not to be touched.

To avoid such overfunding as well as to take advantage of changes in relative values in the bond market occurring since the last major update, it is normally desirable to incorporate the existing fund in the reoptimization. (This is often done even if no overfunding is required in financing the net new liability for the latter reason alone.) We now work with the total new liability stream and may either reoptimize totally or use a simple sequence of trades as described earlier. Similar cost-benefit considerations must be made.

*Call Risk*

When constructing and maintaining a dedicated portfolio, we usually control general portfolio characteristics by selecting the available universe and through the application of constraints on the portfolio—the control approach arising out of the optimization technique normally employed. Call risk is usually controlled through the purchase of noncallable bonds or through the purchase of discount bonds that have natural call protection. We have discussed in an earlier section the review process in which coupons of nearby maturities can actually be increased as the portfolio matures and call protection in nearby maturities can be reduced. Here we discuss alternative forms of call protection.

It can be readily argued that obtaining call protection via discount bonds is suboptimal for any nontaxable entity. The reason is that discount bonds—while unlikely to be called because rates must fall a great deal—also hold advantages to taxable buyers because a greater portion of a discount bond's total return is in the form of capital gain as opposed to current income. Thus taxable buyers prefer discount bonds because capital gain tax rates are lower than ordinary income tax rates. Discount bonds therefore sell at lower yields than comparable high coupon issues because of the presence of taxable buyers. Thus, when a tax-exempt institution purchases a discount bond for call protection, it is also purchasing a tax advantage that it does not need.

To avoid this we must restrict attention to current coupon bonds. Our problems would be solved if there were an adequate supply of noncallable current coupon bonds of all maturities and all credit levels. Such noncallable bonds would be more expensive than comparable callable bonds, as they should be. But this additional cost would be the right price to pay. The interesting fact is that financial theory implies that our returns will be larger (though less certain) on callable current coupon issues than on comparable noncallables so that the nonexistence of a large universe of noncallables may not be a problem.

To see this, the equilibrium market prices of callable and noncallable bonds will be such that the risk adjusted total expected returns from each are the same. Suppose that the annualized expected compound return on a ten-year callable bond over ten years is 12 percent. The expected return on the noncallable bond would be less, say, 11 percent because it is less risky and has a higher initial price. This implies that on an expected value basis we are better off by overfunding with callable bonds than by precisely funding with noncallables.

To summarize our argument, yields as well as expected total pretax returns are higher on current coupon bonds than on discount bonds. Similarly, yields and expected total returns are higher on callable than noncallable bonds. This suggests that rather than fund with discount bonds, we should purchase (using the same total investment) a larger number of current coupon callable bonds (when noncallables are not available). The excess cash flow in early years should be reinvested. If the bond is not called, we clearly come out ahead. If the bond is called, the call price plus accumulated excess income is reinvested (with payouts to match liability outflows) up to the original maturity date of the bond. If after the final payment on this date, we have excess cash, we obviously still came out ahead—in part a result of the savings from not paying for the tax advantage of discount bonds. Of course, we may come out behind through not being able to meet as many payments as the discount bond would have. On an expected value basis we should come out ahead. The degree of downside risk can also be controlled by specifying conditions that must be met so that the risk can be taken. For example, many current coupon ten-year bonds have seven years of call protection. Assuming call in seven years, we could compute the reinvestment rate necessary over the last three years for this bond to just underperform a ten-year, lower-yielding discount bond. We could specify a threshold rate level below which the risk of call would be accepted.

This type of call risk analysis can and should be used in conjunction with normal call risk monitoring. In that process, the degree of call protection is evaluated by comparing current yield levels with projections for yield in the future. If yields are expected to fall beyond the levels initially envisaged as minimum levels at the time the program was purchased, some restructuring may have to take place to increase the call protection. In many cases, a threshold interest rate analysis as described earlier may dictate that the higher (that is, prudent risk adjusted) return occurs by leaving particular bonds in the portfolio. A threshold yield level analysis done at the inception of a dedicated portfolio can illustrate that certain callable bonds will be risk free in the sense that we will still earn the target rate even if the bond is called.

### Precision of the Match and Rewards to Rebalancing

We have discussed now in several contexts the role and effect of the exact cash match concept involved in the standard problem solution. Although it may be the necessary approach for actuarial or other reasons, it tends to impose additional costs on overall performance. Initial setup costs can be larger through dilution of the financing rate with the reinvestment rate—and through the prohibition of hedged or unhedged borrowing from future periods. A general reduction in flexibility tends to preclude swap opportunities. The section on liability updating illustrated the strong prospect that mismatch may inevitably arise through unpredictable changes in the liability stream. The section on call risk illustrated that higher expected returns may be possible with little risk if some imprecision is allowed in payoffs from certain callable bonds.

These remarks stress that the elimination of flexibility in the cash match portfolio may have substantial costs. The instrument by which these costs are imposed is the failure to appreciate the role for portfolio management in the rebalancing process in future years. Thus disallowance of minor mismatches (when these will inevitably occur because of liability updates) precludes the manager from making many profitable swaps, and it can eliminate one of the most important vehicles for controlling call risk. It is extremely difficult to quantify this cost, but our experience is that it could be as large as several times the fee normally paid for dedicated portfolio services.

*Choosing the Reinvestment Rate*

It is common to require in a cash match that the reinvestment rate of cash flows from time of receipt to time of disbursement be quite low. This is a measure of conservation normally deemed appropriate especially when the assumed actuarial rate is being increased on the basis of the dedication. In fact, a different approach may be appropriate with no loss of conservatism.

Using a low reinvestment rate may cause the selection of bonds that are overpriced on a yield basis but that have favorable maturity characteristics. Thus a bond maturing between two adjacent bonds could be overpriced based on yield curve considerations but still cheaper than the shorter bond given reinvestment at the low rate employed. Using a higher rate, one near the forward rate, would correct this deficiency but would expose the portfolio to the risk that the actual short rate at the future point would be below the forward.

To remedy this situation, one could compute the total cost of the portfolio using both the low reinvestment rate and the forward rates. Clearly, the latter total cost would be lower. Next, buy the portfolio based on the forward rate calculation. The savings thus incurred could be used in part or in total to create a separate long duration fund for the purpose of hedging the rate risk. If rates rise over the period, the fund would never be used. If rates decline below the forward rates used, the fund would appreciate in value to a degree sufficient to offset the revenue shortfall as long as the duration of the fund was large enough. The appropriate duration for the fund could be determined by first estimating what the period-by-period cash shortfall would be if the forward rate were not in fact realized, but instead some lower rate. This cash shortfall schedule could then be duration matched. Alternatively, one could compute the duration of the portfolio and that of the liabilities. The duration of the liabilities would be larger. One would then determine what the duration of the separate fund would have to be for the duration of the total fund to equal that of the liabilities. Using the savings to purchase a separate fund with this duration would cause the portfolio to be duration matched.

**Note**

1. Franco Modigliani and Mertan H. Miller, "The Cost of Capital, Corporation Finance and the Theory of Investment," *American Economic Review* (June 1950), pp. 261–295; and "Corporate Income Taxes and the Cost of Capital: A Correction," *American Economic Review* (June 1963), pp. 433–443.

# 8

# Immunization in Foreign Exchange Management

The bullet immunization analyses that were discussed in chapters 1 through 4 demonstrate how the risk in long-run compound return on a bond portfolio can be virtually eliminated over predefined horizons. The target rate of return identified at the start of the horizon is locked up by applying the immunization technique. In this chapter, we demonstrate how the same mathematical concepts underlying bond portfolio immunization are applicable to problems in the area of foreign exchange management. In particular, how is it possible to eliminate exchange rate risk over horizons that are well beyond the reach of forward and futures contracts? Throughout, our objective is to demonstrate how concepts of immunization can be used to lock in the exchange rate. Assuming that one has a stream of foreign currency that must be converted into dollars, our results are divided into four sections.

Under simplified assumptions regarding the hedging process, first we demonstrate how the average realized exchange rate may be locked up at today's rate, abstracting from questions regarding the time value of money. Next, we extend the analysis to show how the future value of a stream of currency may be locked up at today's exchange rate. That is, the time value problem is solved. Third, we adopt more realistic assumptions regarding the hedging process and restate our results for this case. Finally, we summarize the analysis, illustrate potential applications of the technique, and offer extensions to the case of uncertainty in interest rates and currency flows.

**Locking in the Average Exchange Rate**

Suppose we have 1 million (MM) deutsche marks (DM) to be converted to dollars each month for the next five years. To make matters simple, suppose that the dollar-DM (\$/DM) exchange rate $f$ is expected to change in an unpredictable way just once over the next month and remain at the new level for the remainder of the five-year period. The current payment will be exchanged at the current rate, $f_0$, and the remaining payments (totaling 59 million DM) will be exchanged at the new rate, $f_1$.

It seems clear that to lock in today's exchange rate, we should short 59 million DM at today's rate (using, say, the nearby futures contract). The immediate gain (loss) on this transaction will then offset the loss (gain) on our long position in DM. Assuming that we can short DM at the rate $f_0$, the realized exchange rate on the total transaction will be

$$\frac{1}{60}\{f_0 + 59f_1 - 59(f_1 - f_0)\} = f_0$$

That is, the average realized rate equals the initial rate. What is important to recognize at this point is that we can now view the whole process as starting over with fifty-nine months to go. We exchange the current payment at the new rate $f_1$, and short 58 million DM at this same rate. We are now protected over the next month for any additional change in the exchange rate. This process starts over each month. We exchange the current payment at the existing rate and collect (pay) an amount on our remaining short position that exactly compensates for the loss (gain) on our remaining long position.

To summarize, we have an unhedged long position in DM to be received over a period of time. We maintain at each point in time an offsetting short position. The critical insight is that our short position need not be payable over the same horizon as the long position. That is, we do not require a long-term hedge because we have demonstrated that an appropriate series of short hedges works as well. What we do require is that we can, at each point, short DM at the spot rate, and that gains or losses on the short position reflect the new spot rate very closely. Continued use of the nearby futures contract may be satisfactory for this purpose. Although some slippage would no doubt exist, it may be small relative to the magnitude of the unhedged rate change that this overall exercise is seeking to avoid. Later in this chapter, we model the case where we cannot short DM at the spot rate. Similarly, questions regarding the timing of the gains and losses have been ignored and will be taken up in the next section; in the balance of this section we explore the mathematics of the present example before going to a higher level of complexity.

What is interesting is that the steadily declining short position that we have described bears a close resemblance to the steadily declining duration in an immunization problem. In fact, the mathematics are identical, as we shall demonstrate in a simple example. Consider a five-year zero coupon bond paying $1 at maturity. The continuously compounded return $y$ is defined by

$$\text{Price} = e^{-y \cdot 5}$$

As time passes, $y$ will change and the 5 in exponent will decline steadily so that as a more general formula

$$P(t) = e^{-y(t)(5-t)} \tag{8.1}$$

where $t$ denotes time, $0 \le t \le 5$. Price and yield are now a function of time and $5 - t$ is the time until maturity. The five-year continuously compounded return is, by definition, $y(0)$. The instantaneous return on the bond (mathematically, $dP/P$) is the return earned over a very short time interval (denoted $dt$) and allowing a very small change in yield to take place over $dt$. Denote this yield change by $dy$. By computing the total differential of $P(t)$ and dividing by $P(t)$ the instantaneous return is found to be

$$\frac{dP}{P} = y(t)dt - (5 - t)dy \tag{8.2}$$

That is, the return over a short period of time $(dt)$ is composed of a part resulting merely from the passage of time, and a part from the change in yield. The expression $dP/P$ merely denotes the change in price $dP$ divided by price $P$ to give the rate of return. Now, it turns out that if we sum the instantaneous returns given by equation 8.2 and divide by the time horizon, 5, we will produce our continuously compounded five-year return. We know in advance that this must be $y(0)$. In other words, integrating equation 8.2 and dividing by 5 we have

$$y(0) = \frac{1}{5}\left\{ \int_0^5 y\,dt - \int_0^5 (5 - t)dy \right\} \tag{8.3}$$

Although this can be proven directly, it can also be seen by noting from equation 8.1 that the five-year continuously compounded return is defined by

$$y(0) = \frac{\ell n(\$1/P(0))}{5} \tag{8.4}$$

(and this must equal $y(0)$) when $\ell n$ denotes natural logarithm. Using properties of logarithms this equals

$$\frac{1}{5}\{\ell n(\$1) - \ell n(P(0))\} \tag{8.5}$$

This quantity merely equals the sum of all the changes in $\ell n(P)$, (denoted $d\ell n(P)$), divided by 5. That is

$$\frac{1}{5}\{\ell n(\$1) - \ell n(P(0))\} = \frac{1}{5} \int_0^5 d\ell n(P(t)) \tag{8.6}$$

But another mathematical fact is that

$$d\ell n(P(t)) = \frac{dP(t)}{P(t)} \tag{8.7}$$

Hence combining equations 8.2 through 8.7 yields

$$y(0) = \frac{1}{5}\left\{\int_0^5 \frac{dP}{P}\right\} = \frac{1}{5}\left\{\int_0^5 y(t)dt - \int_0^5 (5 - t)dy\right\} \tag{8.8}$$

We have just proved that if you link the instantaneous returns on a zero-coupon bond, the continuously compounded return equals the internal rate at time of purchase, as it should be. This same observation lies at the heart of immunization theory. If the yield to maturity of the bond portfolio moves continuously through time without jumps, we have an instantaneous return

$$y(t)dt - \text{duration} \cdot dy$$

where by assumption, (if the horizon is five years)

$$\text{Duration} = 5 - t$$

so that the instantaneous return becomes

$$y(t)dt - (5 - t)dy \tag{8.9}$$

But from equation 8.8 we know that the continuously compounded return on the portfolio must be

$$\frac{1}{5}\left\{\int_0^5 y(t)dt - \int_0^5 (5 - t)dy\right\}$$

and this in turn has been shown to equal $y(0)$, regardless of the actual changes in yield, $dy$, even though the portfolio does not consist of a single five-year zero coupon bond. $y(0)$ is in this case the immunized (target) return estimated at the outset of the period.

Now, in the case of our foreign exchange example, the flow of dollars consists of the 1 million DM exchanged at the spot rate $f(t)$, plus gains (losses) from the remaining short position. That is

$$f(t) \cdot 1\text{MM} - (60 - t)df$$

where $t$ now represents the total amount exchanged thus far, 1 million DM replaces $dt$ and $df$ denotes the instantaneous and unpredictable change in the exchange rate $f(t)$, which is assumed to move in a random but continuous fashion. If we sum this flow (via integration) and divide by the total number of DM transferred, we arrive at the average (realized) exchange rate, $\bar{f}$. Thus

$$\bar{f} = \left\{ \frac{1}{60} \int_0^{60} f(t)dt - \int_0^{60} (60 - t)df \right\}$$

But we now know that this integral equals $f(0)$, hence

$$\bar{f} = f(0)$$

We have proved our intuitive result regarding locking up today's exchange rate by showing that the average rate will equal the initial rate as long as the appropriate short position is always maintained, as long as exchange rate movements are smooth enough (with nearby futures contracts in step with spot rates) so that the transactions implicit in the mathematics can take place, and as long as we can short currency at the spot rate.

The simplified circumstances of the even flow example assisted intuition in coming up with the solution. We would like to generalize this to the case of an uneven flow of currency. Intuition again suggests that this is possible when we consider applying the approach we have taken above to the case of a single payment of 60 million DM in five years. That is, we short 60 million DM at today's rate and continue to roll over the short position for five years. The spot payment exchanged in five years at the future spot rate $f(5)$, plus the gain (loss) on the short position is then

$$60\text{MM} \cdot f(5) - 60\text{MM} \cdot (f(5) - f(0))$$

which, of course, equals $60\text{MM} \times f(0)$. We have locked in today's exchange rate. This example suggests that in an uneven flow case we should take the approach of maintaining a short position equal to the total amount of DM still to be transferred.

Suppose that the rate of flow of DM to be transferred per unit of time is the continuous function $c(t)$. The actual volume over a small unit of time $dt$ is then $c(t)dt$. The cumulative flow over a period of time 0, $h$ is then the sum (integral) of all the small flows $c(t)dt$ over that period. Denoting this cumulative flow $C(h)$, we have

$$C(h) \equiv \int_0^h c(t)dt$$

The total unexchanged volume of DM at any time $t$ is then $C(5) - C(t)$. If we follow the previous suggestion, then over an interval $dt$ the total flow into dollars from both the current flow exchanged at spot plus gains (losses) on the short position is then

$$f(t)c(t)dt - (C(5) - C(t))df \qquad (8.10)$$

The total flow into dollars is the sum (integral) of these flows, and the average exchange rate is then this total sum divided by the total DM exchanged, or $C(5)$. Thus the average exchange rate is

$$\bar{f} = \frac{1}{C(5)} \left\{ \int_0^5 f(t)c(t)dt - \int_0^5 C(5) - C(t)df \right\} \qquad (8.11)$$

Unlike the case of the even flow, we have no other phenomena to which we can refer to deduce the value of this integral. It possesses a simple solution, however, as proven by theorem 8A.1 in appendix 8A, and as no doubt suspected by now

$$\bar{f} = f(0) \qquad (8.12)$$

We have solved the case of an uneven flow of exchange to be locked up at today's exchange rate. By letting the rate of flow vary, we may replicate any reasonable flow, including (in the limit) a series of lump sum payments. To reiterate, we have shown that the average exchange rate will equal the initial rate, without regard to the timing of flows or hence the future value of the flow. The timing question is considered now.

**Locking in the Future Value of a Flow of Exchange**

The foregoing analysis abstracts from the timing of the recognition of gains and losses on the long and short currency positions. For example, a currency appreciation will produce an instantaneous loss on the short position and a deferred gain on the long position. The realized exchange rate is unaffected but in a present value sense we are worse off. Fortunately, this is simple to correct, leading to modified rules for the size of the short position to be maintained in order to hedge future value.

We adopt a simple nonstochastic world in which the rate for borrowing or lending on a pure discount bond with maturity $T - t$ is $y(t)$ as of time $t$. The opportunity rate for the owner of the DM position should be $y(t)$. For a U.S. resident converting DM to dollars, this would presumably be the U.S. rate. The future value as of time $T$ of the currency transferred over the interval $dt$ at time $t$ is therefore (using the first term in equation 8.10)

$$f(t)c(t)e^{y(t)(T-t)}dt$$

The future value of the entire stream is thus

$$\int_0^T f(t)c(t)e^{y(t)(T-t)}dt \tag{8.13}$$

Equation 8.13 depends on the future unknown movements in the exchange rate $f(t)$. We would like a hedging strategy that eliminates this risk or one that would allow us to substitute $f(0)$ (the initial exchange rate) in place of $f(t)$ in equation 8.13. That is, we seek a strategy whose future value is

$$\int_0^T f(0)c(t)e^{y(t)(T-t)}dt \tag{8.14}$$

To develop such a strategy, note that if $S(t)$ denotes the short position at time $t$ for the future value problem, the future value of the total flow into dollars over the interval $dt$ is (from equation 8.10)

$$e^{y(t)(T-t)}f(t)c(t)dt - e^{y(t)(T-t)}S(t)df \tag{8.15}$$

and the future value of the entire stream is

$$\int_0^T f(t)c(t)e^{y(t)(T-t)}dt - \int_0^T S(t)e^{y(t)(T-t)}df \tag{8.16}$$

We would like to use theorem 8A.1 to prove the equivalence of expressions 8.16 and 8.14 when $S(t)$ is appropriately chosen. To put expression 8.16 in the appropriate form, let

$$c^*(t) = c(t)e^{y(t)(T-t)}$$

and

$$C^*(h) = \int_0^h c^*(t)dt$$

Expression 8.16 becomes

$$\int_0^T f(t)c^*(t)dt - \int_0^T S(t)e^{y(t)(T-t)}df \tag{8.17}$$

From the theorem, $S(t)$ must obey

$$e^{y(t)(T-t)}S(t) = C^*(T) - C^*(t)$$

or

$$S(t) = e^{-y(t)(T-t)}\int_t^T c(h)e^{y(h)(T-h)}dh \tag{8.18}$$

so that expression 8.17 may be written in a form that satisfies theorem 8A.1.

$$\int_0^T f(t)c^*(t)dt - \int_0^T C^*(T) - C^*(t)df \qquad (8.19)$$

Equation 8.18 is our solution for the short position to be maintained at each point in time. $S(t)$ is precisely the present value of the currency yet to be exchanged as of time $t$. This provides an appealing symmetry insofar as we are now seeking to hedge the future value of our position rather than the average exchange rate. Moreover, this adjustment to the short position size agrees with intuition insofar as gains (losses) are instantaneous and hence should be controlled to equal the future value of the future offsetting losses (gains).

**Shorting Currency at Nonspot Rates**

The foregoing sections assumed that DM could be shorted at the spot rate. In general, this will not be possible unless the determinants of forward exchange rates imply that there is no expected change in exchange rate. In other words, over any horizon, we can only short DM at the forward rate applicable to that horizon, and this need not be the spot rate. Let us assume that rather than shorting at the spot rate, $f(t)$, we short at the rate $f^*(t,h)$ for an $h$ period contract. Thus, our gain or loss on a single $h$ period contract is

$$- (f(t + h) - f^*(t,h))$$

instead of

$$- (f(t + h) - f(t))$$

The difference $f(t) - f^*(t,h)$ is the forward premium or discount (denoted $p(t,h)$) for an $h$ period contract as of time $t$. Consequently our gain or loss may be written

$$- (f(t + h) - (f(t) - p(t,h)))$$

or

$$- (f(t + h) - f(t)) - p(t,h)$$

Now, over successively smaller contract periods, the discount $p(t,h)$ must converge to zero. This is a critical observation because most of our analysis is performed in continuous time. Thus, we define the *instantaneous rate of forward discount or premium* as

$$p(t) \equiv \lim_{h \to 0} \frac{f(t) - f^*(t,h)}{h}$$

Using these definitions, the instantaneous gain or loss on a one contract short position that is rolled over instantaneously is

$$-df - p(t)dt$$

If we substitute this into equation 8.19 in place of $-df$ we find that our hedging technique provides a future value (using theorem 8A.1) of

$$f(0)C^*(T) - \int_0^T (C^*(T) - C^*(t))p(t)dt \tag{8.20}$$

Let us define

$$P(h) = \int_0^h p(t)dt$$

so that

$$p(t)dt = dP(t)$$

Theorem 8A.1 now implies that

$$-\int_0^T (C^*(T) - C^*(t))p(t)dt = P(0)C^*(T) - \int_0^T P(t)c^*(t)dt$$

which equals

$$-\int_0^T P(t)c^*(t)dt$$

because by definition, $P(0) = 0$.

Hence equation 8.20 becomes

$$f(0)C^*(T) - \int_0^T P(t)c^*(t)dt \tag{8.21}$$

or making use of the definition of $C^*(t)$

$$\int_0^T (f(0) - P(t))c^*(t)dt \tag{8.22}$$

The effective exchange rate for a flow occurring at time $h$ in the future is therefore

$$f(0) - P(h) \qquad (8.23)$$

This is precisely equal to the initial rate minus the cumulative instantaneous discount.

Equations 8.22 and 8.23 are an important modification to the basic results of the previous section because they reflect the role of exchange rate theory in determining the exchange rate that may be locked up by our hedging technique. In a world of certainty, equation 8.23 must precisely equal the forward exchange rate that exists at time 0 for delivery at time $h$ in the future. If the forward rate had some other value, arbitrage would take place by someone using the hedging vehicle to lock in the difference between the actual forward rate and that given by formula 8.23. Equation 8.23 also shows that using the hedging method, the realized rate would equal the forward rate if that latter market in fact existed over the desired horizon. These results demonstrate that in a world of certainty, the forward rate schedule develops out of the cumulative impact of the instantaneous forward discount $p(t)$.

### Summary, Extensions, and Applications

Developments in this chapter were motivated by the similarity between certain aspects of bond immunization strategies and our intuitive approach to solving some foreign exchange management problems. The precise mathematics (especially in appendix 8A) is an adaptation of some of the mathematics of immunization. The results demonstrate how one can lock up the exchange rate when exchanging an arbitrary flow of foreign exchange to be received in the future. Specifically, the results demonstrate that as long as an appropriate short position can be maintained to offset the long position (referring to the exchange to be received in the future), the future value of the position will be locked in at a value equivalent to that which would occur if the exchange rate remained equal to the current rate, as long as the exchange rate can be shorted at the spot rate. The fully dynamic rule is to maintain at each point a short position equal to the present value of the long position. The results do not require that any particular exchange rate theory hold although the precise nature of the results are affected by such differences.

When we cannot short the exchange rate at the spot rate, we show that the foregoing hedging rule implies that for a particular horizon we create a rate equal to the spot rate less the cumulative impact of the instantaneous forward discount (premium). In a world of certainty, this adjusted rate must equal the forward for this same horizon or else arbitrage will come into play. Thus, we have indirectly demonstrated that the theory of forward rates follows from the cumulative impact of the instantaneous discount (premium) in a world of certainty. In actual markets the hedged rate cannot be known in advance. However, statistical theory reveals that this rate is, of necessity, far more certain (or less volatile) than fluctuation in the underlying spot rate itself over the full horizon. Thus, our hedging approach continues to have merit.

What is interesting about our results is that, contrary to first reactions, long-term forward or future markets are not necessary to reduce the uncertainty in exchange rate transactions. What is required is the ability to earn on every short position the precise change in the executed spot rates or the difference between the shorted rate and the subsequent realized rate. That is, if the spot rate changes against us, we must actually be able to earn (on our short position) the full value of the change as applied to the foreign exchange yet to be transferred. Continued use of the forward market or the nearby futures contract may be satisfactory in practice.

As a practical matter, one is likely to use forward contracts or the futures market to hedge currency flows over horizons for which such markets are available, rather than adopt the approach laid out here. This work then applies to those flows beyond the reach of these markets. In reality, a fair degree of slippage is likely to occur because actual events fail to meet the assumptions of the mathematics regarding such factors as continuity of market movements. Yet we believe that the approach remains of considerable interest to those with serious foreign exchange problems.

The developments of the first two sections were made under the assumption of certainty regarding the volume of foreign exchange to be transferred. The changes in the exchange rate were taken to be uncertain and continuously varying. These assumptions may be generalized to the case of uncertain rates and flows. In more advanced treatments we have made such generalizations to the case where interest rates and exchange rates follow Ito processes, and where currency flows are random functions of a somewhat different type. The critical finding is that the appropriate short position continues to equal the present value of the future position.

In addition, it is quite simple to demonstrate that the same short position remains optimal whether one seeks to render certain either the present value or the future value of the exchanged position. In the case of interest rate certainty that we developed here, this statement is obvious because the future value is simply the present value reinvested at a known rate. In both cases (present value or future value), we are able to achieve (lock in) an adjusted exchange rate. In the case of interest rate uncertainty, a further adjustment to the rate achieved is required because of the correlation of interest rates and exchange rates.

# Appendix 8A:
# Proof of Equation 8.12

THEOREM 8A.1. *If $f(t)$ and $c(t)$ are continuous over $0, T$ and*

$$C(h) = \int_0^h c(h)dt$$

then

$$\int_0^T f(t)c(t)dt - \int_0^T C(T) - C(t)df = f(0)C(T)$$

*Proof.*

$$\int_0^T f(t)c(t)dt - \int_0^T C(T) - C(t)df$$

$$= \int_0^T f(t)c(t)dt - C(T)\int_0^T df + \int_0^T C(t)df$$

$$= \int_0^T f(t)c(t)dt - C(T)(f(T) - f(0)) + \int_0^T d(C(t)f(t)) - \int_0^T f(t)dC(t)$$

$$= \int_0^T f(t)c(t)dt - C(T)(f(T) - f(0)) + C(T)f(T) - C(0)f(0)$$

$$- \int_0^T f(t)c(t)dt$$

$$= f(0)C(T)$$

# 9

# Using Financial Futures and an Approach to Nonstandard Rate Shifts

Financial futures are one of the most important developments in the capital markets in recent years. Like commodity futures, they are a significant risk control device; they enhance the liquidity of the markets generally, and, because of institutional structures such as leverage restrictions for many investors, they allow positions to be taken that could not otherwise be held. The theoretical pricing of futures centers on the arbitrage process. The price of the futures contract is linked to the cash market because one could create the rate obtained on the future through an appropriate long and short position in the cash market. These theoretical analyses have been extended in more recent continuous time analyses of the term structure of interest rates.

The analysis in this chapter applies some of the existing theoretical work to demonstrate how futures can be used to lengthen or shorten a portfolio. For our most basic results we employ no specific assumptions regarding futures pricing and the simplest assumption regarding the nature of yield curve shifts—that is, parallel changes in forward rates. In this case, the conclusions of the analysis are quite simple. We show that if two cash flow streams have the same initial market value but different time profiles (and, for instance, different durations), futures can be used to cause them to have identical present values over time despite interest rate charges. We could view the cash flow streams as two different portfolios that we seek to make equivalent; or, as we do in the present case, we could view one stream as a liability stream and the other as a portfolio intended to finance the liabilities. This latter interpretation underscores the role of futures in immunization. In either case, our conclusion is that the optimal number of futures to hold at each point in time is that which causes the instantaneous price volatility of the desired cash flow stream (due to a parallel shift in forward rates) to equal the instantaneous price volatility of the portfolio plus futures. Specifically, we require that the duration of the desired cash flow equal the duration of the portfolio plus the contribution to price volatility made by the futures. Defining the duration of the futures to equal this sensitivity for a single contract, this contribution equals the futures duration times the ratio of the market value of the securities underlying the total futures position to the market value of the portfolio. This equation is then solved for

233

the number of contracts to hold. Futures are used in this way if it is either impossible or inefficient to rebalance the portfolio so that the durations are the same throughout time.

These results, which are developed in the first section of this chapter, are highly intuitive and emerge from a simple application of conventional theory. In practice, however, the risk of nonparallel yield shifts can cause doubt regarding the adequacy of these methods. Accordingly, in the second section we illustrate how the technique may be generalized to reflect additional sources of uncertainty. Emerging from the analysis is the requirement that one additional constraint hold on the portfolio plus futures position (besides the duration constraint) for each additional source of yield curve risk. This fact also emerges from the application of conventional theory. Again, futures are only necessary if the same set of constraints cannot be satisfied through portfolio rebalancing.

### Results for Parallel Shifts in Forward Rates

We shall assume that we are given a liability stream and a portfolio with initially equal present values. The cash flow profiles, however, are assumed different, so that the changes in market value caused by a parallel shift in forward rates are not necessarily equal. Let the liability stream be given by $\ell(s)$, $t \leq s \leq T_\ell$; let the cash flow stream on the portfolio be given by $c(s)$, $t \leq s \leq T_c$; and let the forward rate be given by $r(s)$, $t \leq s \leq \infty$. We shall assume that the forward rate curve continuously shifts in a parallel fashion by the amount $dS(h)$ at time $h$. Taking the current time to be time $t$, these assumptions imply that the forward rate at time $t$ applicable to a payment at time $s$ in the future is $S(t) + r(s)$, where $S(t)$ is the integral of $dS$ from the same starting time 0 through time $t$. That is

$$S(t) = \int_0^t dS(h) \tag{9.1}$$

and the present values of the portfolio and liability stream are defined by

$$L(t,S) = \int_t^{T_\ell} \ell(h) e^{-\int_t^h S(t) + r(k)dk} dh \tag{9.2}$$

$$C(t,S) = \int_t^{T_c} c(h) e^{-\int_t^h S(t) + r(k)dk} dh \tag{9.3}$$

By assumption we have $L(t, S) = C(t, S)$ at our starting point $t$. If there are no future yield curve shifts (that is, $dS(h) = 0$, $h \geq t$), the present values of the portfolio and the liabilities will continue to equal one another. To see this, liabilities (at time $t$) are paid off at the rate $\ell(t)$, (which decreases $L(t, S)$), but the remaining liabilities ($\ell(h)$, $h > t$) are now nearer to maturity and are thus increasing in value at the rate $S(t) + r(t)$. Denoting the change in total liability at time $t$ as $dL(t, S)$, this may be written as

$$dL(t,S) = -\ell(t)dt + (L(t,S) - \ell(t)dt)(S(t) + r(t))dt$$

Dropping terms containing $dt^2$, this may be written

$$\frac{dL(t,S)}{dt} = -\ell(t) + L(t,S)(S(t) + r(t)) \tag{9.4}$$

which is precisely equal to the derivative of equation 9.2 with respect to $t$.

As for the portfolio, we sell off assets at the rate $\ell(t)dt$ to pay liabilities, and reinvest the balance to earn at the rate $S(t) + r(t)$. Thus we may write

$$dC(t,S) = \ell(t)dt + (C(t,S) - \ell(t)dt)(S(t) + r(t))dt$$

which may be written (dropping terms containing $dt^2$)

$$\frac{dC(t,S)}{dt} = -\ell(t) + C(t,S)(S(t) + r(t)) \tag{9.5}$$

Because $C(t, S) = L(t, S)$, equations 9.4 and 9.5 are identical so that the portfolio and liabilities must also have the same value over time.

When we allow changes in the shift parameter $S$, we must reevaluate the formula for the change in portfolio value and liability value. In particular, we now have

$$dL(t,S) = \frac{dL(t,S)}{dt}dt + \frac{dL(t,S)}{dS}dS \tag{9.6}$$

and

$$dC(t,S) = \frac{dC(t,S)}{dt}dt + \frac{dC(t,S)}{dS}dS \tag{9.7}$$

where the derivatives are now partial derivatives. Because the first term on the right-hand side of equations 9.6 and 9.7 are equal (from examining equations 9.4 and 9.5), equations 9.6 and 9.7 will be equal if we have

$$\frac{dL(t,S)}{dS}dS = \frac{dC(t,S)}{dS}dS \qquad (9.8)$$

From equations 9.2 and 9.3 we have

$$\frac{dl\,(t,S)}{dS} = -\int_{t}^{T_{\ell}}(h-t)\ell(h)e^{-\int_{t}^{h}S(t)+r(k)dk}\,dh \qquad (9.9)$$

and

$$\frac{dC(t,S)}{dS} = -\int_{t}^{T_{c}}(h-t)c(h)e^{-\int_{t}^{h}S(t)+r(k)dk}\,dh \qquad (9.10)$$

Noting that the durations of the liabilities and portfolio are defined by

$$D_{L}(t,S) \equiv \frac{1}{L(t,S)}\int_{t}^{T_{\ell}}(h-t)\ell(h)e^{-\int_{t}^{h}S(t)+r(k)dk}\,dh \qquad (9.11)$$

and

$$D_{C}(t,S) \equiv \frac{1}{C(t,S)}\int_{t}^{T_{c}}(h-t)c(h)e^{-\int_{t}^{h}S(t)+r(k)dk}\,dh \qquad (9.12)$$

equations 9.9 and 9.10 may be written

$$\frac{dL(t,S)}{dS} = -D_{L}(t,S)L(t,S) \qquad (9.13)$$

and

$$\frac{dC(t,S)}{dS} = -D_{C}(t,S)C(t,S) \qquad (9.14)$$

Because $L(t, S) = C(t, S)$, equation 9.8 will only be satisfied if $D_L(t, S) = D_c(t, S)$. This will be true if we are able to continously manage the portfolio through time in an appropriate way. However, this may be inefficient or even impossible if, for instance, the duration of the liabilities is longer than what is possible using traded instruments.

It is at this point that we consider financial futures. Because no investment is required to hold a futures position (aside from margin that may be kept in the form of earning assets), futures may be used to extend (shorten) the duration of the portfolio to achieve the required equality.

Specifically, we require a futures position for which the combined sensitivity to a forward rate shift $dS(t)$ is $dL(t, S)/dS$. The contract that should be used is that which is most predictably related to shifts in $S$. This is the only characteristic of the contract which is employed. In particular, we do not require any specific maturity of the future relative to the mismatch of cash flows of assets versus liabilities unless motivated by reason of correlation with $dS$.

To proceed, let $f(t, S)$ denote the price of a single futures contract. If $X(t, S)$ is the number of such contracts held at time $t$, then the total response of portfolio value (with futures) to a shift $dS$ is

$$\frac{dC(t,S)}{dS}dS + X(t,S)\frac{df(t,S)}{dS}dS \tag{9.15}$$

From equations 9.6 and 9.7, we must have

$$\frac{dL(t,S)}{dS}dS = \frac{dC(t,S)}{dS}dS + X(t,S)\frac{df(t,S)}{dS}dS$$

Making use of equations 9.13 and 9.14 and rearranging, this becomes

$$D_L(t,S) = D_C(t,S) + \frac{X(t,S)}{C(t,S)}\left\{\frac{-df(t,S)}{dS}\right\} \tag{9.17}$$

or solving for $X(t, S)$

$$X(t,S) = \frac{C(t,S)}{-df(t,S)/dS}\left\{D_L(t,S) - D_C(t,S)\right\} \tag{9.18}$$

Equation 9.17 illustrates the interpretation that the effect of the futures is solely to alter the duration of the portfolio so as to equal that of the liabilities, and the sole characteristic of the futures contract that is employed is its price sensitivity. The expression $df(t, S)/dS$ (which is the price sensitivity of the futures contract to shifts in forward rates) requires a theory of futures pricing for exact determination. Assuming the term structure theory employed previously in computing present value and duration, the price of a $T$-year security to be received at a future time $t + k$ with cash flows ($m(h)$, $t + k \le h \le T + t + k$) would be

$$f(t,S,k,T,m) = \int_{t+k}^{t+k+T} m(h)e^{-\int_{t+k}^{h} S(t)+r(z)dz}dh \tag{9.19}$$

Thus, $df/dS$ would be

$$\frac{df}{dS} = - \int_{t+k}^{t+k+T} (h - t - k)m(h)e^{-\int_{t+k}^{h} S(t) + r(z)dz} dh \qquad (9.20)$$

To interpret these results, equation 9.19 states what the price of a T-year security will be at time $t + k$, assuming no shift in the term structure after time $t$. Equation 9.20 is similar to the duration calculation in equation 9.12. In fact, we may define the duration of the future as

$$D^f(t,S) \equiv \frac{df}{dS} \bigg/ f(t,S,k,T,m)$$

Notice from equation 9.20 that this number may differ from the duration of the cash market instrument underlying the contract because the interest rates used in this calculation may differ from current rates. In particular, a systematic pattern of change in this quantity could emerge as the contract draws closer to expiration. Thus, just as variation in the spread between long and short rates can cause fluctuations in the difference between futures and cash market prices, similar fluctuations can exist in the difference in duration. Price and duration differences shrink, however, as expiration draws near. For a nearby contract ($k \approx 0$) this sensitivity is nearly the same as for the cash market instrument (the difference converges to zero on expiration) and we may therefore approximate

$$\frac{df}{dS} \approx -P_f(t,S)D_f(t,S) \qquad (9.21)$$

where $P_f(t, S)$ is the price and $D_f(t, S)$ is the duration of the current cash market instrument underlying the contract. Consequently, for a nearby contract, formulas 9.17 and 9.18 become[1]

$$D_L(t,S) = D_C(t,S) + \frac{X(t,S)}{C(t,S)} P_f(t,S)D_f(t,S) \qquad (9.22)$$

and

$$X(t,S) = \frac{C(t,S)}{P_f(t,S)} \left\{ \frac{D_L(t,S) - D_C(t,S)}{D_f(t,S)} \right\} \qquad (9.23)$$

In the event that the term structure assumption is inadequate for determining $df/dS$, some other, perhaps simulated, technique may be used. Use of the nearby contract seems to produce reliable results in practice. The primary drawback of the use of this contract is the requirement of frequently rolling the position over into the next contract on expiration of the current contract.

### Results for Nonparallel Shifts in Forward Rates

A general assumption for the nature of nonparallel shifts that includes all cases of interest is that where the cumulative forward rate shift $(S(t, h))$ measured as of time $t$ and applying to time $h$ $(h \geq t)$, is given by

$$S(t,h) = \sum_{i=0}^{\infty} a_i(t)(h - t)^i$$

where

$$a_i(t) = a_i(0) + \int_0^t da_i$$

This allows for up to an infinite number of sources of yield curve risk. The present value of the liabilities and portfolio are now

$$L(t,a_i) = \int_t^{T_\ell} \ell(h)e^{-\int_t^h S(t,k) + r(k)dk} dh \tag{9.24}$$

$$C(t,a_i) = \int_t^{T_c} c(h)e^{-\int_t^h S(t,k) + r(k)dk} dh \tag{9.25}$$

The counterparts of equations 9.6 and 9.7 are

$$dL = \frac{dL}{dt}dt + \sum_{i=0}^{\infty} \frac{dL}{da_i} da_i \tag{9.26}$$

$$dC = \frac{dC}{dt}dt + \sum_{i=0}^{\infty} \frac{dC}{da_i} da_i \tag{9.27}$$

Consequently, to eliminate all interest-rate risk, we require that $L(t,a_i) = C(t,a_i)$ and

$$\frac{dL}{da_i} = \frac{dC}{da_i} \quad i = 0, \ldots, \infty \tag{9.28}$$

Now, $dL/da_i$ and $dC/da_i$ are computed from equations 9.24 and 9.25 as

$$\frac{dL}{da_i} = -\int_t^{T_\ell}(h - t)^{i+1}\ell(h)e^{-\int_t^h S(t,k) + r(k)dk}dh \qquad (9.29)$$

$$\frac{dC}{da_i} = -\int_t^{T_c}(h - t)^{i+1}c(h)e^{-\int_t^h S(t,k) + r(k)dk}dh \qquad (9.30)$$

Hence, equation 9.28 becomes

$$\int_t^{T_\ell}(h - t)^{i+1}\ell(h)e^{-\int_t^h S(t,k) + r(k)dk}dh = \int_t^{T_c}(h - t)^{i+1}c(h)e^{-\int_t^h S(t,k) + r(k)dk}dh$$

$$i = 0, 1, 2, \ldots, \infty \qquad (9.31)$$

Defining

$$D_i^L(t,S) \equiv \int_t^{T_\ell}(h - t)^{i+1}\ell(h)e^{-\int_t^h S(t,k) + r(k)dk}dh \qquad (9.32)$$

and

$$D_i^C(t,S) \equiv \int_t^{T_c}(h - t)^{i+1}c(h)e^{-\int_t^h S(t,k) + r(k)dk}dh \qquad (9.33)$$

the condition for immunization may be written

$$D_i^L(t,S) = D_i^C(t,S) \qquad i = 0, \ldots, \infty \qquad (9.34)$$

This development reveals the theoretical structure but is obviously not practical. We would hardly think of identifying and measuring a countable infinity of risk measures! However, it may be reasonable for us to conclude that some manageable number of the $a_i$ are nonzero, and the rest are zero. Suppose we assumed that only the first three were nonzero. Our assumptions regarding forward shifts may then be written

$$S(t,h) = \sum_{i=0}^{2} a_i(t)(h - t)^i \qquad (9.35)$$

and to be immunized we must have

$$D_i^L(t,S) = D_i^C(t,S) \qquad i = 0, 1, 2 \qquad (9.36)$$

If this could not be achieved with the portfolio itself, we could now use futures to achieve the same result. First, choose three futures contracts that are independent in the sense that no single contract has a price sensitivity profile that is equal to some linear combination of the profiles of the other two. Then form the set of equations

$$
\begin{bmatrix}
\dfrac{df_1}{da_0} & \dfrac{df_2}{da_0} & \dfrac{df_3}{da_0} \\[2ex]
\dfrac{df_1}{da_1} & \dfrac{df_2}{da_1} & \dfrac{df_3}{da_1} \\[2ex]
\dfrac{df_1}{da_2} & \dfrac{df_2}{da_2} & \dfrac{df_3}{da_2}
\end{bmatrix}
\begin{bmatrix}
X_1 \\[2ex] X_2 \\[2ex] X_3
\end{bmatrix}
= -
\begin{bmatrix}
D_0^L - D_0^C \\[2ex]
D_1^L - D_1^C \\[2ex]
D_2^L - D_2^C
\end{bmatrix}
\tag{9.37}
$$

where $df_j/da_i$ is the sensitivity of the $j$th future with respect to the $i$th source of uncertainty. We summarize this system as

$$
\left[ \frac{df}{da} \right] \underset{\sim}{X} = - (\underset{\sim}{D}^L - \underset{\sim}{D}^C) \tag{9.38}
$$

The solution for the optimal number of futures of each type is then

$$
\underset{\sim}{X}^* = - \left[ \frac{df}{da} \right]^{-1} (\underset{\sim}{D}^L - \underset{\sim}{D}^C) \tag{9.39}
$$

As in the first section of this chapter, a specific evaluation of equation 9.39 requires a theory of futures to specify $df_j/da_i$. Generalizing equation 9.19 to the nonparallel shift case produces

$$
f_j = \int_{t+k_j}^{t+k_j+T_j} m_j(h) e^{-\int_{t+k_j}^{h} S(t,z) + r(z)dz} dh \quad j = 0, 1, 2 \tag{9.40}
$$

so that

$$
\frac{df_j}{da_i} = - \int_{t+k_j}^{t+k_j+T_j} (h - t - k_j)^{i+1} m_j(h) e^{-\int_{t+k_j}^{h} S(t,z) + r(z)dz} dh \tag{9.41}
$$

## Note

1. This simplified form is in common use, often without acknowledging the potential problems caused by fluctuations in the spread between

long and short rates. See G.O. Bierwag, George G. Kaufman and Alden Toevs, "Duration: Its Development and Use in Bond Portfolio Management," *Financial Analysts Journal* (July–August 1983), pp. 15–35. Also, extensions to additional sources of risk, as treated later in this chapter, have not been made.

# Index

Active immunization: defined, 5; vs.
objective immunization, 31–34;
optimization in, 5, 21
Active management: of dedicated bond
portfolios, 203–206; defined, 5; vs.
objective immunization, 34–35;
optimization in, 5, 21; and triggering, 91
Actuarial rate, 12, 13, 197–198
Aggressiveness. *See* Risk
Arbitrage, 228, 229
Asset, benchmark, 17
Asset mix: in dedicated bond portfolio,
12–14, 192–196; and yield
discontinuities, 68–70
Asset-liability match, 206–213

Basis points (bp), 157
Benchmark asset, 17
Benefit payments, present value of future,
194–195
Bet size: defined, 9–10; and floor return,
91, 92, 153; and forecast accuracy, 91,
154, 155–156; mathematical formula for,
86–88; in return distribution, 90, 99;
simulation of, 153, 155
Bond universe: in bullet immunization, 23;
in dedicated bond portfolio, 190
Bonds: coupon, 2, 40, 215–216; discount,
205, 215–216; noncallable, 205, 215
Borrowing, in cash-matched portfolio,
212–213
Bullet immunization: active, 5, 21, 31–34;
active management, 5, 21, 34–35; and
foreign exchange hedging, 15–16; goal
of, 2; objective, 5, 21, 26–35;
optimization criterion for, 5, 21;
risk-minimizing strategy for, 4–5;
simulation of, 22–35; techniques of,
4–7; theory behind, 2–4

Call protection, 205, 214–216
Capital budgeting, 199–203
Cash flow variance minimization: vs.
curvature minimization, 39–41, 42; as
target return, 30–31, 34–35
Cash-flows: in dedicated bond portfolios,
200–201; in financial futures, 233
Cash match, 10–11, 190–191, 206–208;
borrowing or lending with, 212;
precision of, 216–217

Classic immunization. *See* Bullet
immunization
Contingent immunization: defined, 7;
mathematical analysis of, 8–10, 85–93;
return distributions for, 95–149,
157–187; simulation of, 8–10, 151–156;
theory of, 7–8
Contribution rate, 12–14; and capital
budgeting problem, 199–203; optimal
adjustments to, 197–198; suboptimal
adjustment to, 198–199
Costs: of capital, 202; of equity, 200;
normal, 195; transaction, 24, 213–214
Coupon bonds, 215–216; zero, 2, 40
Coupon stripping, 2
Credit diversification, 25, 204–205
Curvature: minimization of, 39–41, 42; and
total return, 70–72

Dedicated bond portfolios: active
management of, 11, 203–206; asset-
liability match in, 206–213; call
protection with, 205, 214–216;
computations for, 190; decision to use,
11–13, 192–203; defined, 10, 189;
effect on contributions of, 197–203;
liability updating with, 213–214;
optimal, 189; rebalancing of, 214,
216–217; reinvestment rate in, 206–212,
217; setting constraints in, 190–192;
techniques of, 10–11; universe selection
in, 190
Degrees of freedom, 88, 99
Diffusion models, 93, 95–98
Discontinuities: in asset duration, 68, 69;
in asset proportions, 68; in yields,
65–70
Discount bonds, 205, 215–216
Discount rate, 200–202, 210–212
Duration constraint: in bullet
immunization, 25, 27, 29; in contingent
immunization, 155
Duration matching, 11, 17, 191, 208–212,
217
Duration of portfolio: in bullet
immunization, 3, 4–5, 23–24, 27, 28;
of future, 23, 27, 238; generalized
measures of, 17–18; Khang's log-, 27;
mathematical formula for, 62; in total
compound return, 40, 63; weighted

243

# About the Author

**Michael Granito** is the head of quantitative research in the money management division of the Morgan Bank. Mr. Granito developed a bond immunization group at Morgan as well as the analytical techniques employed there in the management of immunized portfolios. He is an adjunct professor of finance at New York University and also taught at the Wharton School while completing doctoral studies in finance at the University of Pennsylvania.